MEXICO'S PIVOTAL DEMOCRATIC ELECTION

A co-publication of Stanford University Press and the
Center for U.S.-Mexican Studies, University of California, San Diego

Mexico's Pivotal Democratic Election

Candidates, Voters, and the Presidential Campaign of 2000

Edited by

Jorge I. Domínguez and Chappell Lawson

STANFORD AND LA JOLLA, CALIFORNIA

Stanford University Press
Center for U.S.-Mexican Studies, UCSD

Stanford University Press
Stanford, California

© 2004 by the Board of Trustees of the
Leland Stanford Junior University

Printed in the United States of America
on acid-free, archival-quality paper.

Library of Congress Cataloging-in-Publication Data

Mexico's pivotal democratic election : candidates, voters,
    and the presidential campaign of 2000 / edited by Jorge I.
    Domínguez and Chappell H. Lawson.
        p. cm.
    Includes bibliographical references and index.
    ISBN 0-8047-4973-6 (alk. paper) —
    ISBN 0-8047-4974-4 (paper : alk. paper)
    1. Presidents — Mexico — Election — 2000. 2. Elections —
Mexico. 3. Mexico — Politics and government — 1988-
4. Political campaigns — Mexico. 5. Political parties —
Mexico. I. Domínguez, Jorge I., 1945-   II. Lawson,
Chappell H., 1967-
JL1292 .M527   2004
324.972'0841 — dc22

                                                2003017240

Original printing 2004

Last figure below indicates year of this printing:
13 12 11 10 09 08 07 06 05 04

To our families

Contents

Part III. Campaign Messages and Voter Responses

Illustrations

FIGURES

TABLES

Preface

This project began in the wake of Mexico's 1997 midterm elections, in which the long-ruling Institutional Revolutionary Party (PRI) lost control of the lower house of Congress and the mayoralty of Mexico City. At that time, it still looked like the PRI would retain the presidency in the 2000 elections. But the remarkable shifts that occurred within the electorate over the course of the 1997 campaign—especially in Mexico City—suggested that the outcome of the 2000 race might be unpredictable. The potential importance of campaign effects was confirmed by analysis of a panel study in Mexico City (conducted by Lawson in conjunction with *Reforma* newspaper) that revealed both substantial volatility within the electorate and an important role for television coverage in shaping electoral choices.

We seek in this book to understand how a campaign might shape the results of a presidential election in an emerging democracy. Our goal was to verify whether what we had observed in 1997 was unique, and to what extent elections in Mexico might depart from the more "modest effects" paradigm for understanding national election campaigns that has dominated the Americanist and comparativist scholarly literature on campaigns. Mexico's 2000 race seemed like the ideal candidate for such a study.

That contest also had profound implications for the study of democratization. From the late 1970s to the early 1990s, constitutional governance—with presidents and parliaments elected in free and fair elections, based on universal suffrage and political liberties—came to Argentina, Bolivia, Brazil, Chile, Ecuador, Peru, and Uruguay. Slowly in the 1980s and more decisively in the 1990s, El Salvador, Guatemala, Honduras, Panama, and (more dubiously) Paraguay transited from governments led by military presidents or principally dominated by the military toward constitutional democratic regimes. South American transitions from military regimes tended to have a birth date: a single election. Transitions associated with the end of civil wars (as in Central America) did too: the signing of a peace agreement and an associated election. The outcome of these founding elections often played an important role in shaping post-transition politics, defining lines of cleavage and the boundaries of democratic reform.

The Mexican transition had no single birth date but many. Mexico had had no military coups since its revolution in the second decade of the twentieth century, and the last president who had been a general at some point in his career stepped down from office in 1946. Democratization of Mexico's civilian, one-party regime was protracted, lasting at least since the mid-1980s to the 2000 election. It involved three presidential races, two nationwide congressional campaigns, and countless subnational contests. But only after the 2000 election could most Mexicans boldly and confidently assert that their political regime, too, had changed decisively. For this reason, the 2000 election offered important insights into how campaigns and elections might shape democratization.

Most of the authors featured in this volume—Roderic Camp, Wayne Cornelius, Joseph Klesner, Beatriz Magaloni, James McCann, Alejandro Moreno, and the two of us—were participants in the project from the beginning. Federico Estévez, Alejandro Poiré, Miguel Basáñez, and Pablo Parás were also core members of the project team and participated throughout in designing and implementing the surveys. Poiré joined the team of authors. Kathleen Bruhn also agreed to participate in the book; her analysis of party strategy filled a crucial missing gap in the project.

A number of scholars who study elections in other countries also proved extremely generous with their time. Paul Sniderman of Stanford University and Tom Piazza of the survey research center at the University of California, Berkeley offered invaluable suggestions on project design and conceptualization. Lynda Lee Kaid of the University of Oklahoma made especially constructive comments on several aspects of the project that related to political communication. Neal Beck of the University of California, San Diego thoughtfully reviewed both the structure of the polls and the survey instruments. Finally, five anonymous reviewers of the original proposal to the National Science Foundation made valuable suggestions that were ultimately reflected in project design and implementation.

The National Science Foundation provided the largest fraction of funding for the project (SES-9905703). This funding covered a substantial portion of survey research, translation, photocopying of survey forms, project-related travel expenses, and data distribution. The Woodrow Wilson School and the Center for Latin American Studies at

Princeton University provided additional funding for a project planning conference, where details of the survey design and instrumentation could be hashed out. Harvard University's Weatherhead Center for International Affairs hosted a conference in December 2000 at which many of the chapters in this volume were presented for the first time. Domínguez in particular thanks the Weatherhead Center for general support of his research, and Harvard's David Rockefeller Center for Latin American Studies for complementary support. Lawson likewise thanks the Massachusetts Institute of Technology for general research support and for covering certain costs of project planning and administration, as well as the Hoover Institution (where final revisions to the volume were completed). We both thank Kathleen Hoover (Weatherhead Center) for her excellent work in the production of this manuscript.

We owe perhaps our greatest debt to *Reforma* newspaper, which conducted the bulk of the polling and covered approximately half the cost of that work. We are especially grateful to Rosanna Fuentes, then an editor at the paper, who contributed to the project as a partner and adviser as well as a contractor. We hope that *Reforma* earns recognition and distinction as a private media outlet that takes seriously its public role.

We also wish to acknowledge the leadership and skill shown by Alejandro Moreno at *Reforma* in conducting a massive panel survey under extremely challenging circumstances. Pollsters in Mexico face obstacles that their counterparts in developed democracies rarely consider, let alone confront. Alejandro managed these problems—phone calls from irate politicians with unsavory reputations who were unhappy with the survey results, interviewers abducted at gunpoint in crime-ridden areas, polling sites populated entirely by monolingual Tzotzil speakers, and so forth—without complaint and without compromising his standards.

Finally, we thank the Mexicans who agreed to be interviewed for this project, in formal surveys or in informal interviews. Whether the Mexican voter was the crucial actor in that country's political transition may be debatable; that ordinary voters were the key to this project is not.

JORGE I. DOMÍNGUEZ, CHAPPELL LAWSON

Acronyms

AC	Alliance for Change (electoral coalition of the PAN and the PVEM)
AM	Alliance for Mexico (electoral coalition led by the PRD)
CD	Democratic Convergence
CEOP	Center for the Study of Public Opinion
CIDE	Center for Economic Research and Instruction
COFIPE	Federal Code of Electoral Institutions and Procedures
CONACYT	National Council on Science and Technology
CONAPO	National Population Council
CT	Workers' Central (peak labor organization affiliated with PRI)
CTM	Confederation of Mexican Workers (peak labor organization affiliated with PRI)
D.F.	Federal District
FDN	National Democratic Front (precursor to PRD)
FLACSO	Latin American Faculty for Social Sciences
IFE	Federal Electoral Institute
INEGI	National Institute for Statistics, Geography, and Informatics
ITAM	Autonomous Technical Institute of Mexico
LICONSA	Industrialized Milk of the National Company for Basic Products (state-owned corporation and federal program that distributes milk at subsidized prices to poor families with young children)
MORI	Market and Opinion Research International (private polling company)
NSF	National Science Foundation
OLS	ordinary least squares regression
PAN	National Action Party
PARM	Party of the Authentic Mexican Revolution
PAS	Social Alliance Party
PCD	Democratic Center Party
PDS	Social Democratic Party

PMS	Mexican Socialist Party
PRD	Party of the Democratic Revolution
PRI	Institutional Revolutionary Party
PROCAMPO	Federal cash-support program for small farmers
PROGRESA	Federal Program for Education, Health, and Nutrition (for poor families)
PRONASOL	National Solidarity Program (federal grassroots development program)
PSN	Nationalist Society Party
PT	Labor Party
PVEM	Green Ecologist Party of Mexico
R	Respondent
TELEVISA	largest private television network
TELMEX	Mexican telephone company
UNAM	National Autonomous University of Mexico

Mexican Words and Phrases

acarreo	busing of voters to the polls
alquimia	alchemy (electoral fraud)
beca	cash stipend
cacique	local boss
cambio	change
cardenismo	the political and social system favored by former president Lázaro Cárdenas and, by extension, his son Cuauhtémoc
cardenista	supporter of Cárdenas; of or pertaining to Cárdenas
Casa Rosada	Argentine presidential palace
caudillismo	rule by a strongman or strongmen
caudillo	strongman
compra y coacción del voto	vote-buying and coercion
credencial	voter identification card
dedazo	hand-picking of his successor by the outgoing president
destape	unveiling of the president's chosen successor
foxista	supporter of Fox
hoy	today
labastidista	supporter of Labastida
Los Pinos	Mexican presidential compound
macho	masculine, manly
madracista	supporter of Madrazo
mariquita	sissy, pansy
mitines	meetings, rallies
oficialista	pro-government or establishment-oriented
panista	supporter of the PAN
partida secreta	president's secret discretionary budget
perredista	supporter of the PRD

político	a politician; a member of the political elite whose career has been mainly in elected rather than appointed office
precandidato	pre-candidate; a primary election contender
priísta	supporter of the PRI
retroceso	retrogression
revisión del voto	observing how someone voted
Secretaría de Gobernación	Mexican Ministry of Government or Interior Ministry
sexenio	six-year presidential term
técnico	a technocrat; a member of the political elite whose career has been mainly in appointed rather than elected office, often in economic policy
voto de miedo	fear vote
voto útil	useful vote; a vote that matters
ya	already (or, more loosely, right now)

Contributors

Kathleen Bruhn is Associate Professor of Political Science at the University of California, Santa Barbara. She is author of *Taking on Goliath: The Emergence of a New Left Party and the Struggle for Democracy in Mexico* (1997) and co-author (with Daniel C. Levy) of *Mexico: The Struggle for Democratic Development* (2001).

Roderic Ai Camp is the Philip McKenna Professor of the Pacific Rim at Claremont McKenna College. He is the author of numerous books, including *Mexico's Mandarins, Crafting a Power Elite for the 21st Century* (2002), *Politics in Mexico, the Democratic Transformation* (2002), *Citizen Views of Democracy in Latin America* (2001), and *Crossing Swords: Politics and Religion in Mexico* (1997). He directs the Hewlett Foundation project on "Democracy through Mexican and United States Lenses."

Wayne A. Cornelius is the Theodore Gildred Professor of Political Science and International Relations, Director of the Center for U.S.-Mexican Studies, and Director of the Center for Comparative Immigration Studies at the University of California, San Diego. He is co-author and co-editor (with Todd Eisenstadt and Jane Hindley) of *Subnational Politics and Democratization in Mexico* (1999) and (with David Myhre) of *The Transformation of Rural Mexico* (1998).

Jorge I. Domínguez is the Clarence Dillon Professor of International Affairs and Director of the Weatherhead Center for International Affairs at Harvard University. He is also co-author (with James McCann) of *Democratizing Mexico: Public Opinion and Electoral Choices* (1996) and co-author and co-editor (with Alejandro Poiré) of *Toward Mexico's Democratization: Parties, Campaigns, Elections, and Public Opinion* (1999).

Joseph L. Klesner is Professor of Political Science at Kenyon College. He has written several essays on Mexican electoral politics, political parties, public opinion, and democratization, which have appeared in *Comparative Politics, Electoral Studies, Latin American Research Review*, and *Mexican Studies/Estudios Mexicanos*, as well as in edited books.

Chappell Lawson is Associate Professor of Political Science at the Massachusetts Institute of Technology, where he holds the Class of 1954 Career Development Chair. He is the author of *Building the Fourth Estate: Democratization and the Rise of a Free Press in Mexico* (2002). He served as principal investigator for the Mexico 2000 Panel Study.

Beatriz Magaloni is Assistant Professor of Political Science at Stanford University. She is co-author (with Alberto Díaz-Cayeros) of "Party Dominance and the Logic of Electoral Design in the Mexican Transition to Democracy," *Journal of Theoretical Politics* (2001). In 1998 she won the Gabriel Almond Award for the Best Dissertation in Comparative Politics and, in 2001 (with Alberto Díaz-Cayeros and Barry Weingast), the prize for the best paper in comparative politics at the meeting of the American Political Science Association.

James A. McCann is Associate Professor of Political Science at Purdue University. He conducts research in the areas of public opinion, electoral behavior, and political parties. His articles have appeared in a variety of academic journals. He is co-author (with Jorge I. Domínguez) of *Democratizing Mexico: Public Opinion and Electoral Choices* (1996).

Alejandro Moreno is Professor of Political Science at the Instituto Tecnológico Autónomo de México (ITAM) and head of the department of polling at the newspaper *Reforma* in Mexico City. He is the author of *Political Cleavages: Issues, Parties, and the Consolidation of Democracy* (1999) and co-author (with Ronald Inglehart and Miguel Basáñez) of *Human Values and Beliefs: A Cross-Cultural Sourcebook* (1998).

Alejandro Poiré is Professor and Chair of the Political Science Department at the Instituto Tecnológico Autónomo de México (ITAM). He is co-author and co-editor (with Jorge I. Domínguez) of *Toward Mexico's Democratization: Parties, Campaigns, Elections, and Public Opinion* (1999).

1

Introduction

CHAPPELL LAWSON

On July 2, 2000, Mexican voters brought to a definitive end the world's
oldest one-party regime. By a margin of more than 6 percent, they
elected opposition candidate Vicente Fox over Francisco Labastida of
the Institutional Revolutionary Party (PRI). For many observers, the
campaign of 2000 was a critical turning point in Mexican democratization, with far-reaching consequences for political life.

THE PUZZLE

Fox's victory was something of a surprise for many Mexicans. A range
of opinion polls had shown Labastida running ahead of Fox, with a gap
of at least 15 points through January 2000. And although this lead
eroded in the months that followed, most polls showed Labastida edg-
ing out his main rival until the official end of the campaign (one week
before election day), after which opinion surveys may not be published. Several private polls failed to anticipate the magnitude of Fox's
victory after that. Surveys conducted by the government and the ruling
party, for instance, predicted that their candidate would win by a significant margin, and even polls by the Fox campaign showed a statistical dead heat as late as three days before the election.[1] Labastida subsequently acknowledged that, until early returns on election day revealed
a sweeping Fox victory, he had never doubted that he would be the
next president of Mexico.[2]

A number of factors justified Labastida's optimism. For over seventy years, ruling party candidates had won every single presidential

contest in Mexico, in most cases without resort to widespread fraud. Until the late 1980s, they had also won every single governorship and an overwhelming majority of local and legislative posts. Although the PRI's vote share had declined steadily during the 1980s, it appeared to have bottomed out at approximately 40 percent by 2000. Even in the 1997 elections, the first national contest held after the disastrous peso devaluation of 1994 and the watershed electoral reforms of 1996, the PRI had managed to garner over 39 percent of the valid vote. As the representative of Mexico's postrevolutionary political establishment, the PRI remained by far Mexico's largest party, with a substantial reservoir of popular support.

The ruling party's prospects in 2000 were, if anything, brighter than they had been three years before. Mexico's economy had grown steadily since 1997, and by July 2000 per capita income had recovered from the peso crash. Moreover, all indications were for continued economic growth along free market lines. During the first quarter of 2000, for instance, gross domestic product expanded at an annualized rate of 8 percent. Although repeated crises had left many Mexicans skeptical of the PRI's economic stewardship, conditions had clearly improved since 1997.

To the economic achievements of the presidency of Ernesto Zedillo (1994–2000) must be added several notable political achievements. Guerrilla insurgencies in Chiapas and elsewhere, though still technically active, had been largely contained and did not appear to threaten social stability. The political turmoil of 1994–1996—including the assassinations of PRI presidential candidate Luis Donaldo Colosio and PRI president José Francisco Ruiz Massieu, as well as rumors of a military coup attempt—had calmed substantially. Mexico was no longer "bordering on chaos," to use the phrase of journalist Andres Oppenheimer.[3]

The most widely touted political achievement of Zedillo's term, however, came in the sphere of democratization. Profound reforms in 1996 had effectively transformed Mexico's electoral system into one worthy of emulation by many established democracies. Opposition parties had won a majority of seats in the lower house of Congress (the Chamber of Deputies), as well as more than a third of the country's state-level governments (including the mayoralty of the Federal District). And freedom of expression, which had never been completely suppressed even during the worst periods of one-party rule, was remarkably robust.[4] By 2000, government officials could plausibly claim that Mexico had already become a democracy despite the PRI's contin-ued control of the presidency.[5]

A series of dramatic changes within the ruling party itself rein-forced this claim. Perhaps the most important of these was the estab-lishment of an open primary system for nominating the PRI's presiden-tial candidate, previously handpicked by the outgoing president. The PRI's primary was held in November 1999, and it was generally con-sidered a success. Francisco Labastida won handily; the three losing "pre-candidates" quickly accepted the results, and none defected to the opposition. Meanwhile, grassroots mobilization and a flood of media coverage surrounding the primary substantially boosted Labastida's support, especially among undecided and independent voters. Mex-ico's old ruling party, it seemed, had learned to play by new rules of the game.

The combination of prosperity, stability, and democratization earned Zedillo a high approval rating. Presidential popularity reached almost 60 percent during the campaign, peaking around the time of the election itself.[6] Figure 1.1 shows average quarterly ratings of Zedillo's job performance from March 1995 (after his first one hundred or so days in office) to March 2000 (in the middle of the campaign). The sur-veys, conducted by *Reforma* newspaper, asked respondents to rate the president on a scale of one to ten (with ten indicating a favorable evaluation). As figure 1.1 shows, average evaluations of Zedillo im-proved consistently after the economic crisis of 1995–1996, reaching their highest level during the campaign. Given the well-documented link between presidential approval and electoral support for the PRI in Mexico, Zedillo's popularity clearly constituted an asset for the ruling party in 2000.[7]

Even more important than the regime's achievements was the fail-ure of Mexico's political opposition to form a united front. Two large opposition factions—led by the center-right National Action Party (PAN) and the center-left Party of the Democratic Revolution (PRD)—fielded candidates, and three less well-known opposition figures also entered the race. Aside from Fox, the most important opposition con-tender was Cuauhtémoc Cárdenas, who had represented Mexico's Left in the presidential campaigns of 1988 and 1994. The son of revered former president Lázaro Cárdenas (1934–1940), his name retained a certain cachet among many Mexicans. In the midterm elections of 1997, when Cárdenas won the mayoralty of Mexico City, his coattails had carried the PRD to almost 26 percent of the national vote—just 1 percent less than the PAN. Although Cárdenas consistently trailed both Fox and Labastida in the polls in 2000, he remained a serious contender and was treated as such by the mass media.[8] Cárdenas's PRD-led coalition thus had the potential to play a spoiler role, robbing Fox of votes needed to defeat the PRI. This scenario seemed increasingly plausible as the campaign progressed, with Cárdenas spending as much energy attacking Fox as he did Labastida.

Figure 1.1. Average Evaluation of Ernesto Zedillo, 1995–2000

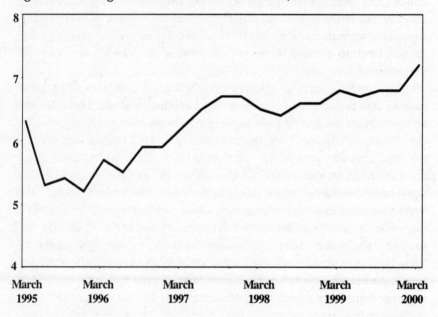

Such opposition divisions represented electoral salvation for Mexico's political establishment. Mexico had no runoff election for president—a reform proposed by the opposition and successfully resisted by the PRI. In a plurality-winner contest, simple arithmetic favored the ruling party. With a solid base of 40 to 45 percent (or so PRI leaders thought) and each major opposition faction able to count on 15 to 20 percent of the electorate, it seemed improbable that either Fox or Cárdenas could defeat the PRI.

Recent state-level elections lent support to this conviction. Between the midterm race of 1997 and the July 2000 presidential contest, seventeen of Mexico's thirty-one states held gubernatorial elections. The

PRI's share of the vote in these states ranged from a low of 38 percent (the July 1999 elections in Baja California Sur) to a high of 53 percent (the February 1999 Hidalgo elections). Perhaps the most obvious analogy was the hotly contested July 1999 race in México State, Mexico's largest and most diverse subnational entity. The PRI won that gubernatorial contest with just under 41 percent of the vote, while the PAN and the PRD split the opposition vote (34 and 21 percent, respectively).

For several reasons, the PRI seemed likely to do at least as well in the presidential race as it had done at the gubernatorial level. Whereas undecided voters might have been willing to cast a ballot against the PRI for governor or federal deputy, where the stakes were relatively low, they were more reluctant to turn over control of the highest office in the land to untested opposition parties.[9] The importance of the presidential race also meant that the PRI was likely to pull out all the stops in an effort to retain power. A number of state-level PRI organizations had engaged in fraud, coercion, vote buying, and similar tactics in the past, as well as in various legitimate forms of electoral mobilization; there was no reason to suspect that the PRI's traditional machinery would suddenly collapse when crucial federal offices were at stake.

As the campaign heated up, these prognostications proved correct. President Zedillo scurried around the country inaugurating public works projects in a series of appearances that looked suspiciously like campaign stops.[10] Other public works were suspended pending the outcome of the elections, with signs posted nearby bearing suggestive phrases like "To be completed on July 3."[11] Such tactics were accompanied by a massive government-sponsored advertising campaign aimed at celebrating the administration's achievements.

Meanwhile, traditional clientelism took on a harsher edge. Beneficiaries of federal welfare programs—from small farmers to mothers with young children to desperately poor recipients of the PROGRESA welfare program—were reminded by their local representatives that these were "PRI programs." In many cases, individual recipients were threatened with a cutoff of much-needed aid if they failed to vote for the ruling party.[12] And ordinary voters were offered every kind of inducement to get to the polls; food, favors, gifts, and cash were all traded for promises of votes.[13] In the state of Yucatán, PRI governor Víctor Cervera even distributed washing machines to party supporters at a June 11 rally in the town of Umán.[14]

Some of these transactions fell within the legal gray zone and were difficult to prosecute. Even where they were plainly illegal, however, the special prosecutor for electoral crimes (a post created as part of the 1996 electoral reform) surpassed himself in dawdle and obfuscation. As of May 2000, not a single violation of electoral law from the 2000 campaign had been successfully prosecuted, nor had a single case of vote buying from *any* election in any part of the country been won.[15] Consequently, vote buying and coercion continued despite protestations from Mexico's opposition and civic groups.

So did campaign finance abuses. Parties and candidates were not legally required to report their expenditures until the end of the year, increasing the opportunities for mischief.[16] Predictably, PRI spending on political advertisements ballooned as the race tightened. According to *Reforma*'s monitoring of television advertisements, PRI spots dwarfed those of both major opposition alliances during the final months of the campaign, despite the fact that all three parties had received roughly equal public funding.[17] Although the true scope of the PRI's campaign finance violations in 2000 may never be known, they appear to have been substantial.[18] Indeed, subsequent revelations about massive diversions of funds from the state-owned oil company, Pemex, to the Labastida campaign triggered a political scandal in 2002.

Finally, certain limited opportunities for old-fashioned fraud remained, even in the reformed electoral system. By 2000, registered observers from opposition parties, civic groups, and international delegations were able to cover perhaps 90 percent of all polling stations for at least part of election day—a remarkable tribute to years of grassroots mobilization by pro-democracy activists.[19] Unfortunately, that still left some 10 percent of polling stations uncovered, typically in remote areas dominated by the PRI. In a tight race, fraud and coercion in these areas could have pushed the ruling party over the top. Although Fox was exaggerating the potential scope of manipulation when he remarked that the PRI would need to win by at least 10 percent for its victory to be credible, many observers felt that a PRI victory of 1 to 2 percent would fall within the margin of fraud.

In short, Francisco Labastida's prospects looked good at the beginning of the presidential campaign. He needed only to retain the PRI's substantial core base and to attract his fair share of undecided voters. With a strong economy, a popular president, a divided opposition, and a few of the PRI's usual tricks, these aspirations did not seem especially ambitious.

To be sure, certain factors worked against the PRI in 2000. Perhaps most problematic was the PRI's reputation for corruption, authoritarianism, and economic mismanagement among sizable segments of the electorate. Despite the reforms of the Zedillo era and recent economic growth, many people were simply fed up with the ruling party. But Mexicans did not seem to be particularly more fed up with the PRI in 2000 than they had been in 1997, and they remained skeptical of the main opposition parties. The PRI thus seemed well positioned to exceed its midterm vote share.

Another potential problem for the PRI was its nominee. Gray and *oficialista*, Labastida was not a particularly inspiring figure. Half a foot shorter than Fox, he sometimes seemed psychologically as well as physically overshadowed—something that became clear during the presidential debates. The PRI's candidate was not, however, notably more dull or unappealing than his predecessors. Certainly by comparison to Ernesto Zedillo (1994), Carlos Salinas (1988), and Miguel de la Madrid (1982), Labastida hardly lacked charisma. In 1986, for instance, he had soundly defeated PAN candidate Manuel Clouthier in the Sinaloa gubernatorial race (69 to 29 percent).

Nor was Labastida particularly vulnerable to charges of corruption. Despite aggressive investigation by Mexico's independent print media, no credible allegations of dirty dealing surfaced. Although rumors circulated about unsavory connections during his tenure as governor of Sinaloa (1987–1992)—a state known for its drug cartels—Labastida's track record on the drug issue was solid enough for public consumption. As governor, for instance, he had been the target of an assassination attempt by drug traffickers, and he briefly left the country (as ambassador to Portugal) after his term ended.

Perhaps the opposition candidates were better than past contenders. In the case of the Left, challenger quality remained similar; Cárdenas had been the Left's candidate in the two previous presidential contests as well. In some respects, Cárdenas looked better in 2000 than in the previous campaigns, given the PRD's large war chest and its better-developed grassroots party organization. Changing media coverage also boded well for the PRD, as hostility toward the Left on the major television networks had diminished somewhat since the early 1990s. In other respects, though, Cárdenas had become a weaker candidate, burdened by his poor record as Mexico City's mayor. Overall, then, there was no reason to assume that leftist challenges to the PRI would prove wildly more appealing to voters than they had in past elections.

Fox's candidacy was potentially more problematic for the PRI. Fox had already demonstrated his ability to draw support from across the opposition spectrum, winning the governorship of Guanajuato State in 1995 by a margin of 25 percent (58 percent against the PRI's 33 percent). Undeniably, he represented a new and potentially attractive alternative to the ruling party. The PAN's candidates in the last two presidential elections, however, had also been solid contenders: Diego Fernández de Cevallos, famous for his vigorous performance in Mexico's first televised presidential debate in 1994, and Manuel Clouthier, the PAN's charismatic 1988 nominee (who was later killed in an automobile accident). Both Fernández and Clouthier had demonstrated their ability not only to mobilize the party's conservative base but also to inspire voters outside its traditional constituency. Having a strong, centrist PAN candidate on the ballot in 2000 certainly threatened Labastida, but it did not appear to doom him.

All told, conditions in 2000 were at least as favorable to the PRI as they had been in 1997. Labastida should have been able to count on at least 40 percent of the vote, and perhaps substantially more than that if he ran a good campaign. Although the opposition as a whole would almost surely win more votes than the PRI, these votes would be divided among two major and three minor candidates, effectively handing the PRI another six-year presidential term.

THE CAMPAIGN

Polls at the beginning of the campaign confirmed that the PRI began the race in good fighting shape. Two surveys by *Reforma*—whose public opinion research team was consistently one of the most reliable in Mexico—showed Labastida with a lead of 8 to 12 percent over Fox in February. Averaging across all published, professional polls, and factoring out undecided voters, Labastida retained between 45 and 50 percent of the vote during January, February, March, and even (according to some surveys) early April. Figure 1.2 shows the results of this "poll of polls."

Part of Labastida's support at the beginning of the campaign may have reflected the lingering effects of his "primary bounce." But many events had occurred in the intervening months that should have erased this effect: the Christmas holidays, the registration of the candidates, substantial press coverage of the early stages of the presidential campaign, the occupation of the National University by federal police, and so on. A more plausible explanation is that Labastida was getting about the share of the vote in February that one would have expected, given preexisting partisan cleavages.

Figure 1.2. The "Poll of Polls"

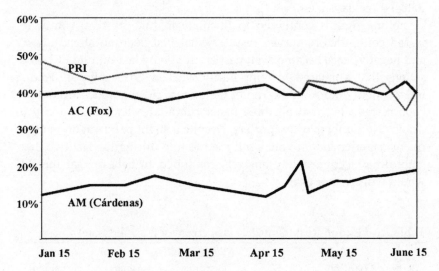

He maintained this lead until about mid-March. At that point, Fox's support began to creep up, and by mid-April, Labastida's support started to slump. The turning point came around the time of the first presidential debate, a widely watched event that included all six presidential candidates. Not only did Fox perform well, but the five opposition candidates joined him in excoriating the ruling party. The first debate thus helped ensure that Mexico's 2000 presidential election would be framed as a referendum on PRI rule, a highly favorable outcome for the PRI's top challenger. By the end of April, just after the debate, Fox and Labastida were neck and neck in the polls.

They remained so through the vicissitudes of the last eight weeks of the campaign. In early May, increasingly negative television coverage of Fox, a vigorous Labastida advertising campaign, and grassroots assistance from the PRI's old guard (the "dinosaurs") helped Labastida regain the lead. On May 17, however, minor-party opposition candidate Porfirio Muñoz Ledo withdrew from the race in favor of Fox, and polls tightened again.

Jockeying for first place continued throughout the rest of May and June. Fox's support ebbed after the so-called Black Tuesday episode of May 23, a live-televised negotiation between the three major candidates about logistics for the second televised debate that left Fox looking foolish. Indeed, many pundits believed that Fox might have cost himself the election that afternoon. But he went on to perform well in the second televised debate (which included only the three major candidates) three days later.

Polling figures continued to fluctuate in June as rival camps released contradictory survey results. What had been an already nasty and negative race became even nastier, driven by last-minute PRI accusations that appeared to temporarily weaken Fox's support among independent voters. At the end of the month, closing rallies around the country revealed that all three major candidates had the capacity to draw vast numbers of supporters. Despite a slight bandwagon in favor of Fox as independent voters returned to him during the last two days before the election, many analysts continued to believe that the PRI would win another term.

Table 1.1. Election Results in 2000 (as percent of the valid vote)

Party or Coalition	Chamber of Deputies	Senate	President
Alliance for Change	39.20	39.09	43.43
PRI	37.77	37.52	36.89
Alliance for Mexico	19.11	19.29	17.00
Others (includes nonregistered candidates)	3.92	4.10	2.68
Total	100.0%	100.00%	100.0%
Total votes cast (including invalid votes)	37.41M	37.52M	37.60M

Notes: Data taken from www.ife.org.mx/wwwore/esta2000, accessed January 12, 2003; votes for the Senate and the Chamber of Deputies represent the proportional representation tallies for those houses. All party shares are percentages of the valid vote; approximately 2.10 percent of the presidential vote, 2.28 percent of the proportional representation Senate vote, and 2.32 percent of the proportional representation congressional vote were ruled invalid.

They were wrong. On election day, opposition supporters turned out in higher-than-usual numbers, and PRI supporters proved more inclined to stay home. Because the actual electorate was substantially more pro-Fox than the population as a whole, the resulting margin of victory was larger than even the polls most favorable to the Alliance for Change had predicted.[20] By midnight, Zedillo had announced Fox's victory, and Labastida had gracefully conceded defeat. The final result of the 2000 campaign was thus a decisive and uncontested victory for

Mexico's leading opposition candidate. Although other parties fared relatively better in proportional representation contests for the Senate and the Chamber of Deputies, Fox's strong showing gave his coalition a substantial boost there as well. Official tallies from presidential and congressional balloting are shown in table 1.1.

The course of the race leaves little doubt that campaign messages were responsible for a substantial shift in public perceptions. Even when earlier polls are weighted to make them demographically comparable to the population that actually voted, thus assuming away any campaign effects on turnout, the five months before the election saw at least a 12 percent shift away from Labastida and in favor of Fox. This shift was, of course, substantially larger than Fox's margin of victory. In other words, the campaign of 2000 clearly altered the outcome of the election. And in doing so, it brought to an end seven decades of PRI rule in Mexico.

THE PROJECT

This book explains what happened in 2000 to change voters' minds. It analyzes the effects on voting behavior of bruising primary competition within the PRI, candidate issue positions and traits, television news coverage, presidential debates, negative campaigning, policy issues and positions, and strategic voting by opposition supporters. And it finds compelling evidence that several of these factors exercised a powerful influence on citizens' choices.

The finding that campaigns matter is perhaps not that surprising. Recently, even scholars of American politics appear to have reached the grudging conclusion that campaigns can prove decisive in determining the outcome of close elections.[21] With a few worthy exceptions, however, scholarly research documenting large-scale campaign effects remains sparse.[22] Given the importance of the topic and the relative dearth of rigorous academic studies, the findings presented in this volume have wide-ranging implications for the study of electoral behavior.

This is especially true for countries outside the developed West— that is, for the majority of electoral democracies. Many new democracies in the developing world lack well-established party systems. Even in Mexico—which has one of the most articulated party systems among emerging democracies—levels of partisan attachment remain lower than in countries like the United States, England, Costa Rica, and Germany. Presumably, the relative absence of partisan anchors leaves a greater proportion of the electorate susceptible to campaign influences.[23]

The potential for campaign effects is presumably greater in a high-intensity contest, which reaches people not normally engaged in politics. In Mexico's 2000 presidential race, saturation media coverage and grassroots mobilization by partisan activists offered citizens a range of campaign messages. The three main parties, awash with public funding, overburdened the airwaves with vast numbers of advertisements. Banners flapped from wires strung across major roadways, posters covered lampposts and trees, and murals with political slogans were stenciled on walls in even the poorest and most remote areas. Meanwhile, candidates barnstormed the country, and party activists fanned out across thousands of neighborhoods and villages. Even for those few citizens without access to television—already a small portion of the electorate—it was hard to ignore campaign stimuli.

The combination of weak initial partisan attachments and high levels of campaign exposure argues for pronounced campaign effects. Bluntly put, if the so-called minimal effects model of campaigns looks wrong for established democracies, it looks horribly wrong for Mexico in 2000. Far from being trivial or marginal influences on electoral outcomes, campaign effects can prove highly consequential.

THE DATA

The contributions in this volume rely primarily on data from the Mexico 2000 Panel Study, a project conceived and overseen by the authors themselves. One of the first efforts of its kind in an emerging democracy, the Mexico 2000 Panel Study was explicitly designed to measure campaign influences on voting behavior in the 2000 contest. Given its relevance to this volume, that project merits some explanation here.

The Mexico 2000 Panel Study consisted of approximately 7,000 interviews in five separate polls over the course of the campaign, using a hybrid panel/cross-sectional design. Its first round, conducted between February 19–27 (just after the official beginning of the campaign), polled a national cross-section of 2,400 adults. This sample was then randomly divided into two groups, the first of which was re-interviewed in the second round (April 28–May 7). Because of attrition, this wave included approximately 950 respondents. In the third round (June 3–18), pollsters re-interviewed those in the second randomly selected subset of the first round, plus approximately 400 respondents interviewed in the second round. Finally, in the fourth round (July 7–16), pollsters re-interviewed as many of the participants as possible from all previous rounds. This included almost 1,200 respondents who had been interviewed in the second and third rounds, as well as just over 100 respondents who had only been previously interviewed in the first. We also supplemented the panel sample with a separate cross-sectional survey of approximately 1,200 fresh respondents (see figure 1.3).

Figure 1.3. Mexico 2000 Panel Study

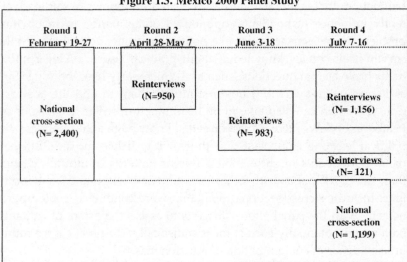

This hybrid design promised substantial benefits over either a pure panel study or a series of cross-sectional polls. The panel nature of the data allows analysts to control for individual-level effects—something crucial for most analyses of campaign influence. In the case of media effects, for instance, self-selection of viewers to media that accord with their preexisting views makes conclusions drawn from cross-sectional data highly suspect. It may be, for instance, that regular listeners of independent talk-radio programs are more likely to vote for the opposition. But these listeners may tune in to such radio programs because they already detest the government, rather than the other way around. With panel data, analysts can tell not only whether people who listen to independent radio shows were more likely to vote for the opposition, but also whether, controlling for other factors, they were more likely to switch to the opposition than their compatriots who relied on more pro-government media.

Of course, relying on panel data alone entails certain trade-offs and sacrifices. Because of attrition, panel surveys are not representative of the general population. The inclusion of a separate cross-sectional poll (embedded in the fourth wave), however, allows researchers to determine whether the sorts of effects identified in the panel also occurred in random cross-sections of the population.

Another potential drawback to pure panel studies is the risk of contamination: that is, the danger that repeated interviews might inadvertently influence respondents' opinions. Contamination is an obvious problem for measuring issues like political learning; not only might the survey itself convey knowledge about political issues, asking respondents basic factual questions (such as "Which party uses the Aztec Sun as its campaign symbol?") might stimulate them to find the answers. Contamination can also take more insidious forms. For instance, if repeated interviews increase respondents' knowledge about politics, and political learning is associated with growing dislike for the PRI, then panel participants might exhibit different patterns of attitude change than nonparticipants with otherwise similar backgrounds and opinions. Including cross-sectional polls that were conducted contemporaneously with the panel allows analysts to assess the extent of contamination and potentially correct for it statistically. (In practice, we found little evidence of contamination or attrition bias.)

Finally, the Mexico 2000 Panel Study covered a wide range of issues relevant to voting behavior: demographic characteristics, media exposure, political knowledge and engagement, opinion about salient public issues, attitudes toward the main parties and candidates, impressions of the electoral process, and (of course) voting intentions. Special attention was paid to campaign influences, such as contact with party activists, media use, exposure to political advertisements, and the presidential debates, as well as to attitudes about the main parties and voting intentions. Several of these questions—for instance, exposure to television news—were repeated in all four waves of the panel.

THE FINDINGS

The chapters that follow use these and other data to understand what happened in Mexico over the course of the campaign. They first provide background on the evolution of the Mexican political system and on partisan cleavages at the start of the 2000 campaign. They then discuss the main parties and candidates before turning to the electoral impact of different elements of the campaign.

In the next chapter, Roderic Camp places the 2000 campaign in the context of Mexico's political transition and democratic consolidation. Camp first reviews how national-level reforms and civic monitoring efforts by nongovernmental organizations and the Catholic Church helped to level the electoral playing field in 2000. He then discusses how the elections themselves changed Mexicans' perceptions of their political system. In February, Mexicans were about evenly divided on the question of whether or not their country was a democracy. After Fox's victory, however, approximately two-thirds of Mexicans felt their system was democratic. The 2000 election was thus both a culmination of decades of political reform and a watershed event in Mexico's democratic transition.

In chapter 3, Wayne Cornelius explores in greater detail the effect of Mexico's new electoral context on voting behavior. Specifically, he demonstrates the increasing ineffectiveness of traditional PRI tactics such as vote buying and coercion. Cornelius notes that a series of political reforms during the 1990s made it more and more difficult for the PRI to rely on vote buying and coercion to win elections. By 2000, artificially "mobilized voters" had become a vanishingly small percentage of the total electorate. Even where the PRI attempted to employ traditional tactics, these tactics had little impact on either turnout or candidate choice.

In chapter 4, Chappell Lawson and Joseph Klesner analyze further how political reforms and the breakdown of authoritarian institutions altered patterns of electoral participation in Mexico. Contrary to the conventional wisdom, they show that turnout rates were not particularly high in 2000. What did change markedly, however, was the composition of turnout: whereas higher turnout used to be correlated with higher levels of PRI support, by the mid-1990s the reverse was true. The elections of 2000 represented the culmination of this trend, as PAN voters participated more and PRI voters less.

Lawson and Klesner identify three main causes of this remarkable reversal in patterns of participation. First, simple fraud and ballot stuffing, which had artificially inflated both aggregate turnout rates and the PRI's share of the vote, declined during the 1990s. Second, political reforms gradually weakened the PRI's traditional machinery, which for decades had delivered rural and union votes. Consequently, previously captured PRI voters were now freer to abstain. Third, these same reforms encouraged opposition faith in the integrity of the electoral process. As a result, those who might once have abstained out of frustration or cynicism showed up on election day to cast their ballots for Fox.

Given the erosion of traditional authoritarian controls, how might Mexicans be expected to vote? In chapter 5, Joseph Klesner describes the partisan cleavages that characterized Mexico on the eve of the 2000 elections. Using both ecological and individual-level data, Klesner argues that the dominant political cleavage in Mexico remained between supporters of the regime (on the one hand) and opposition voters of all ideological persuasions (on the other). In other words, attitudes toward the system explained much more of the variation in individual-level voting behavior than demographic variables or Left-Right ideological divisions. Although those factors continued to divide Mexico's opposition, the pro-regime/anti-regime divide simultaneously offered Fox an exploitable electoral cleavage upon which to base his campaign.

With this electoral context in mind, Kathleen Bruhn discusses the campaign strategies that shaped the course of the presidential race. Bruhn analyzes how Fox was able to articulate a clear message of change that proved crucial to his ultimate victory. Slogans, advertisements, speeches, and a steady stream of other cues all reinforced the same theme. Even personal attacks on Labastida, Bruhn intimates, were part of the Fox campaign's game plan to cut the ruling party down to a beatable size. This overall strategy was consciously crafted to unite opposition voters against the PRI.

By contrast, the behavior of the Cárdenas campaign was contradictory. For instance, the campaign devoted huge sums of money to television advertisements, but Cárdenas himself invested vast amounts of time in one-on-one exchanges with individual supporters and petitioners. The PRD also largely failed to make effective use of its network of local activists, which had served it famously well in 1997. For Bruhn, divisions within Cárdenas's Alliance for Mexico and general incompetence or inexperience on the part of the PRD leadership were crucial factors in preventing Cárdenas from articulating a consistent message. As a result of this failure, the PRD could not fully protect itself from *foxista* inroads.

Neither, it turns out, could the PRI. One crucial element of the PRI's rather lackluster campaign was its ambivalence toward the Zedillo administration. Rather than projecting himself as the successor to a popular president, Labastida half-heartedly embraced Zedillo's economic record while simultaneously attempting to distance himself from neoliberal policies. This strategy, Bruhn argues, may have been appropriate for a front-runner seeking to avoid alienating crucial constituencies. But it had the unintended consequence of allowing Fox to set the agenda for the campaign itself.

One possible explanation for the weakness of Labastida's candidacy is the divisive nature of the PRI's primary contest. In fact, many PRI activists have since charged that holding a competitive primary unnecessarily polarized the party and encouraged supporters of Labastida's main rival, Roberto Madrazo, to defect or stay home on election day. In chapter 7, James McCann explores the effects of the PRI's primary on support for Labastida in the general election. Contrary to the protestations of PRI dinosaurs, McCann finds that the holding of a competitive presidential primary did not alienate PRI voters in the general election. Given that the primary—and the media coverage that surrounded it—presumably increased the PRI's appeal to nonpartisans and undecideds, it can hardly be blamed for the PRI's defeat. Rather, the reasons for Fox's victory lie in signals that voters acquired during the campaign.

The next several chapters address these signals in greater detail. In chapter 8, Chappell Lawson focuses on the nature of television news coverage during the campaign. In keeping with previous studies of Mexican voting behavior, Lawson finds that television news exercised a significant influence on citizens' opinions of the main candidates.[24] Because news coverage, especially on the Televisión Azteca network, was substantially more balanced than in past elections, exposure to TV news boosted support for Fox. Even controlling for a range of other factors, the magnitude of this effect was impressive—possibly large enough to alter the outcome of the election.

In chapter 9, Lawson turns to the effects of the two televised candidate debates. Although debate effects were largely mitigated or overshadowed by subsequent campaign events, both debates seem to have exercised a significant impact on public opinion in the short run. Moreover, they also played an important role in framing the election and altering campaign strategy, which in turn shaped the course of the race.

In chapter 10, Alejandro Moreno analyzes the consequences of negative campaigning for voting behavior. As Moreno points out, the 2000 contest was extraordinarily nasty, punctuated by some rather spectacular examples of mudslinging. Fox's campaign, in particular, was systematically negative—lambasting both the regime in general and his PRI opponent in particular. Moreno finds that these tactics were fairly effective for a crucial subset of the electorate—weak PRI supporters—damaging their evaluations of Labastida and reducing their likelihood of voting. Although not massive, this effect was both statistically significant and electorally consequential, costing the PRI much-needed and traditionally reliable votes.

Presumably, Fox's strategy should also have facilitated strategic defections from the PRD. This is, in fact, what Beatriz Magaloni and Alejandro Poiré find in chapter 11. Despite the fact that much of the coordination between opposition voters occurred before February, Magaloni and Poiré document the continuing relevance of strategic considerations in the five months before the election as well. Although few voters faced a strategic dilemma, in the sense that most believed their favored candidate was likely to win, a significant number of those who did switched their vote. Fox was the principal beneficiary of such strategic voting, which became a modest contributor to his victory.

The story that emerges from these chapters, then, is one of a hard-fought campaign changing the outcome of an election. Although electoral reforms and preexisting political divisions made Fox's victory possible, it was the campaign itself that proved decisive. And by influencing the outcome of the election, the campaign helped propel democratization in Mexico.

In chapter 12, Magaloni and Poiré turn to the meaning of Fox's victory. Apart from the one overriding issue—change—they find little evidence that previously salient issues like economic reform, religion, or crime had much of an impact on voters. Even more remarkably, they find little effect of economic considerations or attitudes toward political reform on voter preferences. Political change—defined by Fox as alternation in power—remained the dominant issue in the course of the campaign. Change, however, took on more of an "ins-versus-outs" flavor than that of a vote for political reform and democracy. Thus Mexico's 2000 election marked the end of heady, high-stakes "transitional" politics and the beginning of electoral "politics as usual." In this new environment, valence issues and candidate characteristics loomed especially large.

In the final chapter, Jorge Domínguez returns to the broader issues that animated this study. In contexts like the Mexican one, Domínguez argues, campaigns can play a crucial role in shaping voters' preferences and behavior. In the absence of deep social cleavages, strong partisan attachments, and economic or political crises, campaign-related stimuli shape whether and how people vote. Campaigns particularly matter, it seems, when candidates are seen to have dramatically different levels of personal appeal, when prospective economic calculations (rather than retrospective punishment votes) take precedence, and when exposure to campaign messages (such as candidate debates, media coverage, and political advertisements) is extensive. This was, of course, the context of Mexico in 2000.

To be sure, Domínguez acknowledges, Mexico's political transition was not purely the product of campaign effects. A number of broader institutional changes set the stage for the 2000 campaign. These included, among other things, electoral reforms culminating in the autonomy of the Federal Electoral Institute (IFE), the development of independent media and polling firms, the emergence and growth of viable opposition parties, and inroads by these same opposition parties at subnational levels. In this new context, opposition parties could expect to compete on roughly equal footing with the PRI and win elections—even presidential elections.

Nevertheless, Domínguez insists, opposition victory was hardly a foregone conclusion. It depended on candidate selection, party strategies, media coverage, and other campaign-related variables. Were it not for these factors, Fox would not have won in 2000. Campaign effects were thus both large and consequential.

For emerging democracies, campaign effects are consequential in another sense as well. In consolidated democracies such as the United States, elections alter the distribution of power within an existing and established political system. In countries undergoing political transition, however, elections also shape the nature of the system itself. Campaigns and elections matter more in emerging democracies because they help to determine how democratic these societies will actually become. Mexico is, of course, a classic case in point; its 2000 election marked a decisive step forward in what had previously been a halting and uncertain process of political transition. The findings presented here thus have broader implications for future research on democratization.

The features that made the campaign of 2000 so crucial are not unique to Mexico. On the contrary, these features are common to many new democracies, and campaign effects are likely to be pronounced in those societies as well. Documenting these effects in a rigorous, compelling way constitutes one of the most important and interesting challenges for political science in the next decade. This volume, we hope, represents an initial contribution to that research agenda.

Notes

1. Interviews by Lawson, Mexico City, June 23–30, 2000.

2. Sam Dillon, "Mexico's Ruling Party Reported to Quash Polls Predicting Its Defeat," *New York Times*, July 17, 2000.

3. Andres Oppenheimer, *Bordering on Chaos* (Boston: Little Brown & Co., 1996).

4. See Chappell Lawson, *Building the Fourth Estate: Democratization and the Rise of a Free Press in Mexico* (Berkeley: University of California Press): 173–77.

5. On the nature and extent of democracy in Mexico, see Chappell Lawson, "Mexico's Unfinished Transition: Democratization and Authoritarian Enclaves in Mexico," *Mexican Studies/Estudios Mexicanos* 16, no. 2 (Summer 2000): 267–87.

6. According to the Mexico 2000 Panel Study, Zedillo's approval ratings were 58 percent in July 2000 (with 24 percent neither approving nor disapproving). In February, they were 59 percent (with 17 percent neither approving nor disapproving).

7. Jorge I. Domínguez and Alejandro Poiré, eds., *Toward Mexico's Democratization: Parties, Campaigns, Elections, and Public Opinion* (New York: Routledge, 1999); Jorge I. Domínguez and James A. McCann, *Democratizing Mexico: Public Opinion and Electoral Choices* (Baltimore, Md.: Johns Hopkins University Press, 1996).

8. For media treatment of Cárdenas, see the chapter on television coverage in this volume.

9. On risk aversion in Mexican voting behavior, see Alejandro Poiré, "Retrospective Voting, Partisanship, and Loyalty in Presidential Elections," in Jorge I. Domínguez and Alejandro Poiré, eds., *Toward Mexico's Democratization*, pp. 32–33; Alberto Cinta, "Uncertainty and Electoral Behavior in Mexico in the 1997 Congressional Elections," in Jorge I. Domínguez and Alejandro Poiré, eds., *Toward Mexico's Democratization*, pp. 174–202.

10. Although campaigning by an incumbent chief executive on behalf of his party would be considered normal in most democracies, in Mexico's transitional context Zedillo's actions raised concerns about official manipulation of the election. In April, electoral authorities wrote the president to request that he refrain from launching public works projects during the rest of the campaign. Author's interviews, Mexico City, June 23–30, 2000.

11. Lawson's personal observation in México State, May 2000; Global Exchange/ Alianza Cívica, "Introduction," in *Pre-electoral Conditions in Mexico in 2000*, June 2000.

12. The impact of these tactics is discussed in Wayne Cornelius's contribution to this volume. For further details on the extent of vote buying and coercion, see Sam Dillon, "In Mexican Campaign, Money Still Buys Votes," *New York Times*, June 19, 2000; Guillermo Correa, "El PRI va por el voto pobre: operan a su servicio 173 programas sociales," *Proceso*, May 14, 2000, pp. 22–24; Ignacio Rodríguez Reyna, "La perfecta armonía entre el Progresa y los votos del PRI," *Milenio*, January 17, 2000, pp. 36–45; Alejandro Almazán, "Los sufragios de la amenaza: 'Si no votan por Labastida, les van a quitar el Progresa'" *Milenio*, May 29, 2000, pp. 25–32; Sergio Flores, "Se distribuyen los cheques del 'Progresa'," *Reforma*, May 9, 1999.

13. Global Exchange/Alianza Cívica, *Pre-electoral Conditions in Mexico in 2000*, June 2000; Alianza Cívica, *First Report of Electoral Irregularities Detected by the Civic Alliance*, Mexico City, June 13, 2000; Alianza Cívica, *Second Report of Electoral Irregu-*

larities Detected by the Civic Alliance, June 30, 2000; Washington Office on Latin America, "Vote-Buying and Coercion of Voters," *Mexico Election Monitor 2000*, No. 4 (May 2000); Washington Office on Latin America, "The Electoral Justice System," *Mexico Election Monitor 2000*, No. 6 (July 2000); Alianza Cívica/Mexico Working Group, *Democracy: The Long and Winding Road* (report by international observers), July 2000; Sam Dillon and Julia Preston, "Mexico Pledges a Clean Vote, but the Old Ways Die Hard," *New York Times*, May 9, 2000; Michael Christie, "Mexico enters final day of campaign ahead of vote," Reuters, June 28, 2000; Sam Dillon, "Clean Vote Vowed in Mexico, but Fraud Dies Hard," *New York Times*, June 28, 2000.

14. Sam Dillon, "In Mexican Campaign, Money Still Buys Votes."

15. Washington Office on Latin America, "The Electoral Justice System"; personal conversation with Special Prosecutor Javier Patiño, Mexico City, May 2000; personal conversation with Deputy Elodia Gutiérrez of the Comisión 2000, Mexico City, May 2000.

16. Washington Office on Latin America, "Campaign Finance," *Mexico Election Monitor 2000*, No. 3 (April 2000).

17. In 2000, the PRI received 921 million pesos (about US$99 million), of which 445 million could be used for campaign expenses. The PAN and the PVEM (Green Party) together were entitled to 940 million pesos (US$107), of which 453 million could be used for campaign expenses. See George W. Grayson, *A Guide to the 2000 Mexican Presidential Election: An Election Studies Report of the CSIS Americas Program*, Mexico Project (Washington, D.C.: Center for Strategic and International Studies, June 2000): 25, 62.

18. Opposition groups, such as the "Friends of Fox," may also have engaged in dubious campaign tactics. See Wayne Cornelius's chapter, this volume, for further details.

19. According to the Federal Electoral Institute, representatives of the Alliance for Change covered 82 percent of polling stations for at least part of election day; the Alliance for Mexico covered 65 percent.

20. See Alejandro Moreno, "En busca de los votantes del 2 de julio," *Enfoque*, August 23, 2000.

21. Christopher Wlezien, "On Forecasting the Presidential Vote," *Political Science and Politics* 24, no. 1 (March 2001): 25–31; James E. Campbell, "The Referendum That Didn't Happen: The Forecasts of the 2000 Presidential Election," *Political Science and Politics* 24, no. 1 (March 2001): 33–38.

22. See Richard Johnston, André Blais, Henry E. Brady, and Jean Crête, *Letting the People Decide: Dynamics of a Canadian Election* (Stanford, Calif.: Stanford University Press, 1992); Lawrence LeDuc, Richard G. Niemi, and Pippa Norris, eds., *Comparing Democracies: Elections and Voting in Global Perspective* (Thousand Oaks, Calif.: Sage, 1996); David L. Swanson and Paolo Mancini, eds., *Politics, Media, and Modern Democracy: An International Study of Innovations in Electoral Campaigning and their Consequences* (New York: Praeger, 1996).

23. See James A. McCann and Chappell Lawson, "An Electorate Adrift? Public Opinion and the Quality of Democracy in Mexico," *Latin American Research Review*, forthcoming.

24. See Chappell Lawson, *Building the Fourth Estate*.

PART I

The Electoral Context

2

Citizen Attitudes toward Democracy and Vicente Fox's Victory in 2000

RODERIC AI CAMP

Mexico witnessed an extraordinary political change on July 2, 2000. In its own way, it can be fairly described as a revolution, because its scope extends well beyond a simple electoral upset to affect citizen attitudes toward democracy, the general political setting, and political processes and behavior in years to come. The changes that Vicente Fox's victory portends go much deeper than Fox the candidate, having been firmly established in the polity during the last decade. Nevertheless, survey research makes clear, with dramatic new data, that the electoral process itself is as important to forming democratic beliefs as are democratic beliefs to the efficacy of competitive, fair elections.[1]

Each of the Mexican presidential elections since 1988 contributed significantly to the altered setting of electoral contests leading up to July 2, 2000. During those twelve years, Mexican voters began to alter their perceptions of the electoral process and, more fundamentally, of democracy. Those influences were especially strong on children, who were being socialized from numerous directions in this pluralistic environment.[2] Voter perceptions came together in a strange chemistry that produced the opposition victory in 2000. The changes that led to that electoral outcome suggest how complicated Mexican democratic attitudes might also be in the future.

This chapter briefly explores Mexico's altered political setting as revealed by recent survey research, describes relevant and sometimes contradictory voter attitudes toward democracy, and assesses the impact of these attitudes on the Fox victory in 2000 and on future political participation generally. These changes in attitudes toward conceptualizing democracy, and translating democratic beliefs into participation, are analyzed in terms of their likely impact in the post-Fox inaugural period and in terms of what a Fox presidency means for democratic participation at the mass level.

WHAT MADE A FOX VICTORY POSSIBLE?

The larger context of the Mexican electoral arena changed dramatically from 1988 through 2000. The single most important political change is the fact that the political opposition had emerged from a marginal status in Mexico's polity, to that of a major, visible actor. In other words, political parties other than the Institutional Revolutionary Party (PRI) began to exert an influence on all political institutions other than the national executive and judicial branches, and this influence could be measured both in policy terms and symbolically. What happened on July 2, 2000, might well be more significant symbolically than for its actual legislative contributions at the local, state, and national levels.

The presence of other political parties—notably the National Action Party (PAN) and the Party of the Democratic Revolution (PRD)—can be seen in the comparative figures that measure their control over political institutions. In 1994, just six years before Fox's victory, opposition parties jointly controlled 11 percent of Mexico's thirty-two gubernatorial posts, 40 percent of the seats in the national Chamber of Deputies, and 26 percent of the Senate positions.[3] In June 2000, just weeks before the election, opposition parties controlled 34 percent of governorships, 52 percent of deputy positions, and 41 percent of Senate seats. These figures represent a dramatic, quantitative increase in the opposition's popularity during the administration of Ernesto Zedillo (1994–2000). Moreover, the figures are deceptive in that they do not readily convey the qualitative impact of opposition political control.

The symbolic and pragmatic presence of opposition leadership immediately prior to the 2000 presidential election is made clear by the fact that, at the state level, opposition figures governed one-third of Mexico's population, and at the local level their governance extended to half of Mexico's population.[4] The economic complement to this statistic is that, although the opposition only controlled eleven states, those states (including the Federal District) accounted for 48 percent of Mexico's gross domestic product.[5]

Grassroots experience becomes a crucial experiential ingredient in determining Mexican attitudes toward the opposition, toward change, and toward democracy's existence and benefits. In other words, if the majority of Mexicans viewed their experiences under the alteration of power as positive (which is not to say all Mexicans found opposition control successful or positive), those experiences might translate into a more receptive environment for democratic experimentation and change. This is particularly noteworthy in the Mexican case because a sizable percentage of Mexicans in past presidential elections, and even immediately prior to the 2000 presidential election, remained fearful of trying something different—specifically a new party in the presidency.[6]

Opposition control at the local and state levels produced policy consequences directly attributable to their leadership. A summary of the impact of the opposition parties' influence in the national legislative branch can be seen in the comparable success of PRI-dominated initiatives compared to all other parties combined. The 1997–2000 legislative sessions approved 89 percent of the PRI-controlled executive branch initiatives, suggesting the incumbent party's excessive dominance over national legislation.[7] In contrast, only 12 to 17 percent of all other parties' legislation passed.[8] However, it is important to note that the volume of executive-branch initiatives dropped during this period compared to previous legislative sessions.

The other major contextual change, a product of opposition party influence in the national legislative branch, was a significant alteration in institutional structures, specifically those institutions responsible for the national electoral process. As a consequence of the 1996 electoral reforms, pushed through under opposition party pressure, Mexico placed the most influential electoral functions into the hands of the Federal Electoral Institute (IFE), led by a highly respected independent council and chairperson, José Woldenberg. Of the many functions assigned to the IFE, the most important included:

- the authority to select participants in the electoral contests (in effect, shaping the party system);

- the power to dictate electoral rules (which establishes the system of representation);

- the responsibility for counting the votes (which determines the actual results); and

- with the Federal Electoral Tribunal, the task of validating the election results (thus establishing the winner's legitimacy).[9]

In addition to the depth of opposition control and the establishment of an autonomous electoral institute, the composition of Mexican political actors was different. In terms of political parties, twelve years ago the PRD did not even exist. The presence of three strong political parties, two of them intensely opposed to the incumbent party, flavored the electoral landscape. Furthermore, eleven political parties participated in the 2000 race, the majority of them forming alliances with the two leading opposition parties, the PAN and PRD. Those alliances proved crucial to the opposition's electoral success, given relevant changes in the campaign finance laws.[10]

The availability of public funds helped to level, for the first time in Mexican election history, the financial playing field among the three leading parties.[11] Each party's performance in the 1997 congressional elections determined the distribution of public funds.[12] For example, although the PRI obtained 40 percent of the vote in those elections, the highest plurality, it received only US$52 million, $4 million more than the PRD's Alliance for Mexico. The PAN-led Alliance for Change, with Fox as its candidate, received almost exactly the same funding levels as the PRI, although the PAN won only 27 percent of the vote in 1997.[13]

The other condition that contributed strongly to an increased perception of a democratic playing field was the fact that the two leading candidates, Francisco Labastida and Vicente Fox, were ranked in a dead heat in the last weeks of the presidential contest.[14] Public opinion polls in Mexico have become a fresh actor in the political process. Given years of electoral fraud and the belief of many Mexicans, even in 2000, that the elections would not be fair, reputable poll results demonstrated the actual strength of the opposition candidates. The PAN, the PRD, and the media since 1994 used polling results as a benchmark for electoral outcomes, making it more difficult for the PRI to commit fraud.[15] Therefore, voters knew in the last week of June that a competitive electoral landscape provided a realistic opportunity for an opposition candidate to win, especially since Labastida himself openly admitted earlier in the campaign that he could lose.

Finally, another influential contextual condition established itself as a component of the voting culture, rather than exclusively as an ideological pattern in society. We do not have a means of determining when this ideological shift began, but it became clear in the late 1990s that Mexicans began to conceive of themselves as being on the right of the political spectrum. Survey research revealed that on a ten-point scale of right to left, the vast majority of Mexicans, 57 percent, considered themselves to be on the right compared to only 20 percent on the left.[16]

This extremely important ideological variable suggests that the only political parties in Mexico that could easily attract the typical voter are parties perceived as center-right or right. What is equally fascinating about this self-identification is that the PRI has replaced the PAN, viewed traditionally as a conservative, Catholic organization, as the far-right party.[17] As a Reforma exit poll demonstrated, voters' ideological preferences were translated into actual candidate choices. Fox received more votes than Labastida from all but one self-identified ideological category, but he obtained the highest support, 59 percent, from center-right voters. Labastida, on the other hand, performed far stronger among far-right voters, from whom he obtained 57 percent of the vote, compared to only 30 percent for Fox.[18]

DEMOCRACY AND THE MEXICAN VOTER IN THE 1990s

As an increasingly competitive and democratic electoral setting began to emerge in the 1990s, analysts were able to identify characteristics of the evolving Mexican voter. These characteristics, translated into voting behavior, interacted with and in part were a product of the newly minted democratic setting.[19] The difficulty in assessing their importance, and in drawing comparisons with voter behavior elsewhere, stemmed from the fact that a truly viable voter, who could hold political leadership accountable, did not emerge until after 1988, when Cuauhtémoc Cárdenas, a coalition candidate, surprised most observers with his strong showing against Carlos Salinas despite widespread fraud.

Prior to the 2000 presidential election, the most influential aggregate variable in determining electoral outcomes was the state of the economy and the individual's assessment of his own economic situation, perhaps the key factor in 1997. Its impact varies from one election to another. But declining economic fortunes were not always associated with voter turnout (as distinct from voter choices), and many Mexican voters in times of economic downturn abstained altogether instead of voting for the PAN or PRD.

The economic setting in July 2000 differed from that in 1997 or 1994. Ernesto Zedillo faced a serious economic crisis in the first year of his presidency, similar to economic difficulties shared by his immediate predecessors. Despite such a difficult beginning, Zedillo's macroeconomic policies eventually led to a steadily improving economy. It is evident that many Mexicans were not the direct beneficiaries of those governmental policies; nevertheless, their overall perceptions of economic conditions generally and personally were more positive in 2000 than in either earlier period.[20] Indeed, their perception of President Zedillo's job performance was quite strong, with 56 percent approving his presidency compared to 23 percent who disapproved. Both of these perceptions should have helped Labastida at the polls.

The interrelationship between democracy and economic performance is apparent when citizens identify what they expect from democracy. In an October 1999 poll conducted by *Reforma* newspaper and sponsored by the Hewlett Foundation, among Mexicans who participated in an open PRI primary to determine its presidential candidate, 36 percent expected economic progress or improvement from democracy, followed by 15 percent who hoped for the rule of law and 15 percent who hoped for equality. If a third of the voters hoped that democracy would lead to an improvement in their personal economic situation, why did this perception not help Labastida?

The reason for this is that, unlike in the 1994 presidential election, voters in 2000 made almost no distinctions between the leading candidates' abilities to implement various economic policies. In contrast, in the race between Ernesto Zedillo and Diego Fernández de Cevallos, the two leading candidates in 1994, Zedillo scored much more favorably.

Voter perceptions of the integrity of the electoral process itself, although increasing positively over the last decade, did not change dramatically between 1994 and 2000. One out of three voters still expressed little or no faith in the balloting process's integrity immediately prior to the July 2000 elections. As James McCann and Jorge Domínguez have demonstrated, "the greater the expectation of fraud, the lower the likelihood of voting."[21] Contrary to many predictions, voter turnout, while reasonably strong at 64 percent, was not as massive as was the case six years earlier, when neither the PAN nor the PRD had any chance of winning.[22] However, in those districts where the Alliance for Change won more than 50 percent of the votes, the turnout was higher than average.[23]

The fact that the candidates themselves did not generate strong partisan sympathies explains the lower turnout. Specifically, Labastida was not able to mobilize the traditional PRI voter. In other words, because most voters clearly could not distinguish between the moral qualities and administrative abilities of the two leading candidates, and economic conditions remained moderately favorable, no immediate incentive appealing to most voters encouraged strong voter turnout.

Indeed, 71 percent expressed little or no interest in the campaign in February 2000. The fact that most Mexicans remained uninterested in politics reinforced a specific lack of interest in the presidential race.[24] Low levels of political interest suggest that, unless something significant piques voters' concerns, turnout will never be massive.

One of the most revealing characteristics of Mexican voters exposed through survey research is their source of political information. Most citizens receive their political information through television—specifically television news programs and campaign advertising. During the campaign, 84 percent of the voters watched television news, and two-thirds of those viewed news programs at least four or more times weekly.[25] Most Mexicans believed that Francisco Labastida received more coverage on television, but in a given time period during the campaign, an equal number, half, saw advertisements for both Fox and Labastida. The qualitative impact on the voter, however, did not correspond to campaign advertising's balanced exposure among citizens.[26] Qualitatively speaking, Fox's advertising achieved a greater impact as measured by the fact that nearly one out of two voters could actually associate his name with his campaign jingle (*Ya, ya, ya, ya es hora del cambio*). In contrast, only 38 percent correctly identified Labastida's motto (*Que el poder sirva a la gente*) despite the fact that Labastida himself was slightly better known than Fox.

It is impossible to prove a specific empirical linkage between voters exposed to the campaign theme of change and those who actually voted for change. But it seems reasonable to argue that Fox's campaign advertising helped to flavor the electoral setting by giving much greater visibility—and, in all probability, legitimacy—to the concept of change. Fox was capitalizing on and reinforcing a remarkable evolution in voter attitudes since 1980.[27]

The *Dallas Morning News* was the first media source, using survey research, to notice a significant voter attitudinal shift toward change. On June 21, 2000, just ten days before the election, the paper reported that 43 percent of the respondents had indicated they would never vote for the PRI, compared to only 30 percent expressing that posture in December 1999. Even more significantly, 72 percent admitted they would support a "radical change" in reforming the political process, compared to only half of all Mexicans six months earlier.[28] The fact that half of the voters ultimately ranked change as the most important reason for voting in the 2000 presidential election is unquestionably linked to voting for Fox since half of all voters, at least on a superficial level, associated his candidacy with such a goal. Fox helped this process of identification by denoting his coalition of parties as the Alliance for Change, thus explicitly linking his motto with his party identification.

The PRI was not as successful as the PAN in conveying its campaign message through advertising. But the PRI, relying on its traditional grassroots strength and larger core of partisan voters, volunteers, and rank-and-file members, used its networking abilities to make personal contacts with voters. The Mexico 2000 Panel Study clearly reveals that twice as many people received party advertising or letters from the PRI compared to the PAN; and more importantly, twice as many PRI representatives as PAN officials actually visited prospective voters in the week prior to the respective polls.

Vicente Fox was able to overcome the PRI's traditional grassroots strength as measured by its self-identified partisan voters. Early in the campaign, 37 percent of prospective voters described themselves as *priístas*, compared to only 21 percent *panistas*.[29] By July, *priístas* had dropped to 33 percent and *panistas* had risen to 27 percent.[30] In 1994, only 23 percent of voters considered themselves PRI partisans, compared to 19 percent PAN partisans. These figures suggested that if Labastida could keep his partisan voters (he received the support of 37 percent of all voters in the actual election), he only had to persuade a small number of independent voters to join his ranks in order to rise above the 40 percent mark. This he failed to do. Labastida retained his die-hard partisans but attracted few other voters. Fox, on the other hand, more than doubled his support beyond PAN partisan voters, a truly remarkable achievement. Among independent voters, Fox garnered 56 percent of the vote.[31]

Party loyalty, as an explanatory variable in the 2000 presidential race, remained crucial for Labastida but less so for Fox. Of the reasons voters gave for supporting their candidates, party loyalty ranked sixth in importance, an explanation given by only a minuscule 5 percent of voters. Of the Mexicans who gave this reason for their presidential choice (in an open-ended question), Labastida won 79 percent of their support.

The interaction between party loyalty and a candidate's personal appeal is clearly apparent in table 2.1. In fact, an inverse relationship exists between party and candidate when comparing Labastida and Fox. The PRI was crucial to Labastida's fortunes, strengthening his appeal as a candidate; half of the voters who gave "party" as a reason for voting cast their ballots for Labastida. In contrast, Fox was much stronger than the PAN. Of the Mexicans who voted for a candidate over their party, slightly over half voted for Vicente Fox.

Table 2.1. Party and Candidate Attractiveness among Mexican Voters in 2000

Reason for Voting[a]	Party[b]			Others
	PRI	PAN	PRD	
For the candidate	28%	52%	17%	3%
For the party	50	35	13	3
For both	39	36	22	3

[a] Respondents were only given these three choices.
[b] Party labels refer to their broader coalitions.

CHANGE, DEMOCRACY, AND VOTING FOR FOX

Who were the Mexicans who voted for Vicente Fox, and what role did change and democracy play in this process? The fundamental variable in this election becomes apparent when voters have the opportunity to express their reasons for voting for their respective candidates. A poll done by *Reforma* after the election reveals the uniqueness of the 2000 presidential race. The data from table 2.2 establish the overwhelming influence of change.[32]

Table 2.2. Why Mexican Voters Cast Their Ballots for President in 2000

Reason for Voting	By Candidate				All
	Fox	Labastida	Cárdenas	Others	
Change	66%	15%	18%	1%	43%
His proposals	37	42	17	4	22
The candidate	28	50	18	4	9
Custom	12	82	5	1	7
Other	34	43	22	2	6
Party loyalty	8	79	12	1	5
Least bad	37	40	20	3	4
Obligation	31	56	13	0	2
Don't know	27	55	14	3	2

The fact that so many Mexican voters identified with change, and that democracy permitted them to make this choice, produced the Fox victory. Mexicans were not voting for Fox, they were not voting for they PAN, and they were not voting for substantive policy issues. They were voting for change, conceptualized pragmatically as an alteration in power, replacing incumbent politicians and the party they represented with something different.

Two pieces of data stand out in a striking way. First, 98 percent of the voters knew why they were voting, and 43 percent of the voters selected change, twice the percentage of the next highest reason given. Two-thirds of those voters selecting change cast their ballots for Fox. Of the eight possible reasons given for voting, this is the only category where both the PRD and the PAN ranked ahead of the PRI. Second, of all the reasons voters gave for choosing their candidates, Labastida won voter support in seven out of eight categories, beating out Fox on his proposals by 42 to 37 percent. Unfortunately for Labastida, only 22 percent of the voters selected their candidate based on his ideas.[33]

How did the traditional variables become less influential in this election and change become such a dominant feature of the electoral landscape? As suggested above, the most influential determinant of this election was the erosion of the so-called fear factor. The strong presence of a belief among a large minority of potential voters that Mexicans would rather go with what they know than risk change always played a role in prior elections. In 2000, nearly a third of Mexican voters favored going with what they knew rather than an alternative that potentially was better but that implied risks. The PRI often capitalized on this underlying fear by implying that a vote for the opposition was tantamount to a vote for political violence. They were particularly effective in using this theme when Cuauhtémoc Cárdenas was the leading opposition candidate in 1988. The severe economic crisis of 1994–95 may well have convinced some previously fearful voters that electing a PRI candidate provided no guarantees of economic stability after 2000.

Opposition parties received help from an unusual ally in allaying this fear of change. The Catholic Church played a fundamental role in converting the setting of Mexican politics to democracy. Since the late 1980s, in hundreds of sermons, public statements, and diocesan letters, the Catholic Church commanded the laity to participate in the electoral process, even arguing that voting was a Christian duty.[34] They were fully aware of the "fear factor" and addressed this issue in their public statements, adding support to the views of independent journalists and to the leading opposition candidates' own voices.[35] In fact, in a national conference organized by the Archdiocese of Guadalajara (one of the most influential centers of Catholicism in the country) attended by nongovernmental and grassroots organizational leaders in May 2000, the Church officially denounced the promotion of the "fear vote" as a sin.[36]

Many independent voters, and voters sympathetic to the PRD or the remaining unaffiliated opposition parties, decided to vote for change. This was the first time that a majority of independent voters became sufficiently convinced that change was of paramount importance and that casting a ballot for change through Fox would effectively be counted. The shift in voter perceptions, or at least the willingness of voters to express their views at the ballot box, occurred after the last legally permitted publication of poll results. But as the advisers to Vicente Fox discovered in their own party polls five days before the election, the percentage of voters admitting that they planned to vote for Fox had begun a small but significant shift in his favor six days before the election.[37]

In 1994 approximately the same percentage of voters, about a fifth of the electorate, remained undecided. But unlike 2000, the undecideds, who turned out in large numbers, voted in the same distributional patterns as the committed voters, contrary to the expectations of some leading pollsters.[38] Consequently, since the undecided voter confounded that expectation in 1994, few analysts considered a different outcome in 2000. It is possible that voter perceptions of electoral fraud, despite many improvements over 1994, may have contributed to more guarded expressions of their preferences to pollsters and to a lower voter turnout.[39]

The neutral role of candidate proposals and abilities marked another major difference between 1994 and 2000. As Joseph Klesner argues, "careful studies of voting behavior have suggested that Mexicans make their voting decisions based on several factors, including partisanship, assessment of candidates' personal qualities, assessments of the state of the economy and their personal economic situations, and their willingness to accept risk."[40] The important substantive issues had changed relatively little from 1994 to 2000, as the comparisons in table 2.3 demonstrate.

Astoundingly, voters made little distinction based on the two leading candidates' primary policy proposals, on their personal or party's ability to implement programs to cope with those issues, and even on their personal qualities. This explains why, immediately before the election, most polls ranked the leading candidates in a dead heat. No researcher was asking directly about change. In contrast, the perceived differences between Ernesto Zedillo and Diego Fernández de Cevallos in 1994 were definitive in all of these categories. Citizens therefore translated these differences into votes at the polling booth.

The data in table 2.3 also explain the lower voter turnout in 2000 compared to 1994. The only voter who had an unusual interest in this presidential election was the voter who strongly desired, or was hopeful for, change. There was no policy reason, or pressing political and economic situation, that encouraged other voters to participate. Since the typical voter could not draw any distinction between Fox and Labastida on any traditional measurement of voter preference, the influence of issues waned.

Other explanations also played a role in Vicente Fox's victory. The role of the urban voter, a voter who accounts for the overwhelming percentage of actual participants (70 percent) compared to their rural counterparts (20 percent), was crucial.[41] Fox scored 17 percentage points higher among urban voters than did Labastida (48 to 31 percent). First-time voters, who accounted for 18 percent of all voters, also supported Fox disproportionately (50 to 32 percent). And finally, Fox performed most strongly among educated voters. Over a third of the Mexican electorate (36 percent) has preparatory or professional education. Among those voters, Fox received 60 percent support, 38 percentage points above Labastida, the single-largest percentage difference in the voter profile among the two candidates.[42]

ELECTORAL CONSEQUENCES FOR DEMOCRACY

Democracy also has a broader relationship to the 2000 presidential election and, potentially, a deeper significance since Fox has taken office. Mexican beliefs in and levels of satisfaction with democracy prior to July 2000 were neither strong nor positive. Despite the significant changes outlined above, in August 1996 nearly two-thirds of Mexicans thought that under Zedillo democratic conditions had not changed or had moved backward; only a third thought Mexico had become more democratic.[43] The following year, 70 percent of Mexicans expressed dissatisfaction with the way democracy was functioning in Mexico, the highest level among eight Latin American countries. Moreover, democracy's ability to solve Mexico's problems was viewed by many Mexicans as inadequate since only 46 percent thought it could resolve issues confronting the country's development, compared to a nearly equal number (43 percent) who believed it could not.[44] A year later, only 51 percent thought democracy was preferable to any other form of government; 28 percent considered an authoritarian model preferable, and 19 percent expressed no preference.[45]

Table 2.3. Comparison of Voter Attitudes, 1994 and 2000

1994 (1 month prior)		2000 (4 months prior)	

- *"What is the most important problem in the country today?"*

Unemployment	24%	Public security	21%
Economy	16	Economy	19
Poverty	15	Poverty	12
Public security	9	Unemployment	9
Corruption	8	Corruption	8

- *"How would you rate the candidates on their honesty?"*

Zedillo	39% most honest	Labastida	40% somewhat, very
Fernández	19% most honest	Fox	39%, somewhat, very

- *"Who is the most capable of governing?"*

Zedillo	50%	Labastida	48% economy 46% crime
Fernández	23%	Fox	45% economy 44% crime

- *"Which of the parties is most capable of improving?"*

Public safety	PRI	48%	Public safety	PRI	46%
	PAN	22%		PAN	44%
Economy	PRI	51%	Economy	PRI	48%
	PAN	18%		PAN	45%
Education	PRI	56%	Education	PRI	50%
	PAN	16%		PAN	48%

Sources: 1994 data are from Belden and Russonello, "Mexico 1994, Summary of a Survey of Electoral Preferences in Mexico," from a national random sample of 1,526 respondents, July 23–August 10, 1994. The 2000 data are taken from the Mexico 2000 Panel Survey, first wave.

By 2000, the satisfaction level with the functioning of democracy had improved considerably since 1997. Nevertheless, among highly educated voters, 62 and 72 percent of preparatory- and university-educated Mexicans, respectively, remained dissatisfied, explaining why they would vote for change in huge numbers. Supporters of the PAN and university graduates, compared to any other partisan or educated group, believed the primary task of democracy was to elect leaders. Therefore, those voters, who already were sympathetic to candidate Fox as an individual representing change, largely viewed the democratic context as providing them with an opportunity to vote such a candidate into office. Not surprisingly, PAN and PRD partisans gave much stronger support when asked to express a preference between a democratic system and an authoritarian system.

The Mexico 2000 Panel Study only included a single question on democracy per se: "Do you believe Mexico is a democracy or not?" Answers to this question, however, reflected a significant change between the three preelection survey results and the one immediately following the July election. Before, the majority of Mexicans believed that a democracy did not exist in Mexico; typically 40 to 48 percent agreed that Mexico was democratic. Mexicans who were most adamant about the lack of democracy in Mexico prior to July 2000, not surprisingly, fit the Fox voter profile. These were individuals who were most interested in politics, who read about politics, and who planned to vote for Fox or Cárdenas. In contrast, the majority of voters who planned to vote for Labastida already believed that democracy existed in Mexico. In fact, Mexicans who were likely PRI partisans, and who had attended a PRI meeting, reflected the strongest level of belief in Mexico's democracy: two-thirds believed Mexico already had achieved a democracy. Interestingly, differing views of substantive policy issues and differences in levels of interpersonal trust did not affect these perceptions.

Immediately following the election, we asked the same respondents about the existence of democracy in Mexico. Those responses reflected a dramatic shift in opinion. Sixty-three percent, an increase of more than half, believed Mexico now had a democracy. Those who considered that Mexico was not a democracy dropped precipitously from 48 to 28 percent. The most marked increases in positive democratic views occurred among rural residents, citizens most interested in politics, those who followed the campaign, the well-informed, and those who expressed trust in their peers (see table 2.4).

Table 2.4. Changing Visions of Democracy in the 2000 Presidential Election

Voter Characteristics	Respondents Answering "Yes" to the Question: "Do you believe Mexico is a democracy?"	
	February	July
All voters	**40**	**63**
Trusts others	44%	79%
Approved of Zedillo's performance	68	75
Strongest political interest	38	72
Followed campaigns intensely	52	71
Watches TV news frequently	41	71
Well-educated	36	70
Favored the PAN	33	69
Urban resident	40	64
Favored the PRI	43	59
Favored the PRD	27	48
Lowest income	42	44
Highest income	36	62

The most fascinating consequence of this change in perceptions of Mexico's political system addresses a fundamental theoretical issue involving the link between culture, political socialization, and politics. For the first time in Mexico's political history, we have empirical evidence of a cause-and-effect relationship between the political system's performance (in this case, a presidential election) and political values, specifically the perception of whether Mexico was a democracy.

One of the most hotly debated issues in political culture is the extent to which citizen values and attitudes bear on political behavior and structures. This finding does not solve that debate, but it does demonstrate definitively that structures and behavior determine political attitudes. When Mexicans saw their behavior confirmed in the electoral victory of Fox, for those who truly doubted democracy's existence in Mexico (the majority of them Fox sympathizers), the results converted them to democrats and reinforced a new vision. As Harry Eckstein argued in his careful exposition of culture and political change, cultural socialization can occur from an experience.[46]

The reason for changing voter attitudes about democracy, however, raises serious concerns in Mexican politics. The argument can be made that when a voter's candidate wins, suddenly that voter believes in democracy. The counterpoint to that effect is that if their candidate loses, they lose their confidence in the process.[47] This is both a tenuous and immature assessment of democracy. Mexico's dramatic change may reflect a much stronger, permanent shift in that it convinced many voters, after seven decades of the same incumbent governors, that it was not a question of "their candidate" winning, but a question of that candidate representing a more fundamental, underlying change in the political system and process. Given Mexico's historic pattern of governance, and the points set forth above, this interpretation is far more realistic.

Fox's victory implies another major shift in democratic behavior. Mexicans have little respect for political parties, and as our data suggest, Fox's identity both as a candidate and as a symbol for change earned him more than double the support he earned from his party label. To fashion these identities, Fox created an ad hoc organization, the Friends of Fox, in September 1998 to substitute for the internal, organizational, and geographical unevenness of the PAN.[48] This organization succeeded in drawing millions of activists and voters to Fox's side. The success of the Friends of Fox demonstrates another important shift in the larger political setting, an environment favorable to the creation and growth of nongovernmental and citizen groups, building on a flowering of such organizations since the 1985 earthquakes in Mexico City.[49]

CONCLUSION

The 2000 Mexican presidential election produced a remarkable alteration in voter attitudes toward change and democracy. The data analyzed above demonstrate that interactions between citizen views of change and democracy are complex and deep. The panel surveys have only touched the surface of this linkage because they relied on a single question.

The most provocative finding theoretically, of course, is the impact political processes have on political culture. Mexican voters have now convinced themselves in large numbers that a democracy exists in their country because they, through effective suffrage, effected a dramatic change in power. The average voter has indeed perceived a connection between voting, change, and democracy.

The linkage is significant for two reasons. First, the panel data provide empirical information about how political socialization occurs and, specifically, the nature of interaction between political values and attitudes, and political processes. We know from other studies of adult socialization in Mexico that single political events influence citizen perceptions, and they may have long-term consequences on attitudes and behavior.[50] In the case of the 2000 presidential election, the average adult citizen was a participant in the event, not just an observer. The process of voting and observing the results of their participation directly socialized these voters.

The second conclusion that emerges from the linkage between change and democracy is the tenuousness of fundamental political beliefs. The evolution of the Mexican political model from a semi-authoritarian system in the late 1980s to a strongly competitive, electoral democracy in the late 1990s did alter Mexican beliefs in the existence of democracy in their society. But the share of citizens who believed in the existence of democracy reached a certain point and stalled, with fewer than half the population convinced that democracy existed. The July 2 elections produced a remarkable increase in the percentage of Mexicans who considered their polity to be a democracy. Does this increase augur well for democracy's future? The depth of democratic beliefs in Mexico is questionable. A large percentage of "democrats" have moved into that column because of their candidate's victory. Would they back down from their democratic convictions if a PRI candidate were to win in 2006?

The answer to this question remains unknown. As suggested above, it is quite possible that the change in political leadership is so astonishing to most Mexicans, who have never witnessed such a change, that the change itself functions as a starting point for "real" democracy. In other words, as we have argued earlier, if the typical Mexican has voted for change, and not for a specific candidate, democratic beliefs may be on firmer ground.

The fundamental weakness of the intensity of democratic beliefs is tested by citizen expectations of democracy.[51] It is clear in the Mexican case that citizens have high and hopeful expectations of democracy improving their standard of living, providing them with increased personal security, and making their governors accountable. If Fox fails to fulfill those expectations in any significant way, citizen commitment to democracy is likely to waver.

Notes

1. The author would like to acknowledge the support of the National Science Foundation (SES-9905703) and *Reforma* newspaper. Most of the data in this essay are taken from the Mexico 2000 Panel Study, whose participants included Miguel Basáñez, Roderic Camp, Wayne Cornelius, Jorge Domínguez, Federico Estévez, Joseph Klesner, Chappell Lawson (principal investigator), Beatriz Magaloni, James McCann, Alejandro Moreno, Pablo Parás, and Alejandro Poiré.

2. *Reforma* conducted a fascinating poll of 506 children between the ages of nine and sixteen, on April 7–17, 2000. They found that children, compared to adult Mexicans, give much stronger support to democracy and democratic principles, including: "your vote counts," 81 percent agreed; "democracy is the best system," 60 percent agreed; "Mexico is a democracy," 60 percent agreed; and "democracy is a good thing," 75 percent agreed. See "Quieren votar cuando sean mayor de edad," at reforma.com.mx\encuestas, May 5, 2000.

3. The historic figures are even more remarkable. In 1988, opposition parties at the municipal level governed 3 percent of the population. In 1998 that figure increased to 50 percent, a fifteen-fold increase in ten years. See "Un estudio de un consejero electoral revela que los rivales del PRI han crecido 15 veces de 1988 a 1998," *Diario de Yucatán*, November 22, 1999, at www.yucatan.com.mx.

4. Specific data are available on municipalities, population, and local congresses. See *Review of the Economic Situation in Mexico*, April 1999, p. 136.

5. These figures are provided in the *Review of the Economic Situation in Mexico*, March 2000, p. 126.

6. Vicente Fox himself was fully aware of how the PRI had used citizen desire for change to encourage them to vote for their party. See his comments in a campaign speech in "Fox alerta sobre el peligro del 'voto del miedo'," *Diario de Yucatán*, December 13, 1999, at www.yucatan.com.mx.

7. Alfonso Lujambio, "Adiós a la excepcionalidad, régimen presidencial y gobierno dividido en México," *Este País*, February 2000.

8. Jeffrey Weldon further breaks down these data by party initiatives and congressional versus executive initiatives for the legislative sessions from 1988 through 1999. See his "Executive-Legislative Relations in Mexico in the 1990s," forthcoming in Kevin Middle-brook, ed., *Dilemmas of Change in Mexican Politics* (La Jolla: Center for U.S.-Mexican Studies, University of California, San Diego, 2003).

9. María Amparo Casar, "Mexico's 2000 Presidential Election," *Enfoque* (Fall-Winter 2000): 1–2, 16.

10. It is worth noting, however, as Kathleen Bruhn's chapter in this volume argues, that the large number of opposition parties initially weakened the opposition because of the transaction costs to the two largest parties.

11. It is also true that greater equity in television coverage was achieved as an indirect result of electoral reforms.

12. A historical comparison of public financing from 1994 through 2000 is available in Mony de Swaan, "En busca de la equidad, financiamiento público a partidos políticos," *Este País*, March 2000, pp. 12–16.

13. José Antonio Crespo explains how this pattern occurred in his "Raising the Bar: The Next Generation of Electoral Reforms in Mexico," CSIS Policy Papers on the Americas, March 2000, especially pp. 16–17.

14. Sam Dillon, "Polls Show Virtual Tie in the Crucial Presidential Race in Mexico," *New York Times*, June 24, 2000, at www.nytimes.com. According to telephone polls conducted by *Reforma*, Fox had been 8 to 10 percentage points ahead of Labastida since January 2000. These results were not published because they were an unrepresentative sample of urban, better-educated voters. However, those were the voters, according to exit polls, that turned out in much larger numbers, thus determining the outcome on July 2. Personal communication from Alejandro Moreno, July 6, 2000.

15. The role of the media as a crucial actor in the 1994–2000 period, on the basis of personal interviews with many of the pollsters, is nicely developed by Miguel Basáñez, "Public Opinion Research in Mexico," 2000, unpublished. For a comprehensive treatment of these underlying issues, see Roderic Ai Camp, ed., *Polling for Democracy: Public Opinion and Political Liberalism in Mexico* (Wilmington, Del.: Scholarly Resources, 1996).

16. Based on a multi-country project directed by the author and supported by the Hewlett Foundation, "Democracy through Latin American Lenses." The polling occurred in July 1998, of 1,200 Mexicans randomly selected in a national survey with a +/–3 percent margin of error. The results are available on a CD-ROM in Roderic Ai Camp, ed., *Citizen Views of Democracy in Latin America* (Pittsburgh, Penn.: University of Pittsburgh Press, 2001).

17. When asked to rank the parties on the same left-right scale, 67 percent of respondents ranked the PRI as right of center, compared to only 49 percent for the PAN. This report supports the view that the left-right spectrum primarily reflects attitudes toward the existing regime—that is, that the status quo is equated with extreme conservatism. This means that voters are not judging the parties on the basis of their socioeconomic platforms, and, therefore, these patterns do not carry the same level of significance.

18. In his examination of this phenomenon, Chappell Lawson has found that self-reported ideology correlates more strongly with attitudes toward the PRD. See his "Why Cárdenas Won," in Jorge I. Domínguez and Alejandro Poiré, eds., *Toward Mexico's Democratization* (London: Routledge, 1999): 154–55. For further evidence of this, see Ulises Beltrán, "Encuesta Nacional sobre el Votante Mexicano," *Política y Gobierno* 4, no. 2 (1997): appendix. Here, 14 percent of respondents identified themselves as Left, but 28 percent of PRI sympathizers did so.

19. For some valuable comparisons, which place these characteristics in a changing context, see Alejandro Moreno and Keith Yanner, "Predictors of Voter Preference in Mexico's 1994 Presidential Election," presented at the international congress of the Latin American Studies Association, Washington, D.C., September 1995.

20. For a comparison of personal economic situations from 1994 through May 2000, see "Public Opinion prior to the July 2 Elections," *Review of the Economic Situation in Mexico*, June 2000, p. 247. This article concluded that a significant sign of optimism emerged in citizen perceptions of personal economic situations. Based on a Banamex survey of 2,400 respondents, with a +/–4 margin of error, April 26–May 4, 2000.

21. James McCann and Jorge Domínguez, "Mexicans React to Electoral Fraud and Political Corruption: An Assessment of Public Opinion and Voting Behavior," *Electoral*

Studies 17, no. 4 (1998): 499. See also the chapter by Joseph Klesner and Chappell Lawson in this volume.

22. For example, José Woldenberg, president of the Federal Electoral Institute, on the basis of the number of candidates and intensive competition in the presidential race, predicted a huge turnout among the 59 million registered voters. *Diario de Yucatán*, May 19, 2000, at www.yucatan.com.mx.

23. See Joseph L. Klesner and Chappell Lawson, "Adiós to the PRI? Changing Voter Turnout in Mexico's Political Transition," *Mexican Studies/Estudios Mexicanos* 17, no. 1 (Winter 2000): 2; see also the chapter by Lawson and Klesner in this volume.

24. Based on the Mexico 2000 Panel Study, first wave. This pattern has been the case consistently. In a 1998 Latinobarómetro poll of Mexico, 68 percent expressed the same lack of political interest as reported in *Este País*, May 1999, p. 41.

25. Most studies also found that the news coverage on Televisa and TV Azteca was biased in favor of Labastida. For assessments through the spring, see the Washington Office on Latin America, "Mexican Election Monitor 2000," June 2000.

26. Miguel Basáñez, "Rise and Reliability of Opinion Polling in Mexico," presented at the Institute of Latin American Studies, University of Texas at Austin, April 7, 2000. Seventy-one percent of those interviewed by MORI said Labastida received the most coverage.

27. Federico Reyes Heroles, "La cultura política mexicana," *Diario de Yucatán*, May 23, 2000, at www.sureste.com.mx.

28. These results were reported in "Cada vez más fuerte el clamor por el cambio," *Diario de Yucatán*, June 23, 2000, at www.sureste.com.mx.

29. Mexico 2000 Panel Survey, first wave, national random sample of 2,399 Mexicans, February 19–20 and 26-27, 2000.

30. Ultimately, 37 percent of voters changed their loyalty: one-third to another party, one-third from independent to a party, and one-third from a party to independent. "Abandona al PRI uno de cada tres," *Reforma*, July 29, 2000.

31. "La perinola sigue girando," *Reforma*, July 29, 2000, survey of 3,283 voters on July 2.

32. *Review of the Economic Situation in Mexico*, July 2000, p. 266, based on a postelection poll by *Reforma*. Data not provided on the sample or margin of error.

33. In 1994, in the Belden & Russonello poll, 54 percent preferred to retain the PRI and continue with present advances, whereas only 36 percent wanted an opposition party win "in order to bring about change." Ten percent either did not know or did not answer the question.

34. See Roderic Ai Camp, *Crossing Swords, Religion and Politics in Mexico* (New York: Oxford University Press, 1997) and Oscar Aguilar Ascencio, "La iglesia católica y la democratización en México," in José de Jesús Legorreta Zepeda, ed., *La iglesia católica y la política en Méxic de hoy* (Mexico City: Universidad Ibero-Americana, 2000): 145–74. For a recent statement from the episcopate's social pastoral committee, see "El papel de la Iglesia en la transición democrática es fundamental," *Diario de Yucatán*, June 22, 2000, at www.sureste.com.mx. For a complete position, including specific recommendations on democratic values, voting, political parties, political campaigns, and church participation, see Conferencia del Episcopado Mexicano, *La democracia no se puede dar sin tí, elecciones del 2000*, May 2000.

35. Church spokespersons, such as Bishop Genaro Alamilla Arteaga, who regularly write editorials for the Mexican press, suggested to prospective voters that one of the three qualities they should identify in their candidate was the democratic principles on which the individual would rely in governing. "Tres requisitos, ¿por quién debemos votar?" *Diario de Yucatán*, June 27, 2000, at www.sureste.com.mx.

36. "Censura de la Iglesia al vote del miedo," *Diario de Yucatán*, May 10, 2000, at www.sureste.com.mx.

37. As revealed by Jorge Castañeda in an address to the Mexican Association of Business Executives, July 7, 2000, Mexico City.

38. For a detailed and dispassionate discussion of these and other issues that the 1994 and 1997 elections raised in anticipation of polling in the 2000 race, see the excellent article by Seymour Martin Lipset, Robert M. Worcester, and Frederick C. Turner, "Opening the Mexican Political System: Public Opinion and the Elections of 1994 and 1997," *Studies in Comparative International Development* 33, no. 3 (Fall 1998): 70–89, especially p. 86.

39. In 1994, 41 percent and 17 percent, respectively, believed the election would be clean or reasonably clean. In 2000, interestingly, the response was just the reverse: only 14 percent and 41 percent, respectively, viewed the upcoming election as clean and reasonably clean.

40. Joseph L. Klesner, *The 2000 Mexican Presidential and Congressional Elections, Pre-Election Report* (Washington, D.C.: Center for Strategic and International Studies, June 15, 2000): 5.

41. The Mexican census categorizes the rest of the population, 10 percent, as living in mixed rural and urban zones. In the Mexico 2000 Panel Study, these residents are normally treated as rural.

42. Among preparatory-educated voters, the figures were 53 to 28 percent in favor of Fox. *Review of the Economic Situation in Mexico*, July 2000, p. 267, based on data from the Federal Electoral Institute and *Reforma*.

43. The question was: In general, during the last three years, has Mexico become more democratic, less democratic, or hasn't it changed much? A lot or just a little? More = 34 percent, No Change = 41 percent, Less = 19 percent. Los Angeles Times/Reforma survey, August 1996. A survey of 1,500 Mexicans, random national sample, August 1–7, 1996.

44. Marta Lagos, "Actitudes económicas y democracia en Latinoamérica," *Este País*, January 1997, p. 7. For an extensive analysis of Mexican democratic attitudes, see Roderic Ai Camp, "Democracy through Mexican Lenses," *Washington Quarterly* 22, no. 3 (Summer 1999): 229–42.

45. "Latinobarómetro México 1998," *Este País*, May 1999, p. 42, based on a survey of 1,200 randomly selected Mexicans nationally, November 14–December 3, 1998.

46. Harry Eckstein, "A Culturalist Theory of Political Change," *American Political Science Review* 82 (September 1988): 791.

47. One element in these same data that provides stronger hope for confidence in the democratic model is that PRI voters did not change their minds about the system being any less democratic as a result of their candidate losing. On the other hand, PRI voters, in percentages higher than any other group, believed that the election results were fraudulent. *Panistas*, of course, were most convinced of their

cleanliness. See "The Country President Zedillo Leaves Behind," *Review of the Economic Situation in Mexico* 76 (October 2000): 429.

48. Its composition, origin, and staff are described in detail by Francisco Ortiz Pardo and Francisco Ortiz Pinchetti, "En detalle, la gigantesca organización que mueve a Fox," *Proceso*, February 13, 2000, at www.proceso.com.mx.

49. The largest number of Mexicans belong to religious organizations (23 percent), followed by sports groups (9 percent) and cultural institutions (8 percent). Only 4 percent actually belong to parties. See Federico Reyes Heroles, "La cultura política mexicana."

50. Roderic Ai Camp, *The Making of a Government, Political Leaders in Modern Mexico* (Tucson: University of Arizona Press, 1984).

51. For evidence of the importance of expectations, see Roderic Ai Camp, "Democracy through Mexican Lenses."

3

Mobilized Voting in the 2000 Elections: The Changing Efficacy of Vote Buying and Coercion in Mexican Electoral Politics

Wayne A. Cornelius

Mexico is a very poor country with enormous disparities. For a lot of people, one kilo of sugar or beans is more important than a vote. There are unscrupulous political operatives who know these needs and will find ways to capitalize on them. These are facts of life, and we work very hard to get rid of them. Our media campaigns tell the people that their vote is secret and free. We warn them against vote buying and coercion, telling them they should not feel beholden or intimidated. We assure them that when they go to the polling place, no one will be able to see how they vote. So, by election time, even people who received gifts will know that nobody else will be able to tell how they voted.—José Woldenberg, President, Federal Electoral Institute, June 25, 2000[1]

One factor contributing to the defeat of Mexico's Institutional Revolutionary Party (PRI) in 2000 was the diminished role of "mobilized" voters—people whose electoral participation (turnout) and/or candidate choices were induced by vote buying and coercion. Another key actor was the nonvoter, especially the erstwhile *priísta* voter whose failure to turn out on July 2, 2000, doomed the PRI's chances of retaining control of the presidency. Here, too, we can see how old-style machine politics have reached their limit in Mexico, at least in terms of assuring an adequate turnout for the PRI.

From the party's creation in 1929 until the early 1990s, authoritarian mobilization of voters was a key ingredient of the PRI's electoral success.[2] A steadily shrinking but still crucial bloc of voters, concentrated in the country's most economically underdeveloped electoral districts, routinely voted for the ruling party's candidates in response to pressures from local *caciques* and PRI-affiliated peasant and labor leaders. Particularistic material rewards—everything from minor kitchen appliances to land titles and public-sector jobs—were routinely and systematically used to purchase electoral support. Some destitute Mexicans, especially in rural areas, freely sold their votes in return for handouts from local officials.

The PRI came to rely increasingly on such tactics (especially vote buying) in the 1990s as its options for manipulating election results were narrowed by sweeping reforms of the electoral law and increased monitoring of the electoral process by independent observers. PRI state governors took advantage of fiscal decentralization measures in the 1990s to strengthen their party's vote-getting machine by channeling funds received from federal programs to their core constituencies. In the state of Puebla, for example, Governor Manuel Bartlett (1993–1999) crafted a state law to divert the lion's share of federal revenue-sharing funds from cities controlled by the National Action Party (PAN) to rural areas where it was easier for the PRI to harvest votes.[3] In Yucatán State, Governor Víctor Cervera Pacheco (1993–2001) breathed new life into the PRI's clientelistic networks by using them to distribute major new resources provided to the state through federal antipoverty and temporary employment programs.[4]

In the run-up to the 2000 elections, PRI operatives in many parts of the country attempted to head off a victory by PAN presidential candidate Vicente Fox, warning that the flow of benefits to low-income families through three high-profile federal poverty alleviation programs would be ended if the PRI lost the presidency. The PROGRESA program, created during the presidency of Ernesto Zedillo (1994–2000) as the successor to President Carlos Salinas's National Solidarity Program (PRONASOL), provides a food stipend, nutritional supplements, and primary health care for low-income rural families, as well as a cash stipend (*beca*) for families with school-age children. By December 2000, 2.4 million families (equivalent to 40 percent of the rural population) were participating in PROGRESA. PROCAMPO, launched during the

Carlos Salinas presidency, is a cash income support program that benefits approximately three million small-scale agricultural producers each
year. LICONSA, established in its present form by the Zedillo administration in 1995, distributes subsidized milk to 2.6 million low-income
families throughout the country who have children under age twelve.[5]

In theory, the millions of Mexicans who benefited from these federal
antipoverty programs constituted the largest potential reservoir of
votes for the PRI. But the traditional calculus of vote buying and coercion changed radically in the 2000 election, and those who followed the
old rules perished with them. The new rules were aptly summarized
during the campaign by opposition party candidates who repeatedly
advised voters to "take the gift, but vote as you please." PRI operatives
delivered a starkly different message: "We've helped *you*; now you
help *us*!"

This chapter seeks to document the declining efficacy of vote buying and coercion (*compra y coacción*) in Mexican electoral politics, particularly as demonstrated by the 2000 presidential election. I first discuss the incidence of *compra y coacción* in the 2000 election and describe
some of the new forms that such tactics took in 2000. I then develop an
empirical profile of the voter most likely to be subject to authoritarian
mobilization in 2000, and highlight interparty differences in use of vote
buying and coercion. Finally, I assess the effectiveness of these tactics
in determining candidate choice and propensity to vote in 2000.

DEFINITIONS AND DATA

Vote buying involves the trading of material benefits and services for
votes. The goods and services provided by PRI leaders in recent elections have included cash handouts, foodstuffs, cloth, bags of cement,
fertilizer, seeds, irrigation pumps, fumigators, cement flooring, sewing
machines, blenders, portable washing machines, bicycles, school sup-
plies, breakfasts and lunches on election day, bus transportation from
outlying areas to polling places (*acarreo*), vocational training, and a
variety of other government-provided or subsidized services. Household appliances were routinely raffled off at PRI campaign rallies. As
discussed above, the resources for such giveaways often came from
federal government antipoverty programs, manipulated by PRI state
governors.

Coercion refers to a set of activities ranging from violations of ballot
secrecy inside polling places to intimidation of voters outside polling
places, confiscating voter credentials and/or recording the numbers of

voter credentials during home visits in the preelection period, conditioning the receipt of some government service or benefit upon voting for a specific party or candidate, and threats of physical violence.

Not all of these actions are illegal under federal election law (COFIPE). Indeed, one postelection survey found that only 21 percent of vote buying and coercive acts reported by interviewees were technically illegal.[6] PRI politicians engaging extensively in vote buying (like Yucatán's governor Víctor Cervera Pacheco) seized upon the ambiguities in the COFIPE to defend their conduct as routine, perfectly legal distributional functions of the governments that they headed.[7]

Other stratagems, such as transporting voters to the polls and visiting them at home in the run-up to the election, are not inherently coercive but historically have been instruments of authoritarian mobilization in Mexico. This is why the electoral code reforms of the 1990s made some of these practices (such as *acarreo*) illegal. Similarly, visiting a voter at home is a common practice in democratic political systems, but in Mexico the arrival of a PRI representative at the door traditionally has aroused fear that "the government is watching" and actively trying to keep track of how people vote. When a home visit involves taking down the voter's name and voting credential number, the intent to intimidate is clear.

This chapter synthesizes the evidence relating to vote buying and coercion in recent Mexican elections from five main sources:

- The Mexico 2000 Panel Study, supported by the U.S. National Science Foundation and the Mexican newspaper *Reforma*. Data from the fourth wave of the panel survey (N = 1,260) and the postelectoral cross-section survey (N = 1,199) were analyzed for this chapter. Questions relevant to vote buying and coercion were: "In the last few weeks of the campaign, did a representative of any political party or candidate visit you?" and "In the last few weeks of the campaign, did you receive a gift or other assistance from any political party?"[8]

- A nationwide exit poll conducted by a private polling firm, Consulta Mitofsky. Face-to-face interviews were conducted with a sample of 6,145 persons leaving the polls on July 2, 2000. The series of questions relating to vote buying and coercion was: "Did anyone from the campaign teams of the presidential candidates ... visit your home to promote your vote? help you get to the polling station to vote? threaten you if you did not vote for him? give you any gift? promise you something if you voted for him? invite you to breakfast so that you would go to vote together? or check which party you voted for today?"[9]

- A national probability sample of election observers who worked on July 2, 2000, under the auspices of Civic Alliance (Alianza Cívica), a national coalition of nongovernmental organizations that has conducted independent election observation in Mexico since 1994, who were interviewed by telephone on election night.[10] Most of the questions related to violations of ballot secrecy and persons who were observed *"haciendo alguna forma de presión"* (pressuring voters in some way).

- A national survey of voters in the July 2000 election, conducted by Investigaciones Sociales Aplicadas S.C. for an academic institution, FLACSO (Latin American Faculty for Social Sciences), with funding from the Federal Electoral Institute (IFE).[11] Respondents in a stratified sample of municipalities were interviewed in person during December 2000.

- Ethnographic observations and interviews conducted by myself and other academics who observed the preparations for the July 2000 federal elections and the balloting process on election day.[12]

Two major caveats are in order. First, the extant data on vote buying and coercion from sample surveys (including exit polls) are limited in both quantity and quality. Measurement problems abound; coercion, especially, is not measured adequately in any of these surveys. Survey items tend to be ambiguous and poorly worded. Most preelection and exit polls do not include any relevant questions. In those that do, the reported incidence of coercive or manipulative campaign tactics is so low that the number of cases becomes a problem in rigorous multivariate analysis. Second, we lack quantitative data on the frequency of vote buying and coercion *before* the 2000 elections. The incidence of such acts reported by respondents interviewed in 2000 presumably is lower than in previous Mexican electoral contests, due to more intense scrutiny by the IFE, the mass media, NGOs, and opposition-party poll watchers (for example, representatives of the PAN and/or the Party of the Democratic Revolution [PRD] were present in about 90 percent of the country's polling places on July 2, 2000, compared with 69 percent in the 1994 presidential election), but systematic time series data are not available.[13]

FINDINGS

Within the limitations of the available data, what can be said about the frequency and efficacy of vote buying and coercion in the 2000 election? The evidence suggests that vote buying and coercion have by no means disappeared from Mexican elections, but the incidence of such practices has probably fallen enough, and their actual impact on voter behavior has become sufficiently attenuated, that voters subject to authoritarian mobilization are unlikely to affect most election outcomes. The percentage of voters in the 2000 federal election who were exposed to any of a variety of manipulative practices ranges from 4.7 percent in the FLACSO/IFE postelection survey to 11 percent in the Consulta Mitofsky exit poll and 26.1 percent in the Mexico 2000 Panel Study's postelectoral cross-section survey. In the Mitofsky poll, most cases involved what the pollster characterized as *"revisión del voto"* ("Did anyone check for whom you voted today?"). The referent of this question is unclear, but 9 percent of the voters interviewed by Mitofsky claimed that they had experienced it. Civic Alliance observers reported some degree of violation of vote secrecy in 22 percent of the polling places, but this could include anything from a single ballot that might have been shown to a precinct official before being deposited in a ballot box on up to more systematic violations.

Vote-buying attempts in 2000 appear to have been on a more modest scale than in previous Mexican elections.[14] In Mitofsky's exit poll, fewer than 5 percent of the voters reported having received some type of individualized, material benefit from any of the competing parties. In the Mexico 2000 Panel Study, 14.7 percent of respondents in the fourth (postelection) wave of interviews reported receiving a gift or some form of assistance from a political party in the run-up to the election (see table 3.1).

These national-level results mask significantly higher frequencies of vote buying and coercion in some states and localities. In Oaxaca and Yucatán, for example, gift giving was rampant in the months preceding the 2000 election and even on election day, in the form of free breakfasts and lunches for voters. Strategically timed distribution of checks to beneficiaries of federal government social programs (especially PROGRESA, the cash assistance program to low-income families with school-age children) was another tactic used by PRI governors in these impoverished southern states. Shameless intimidation tactics were also used systematically in the states of Yucatán and Puebla, most commonly in the form of threats that PROGRESA benefits would be cut off if people voted for PAN presidential candidate Vicente Fox. In some cases, PRI activists reportedly used lists of PROGRESA beneficiaries to mobilize participation in campaign rallies and to get out the vote on election day. Elsewhere, PRI operatives went house to house asking for and recording the numbers of IFE-issued voter credentials, apparently in an attempt to convince voters that their candidate choices on July 2 would be known to election officials.[15]

Table 3.1. Received Gifts from Political Parties or Presidential Candidates' Campaigns in 2000 (Mexico 2000 Panel Study)[a]

	Second Wave N = 959		Third Wave N = 976		Fourth Wave N = 1,260		Postelection Cross-section N = 1,199	
PRI/ Labastida	3.2%	(31)	6.6%	(64)	8.8%	(111)	15.3%	(184)
PAN/ Fox	0.9	(9)	2.2	(21)	3.1	(39)	4.4	(53)
PRD/ Cárdenas	0.9	(9)	1.4	(14)	2.1	(26)	3.3	(39)
Other parties	0.3	(3)	0.4	(4)	0.7	(9)	3.1	(37)
Total	5.3	(52)	10.6	(103)	14.7	(185)	26.1	(313)

[a] Cell entries are valid percentages for each sample (wave) in the Mexico 2000 Panel Study. No data are available for the first wave because the question about receipt of gifts was not asked in that wave. Numbers in parentheses are frequencies for each response.

Arguably the most serious kind of abuse in the 2000 federal election was the purchase or "renting" of voter credentials by local PRI officials or PRI-affiliated labor union leaders, with credentials being returned only after the election. This tactic was used to prevent potential opposition-party voters from casting a ballot. But the incidence of voter credential confiscation seems to have been low. The FLACSO/IFE post-election survey found that only 5 percent of the 5 percent of respondents who had been exposed to some form of vote buying or coercion had experienced it in that particular form.

The evidence from 2000 suggests that there has been a modernization of vote buying and coercion in Mexican elections. Ninety percent of such activity now happens *before* election day, not at the polling places. Even *acarreo*—the illegal transportation of voters to the polls by a political party—has become more sophisticated. On election day in the states of México and Yucatán, for example, PRI-chartered buses were observed stopping and unloading their passengers a block or two from a polling place, thereby skirting the legal prohibition on *acarreo*. Free lunches for voters were provided under the guise of "birthday parties" for PRI operatives, a remarkable number of whom claimed to have been born on July 2.

What kinds of people were most likely to have their votes bought or coerced in the 2000 election? The following profile of the voter most likely to be subject to authoritarian mobilization was constructed from data from the Mitofsky exit poll and the Mexico 2000 Panel Study (fourth wave interviews):

- older voter (fifty or more years of age);
- male (although the gender difference was very small);
- medium-educated (complete secondary education or some pre-college preparatory education);
- lower-income; and
- urban dweller (especially for gift receiving).

Some of these demographics are consistent with the stereotypical artificially mobilized *priísta* voter in Mexico.[16] Others, however, are not, particularly urban residence. This finding demonstrates the extent to which all political parties contending for the presidency in 2000 viewed the cities as the primary battleground. Low-income urban neighborhoods were the places where the parties could buy the most votes most efficiently. (The urban sector accounted for nearly 70 percent of total votes in 2000.) Although the premodern sector of the electorate may have been most exposed to vote buying and coercion in 2000, most of the artificially mobilized votes came from urban areas.

Who practices vote buying and coercion? The survey data suggest that all three of the major parties did it to some extent in 2000. As shown in table 3.1, the PRI engaged in vote-buying efforts more than any other party, but the PAN and the PRD were not completely out of the vote-buying game in 2000. Moreover, all parties were more prone to engage in vote buying in states where they controlled the governorship. This was especially true of the PRI, whose state governors clearly pulled out all the stops to preserve their own power and access to federal government resources via a PRI president. Manipulative activities by the PAN were much more evenly distributed across the country, perhaps because the source of most vote buying in behalf of Vicente Fox was not the PAN itself but the highly decentralized Friends of Fox (Amigos de Fox) campaign apparatus.[17]

In 2000 the parties also differed in terms of their preferred mode of vote buying and coercion. The PRI was responsible for most acts of *acarreo*, threats to cut off government benefits, and election-day breakfasts for voters—that is, old-style clientelist tactics. In the Mitofsky exit poll, the PAN was most responsible for cases of *revisión del voto* (observing how one voted).[18] However, as previously noted, this is an ambiguous indicator of coercion since there is no way to know whether there was a prior arrangement between the voter and the observer to vote for a particular candidate.

There are also some very interesting interparty differences in the *effectiveness* of vote buying and coercion in the 2000 election. The PRI clearly got the smallest payoff from these tactics. An analysis of the Mitofsky exit poll data reveals that less than 50 percent of the voters who had experienced vote buying or coercion by the PRI voted for its presidential candidate, Francisco Labastida, while 82 percent of the voters who had been targeted by the PAN voted for Vicente Fox. Even the PRD got more bang for its bucks than the PRI: 62 percent of voters who had been targeted by the PRD eventually voted for its presidential candidate, Cuauhtémoc Cárdenas. Those who were targeted by both the PRI and the PAN were more likely to have voted for Fox. Those who were threatened by the PRI were also more likely to have cast a vote for Fox, as was true of those who had been invited to an election-morning breakfast by the PRI. Even transportation to the polls by PRI-rented buses was not a significant predictor of voting for Labastida.[19]

A multinomial logit analysis of data from the fourth wave of the Mexico 2000 Panel Study reveals the same pattern of efficacy. Table 3.2 shows that, while seeking out voters in their homes benefited all three presidential candidates, only the PRD candidate benefited significantly from gifts provided by his party. In table 3.3 we see that benefits from the PROGRESA and LICONSA programs helped PRI candidate Labastida more than the PAN's Fox, but PROCAMPO benefits were not significantly related to the Fox-versus-Labastida choice.

Although the sign and statistical significance of the coefficients in the multinomial logit analyses show how voter choice in 2000 was affected by gift giving and possible coercion (in the form of home visits by campaign workers), it is easier to interpret the probabilities predicted

Table 3.2. Influence of Gifts and Home Visits on Candidate Choice in the 2000 Presidential Election (multinomial logit model)[a]

Independent Variables	Fox vs. Labastida		Cárdenas vs. Labastida	
	Coefficients	Std. Errors	Coefficients	Std. Errors
Women	−0.3661*	0.1522	−0.6863**	0.2098
Education	0.1497*	0.0729	−0.0401	0.1046
30–49 years old	−0.5204**	0.1746	−0.1428	0.2539
50 years old+	−0.5926**	0.2218	−0.0985	0.3076
Socioeconomic level of dwellings[b]	−0.1023	0.0832	−0.0505	0.1200
Rural locality	−0.9723**	0.1929	−0.2053	0.2519
Was visited by a PRI representative	−0.4024†	0.2421	−0.1950	0.3361
Was visited by a PAN representative	0.9026	0.3577	−0.7448	0.6819
Was visited by a PRD representative	0.0262	0.4025	1.1172*	0.4623
Received a gift from the PRI	0.0373	0.2695	−0.1793	0.3901
Received a gift from the PAN	0.5380	0.4535	−1.6906	1.1116
Received a gift from the PRD	−0.1870	0.6112	1.3296†	0.6906
Constant	1.0483†	0.5570	−0.1200	0.7957

[a] Data are from the fourth wave of the Mexico 2000 Panel Study. N = 961, LL = −898. Other parties were omitted from the analysis since they did not account for any observations of gift receiving and home visits.
[b] Higher values mean lower levels of dwellings and neighborhoods.
** $p < .01$, * $p < .05$, † $p < .10$.

by the model, which are reported in tables 3.4 and 3.5. When people were visited only by the PAN, their probability of voting for Fox was 73 percent, while just 46 percent of those visited (only) by a PRI representative were likely to have voted for Labastida. Similarly, among those who received a gift from the PAN (only), their probability of voting for Fox was nearly 68 percent, while just 37 percent of those who received a gift only from the PRI were likely to have voted for Labastida.

Table 3.3. Influence of Benefits from Federal Social Programs on Candidate Choice in the 2000 Presidential Election (multinomial logit model)[a]

Independent Variables	Fox vs. Labastida		Cárdenas vs. Labastida	
	Coefficients	Std. Errors	Coefficients	Std. Errors
Women	−0.3379*	0.1531	−0.6573**	0.2103
Education	0.0969	0.0738	−0.0338	0.1061
30–49 years old	−0.5386**	0.1767	−0.1034	0.2553
50 years old+	−0.7005**	0.2243	−0.1146	0.3108
Socioeconomic level of dwellings[b]	−0.0520	0.0838	−0.0382	0.1191
Rural locality	−0.8900**	0.1987	−0.2943	0.2597
Beneficiary of PROGRESA	−0.7411**	0.2871	0.1337	0.3184
Beneficiary of PROCAMPO	−0.2355	0.2551	0.0045	0.3138
Beneficiary of LICONSA	−0.5392*	0.2653	0.0890	0.3441
	1.1431	0.5567	−0.2234	0.7911

[a] Data are from the fourth wave of the Mexico 2000 Panel Study. N = 961, LL = −898. Other parties were omitted from the analysis since they did not account for any observations of benefits received from federal social programs.
[b] Higher values mean lower levels of dwellings and neighborhoods.
** $p < .01$, * $p < .05$, † $p < .10$.

Table 3.4. Predicted Probabilities of Voting for Each Presidential Candidate Associated with Receipt of Gifts and Home Visits, 2000[a]

	Labastida (PRI)	Fox (PAN)	Cárdenas (PRD)
Average	37.1	49.4	13.5
Was visited by a representative from …	45.6	73.2	33.3
Received a gift only from …'s party	37.3	67.7	40.9

[a] Data are from the fourth wave of the Mexico 2000 Panel Study.
Note: All variables were set at their means, except for the specified variable.

Table 3.5. Predicted Probabilities of Voting for Each Presidential Candidate Associated with Being a Beneficiary of a Federal Social Program, 2000[a]

	Labastida (PRI)	Fox (PAN)	Cárdenas (PRD)
Average	36.7	49.1	14.1
Only a beneficiary of PROGRESA	46.0	34.3	19.8
Only a beneficiary of PROCAMPO	38.3	47.3	14.5
Only a beneficiary of LICONSA	43.0	39.3	17.7

[a] Data are from the fourth wave of the Mexico 2000 Panel Study.
Note: All variables were set at their means, except for the specified variable.

Table 3.5 shows that government social programs closely identified with the PRI did not give Labastida the expected boost. The PRO-GRESA and LICONSA programs were more advantageous to Labastida than to Fox, but not overwhelmingly so, and those who had received payments from PROCAMPO were more likely to have voted for Fox. On average, beneficiaries of these three government programs had a higher probability of voting for Fox (49 percent) than for Labastida (37 percent) or Cárdenas (14 percent). The failure of these programs to deliver many votes to the PRI in 2000 may be explained by the beneficiaries' perception that the programs were "official" government programs for which the PRI should not be credited, or that they were entitlements rather than special gifts to the poor.

Neither did vote buying and seeking out voters in their homes enhance the PRI's ability to get out its vote on July 2, 2000. Table 3.6 reports results from a probit analysis of data from the Mexico 2000 Panel Study. The usual sociodemographic variables (education, age) were the statistically significant determinants of having voted in the 2000 election. Neither receiving a gift from the PRI (or any other party) nor being visited at home by a party representative is related to turnout. Similarly, receiving benefits from the PROGRESA, PROCAMPO, and LICONSA programs did not increase one's probability of voting (see table 3.7). Again, only standard sociodemographic attributes are statistically significant predictors of turnout. These results are consistent with Klesner and Lawson's analysis of the data from two waves of the Mexico 2000 Panel Study, which demonstrates that while beneficiaries of federal social programs were significantly more likely to state an *intention* to vote, in February 2000 interviews, they were not significantly more likely to actually vote in July 2000.[20]

Table 3.6. Influence of Gifts and Home Visits on Turnout (people who cast a vote for any presidential candidate; probit model)[a]

Independent Variable	Coefficients	Std. Errors
Women	0.0508	0.0996
Education	0.1888**	0.0524
30–49 years old	0.5541**	0.1119
50 years old+	0.7132**	0.1481
Socioeconomic level of dwellings[b]	−0.0352	0.0559
Rural locality	0.1721	0.1239
Was visited by a PRI representative	−0.0537	0.1574
Was visited by a PAN representative	−0.1842	0.2146
Was visited by a PRD representative	0.4462	0.2862
Received a gift from the PRI	0.0236	0.1793
Received a gift from the PAN	−0.2325	0.2807
Received a gift from the PRD	0.3299	0.4127
Constant	0.3176	0.3757

[a] Data are from the fourth wave of the Mexico 2000 Panel Study. $N = 1{,}142$, $LL = -419$.
[b] Higher values mean lower levels of dwellings and neighborhoods.
** $p < .01$, * $p < .05$, † $p < .10$.

Table 3.7. Influence of Federal Social Programs on Turnout (people who cast a vote for any presidential candidate; probit model)[a]

Independent Variable	Coefficients	Std. Errors
Women	0.0586	0.1001
Education	0.1944**	0.0529
30–49 years old	0.5573**	0.1122
50 years old+	0.7154**	0.1484
Socioeconomic level of dwellings[b]	−0.0330	0.0562
Rural locality	0.1599	0.1270
Beneficiary of PROGRESA	0.0740	0.1691
Beneficiary of PROCAMPO	−0.0538	0.1595
Beneficiary of LICONSA	−0.0319	0.1627
Constant	0.2863	0.3739

[a] Data are from the fourth wave of the Mexico 2000 Panel Study. $N = 1{,}130$, $LL = -417$.
[b] Higher values mean lower levels of dwellings and neighborhoods.
** $p < .01$, * $p < .05$, † $p < .10$.

DISCUSSION AND CONCLUSIONS

These findings concerning the efficacy of vote buying and coercion demonstrate the weakness of the PRI apparatus by the time of the 2000 federal election. In the run-up to this election, the PRI invested heavily in activities that had a very poor return. The Mexican voter in 2000 was, if anything, repelled by *compra y coacción* engineered by the PRI, and more likely to vote for the PAN's presidential candidate. This counterproductive effect may apply particularly to *priístas* who supported Roberto Madrazo, the very popular former governor of Tabasco, in the PRI's presidential primary election in November 1999. In general, the evidence from sample surveys and informal interviewing suggests that PRI threats and attempts at vote buying are viewed as more pernicious than those of other parties. This perception is, undoubtedly, the legacy of seven decades of "electoral alchemy" and authoritarian rule by PRI governments. Ironically, the PRI seems to be the only party for which antidemocratic practices no longer work.

Another generalization supported by the various bodies of evidence is that gift giving and partisan manipulation of federally funded social welfare programs were not significant determinants of voter choice or turnout in the 2000 election, all else being equal. This may tell us something important about the transformation of Mexican political culture during the period of rising competitiveness. Even though scientifically credible baseline data are not available, the electoral efficacy of traditional clientelist practices appears to have declined, especially in terms of mobilizing the PRI's vote. Indeed, these practices are likely to be counterproductive in the highly competitive electoral environment faced by the PRI in the twenty-first century.[21]

Such findings highlight the importance to the PRI's survival of shedding its authoritarian image and trying to conduct itself as a modern, inclusive, democratic party. Continued reliance on open primaries to select the party's presidential (and perhaps gubernatorial) candidates, avoiding traditional practices like *acarreo* and small-scale, particularistic gift giving, and rules changes that enhance the role of young people and women in the party's governance would all advance the PRI's transformation.[22]

Voter turnout is the Achilles' heel of the PRI's rebuilding effort. The data presented in this chapter show that the PRI can no longer rely on traditional clientelism to turn out its vote in federal elections. Since the debacle of July 2, 2000, the PRI has been able to use traditional clientelist tactics to win low-turnout (below 60 percent) elections for state and municipal offices in Tamaulipas, Oaxaca, Chiapas, Tabasco, and other states; but this is not a formula for regaining power at the national level. In most of the country's electoral districts, the PRI's traditional turnout advantage over its principal competitor, the PAN, has virtually disappeared.[23] Candidate choice was very important to turnout for all parties in the 2000 election, according to the Mexico 2000 Panel Study, and running an attractive, credible presidential candidate with broadly based grassroots support in 2006 will be essential to a PRI recovery at the national level.

Figure 3.1. The President's "Secret" Budget, 1993–2000

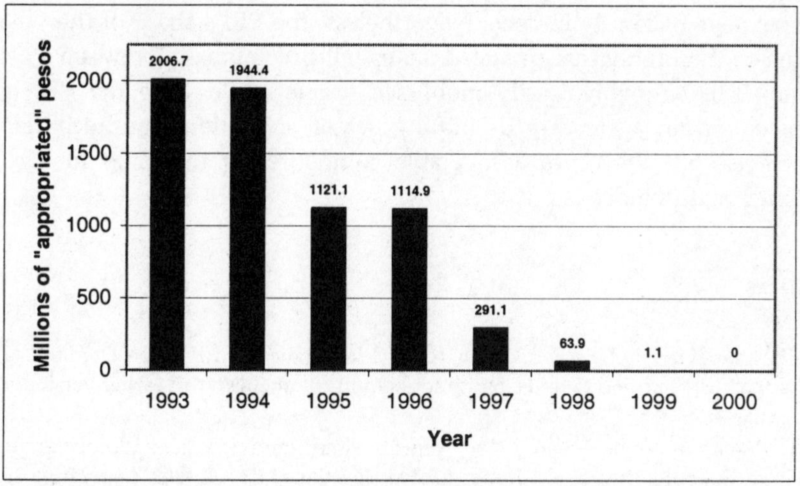

Source: Santiago Levy, "El presupuesto de egresos de la Federación," *Este País*, October 2000, p. 3.

The principal alternative to modernizing and democratizing the party along these lines would be to focus on maintaining control of the PRI's remaining fiefdoms at the state and local levels,[24] but such a strategy may no longer be realistic. PRI machines at the state and local levels have traditionally relied on largesse dispensed through the presidency—now controlled by the PAN—and on political control exercised by leaders of the PRI's sectoral (peasant and labor) organizations. The president's "secret" budget (*partida secreta*) used to be a major source of campaign financing for state-level PRI organizations, but by 2000 this discretionary presidential fund had ceased to exist, mainly as a result of pressure since 1997 from a Congress no longer controlled by the PRI (see figure 3.1). And the PRI's sectoral organizations cannot be relied upon to deliver enough votes to the party's candidates to win strongly contested elections in most parts of the country. Already in a seriously weakened state, these organizations are likely to experience significant defections now that their umbilical cord to the presidency has been severed.

Using traditional structures and methods of voter mobilization, the PRI will be hard pressed in future national elections to improve upon its performance in 2000, when it won only the country's most impoverished states and lost a major portion of its vote share even in these marginalized states.[25] It is in these parts of the country that significant numbers of voters remain vulnerable to economic coercion, especially in the form of threats to deny transfer payments that constitute a large percentage of family income. Nevertheless, the PRI's share of the vote even in the highly marginalized states fell precipitously between 1994 and 2000. Arguably, easily mobilized voters could keep the PRI in power within a steadily dwindling set of subnational authoritarian enclaves, but its future as a viable competitor at the national level would be dim indeed.

Notes

I am indebted to Luis Estrada for research assistance and to Jorge Domínguez, Chappell Lawson, and Peter H. Smith for helpful comments on an earlier version of this chapter.

1. Quoted in Sergio Muñoz, "Los Angeles Times Interview: José Woldenberg—Mexico Holds Its Breath and Hopes for Fair Elections," *Los Angeles Times*, June 25, 2000.

2. This feature of the Mexican system as it operated until the 1990s is common to authoritarian regimes elsewhere. Most citizen participation in the electoral process is mobilized by the government itself; unorganized popular participation is low. Some authoritarian regimes—like Mexico under PRI dominance—develop complex, all-embracing networks of organizations and activities whose purpose is mobilization of the population, although the periods of mobilization are usually shorter and less intensive than in a totalitarian regime. See Juan J. Linz and Alfred Stepan, *Problems of Democratic Transition and Consolidation* (Baltimore, Md.: Johns Hopkins University Press, 1996): 49–50. In PRI-dominated Mexico, intensive mobilization generally was limited to the six months preceding elections.

3. See Peter M. Ward and Victoria E. Rodríguez, *New Federalism and State Government in Mexico: Bringing the States Back In* (Austin: Lyndon Baines Johnson School of Public Affairs, University of Texas at Austin, 1999): 114–15; and Wayne A. Cornelius, "Blind Spots in Democratization: Subnational Politics as a Constraint on Mexico's Transition," *Democratization* 7, no. 3 (Autumn 2000): 125–26.

4. See Rose J. Spalding, "Political Parties in Yucatán: Regionalism, Strategy, and Prospects for the PRI," pp. 20–22, presented at the international congress of the Latin American Studies Association, Chicago, Ill., September 24–26, 1998.

5. For more detailed descriptions of the benefits, administration, and electoral consequences of these federal social programs, see Juan Molinar Horcasitas and Jeffrey A. Weldon, "Electoral Determinants and Consequences of National Solidarity," in Wayne A. Cornelius, Ann L. Craig, and Jonathan Fox, eds., *Transforming State-Society Relations in Mexico: The National Solidarity Strategy* (La Jolla: Center for U.S.-Mexican Studies, University of California, San Diego, 1994); Alberto Díaz-Cayeros, Federico Estévez, and Beatriz Magaloni, "A Portfolio Diversification Model of Electoral Investment: Competition and Policy Choice in Mexico's PRONASOL, 1989–1994," presented at the meeting of the American Political Science Association, San Francisco, August 30–September 2, 2001; Alina Rocha Menocal, "Do Old Habits Die Hard?—A Statistical Exploration of the Politicization of PROGRESA, Mexico's Latest Federal Poverty-Alleviation Program," *Journal of Latin American Studies* 33 (2001): 513–38; Spalding, "Early Social Policy Initiatives in the Fox Administration"; and David Myhre, "The Achilles' Heel of the Reforms: The Rural Finance System," in Wayne A. Cornelius and David Myhre, eds., *The Transformation of Rural Mexico: Reforming the Ejido Sector* (La Jolla: Center for U.S.-Mexican Studies, University of California, San Diego, 1998).

6. FLACSO-IFE, "Estudio sobre la participación ciudadana y las condiciones del voto libre y secreto en las elecciones federales del año 2000," Mexico City, 2000.

7. On the case of Cervera Pacheco, the PRI's most accomplished vote buyer in the late 1990s, see Rose J. Spalding, "Political Parties in Yucatán: Regionalism, Strategy, and Prospects for the PRI," pp. 20–22; and Tim Weiner, "In Old-Time Boss' Redoubt, Mexico Tests Political Wind," *New York Times*, May 27, 2001.

8. In Spanish, *"¿En las últimas semanas de la campaña, a usted lo visitó un representante de algún partido político o candidato a la presidencia?"* and *"¿En las últimas semanas de la campaña, usted recibió regalos o asistencia de algún partido político?"* Respondents who answered affirmatively were then asked to name the parties or candidates.

9. In Spanish, *"¿Alguno de los equipos de campaña de los candidatos a la Presidencia de la República ... visitó su domicilio para promover el voto?, lo ayudó a venir a la casilla votar?, lo amenazó si no votaba por él?, le dio algún regalo?, le prometió algo para usted si votaba por él?, lo invitó a desayunar para venir juntos a votar?, revisó por cual partido votó hoy?"*

10. Alianza Cívica, *Reporte del 2 de julio*, at http://www.laneta.apc.org/alianza/. For a description of Civic Alliance's election observation procedures, see Sergio Aguayo Quezada, "Electoral Observation and Democracy in Mexico," in Kevin J. Middlebrook, ed., *Electoral Observation and Democratic Transitions in Latin America* (La Jolla: Center for U.S.-Mexican Studies, University of California, San Diego, 1998).

11. FLACSO-IFE, "Estudio sobre la participación ciudadana."

12. These reports by international election observers include: Alianza Cívica/ Mexico Working Group, *Democracy: The Long and Winding Road* (Mexico City, July 2000); Wayne A. Cornelius, "Mexicans Would Not Be Bought, Coerced," in Gilbert Joseph and Timothy Henderson, eds., *The Mexico Reader: History, Culture, Politics*

(Durham, N.C.: Duke University Press, 2002); Global Exchange/Alianza Cívica, *Pre-electoral Conditions in Mexico in 2000* (Mexico City, June 2000); Chappell Lawson, "What's New about the 'New' Mexico?—Reflections on the July 2 Election," *ReVista: Harvard Review of Latin America* 1, no. 1 (Fall 2001): 8–10; Jean F. Mayer and Thomas Legler, "The 2000 Mexican Elections: The Persistent Urban-Rural Divide" (Toronto: Centre for Research on Latin America and the Caribbean, York University, 2000); National Democratic Institute for International Affairs, "Report of the National Democratic Institute's International Delegation to Mexico's July 2, 2000 Elections" (Washington, D.C., 2000); Washington Office on Latin America, "Vote-buying and Coercion of Voters," *Mexico Election Monitor 2000*, No. 4 (May 2000); Washington Office on Latin America, "The Electoral Justice System," *Mexico Election Monitor 2000*, No. 6 (July 2000); María de los Angeles Crummett and Veronica Wilson, "Promoting the Free and Secret Vote in Oaxaca: Voting Rights in the 2000 Mexican Presidential Elections," presented at the international congress of the Latin American Studies Association, Washington, D.C., September 6–8, 2001.

13. In a national exit poll conducted by Mitofsky International for the August 1994 presidential election, 7 percent of the respondents reported that someone had tried to coerce them into voting for a specific candidate or party (Jorge I. Domínguez and James A. McCann, *Democratizing Mexico: Public Opinion and Electoral Choices* [Baltimore, Md.: Johns Hopkins University Press, 1996]: 208). However, Civic Alliance observers noted attempts to coerce voters in 25 percent of the precincts, nationwide. Civic Alliance also found that support for the PRI dropped by as much as 30 percent in rural areas of some states when election observers were present (Aguayo Quezada, "Election Observation," p. 181).

14. For example, vote buying in the 1994 federal elections was pervasive in some regions, especially through the PROCAMPO cash subsidy program benefiting rural dwellers. See Lynn Stephen, *Zapata Lives! Histories and Cultural Politics in Southern Mexico* (Berkeley: University of California Press, 2002): 298–300.

15. See Rose J. Spalding, "Early Social Policy Initiatives in the Fox Administration," presented at the international congress of the Latin American Studies Association, Washington, D.C., September 6–8, 2001, pp. 6–7; Cornelius, "Mexicans Would Not Be Bought"; and Mayer and Legler, "The 2000 Mexican Elections," pp. 5–6.

16. See, for example, Ann L. Craig and Wayne A. Cornelius, "Political Culture in Mexico: Continuities and Revisionist Interpretations," in Gabriel A. Almond and Sidney Verba, eds., *The Civic Culture Revisited* (Newbury Park, Calif.: Sage, 1989): 362–71.

17. For an analysis of interstate and rural/urban differences in vote buying and coercion in the 2000 election based on data from the Mitofsky exit poll, see Martha Patricia Gómez Straffon, "La compra y coacción del voto en las elecciones federales del año 2000: resultados de una encuesta de salida" (Bachelor's thesis, Instituto Tecnológico Autónomo de México, 2001): 59–62. On the Friends of Fox campaign organization, see David A. Shirk, "Vicente Fox and the Rise of the PAN," *Journal of Democracy* 11, no. 4 (October 2000): 25-32; and David A. Shirk, "Mexico's Democratization and the Organizational Development of the National Action Party," in Kevin J. Middlebrook, ed., *Party Politics and the Struggle for Democracy in Mexico:*

National and State-Level Analyses of the Partido Acción Nacional (La Jolla: Center for U.S.-Mexican Studies, University of California, San Diego, 2001).

18. Gómez Straffon, "La compra y coacción del voto," pp. 55–58.

19. Ibid., pp. 77, 88–93.

20 See Joseph L. Klesner and Chappell Lawson, "Adios to the PRI? Changing Voter Turnout in Mexico's Political Transition," *Mexican Studies* 17, no. 1 (Winter 2001): appendix C, pp. 35–36. See also Lawson and Klesner's contribution to this volume.

21. On optimal campaign strategies for the PRI and Mexico's other major parties in future elections, see Joseph L. Klesner, "Electoral Competition and the New Party System in Mexico," presented at the meeting of the American Political Science Association, San Francisco, August 30–September 2, 2001.

22. The PRI's recent experience with a radically decentralized presidential nomination procedure is analyzed in Joy Langston, "Why Rules Matter: Changes in Candidate Selection in Mexico's PRI, 1988–2000," *Journal of Latin American Studies* 33 (2001): 485–511. On the use of the open primary system to rebuild support for the PRI at the state level, see Yemile Mizrahi, "La alternancia política en Chihuahua: el regreso del PRI," in Víctor Alejandro Espinoza Valle, ed., *Alternancia y transición política: ¿cómo gobierna la oposición en México?* (México City: Plaza y Valdés/El Colegio de la Frontera Norte, 2000). At its most recent national assembly, held in November 2001, the PRI adopted rules requiring that 50 percent of its candidates for elective office must be women and 30 percent persons under the age of thirty. It also reaffirmed a 1996 change in nomination rules requiring PRI presidential candidates to have at least ten years of activism in the party and to have held at least one elective office.

23. See Klesner and Lawson, "Adiós to the PRI?"

24. See Wayne A. Cornelius, Todd Eisenstadt, and Jane Hindley, eds., *Subnational Politics and Democratization in Mexico* (La Jolla: Center for U.S.-Mexican Studies, University of California, San Diego, 1999).

25. In the 2000 presidential election, the PRI won an absolute majority in only two states, Nayarit and Sinaloa, the latter being the home state of its presidential candidate.

4

Political Reform, Electoral Participation, and the Campaign of 2000

CHAPPELL LAWSON AND JOSEPH L. KLESNER

Mexico's election results of July 2000 came as a surprise, if not a shock, to many observers. Although national polls had revealed a close race between Francisco Labastida and Vicente Fox, even those surveys released by Fox allies substantially underestimated their candidate's actual margin of victory. One reason, as leading pollster Alejandro Moreno pointed out, was that the composition of the electorate was quite different from the general population that pollsters surveyed.[1] In the end, Fox supporters were disproportionately likely to vote on election day, while potential PRI voters were more inclined to stay home.

The geographic distribution of participation in figure 4.1 bears witness to a pro-Fox bias in turnout. Participation as a percentage of registered voters was unusually high in the conservative, Catholic states of the central Bajío region (which includes Fox's home state of Guanajuato). It was relatively—and unexpectedly—weak in several traditional strongholds of the long-ruling Institutional Revolutionary Party (PRI) in Mexico's poorer, more rural south. In fact, turnout was lowest of all (52.5 percent) in the turbulent southernmost state of Chiapas, which includes communities where the PRI had tallied over 100 percent of the eligible electorate only a decade before.[2] Clearly, something significant had changed in Mexican voting patterns.

The 2000 presidential election represented the culmination of recent trends in political participation. Whereas Mexico's ruling party could once rely on fraud, clientelism, and corporatism to boost its support,

electoral reforms during the 1990s undermined these traditional instruments of PRI mobilization. At the same time, political reform and
vigorous electoral challenge convinced increasing numbers of opposition and unaffiliated voters that their votes might actually determine
who governed Mexico. Finally, market-oriented reforms, repeated economic crises, and increasing factionalism within the PRI presumably
undermined the party's ability to turn out voters. The result was a remarkable reversal in patterns of electoral participation. Although
higher official turnout levels had historically been associated with support for the dominant party, on July 2, 2000, supporters of Vicente Fox
were more likely to participate.[3]

Figure 4.1. Geographic Distribution of Turnout in 2000

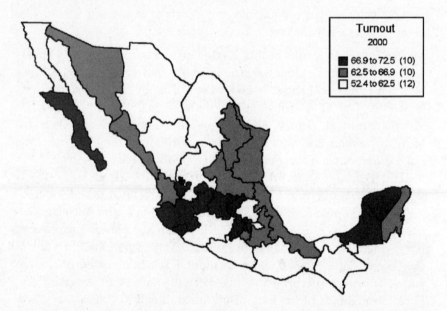

In this chapter, we discuss how Mexico's protracted process of electoral reform contributed to the opposition victory in 2000 by altering
turnout patterns. The first section uses aggregate-level data and publicly available opinion polls to show how turnout patterns shifted during the 1980s and 1990s. The second section focuses on electoral participation in 2000, highlighting the factors that shaped turnout in that
pivotal contest. The third section analyzes campaign-induced changes
in the likelihood of voting between February and June 2000. Drawing

on data from the Mexico 2000 Panel Study, we show how sympathy for Vicente Fox, exposure to campaign messages on television, and increasing confidence in the electoral process among opposition voters contributed to higher rates of political participation. We conclude that both historical and campaign-induced changes in turnout patterns helped propel Fox to victory.

TURNOUT IN MEXICO

For decades, the PRI's electoral dominance depended on a political machine able to get out the vote on election day. Thanks to fraud, state corporatism, clientelism, and other traditional instruments of social control—as well as substantial genuine attachment to the ruling party—official participation rates remained high despite the absence of real competition.[4] In the 1960s, for instance, official turnout in national elections averaged approximately two-thirds of registered voters, and in some states participation surpassed 90 percent.[5]

As Mexico modernized and the ruling party's political machine began to weaken, turnout tended to decline. As figure 4.2 shows, participation rates dropped fairly steadily during the 1960s and 1970s, even before the economic crises of the 1980s. Presidential races (1964, 1970, and 1976) attracted more attention than midterm contests, but each election of the same type saw a larger proportion of the electorate abstain. Turnout bottomed out in the contested elections of 1988, when official participation as a percentage of registered voters sunk to 50 percent.

Aside from this secular downward trend, turnout levels responded primarily to PRI-inspired registration and voter mobilization drives. Registration drives boosted participation temporarily by galvanizing the PRI's grassroots political machinery. But turnout rates tended to decline sharply afterward, as registration drives mechanically raised the number of eligible electors and as an increasingly unpopular ruling party proved unable to maintain high levels of participation (whether real or manufactured). Electoral reforms tended to reinforce these effects by purging the registration lists of voters who, though consistently loyal to the PRI, also happened to be dead.[6]

Electoral reforms tended to have the opposite effect on opposition voters. Not only did registration drives and the creation of a new voter list close the gap between PRI and opposition registration rates, they also helped convince opposition supporters that their votes might actually count. According to Gallup's 1991 national preelection poll, for

Figure 4.2. Official Turnout as a Percent of Registered Voters

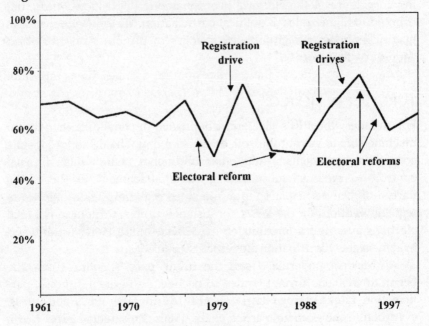

Figure 4.3. Turnout in Urban and Rural States

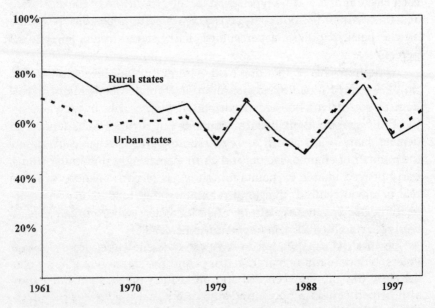

instance, slightly less than 51 percent of opposition voters believed that there would be little or no fraud in the elections that year.[7] By February 2000, according to the first wave of the Mexico 2000 Panel Study, that figure had increased to 58 percent. As discussed further below, increasing perceptions of electoral integrity proved to be an important stimulant to participation.

As a consequence of these larger political changes, the composition of Mexico's electorate began to shift. Whereas support for the opposition had once correlated negatively with official turnout rates, in the 1990s that pattern reversed. Figure 4.3 compares average turnout in the five most rural states (where PRI instruments of social control tended to work most effectively) with average turnout in the five most urban states (where these instruments tended to be weaker).[8] Although initially higher, turnout declined more rapidly in heavily rural states during the 1960s and 1970s. In the 1980s, turnout levels were approximately the same for both sets of states, and by the 1990s, turnout was higher in heavily urbanized states. "Normal" patterns of turnout evident in more developed democracies thus emerged as the old regime broke down.

Table 4.1 provides further documentation of changes in the social composition of electoral participation, using district-level data. As the bivariate correlations in table 4.1 indicate, official turnout rates did not differ substantially between urban and rural districts until the late 1980s. In the 1990s, however, urban areas registered higher participation. Trends for other measures of modernization, such as literacy and the percentage of the workforce employed in agriculture, were even more pronounced. The poorer, less educated, rural communities that had long constituted PRI strongholds thus fell from some of the highest turnout regions to some of the lowest.

This transformation had predictable effects on the partisan composition of the vote. As table 4.1 shows, turnout was correlated positively with the PRI's share of the vote for most elections through the 1980s. In the 1990s, however, turnout correlated negatively with PRI support and positively with support for the National Action Party (PAN).

Importantly, these partisan effects persist when modernization-related factors that also determine turnout are taken into account. Table 4.2 reports the results of OLS regression on turnout across Mexico's electoral districts since 1988. As the data show, turnout was negatively associated with PAN voting in 1988, but positively associated with PAN voting thereafter. For the PRI, this relationship was reversed.

Table 4.1. Correlates of District-Level Turnout, 1979–2000

Variable	1979	1982	1985	1988	1991	1994	1997	2000
Urbanization (>50,000)	.04	.03	-.04	.12*	.22*	.31*	.42*	.50*
Literacy	-.15*	-.02	-.07	-.12*	.18*	.54*	.52*	.55*
% EAP in agriculture	.01	-.12*	-.02	.07	-.19*	-.58*	-.51*	-.58*
PRI vote	.09	-.07	.13*	.13*	-.51*	-.43*	-.57*	-.57*
PAN vote	-.15*	.01	-.24*	-.13*	.35*	.55*	.41*	.55*

Notes: EAP = economically active population. * $p < .05$ level.

Table 4.2. Multivariate Analysis of District-Level Turnout, 1988–2000

Variable	1988	1991	1994	1997	2000	1991	1994	1997	2000
Constant	.43*	.91*	.51*	.58*	.55*	.51*	.33*	.60*	.47*
Literacy	-.12	-.05	-.00*	.29*	.28*	.21*	.34*	.19*	.16*
Urbanization	.17*	.06	.12*	.03	-.03	.04*	.00	.00	.02
PRI Vote	.08*	-.43*	—	-.16*	-.35*	—	—	-.23*	—
PAN Vote	—	—	.29*	—	—	.20*	.15*	—	.15*
Adjusted R²	.06	.26	.15	.39	.36	.42	.32	.38	.38
F statistic	7.0	35.5	19.1	63.9	57.5	73.0	46.8	61.6	60.7

* $p < .05$ level.

Opposition voters thus became relatively more likely to participate over the course of the 1990s. Presumably, decreases in authoritarian mobilization, coupled with increasing participation among previously cynical opponents of the regime, were primarily responsible for these shifts.

Table 4.3. Bivariate Correlates of Individual-Level Turnout in the 1990s

	1991	1994	1997	2000 (July)
Education	−.02	.06*	.06*	.07*
Income proxy	.09*	.04*	.06*	.07*
Urban resident	.05*	.01	−.01	.02
Perceptions of fraud	−.08*	−.22*	−.12*	−.09*
Net evaluation of PRI	.07*	.06*	−.02	−.01

Note: Data for 2000 represent the combined fourth wave of the panel and postelectoral cross-section.

* $p < .05$.

Individual-level data to corroborate these suppositions are not available before 1988 (when Gallup conducted the first professional, publicly accessible election poll in Mexico).[9] The data that are available from the 1990s, however, confirm the principal findings of ecological analysis at the state and district levels. Wealthier, more educated citizens tended to vote more regularly during the last decade; urban residents also appeared slightly more likely to vote, although that effect was much less clear. Perceptions of electoral integrity remained a consistent and powerful predictor of participation; even controlling for other factors, those who believed the elections might be fraudulent were substantially less likely to vote.[10] Finally, the partisan composition of turnout appears to shift away from the PRI. In the early 1990s, relative affinity for the PRI (as measured by the difference between evaluations of the PRI and evaluations of the opposition parties) was positively associated with turnout.[11] In the second half of the decade, the reverse was true. These findings are shown in table 4.3.

VOTER TURNOUT IN 2000

Evidence from the last several decades thus suggests that Mexico's changing political context had an important influence on patterns of electoral participation. As political reforms deepened, the PRI's ability to inspire, cajole, coerce, or fabricate participation declined. Meanwhile, opposition voters became more inclined to participate in an increasingly competitive and honest process. These trends come through clearly in both individual-level and aggregate data.

Data from 2000 demonstrate that these trends were especially strong in that election. Table 4.4 summarizes the relationship between turnout and partisan support using data from Mexico's three hundred electoral districts.[12] As the table shows, turnout was highest where Fox's Alliance for Change did well, and lowest where the PRI remained strong.

Table 4.4. Turnout and Partisan Support by District in 2000

Districts Where Party's Share Was	Average Turnout of Registered Voters	
	Alliance for Change	PRI
> 50%	67.1	59.9
40–50%	64.0	59.3
30–40%	64.3	63.7
20–30%	60.9	68.4
< 20%	56.0	72.2

As in other recent elections, the relationship between partisan support and turnout in 2000 was not purely a product of modernization-related variables. Table 4.5 presents the results of OLS regression on turnout across Mexico's three hundred electoral districts in 2000. As the table shows, education was positively associated with turnout; agricultural employment was negatively so. Controlling for these factors, however, PAN voting was positively correlated with turnout, while PRI support exercised a strongly negative effect. These data provide further evidence that the PRI's electoral machine continued to deteriorate while the capacity of opposition parties (especially the PAN) to mobilize their supporters increased.

Table 4.5 also shows that these results persist when we control for certain data that were not always available in earlier years. For instance, participation was higher in more heavily Catholic areas—hardly a surprising finding given the Church's repeated exhortations to vote. Aggregate participation rates also paralleled turnout in the PRI's internal primary of November 1999, indicating that participation continued to be higher in those remaining zones where the PRI's apparatus survived. Regardless of which variables are included, though, PAN voting remains positively related to turnout, and PRI voting inversely so.

Table 4.5. Multivariate Analysis of District-Level Turnout, July 2000

Variable	PAN (1)	PAN (2)	PAN (3)	PRI (1)	PRI (2)	PRI (3)
Constant	.57*	.40*	.34*	.70*	.48*	.45*
Percent of EAP in primary sector	−.05*	−.03	−.05*	−.06*	−.03	−.06*
Percent with higher education	.37*	.37*	.33*	.27*	.30*	.23*
Percent Catholic		.23*	.26*		.25*	.27*
Turnout in PRI primary			.24*			.28*
PAN share of vote	.14*	.10*	.12*			
PRI share of vote				−.18*	−.14*	−.20*
Adjusted R²	.41	.46	.50	.40	.46	.51

Notes: N = 300 federal electoral districts; census data from 1990 census available at http://www.inegi.gob.mx; electoral data taken from http://www.ife.org.mx.
* $p < .05$.

Individual-level data from the Mexico 2000 Panel Study both support these conclusions and highlight several other demographic and attitudinal factors associated with turnout. For the first three waves of the panel (February, April, and June), respondents were asked their likelihood of voting—on a scale of zero to ten, with zero indicating no chance of voting and ten indicating that they would definitely cast a ballot. Because the distribution of these responses was highly skewed (with approximately 68 percent of those surveyed rating their likelihood of voting at a ten), the following analysis regroups these responses into four categories: those who rated themselves at a three or less (approximately 12 percent); those who rated themselves at four through six (approximately 8 percent); those who rated themselves at seven through nine (approximately 14 percent); and those who rated themselves at ten. We then analyze this new scale using ordered logit regression; the results are presented in table 4.6.[13]

Approximately 89 percent of the entire sample reported being registered to vote in February (that is, they reported having an up-to-date voter identification card for the area in which they lived).[14] In order to differentiate between the effects of registration and the likelihood of voting among those already registered, table 4.6 presents two models (which are identical except for the registration variable). As the table shows, however, the influence of most variables is similar whether or not registration is included.

Table 4.6. Likelihood of Voting in February 2000

Variable	Beta	p-value	Beta	p-value
Threshold 1 (Will not vote)	−6.296	.00	−6.196	.00
Threshold 2 (Might vote)	−5.575	.00	−5.432	.00
Threshold 3 (Likely to vote)	−4.680	.00	−4.501	.00
Year of birth	−0.026	.00	−0.022	.00
Male	−0.211	.04	−0.241	.02
Socioeconomic status	−0.043	.32	−0.065	.14
Education	0.095	.09	0.116	.04
Church attendance	0.094	.03	0.087	.05
Nonunionized	−0.201	.21	−0.153	.34
Rural resident	0.299	.02	0.294	.02
Northern region	−0.180	.20	−0.049	.73
Central region	−0.105	.46	−0.042	.77
Metropolitan region	−0.091	.51	−0.047	.73
Opinion of Labastida	0.012	.47	0.008	.63
Opinion of Fox	0.036	.05	0.041	.03
Opinion of Cárdenas	−0.027	.12	−0.024	.17
Interpersonal trust	0.503	.00	0.459	.01
Perceptions of fraud	−0.116	.05	−0.108	.07
Political interest	0.289	.00	0.316	.00
Attention to campaign	0.185	.01	0.152	.07
Weekly television viewing	0.026	.06	0.029	.03
Visited by party representative	0.325	.62	0.389	.55
Registered to vote	—	—	−1.412	.00
Cox and Snell		.09		.13
Chi-squared statistic		172		261
Valid N		1,904		1,904

Note: Base case = will definitely vote.

Propensities to vote in February 2000 generally conform to standard predictions of participation in Mexico and elsewhere.[15] In most cases, the factors that predicted turnout in February remained significant in subsequent waves of the panel and in a separate postelectoral cross-section of the population. By far the most powerful demographic factor was age: older people voted more, controlling for other factors, and younger people were less likely to participate. To some extent, this difference reflects registration rates; approximately 22 percent of those twenty-three years of age and younger were not registered, whereas only 6 percent of those over forty were not. But age continued to exercise a significant influence over participation when registration levels were taken into account, suggesting that past habits of voting (from an era when turnout was higher) continue to govern behavior today. Although the importance of age declined somewhat over the course of the campaign, as the Fox campaign focused on galvanizing youth support, it remained important.

The effects of gender, by contrast, were not particularly robust. Although men reported being less likely to vote in February, all else equal, in other models and at other phases in the campaign they were more likely to report doing so. Socioeconomic status had no significant effect once other factors were taken into account.[16] Education worked in the expected direction, with more educated citizens being more likely to cast ballots, but its effects were only marginally significant. The same held for union membership, which was once an important predictor of turnout in a country where the ruling party controlled most unions; presumably, neoliberal reforms and declining official control of unions weakened the unions' ability to deliver votes. Church attendance, by contrast, remained a significant and powerful influence on participation. Reflecting clerical appeals, those more consistently exposed to religious messages and more integrated into church life were substantially more likely to participate.

Perhaps surprisingly, rural residents were more likely to vote than urbanites once other factors are held constant. This gap does not appear to be a function of differences in registration rates alone, despite the fact that rural dwellers are slightly more likely to be registered (90 percent versus 88 percent for urban residents). More probably, it reflects the persistence of clientelistic networks in some parts of the countryside.

Regional differences, which may at first appear suggestive, seem to be a product of differences in registration rates.[17] About 15 percent of northerners were not registered in 2000, compared to between 10 and 11 percent of those in other regions—a difference that presumably reflects the greater transience of residence in border areas. Once registration levels are taken into account, there is little evidence of strong regional biases in participation. Thus the fact that most of northern Mexico is effectively a two-party system of the PAN and PRI—while parts of southern Mexico are effectively a two-party system of the PRI and leftist Party of the Democratic Revolution (PRD), and the metropolitan area is essentially a three-and-a-half-party system—seems to matter little for participation rates.

Other features of the political context do seem to matter, however. Opinions of Fox, for instance, were strongly and significantly related to turnout. Opinions of Labastida had a much more muted effect, and attitudes toward Cárdenas were negatively associated with participation (other things being equal). It thus appears that the relative attractiveness and viability of the main candidates played a role in mobilizing or demobilizing voters. Cárdenas's supporters were clearly less enthusiastic about participating in what was, by February, already a two-man race; likewise, Labastida's candidacy failed to galvanize his base.

Two other attitudinal factors—interpersonal trust and perceptions of electoral integrity—also played important roles in encouraging participation. The more likely respondents were to find their fellow citizens trustworthy, the more likely they were to participate. And as expected, perceptions of how clean the elections would be were significant predictors of voting. In other words, structural changes in Mexico's electoral context continued to translate into perceptions of electoral integrity and, ultimately, propensities to vote.

Campaign stimuli varied in their impact. Interest in politics and attention to the 2000 campaign were both positively related to turnout, the first more reliably so. Exposure to television news—which included substantial coverage of the race—was also significant, indicating an important priming function of Mexico's most important medium. Canvassing by grassroots party activists, by contrast, appeared to exercise little influence on participation.

Analysis of self-reported turnout in July (after the elections) supports these findings. As with most surveys, self-reported turnout was highly inflated in our data—about 83 percent of the sample reported voting, compared to less than 60 percent of the adult population. As a result, there is substantially less variation to analyze than in February, and obvious biases in the data make conclusions drawn from July somewhat less reliable than those drawn from survey responses in February. On the other hand, responses in July theoretically capture self-reported *behavior* rather than simply respondents' propensities or dispositions.

The following analysis relies on binary logistic regression on self-reported turnout. In order to maximize the sample size, it combines the fourth wave of the panel with a separate postelectoral cross-sectional poll from the Mexico 2000 Panel Study, conducted at the same time with roughly the same number of respondents (approximately 1,200 each). To control for the potential influence on turnout of participation in the panel itself, this analysis includes a variable measuring the number of times each respondent was interviewed (from one to four). It excludes certain items that were not included in both surveys (such as union membership and self-reported registration, for example), but it otherwise incorporates the relevant variables from table 4.6. The results of the analysis are reported in table 4.7.

Table 4.7. Self-Reported Turnout, July 2000

Variable	Coefficient	p-value
Year of birth	−0.020	.00
Male	0.146	.25
Socioeconomic status	−0.023	.67
Education	0.088	.22
Church attendance	0.122	.03
Rural resident	0.041	.78
Northern region	0.276	.14
Central region	0.162	.36
Metropolitan region	0.038	.82
Opinion of Labastida	0.009	.61
Opinion of Fox	0.003	.88
Opinion of Cárdenas	0.021	.32
Interpersonal trust	0.285	.14
Perceptions of fraud	−0.391	.02
Political interest	0.328	.00
Attention to campaign	0.250	.00
Weekly television viewing	0.028	.21
Number of times interviewed in panel	0.039	.52

Cox and Snell = .05

Chi-squared statistic = 110

Valid N = 2,069

All told, the data contain some intriguing findings but little in the way of dramatic surprises. Age, church attendance, political interest, attention to the campaign, and perceptions of electoral integrity (measured dichotomously) remain significant influences.[18] Factors like education, interpersonal trust, and exposure to television news operate in the expected direction, but their effect is not statistically significant (presumably because of colinearity in a sample where very few respondents reported not having voted).

Turnout patterns in 2000 can thus be seen as the continuation of a long-term trend toward clean elections in Mexico. Staple factors (like age, church attendance, and interest in politics) influenced turnout, but factors associated with old-style Mexican politics (such as region, union membership, and rural residency) mattered less. Meanwhile, perceptions of electoral integrity played an important role in shaping who would vote. Partisan competition and electoral reform at the system level thus translated into political behavior at the individual level.

CAMPAIGN INFLUENCES ON TURNOUT IN 2000

These shifts become clearer still if we consider changes in propensities to vote over the course of the campaign. All told, the 2000 campaign itself played an important role in shaping turnout rates across different segments of the population in ways that reinforced existing trends in participation. Comparing across separate waves of the panel allows us to evaluate these changes, and also to understand better how the campaign contributed to Fox's victory by altering turnout patterns.

Overall, the campaign appears to have had a mobilizing effect. Of those respondents who participated in both the first and third waves of the panel, approximately 69 percent indicated that they definitely planned to vote in February. By the third wave of the panel (June), just over 73 percent definitely planned to vote. Despite its generally negative tone, the campaign tended to stimulate political participation.

Much more interesting than this overall change, however, is the shift in the partisan composition of the vote. Among those who identified with the PRI at the beginning of the campaign, increases in their likelihood of voting from February to June paralleled the sample as a whole (about 3.5 percent). Among initial PAN identifiers, however, the increase was almost 7.5 percent; among PRD identifiers, the increase was substantially smaller (1.2 percent). Subtracting the changes in each group from the overall change, we find that—in relative terms—the campaign activated PAN supporters, deactivated PRD supporters, and had little effect on PRI identifiers. These data are shown in table 4.8.

Table 4.8. Shifts in Likely Turnout by Partisan Affiliation, February–June

	PRI	PAN	PRD	Other/None	All
Will definitely vote (February)	73.9%	68.6%	72.7%	65.1%	69.8%
Will definitely vote (June)	77.4%	76.0%	73.9%	67.0%	73.4%
Change	+3.5%	+7.4%	+1.2%	+1.8%	+3.4%
Relative change	+0.1%	+4.0%	−2.2%	−1.6%	—
N	368	204	88	321	981

The campaign thus reinforced patterns already evident in February, when PAN voters seemed galvanized by their candidate. PRI supporters, by contrast, were comparatively unenthusiastic about their nominee, and leftists remained relatively less likely to engage in a race that offered them limited prospects for victory.

Other than partisan affiliation, what factors activated or deactivated potential voters? Table 4.9 reports the results of OLS regression on the change in respondents' likelihood of voting from February to June. This analysis includes all demographic variables from the ordinal logit model discussed above, as well as changes in those variables related to the campaign. It also includes a measure of how negative respondents perceived the tone of the campaign to be (an item not included in the first wave).

Several important results leap out from this analysis. First, few of the variables are clear predictors of change in likelihood of voting. Changes in campaign attentiveness and political interest, contact with grassroots activists, and perceptions of negative campaigning did not significantly alter a respondent's probability of turning out. Nor did most demographic variables (education, socioeconomic status, gender, and so on). Only a handful of factors helped to mobilize or demobilize voters over the course of the campaign.

Table 4.9. Change in Propensity to Vote, February–June

Variable	Coefficient	p-value
Constant	−0.569	.37
Year of birth	0.008	.26
Male	0.038	.84
Socioeconomic status	−0.091	.27
Education	−0.006	.95
Church attendance	−0.079	.34
Union membership	−0.342	.25
Urban resident	0.095	.68
Northern region	0.533	.05
Central region	0.929	.00
Metropolitan region	0.416	.11
Change in opinion of Labastida	0.007	.80
Change in opinion of Fox	0.061	.04
Change in opinion of Cárdenas	0.016	.61
Trust	−0.368	.22
Change in perceptions of fraud	−0.188	.04
Perceptions of negative campaigning	0.032	.82
Change in political interest	−0.088	.41
Change in attention to campaign	−0.022	.81
Change in weekly television viewing	0.038	.07
Change in exposure to party activists	−0.675	.28
N = 748		
Adjusted R-squared = .02		
F-statistic = 1.83		

One such factor was region. In central Mexico—from which Fox hailed and in which PAN governors controlled several state houses—participation rates jumped over the course of the campaign relative to other regions. Grassroots mobilization by the so-called Friends of Fox may have played a role there. Participation also increased, though somewhat less dramatically, in the north and the area around Mexico City—both longtime hotbeds of opposition sentiment. By contrast, participation tapered off in the south, where the PRI's vote-getting machine had traditionally been strongest. The most likely explanation for these changes is that the continuing decline and diminished cohesiveness of the PRI's "apparatus" cost the ruling party participation.

Fox's candidacy itself also seems to have been a powerful draw. The more that people upgraded their perceptions of Fox over the course of the campaign, the more likely they became to vote. By contrast, improvements in opinions of Fox's two principal rivals had little mobilizing effect. Presumably, the prospect of an opposition candidate closing in on Los Pinos (Mexico's presidential residence) helped to turn out voters.

Equally powerful was the effect of increasing perceptions of electoral integrity. As in past contests, the more voters believed that the elections would be clean, the more likely they became to vote. And as in the past, it was opposition supporters who most frequently changed their minds about whether the election would be fraudulent. Although all categories of respondents became increasingly convinced of the integrity of the electoral process, the great bulk of attitude change occurred among respondents who did not identify with the PRI.

One final factor that encouraged turnout was exposure to network television news. This effect appears to have been substantial. Not only was exposure to television news a statistically significant predictor of turnout in February, increasing news viewership over the course of the campaign was associated with an increasing propensity to vote (at the 10 percent level of significance), controlling for other factors. Despite the negative tone of the race, the constant stream of television coverage did seem to pique voter interest.

All told, evidence from the Mexico 2000 Panel Study strongly supports the notion that shifts in turnout helped to undermine PRI rule. These shifts were partly the product of long-run changes in Mexico's political context, such as increases in political competition, growing public confidence in electoral institutions, and a more open media environment. In addition, though, several factors specific to the 2000 campaign helped to shape turnout rates. Among these was Fox himself, who galvanized potential voters to a greater degree than his rivals.

CONCLUSION

In this chapter, we have endeavored to demonstrate how structural changes in Mexico's political system helped to pave the way for the PRI's defeat in 2000. Over the last two decades, the erosion of traditional instruments of authoritarian mobilization altered patterns of political participation in Mexico. As these instruments weakened and electoral reforms took hold, opposition supporters began to participate at relatively greater rates. These changes culminated in the 2000 elections, in which opposition partisans were more likely to participate than supporters of the regime.

We have also endeavored to show how the campaign of 2000 accelerated and reinforced changes in turnout. Throughout the race, Mexicans were repeatedly promised—by the Federal Electoral Institute (IFE), by President Ernesto Zedillo (1994–2000), and by the candidates themselves—that their votes would "count and be counted." Previously skeptical opposition supporters increasingly believed these promises and turned out to vote. In so doing, they made the promise of electoral change a reality: their votes were counted, and they certainly did count.

Notes

The authors thank Miguel Basáñez, Ulises Beltrán, Gallup of Mexico, and the Department of Social Sciences at the Instituto Tecnológico Autónomo de México (ITAM) for making available polling data from 1988 to 1997, and Jorge Domínguez for helpful comments on an earlier version of this chapter.

1. Alejandro Moreno, "En busca de los votantes del 2 de julio," *Enfoque*, August 23, 2000.

2. Turnout data by state for 2000 are given in table 4.10 in the appendix to this chapter.

3. On historic Mexican patterns, see Rogelio Ramos Oranday, "Oposición y abstencionismo en las elecciones presidenciales, 1964–1982," in Pablo González Casanova, ed., *Las elecciones en México: evolución y perspectives* (Mexico City: Siglo Veintiuno, 1985): 193; Barry Ames, "Bases of Support for Mexico's Dominant Party," *American Political Science Review* 64, no. 1 (March 1970): 165; Joseph L. Klesner, "Changing Patterns of Electoral Participation and Official Party Support in Mexico," in Judith Gentleman, ed., *Mexican Politics in Transition* (Boulder, Colo.: Westview, 1987); Wayne Cornelius, *Politics and the Migrant Poor in Mexico City* (Stanford, Calif.: Stanford University Press, 1975): 79–80; Juan Molinar Horcasitas, *El tiempo de la legitimidad: elecciones, autoritarismo y democracia en México* (Mexico City: Cal y Arena, 1991): 76.

4. See Karl M. Schmitt, "Congressional Campaigning in Mexico: A View from the Provinces," *Journal of Inter-American Studies* 11, no. 1 (1969): 93–110; Wayne A. Cornelius and Ann L. Craig, "Politics in Mexico," in Gabriel A. Almond and G. Bingham Powell, Jr., eds., *Comparative Politics Today: A World View*, 3d ed. (Boston: Little, Brown, 1984): 437–41, 451–52.

5. For instance, officially reported turnout was 94 percent in Baja California Sur in 1961, 90 percent in Campeche in 1967, and 90 percent in Quintana Roo in 1970. Participation by state in 1970 is given in table 4.10 in the appendix to this chapter.

6. On electoral reforms in Mexico, see Kevin Middlebrook, "Political Liberalization in an Authoritarian Regime: The Case of Mexico," in Paul Drake and Eduardo Silva, eds., *Elections and Democratization in Latin America, 1980–1985* (La Jolla: Center

for Iberian and Latin American Studies and Center for U.S.-Mexican Studies, University of California, San Diego, 1986).

7. A brief description of the polls referred to in this chapter is presented in table 4.11 in the appendix to this chapter.

8. "Rural" states included Chiapas, Hidalgo, Oaxaca, Tabasco, and Zacatecas. "Urban" states included Baja California, Coahuila, the Federal District, México State, and Nuevo León.

9. Unfortunately, Gallup's 1988 poll contained no explicit measure of turnout. Polling data used here are thus limited to the period 1991–2000.

10. Perceptions of electoral integrity were measured slightly differently across surveys. The Mexico 2000 Panel Study asked respondents how clean they expected the elections to be on a four-point inverse scale. Other polls asked explicitly about the magnitude of fraud.

11. Partisan sympathies were measured differently across the four polls analyzed in table 4.3. In 1991 we relied on items asking whether each of the three major parties was gaining or losing ground. In 1994, partisan sympathies were measured on a four-point scale. The 1997 and 2000 surveys used eleven-point feeling thermometers. Net opinion of the PRI was calculated as the evaluation of the PRI minus the average evaluation of the two major opposition parties.

12. District-level data are taken from the Web site of the Instituto Federal Electoral (http://www.ife.org.mx).

13. The same general relationships hold when other methods are used, such as OLS regression on self-reported probability of voting and logistic regression on whether the respondent definitely planned to vote (that is, a ten on a scale of zero to ten).

14. Those without identity cards could not vote. However, someone whose *credencial* was valid but not updated for his/her current address, or who was outside his/her voting district on election day, could vote for certain offices at special booths.

15. For further information on turnout over time in Mexico, see Joseph L. Klesner and Chappell Lawson, "Adiós to the PRI? Changing Voter Turnout in Mexico's Political Transition," *Mexican Studies/Estudios Mexicanos* 17, no. 1 (Winter 2000): 17–39.

16. Socioeconomic status was measured by a composite of (1) interviewer coding of the respondent's residence, (2) interviewer coding of the respondent's neighborhood, (3) self-reported monthly income per member of the household, and (4) an index of common household items. That index was then chunked into quintiles.

17. Baja California, Baja California Sur, Chihuahua, Coahuila, Durango, Nuevo León, Sinaloa, Sonora, and Tamaulipas were coded as north; Aguascalientes, Colima, Guanajuato, Hidalgo, Jalisco, Nayarit, Querétaro, San Luis Potosí, and Zacatecas were coded as central; the Federal District and México State were coded as metro area; all other states were coded as south.

18. Because perceptions of electoral integrity were so high in the wake of Fox's victory (over 80 percent), responses were grouped into two categories: those who perceived the elections to be basically or totally clean and those who perceived them to be "a little clean" or "not at all clean," or who were not sure.

Chapter 4 Appendix

Table 4.10. Turnout as a Percentage of Registered Voters by State, 1970 and 2000

State	1970	2000
Aguascalientes	60.7%	67.1%
Baja California	59.0	57.6
Baja California Sur	65.4	67.2
Campeche	83.3	69.1
Chiapas	67.6	52.5
Chihuahua	50.8	58.7
Coahuila	58.1	59.1
Colima	45.5	66.9
Durango	67.1	58.6
Federal District	49.4	71.4
Guanajuato	60.6	67.1
Guerrero	64.7	54.4
Hidalgo	78.5	62.4
Jalisco	63.6	67.0
México	62.7	68.6
Michoacán	63.4	61.2
Morelos	65.0	66.0
Nayarit	67.0	63.2
Nuevo León	55.1	63.8
Oaxaca	78.7	59.0
Puebla	63.3	62.8
Querétaro	66.6	70.2
Quintana Roo	90.1	62.6
San Luís Potosí	64.2	63.5
Sinaloa	52.3	65.1
Sonora	49.0	64.7
Tabasco	79.2	61.6
Tamaulipas	58.3	63.4
Tlaxcala	68.5	62.5
Veracruz	73.7	63.7
Yucatán	66.2	72.5
Zacatecas	65.0	61.1
National average	**64.5**	**63.6**

Table 4.11. Description of Principal Polls

Poll	Timing	Date	N	Scope	Turnout Question
Gallup 1991	Preelectoral	July 1991	3,053	National cross-section	Whether R always votes
MORI 1994	Preelectoral	July 1994	3,137	National cross-section	Whether R will definitely vote
ITAM 1997	Post-electoral	July 1994	1,242	National cross-section	Whether R voted
Mexico 2000 Panel, Wave 1	Preelectoral	February 2000	2,355	National cross-section	Likelihood of voting (0–10)
Mexico 2000 Panel, Wave 3	Preelectoral	June 2000	981	Subsample of first wave	Likelihood of voting (0–10)
Mexico 2000 Panel, Wave 4	Post-electoral	July 2000	1,251	Survivors from previous waves	Whether R voted
Mexico 2000 (postelectoral cross-section)	Post-electoral	July 2000	1,199	National cross-section	Whether R voted

PART II

Parties and Candidates

5

The Structure of the Mexican Electorate: Social, Attitudinal, and Partisan Bases of Vicente Fox's Victory

JOSEPH L. KLESNER

Campaign dynamics played a central role in bringing Vicente Fox to power in the July 2000 presidential election. For campaign dynamics to have mattered, however, the right social and political factors had to be in place. If Mexico's former ruling party, the Institutional Revolutionary Party (PRI), had retained the same mobilizational capacity it once demonstrated, it would have continued to capture a clear majority of votes—as it had done in earlier decades.

By the late 1990s, Mexico had reached a "critical juncture" in its political development.[1] That is, shifts in the underlying partisan composition of the electorate and the political rules of the game had made a PRI defeat possible (though not inevitable). Because these bases were in place, campaign strategies and tactics could make the difference between an opposition victory and yet another win by the PRI.

Mexico's ruling party had fought a protracted battle to delay its long-expected demise. But its social base was disproportionately composed of voters from Mexico's traditional sectors, especially the peasantry, the unionized working class, the poor, and the less educated. Consequently, modernization and increased social mobility in the years after World War II had led to the erosion of the PRI's support.[2] By the 1980s the social groups that the PRI could most count on to provide its electoral majorities had diminished significantly in weight as Mexico urbanized, as its workforce moved into the service sector, and as literacy spread.

In addition, a series of spectacular policy failures and episodes of political repression created a deep pro-regime/anti-regime cleavage in the electorate.[3] Repression of the student movement in 1968, the government's inadequate response in the aftermath of the 1985 earthquakes in Mexico City, and electoral fraud perpetrated by the PRI to maintain its hegemony during the economic crisis of the mid-1980s deepened the differences between PRI and opposition supporters. The contested presidential election of 1988 further accentuated opposition sentiment, but it also signaled the emergence of a significant party of the left (the Party of the Democratic Revolution, or PRD) that split the opposition vote with Fox's more conservative National Action Party (PAN). Consequently, the final blows to PRI hegemony came only with the tumultuous events of 1994–1995: the Chiapas rebellion, two high-profile political assassinations, the peso crisis, and the political reforms of the administration of President Ernesto Zedillo (1994–2000). As I will show below, it was not until these incidents that a significant number of voters permanently abandoned the PRI.

The erosion of the PRI's social base contributed to an acceleration of opposition advances in the mid-1990s. Whereas the PRI once could expect to win nearly every congressional district by a wide margin, by the 1990s the competitiveness of the electoral system created many opportunities for opposition victories. Yet winning the presidency, the apex of power in the PRI-dominated hegemonic regime, posed unusual challenges for the opposition PAN and PRD because, as late as 1997, neither had developed the ability to compete with the ruling party in all parts of the country. Fox's accomplishment was to gather the votes of oppositionists across Mexico and thereby defeat his PRI rival, Francisco Labastida.

This chapter sets the stage for the pivotal 2000 presidential campaign by describing the broader forces behind the PRI's precipitous decline in the 1990s. I begin the analysis by documenting the increasing competitiveness of the Mexican party system. I next explore the evolution of partisanship and partisan independence in the past decade and a half. In the third section, I examine the social bases of the parties. Finally, I demonstrate the existence and scale of the pro-regime/anti-regime cleavage in the electorate, a cleavage that Fox successfully exploited.

THE DEVELOPMENT OF COMPETITION IN THE MEXICAN PARTY SYSTEM

Vicente Fox took Mexico's top prize from the PRI when he won the presidency on July 2, 2000. His victory came as the culmination of a long effort by opposition parties, none struggling more diligently or longer than the PAN, to seek power through the electoral process.[4] The battle against the PRI gradually wore down the former ruling party's hegemony at the national level. As figure 5.1 shows, the PRI's decline was quite gradual in the 1960s and 1970s—about 3 percent per election. Had that rate of decline continued, the PRI's vote share would not have dropped below 50 percent until 2003. That trend reflected Mexico's modernization, with the PRI's social bases eroding as the society urbanized and as levels of education rose. However, in the 1980s and 1990s the PRI's decline accelerated rapidly in response to the policy failures of the mid-1980s, as the steeper slope of the PRI vote trend line for the elections of 1985 onward in figure 5.1 indicates.

Figure 5.1. Growth of Electoral Competition at the National Level, 1961–2000

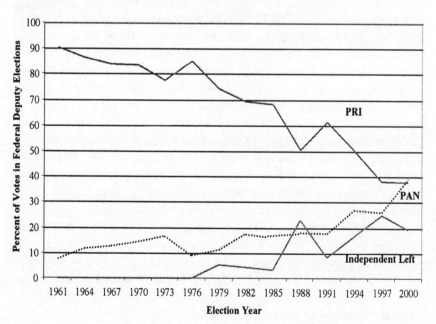

Moving beyond national aggregates, district-level returns provide a more complete assessment of party competition in Mexico. To document how competition in Mexico's party system has increased, I have grouped the three hundred federal deputy election districts into four categories based on Juan Molinar's NP index, following the procedure used by Pacheco Méndez:[5]

- *hegemonic*: districts in which a single party dominates (NP = 1.0 to 1.5);

- *pure bipartism* (or two-party): districts where two parties compete (NP = 1.5 to 2.0);

- *plural bipartism* (elsewhere labeled a two-and-a-half-party system): districts in which two parties compete and are joined by a third which is weaker (NP = 2.0 to 2.5); and

- *tripartism* (or multipartism): districts in which three (or more) parties effectively compete (NP greater than 2.5).

Table 5.1 shows that most electoral districts were hegemonic even as late as 1991; until the 1980s, fully five-sixths of the districts were hegemonic. The growth of competition came gradually until very recently, and in its earliest phases competition existed only in urban and northern border settings. In 1982, for example, all of the ninety-five nonhegemonic districts were in the three largest metropolitan areas (greater Mexico City, Guadalajara, and Monterrey) and urban regions in the states of Baja California, Sonora, Chihuahua (especially in Ciudad Juárez), Coahuila, and Tamaulipas (but only in Nuevo Laredo and Matamoros), as well as the city of Mérida in Yucatán. However, by 1997 fewer than 10 percent of the districts fell into the hegemonic category and opposition parties won six of the twenty-five hegemonic cases—meaning that over 90 percent of the districts had become competitive among two or more parties. The electoral context in the 1990s thus marked a profound change from the 1980s and before.

However, it is also important to recognize that less than 20 percent (fifty-six) of Mexico's three hundred electoral districts fell into the tripartism category in 1997. Mexico may have had a three-party system in the Congress and at the national level, but at the district level most competition remained between two of the three parties. More specifically, competition took place between the PRI and one or the other of the major opposition parties.

Table 5.1. The Rise of Competition in Mexico, 1979–1997

Number of Parties (NP Index)	1979	1982	1985	1988	1991	1994	1997
Tripartism (NP > 2.5)	0	1	3	89	1	33	56
Plural bipartism (2.0–2.5)	5	24	27	38	20	105	112
Pure bipartism (1.5–2.0)	53	70	71	43	92	89	107
Hegemonic (1.0–1.5)	242	205	199	130	187	73	25
Total	300	300	300	300	300	300	300

Notes: Data are from the Instituto Federal Electoral. NP index is defined by Juan Molinar, "Counting the Number of Parties: An Alternative Index," *American Political Science Review* 85, no. 4 (December 1991): 1383–92.

Table 5.2 disaggregates districts for the congressional elections in the 1990s.[6] The extent to which the district contests pitted one or the other opposition party against the PRI became clear by 1997. In that election, the PRI and PAN squared off in slightly over a third of the districts (110 of 300), with the PAN winning 52 and the PRI 58 of those districts. The PRI and PRD competed in roughly the same number of districts, with the PRI taking 58 seats and the PRD capturing 56. It bears emphasizing that by 1997 opposition parties were not just competing against the PRI, but they were *winning* close to half of the time (136 of the 281 districts in which the PRI was not hegemonic). Hence, before the 2000 election the parties of opposition—the PRD and the PAN—finally had developed the capacity to challenge the PRI in enough of the country to pose a credible alternative to the dominant party in federal elections.

In addition to federal legislative races, local contests became distinctly more competitive in the 1990s. During the administrations of Carlos Salinas (1988–1994) and Ernesto Zedillo, the PAN and PRD had seized most of the largest municipal governments and eleven of the nation's thirty-one state houses, plus the government of the Federal District (Mexico City). By mid-1997 the population in *municipios* governed by PRI municipal presidents accounted for just 43 percent of Mexicans, while PAN and PRD municipal governments presided over 35 percent and 19 percent, respectively, of the total population.[7]

Table 5.2. Nature of Competition in Federal Deputy Elections, 1991–1997

Type of District	1991	1994	1997
PRI hegemonic	**187**	**73**	**19**
PRI-PAN competition	**90**	**134**	**110**
PRI wins two-party district	80	120	58
PAN hegemonic	0	0	5
PAN wins two-party district	10	14	47
PRI-PRD competition[a]	**22**	**60**	**115**
PRI wins two-party district	22	55	58
PRD hegemonic	0	0	1
PRD wins two-party district[a]	0	5	56
Tripartism	**1**	**33**	**56**
PRI wins	1	29	29
PAN wins	0	4	13
PRD wins	0	0	14

Source: Instituto Federal Electoral.

[a] Includes one district won by the Labor Party (PT).

Again, though, the evidence suggests that Mexico was less a three-party system than a pair of two-party systems that *may have been* evolving to genuine three-party competition across the nation. This two-party nature of most electoral competition had important consequences for party strategies. As scholars of party systems have often noted, where two parties compete to claim a single prize—a governorship, city hall, or congressional seat in a winner-take-all district, for example—those parties must strive to win majorities, and thus they must appeal to a broad middle of the electorate. There are centripetal forces at work in such situations, encouraging the parties to cast their campaign appeals and ideology in more moderate terms that will engage those voters who sit in the middle of the ideological spectrum.[8] Indeed, to the extent that competition becomes localized, centering on state and local governments, electoral outcomes may begin to turn on issues of experience and capacity to govern, rather than ideology or national policy issues. Competition comes to be framed in terms of "ins" versus "outs." Opposition parties that seek to convince the electorate to punish an incumbent PRI for its corruption, cronyism, and authoritarianism can exploit the ins-versus-outs competition. The PRI, in contrast, has long sought to paint elections for executive posts as contests between an experienced PRI and potentially inept or polarizing oppositionists. Furthermore, once two-party competition with a local and/or state-level dimension has been consolidated, other parties find it difficult to make gains in the electoral arena. Such two-party electoral dynamics seem to have been at work in much of Mexico during Zedillo's term. That two-party competition between ins (almost always the PRI) and outs (either the PAN or the PRD) feeds a rhetoric focused around a pro-regime/anti-regime cleavage in the electorate.

PARTISANSHIP AND PARTISAN IDENTIFICATION

Not only had the parties of opposition created spaces in which they competed effectively with the PRI prior to the 2000 elections, but they had also eroded the PRI's dominance over the partisan attachments of Mexican voters. I have used the term "hegemonic party system" in the sense meant by Sartori—as a system in which the hegemonic party does not envisage its own defeat and treats other parties as second-class, licensed, non-antagonistic opponents.[9] But we should recognize that the PRI was hegemonic in a Gramscian sense too.[10] That is, PRI domination had an ideological or attitudinal dimension to it: Mexicans supported the PRI because its message convinced them far more than did the appeals of the PAN or the smaller parties of opposition that existed in the 1970s and early 1980s. The PRI message that continued to sway voters even as late as 1994 was that PRI candidates, and only PRI candidates, had the experience in governing so needed by the Mexican nation. In the 1994 presidential campaign, for instance, the PRI suggested to voters that the uncertainty of the times required a president with experience in the highest levels of government. So, even as late as 1994, the PRI's dominance seemed secure.

Scholars of U.S. elections built the notion of partisanship or party attachment on the observation that in U.S. electoral politics individuals maintained an identification with a particular party throughout most of their lives.[11] The notion of partisan attachment implies that those who strongly identify with a party will very likely vote for that party regardless of other, more short-term factors that could affect vote choice, such as perceptions of economic conditions, personalities of candidates, or the conduct of political campaigns. One measure of partisan attachment comes from the responses to questions posed by survey researchers

Table 5.3. Partisanship in Mexico, 1986–2000

Survey	1986 New York Times	1989 Los Angeles Times	1991 Los Angeles Times	1994 Presidencia Post-Election	1996 Los Angeles Times	1997 ITAM Post-Election	2000 Mexico 2000 Panel Study, First Wave
PRI	46	32	48	38	31	30	37
PAN	16	15	12	25	22	22	21
PRD[a]		15	7	9	8	22	9
None	32	26	21	22	30	18	29
Don't know / No answer	1	9	10	4	7	5	4
Other	6	3	2	3	2	3	—
N	1,576	1,835	1,546	3,426	1,500	1,243	2,397

Sources: New York Times Mexico Survey, 1986 (ICPSR 8666), October 28–November 4, 1986; Los Angeles Times poll, no. 192, August 5–13, 1989; Los Angeles Times poll, no. 258, September 11–October 2, 1991; Office of the Technical Advisor to the President of Mexico, Postelectoral poll, August 26, 1994; Los Angeles Times poll, no. 381, August 1–7, 1996; Instituto Tecnológico Autónomo de México (ITAM) Postelection poll, July 20–27, 1997; Mexico 2000 Panel Study, first wave, February 19–27, 2000.

Note: All surveys are national except the 1994 postelection poll, which only sampled residents of Mexico City, Guadalajara, Mérida, Monterrey, Tijuana, and Tuxtla Gutiérrez.

[a] The PRD did not come into existence until after 1988. The figure presented for the PRD in 1988 reflects the sum of partisan preferences expressed for the parties composing the National Democratic Front (FDN), those that supported the 1988 presidential candidacy of Cuauhtémoc Cárdenas.

to potential voters: "With which party do you most sympathize?" Table 5.3 presents the responses from seven separate polls conducted in Mexico over the past fifteen years. As this table suggests, in the mid-1980s the PRI claimed the partisan attachment of almost half of Mexicans. Although that number declined significantly in the aftermath of the contested election of 1988, by 1991 the PRI had regained the attachment of nearly half of the voters. Only after the explosive events of 1994 and the opening of the political system under Zedillo did the extent of PRI partisan identification decline significantly and permanently. By 1997 the portion of the electorate willing to express PRI partisanship had fallen by over a third from its level at the beginning of the decade, from 48 percent in 1991 to 30 percent in the aftermath of the PRI's unprecedented defeat in the 1997 congressional elections. PRI partisanship remained at relatively lower levels (in the mid-30s) throughout the 2000 campaign.

In contrast, percentages of the population identifying with the PAN jumped in the mid-1990s from the lower-to-mid-teens to the lower-to-mid-20s. PRD partisanship, meanwhile, has been rather unstable, fluctuating over the last decade along with the fortunes of the party. Nevertheless, both the PAN and PRD claimed substantially fewer adherents than the PRI. Never before the 2000 election did either of the opposition parties approach the number of partisans that the PRI enjoyed.

But more notable for present purposes is the large percentage of voters that remained independent over the last decade, either not identifying with any party or unable to express a partisan affiliation. That figure (the sum of "none" and "don't know/no answer") has varied from around 23 percent to as much as 37 percent of the electorate. Once the PRI identifiers declined to about a third of the electorate, as they did in the 1990s, independents became a large-enough body of voters to swing an election. Thus, as Fox entered the 2000 presidential race, he could hope to hold the 21 percent of voters who said they were PAN sympathizers and to gain as much as possible of the 33 percent who claimed no partisan affiliation or refused to indicate their partisan identity, perhaps peeling off some weak PRD or PRI partisans as well.

To gain a more precise characterization of the electorate that the 2000 presidential candidates faced, consider table 5.4. Partisan identity in February 2000 has been disaggregated according to the strength of partisan attachment—that is, into those who identified strongly or weakly with a particular party, as well as independents who "leaned" toward one or another party.

Table 5.4. Strength of Partisan Attachment in 2000 and Past Voting

Strength of Party Identification	Percent of Electorate	Percent Voting for Own Party, 1994	Percent Voting for Own Party, 1997
PRI	41.1		
Strong PRI	15.8	86.6	80.1
Weak PRI	20.8	76.0	64.0
Lean to PRI	4.5	57.1	42.9
PAN	28.5		
Strong PAN	5.8	67.0	65.5
Weak PAN	15.9	50.4	40.1
Lean to PAN	6.8	35.3	28.7
PRD	10.4		
Strong PRD	2.8	76.4	71.2
Weak PRD	5.6	45.1	41.0
Lean to PRD	2.0	35.9	28.6
Other	0.7	7.1	20.0
Independent	19.4	27.2[a]	34.8[b]

Source: Mexico 2000 Panel Study, first wave, February 2000.

[a] Those who responded "none." Another 33.9 percent responded "don't know" about their 1994 vote.

[b] Those who responded "none." Another 34.8 percent responded "don't know" about their 1997 vote.

Including leaners with partisans lowers the independent, nonpartisan segment of the electorate to about one in five voters (19.4 percent). At the same time, when those who admitted partisan attachments were asked about the strength of those ties, more defined their attachments as weak than as strong. Thus only a quarter of the electorate (24.4 percent) claimed to be strong partisans of one of the three major parties; 42.3 percent said they identified with a party weakly, and 13.3 percent initially said they were nonpartisan but then admitted to leaning toward one of the three major parties. At first glance one might conclude that the PRI retained the clear advantage entering the 2000 presidential race—either a 16 or a 13 percentage point edge over the PAN in partisans, depending on whether a stricter (table 5.3) or looser (table 5.4) definition of partisan attachment is used. Nevertheless, there were opportunities for a compelling opposition candidate. Specifically, 19.4 percent of voters claimed independence and 13.3 percent only *leaned* to a party (for a total of 32.7 percent, or one in three); a further 42.3 percent were only *weakly* attached to a party.

The two columns on the right of table 5.4 suggest that partisanship taps an independent dimension of Mexican political identity beyond the party for which a respondent most recently voted. The weaker the self-reported partisan attachment, the less likely one was to have voted for one's preferred party in recent elections.[12] Yet partisanship obviously shapes voting behavior to a strong degree, especially for PRI partisans, where as many as three-quarters of weak PRI partisans reported having voted for Zedillo in 1994. For the opposition parties, however, weak partisanship did not so directly translate into votes for the party one claimed to be attached to; only half or less of weak PRD and weak PAN partisans reported voting for their party in each of the two past elections. "Leaners," meanwhile, were even less likely to have voted recently for their preferred party. Again reflecting the hegemonic character of the regime, however, PRI leaners were much more likely than opposition leaners to have voted for their party.

Vicente Fox and the PRD candidate, Cuauhtémoc Cárdenas, thus entered a challenging but potentially promising partisan context in 2000. The PRI no longer held the partisan attachments of so large a share of the voters as it once did, and the majority of the voters were not strongly attached to any party. Moreover, voters weakly identifying with one of the opposition parties had a record of voting for parties other than their preferred party. Taking into account opposition identifiers, almost half of the electorate was available for recruitment into one of the two opposition candidates' camps.

SOCIAL BASES OF THE PARTIES

The previous two sections have established that competition had arisen in Mexico well prior to the 2000 elections and that the PRI held the strong allegiance of only a small part of the electorate. Together, these two developments made it conceivable for an opposition candidate to attract enough floating voters to finally oust the PRI.

Which types of voters were most likely to support such an opposition candidate? Were there differences in the social characteristics of PRI partisans and those supporting the other parties? In sum, was there a demographic basis to the opposition's challenge that could be further exploited in 2000?

Scholars have addressed the question of the social bases of electoral behavior by following two different routes: (1) ecological studies relying on aggregate data, and (2) analyses at the level of the individual drawing on survey data. Each approach has strengths and weaknesses. Because of political pressure and the perception that in one-party regimes public opinion just did not matter much, surveys about politics did not emerge until the mid- to late 1980s. Hence early studies of voting behavior in Mexico necessarily relied on aggregate data.[13] Beyond the data availability issue, ecological studies have another advantage. Although the risk of committing an ecological fallacy means that we cannot infer individual behavior from aggregate results, aggregate-level studies can tell us in which kinds of places a particular party tends to perform well or poorly. During the era of one-party hegemony, when the PRI was able to deliver vast numbers of votes through fraud and clientelism, ecological data often produce better insights into the nature and sources of PRI support than do individual-level analyses. For the era of transition to democracy, ecological studies can show us where the opposition was able to make its advances. Of course, if we wish to know the characteristics of the partisans of the major Mexican parties, and if we want to determine the attitudinal bases of support for the PRI or the opposition parties, only individual-level data gathered through polling can provide the necessary evidence. Here I employ both types of data in an effort to shed light on the social bases of partisan identification in Mexico.

Past studies of Mexican voting behavior using aggregate data at the state level and the district level have found that urbanization, industrialization, and education are among the most powerful predictors of the percentage of the vote received by the PRI or opposition parties in federal elections.[14] The multivariate analysis presented below builds upon and extends previous research by using aggregate data gathered at the level of the *municipio*, the Mexican equivalent of a U.S. county.[15] Table 5.5 reports these results for the three federal deputy elections held in the 1990s (before which data are not available).

As in other studies conducted with aggregate data, urbanization (here measured by the percent of the population living in localities with more than 20,000 inhabitants) and industrialization (here measured by the percent of the population employed in manufacturing) prove to be significant predictors of the direction of the vote. Education (here measured by the literacy rate) is also a significant explanatory variable, as it has been in earlier studies with data aggregated at a higher level.[16] In terms of these social structural variables, the PRI did quite well in *municipios* that are more rural and in which literacy is relatively low. In 1991 it finished worse in areas that were more industrial, but in the other elections it performed slightly better in industrial areas, controlling for other factors such as urbanization and literacy. This profile conforms to the broad understanding that the PRI performed best where the population was vulnerable to ruling party appeals because of its lack of education, lack of access to urban-based media, and economic marginality. But controlling for other factors, the PRI's long-standing corporatist relationship with labor boosted its support in areas where a large part of the labor force was engaged in manufacturing.

In contrast, the PAN's best performances were in more urban, industrialized *municipios*. Except for the 1991 election, the PAN also did better in *municipios* with higher literacy rates, as earlier studies had also suggested. Again, this fits with past descriptions of the PAN as a party with an urban, educated, middle-class base.[17]

The PRD's electoral base is less easy to describe in terms of these measures of socioeconomic modernization (note that the adjusted R^2 for the PRD equations is generally lower than for the PRI or the PAN). On the one hand, the PRD has become a party of nonindustrial areas, as the negative coefficients for the industrialization measure indicate. On the other, however, the PRD finished better in areas where the literacy rate was high, unlike the PRI and more like the PAN. This suggests that the PRI did well in rural areas where the population was less educated, while the PRD did better in areas where the manufacturing base was weak but the population was better educated. Again, this confirms the notion that the PRD draws much of its support from the politically engaged poor (as well as residents of Mexico City).

One other variable provides significant explanatory power—the percent of the population that is Catholic. Of course, this variable does not directly measure the intensity of religious sentiment or practice, simply the percentage of respondents who declared themselves Catholic to census takers. However, because the level of aggregation here is relatively low, there is greater variance in this variable than has been available to those conducting ecological analyses of Mexican elections with district- or state-level data. As would be hypothesized given the PAN's history of close identification with the Catholic Church and its social Christian message, the PAN performed well in *municipios* with a higher percentage of Catholics.[18] In contrast, the PRD and the PRI, both

Table 5.5. Aggregate Analysis of Federal Deputy Returns by *Municipio*, 1991–1997

Variable	PAN			PRI			PRD		
	1991	1994	1997	1991	1994	1997	1991	1994	1997
Constant	-.08	-.17	-.31	.76	.37	.87	.11	.47	.26
Percent urban	.13	.10	.10	-.15	-.15	-.14	-.02	-.01	.01
Percent employed in manufacturing	.18	.16	.26	-.07	.11	.10	-.13	-.13	-.33
Percent Catholic	.13	.32	.25	-.03	-.28	-.16	-.03	-.55	-.13
Percent literate	-.02	.08	.19	.01	.19	-.28	.02	.11	.21
North	.09	.02	.09	-.01	.22	.01	-.03	-.08	-.10
South	-.05	-.01	.02	-.02	.15	-.02	.01	.08	.01
Mexico City area	-.08	-.05	-.07	-.12	.23	-.07	.05	.12	.12
Center-west	.06	.03	.12	-.07	.24	-.06	.04	.08	-.05
Adjusted R²	.47	.47	.50	.47	.19	.58	.14	.28	.37
N (number of *municipios*)	2,386	2,385	2,395	2,386	2,385	2,395	2,386	2,385	2,395

Sources: Electoral data from the Instituto Federal Electoral (IFE); demographic and socioeconomic data from the Instituto Nacional de Estadística, Geografía e Informática (INEGI).

Notes: Unstandardized OLS estimates. Cases have been weighted by population. All coefficients are statistically significant at the .001 level. New *municipios* were created in the 1990s, thus changing the number of cases.

strongly secular in their ideology, performed more poorly in districts with higher concentrations of Catholics.

Therefore, we can conclude that electoral competition had increased most in the most developed parts of the nation. These areas presaged the future of Mexico—that is, the PRI was holding on to power on the back of a segment of society that was steadily diminishing in size. As Mexico modernized, the opposition's share of the vote increased.

Yet, although these demographic, socioeconomic, and religious variables prove to be significant explanatory predictors of partisan support, they only contribute about half of the explanatory power of the models displayed in table 5.5. The other half of the explained variance is contributed by the dichotomous variables tapping region.[19] Because this is a multiple regression model, region explained a large portion of the variance in the vote, *even controlling for socioeconomic and demographic variables.*

In table 5.5, the constant indicates the share of the vote that would go to the party in question if the values of all of the other variables were zero in the central region—that is, in the states of Hidalgo, Morelos, Puebla, and Tlaxcala. The regression coefficient for each regional variable indicates what must be added to the constant to obtain that region's intercept. In effect, it indicates the percentage of the vote that the party gains or loses over the base case (the central region) in that particular region. So in the north in 1997, for example, the PAN performed 9 percent better than the base case. In the center-west, the PAN performed 12 percent above the base case, while in the greater Mexico City area it performed 7 percent below. Looking at the three elections together, the PAN regularly over-performed in the center-west and north, and under-performed in Mexico City and the south (controlling for other factors).

Conversely, controlling for other explanatory factors, the PRD often finished by as much as 8 to 10 percent below the base case in the north. However, it over-performed in the southern states, most recently by about 4 percent. In greater Mexico City, the PRD finished as much as 9 to 12 percent above the base case. In the country's center-west, the PRD has strength in Michoacán, a state once governed by PRD leader Cuauhtémoc Cárdenas and by his father, former president Lázaro Cárdenas, before him. Thus the PRD sometimes did better in the center-west than would otherwise be expected. Regionally, then, the PRD's strengths are roughly the converse of the PAN's.

Multiple regression analysis thus supports the argument that Mexico's party system had regional dimensions well beyond what would be expected given the already considerable socioeconomic differences between the regions.[20] In the 1990s the opposition parties divided the labor of creating competitiveness along regional lines. The result was thus less three-party contestation in each part of the country than many examples of two-party competition with the PRI present everywhere.

Table 5.6 provides another source of evidence about the regional dimensions of the party system. Here I use the NP index to divide the three hundred districts into PRI hegemonic districts; districts with two-party competition (those where NP is greater than 1.5 but less than 2.5), divided here according to which opposition party competed with the PRI; and multiparty (usually three-party) districts. Those districts are then distributed into the regions used for the multivariate analysis displayed in table 5.5. A concentration of PRI-PAN competition in the north and the center-west, with PRI-PRD competition clustered in the Mexico City metropolitan area and the south, emerged clearly in 1997. Such a development allowed the PRI to divide and conquer in presidential elections so long as no opposition candidate could transcend his party's traditional regional base.

Table 5.6. Districts Categorized by Extent and Type of Competition, 1997

Type of District	National	North	Center-West	Metro Area	Center	South
PRI hegemonic	19	1	0	2	7	9
PRI-PAN competition	110	59	30	3	7	11
PRI-PRD competition[a]	115	8	9	42	10	46
Multipartism	56	7	20	19	5	5
Total	300	75	59	66	29	71

Source: Instituto Federal Electoral.

[a] Includes one district won by the Labor Party (PT).

The observations made in this section thus far have been based solely on aggregate data. Are these observations supported at the individual level? To provide perspective on individual-level behavior, table

5.7 reports some social characteristics of the partisan groups first identified in table 5.4. For the most part, these individual-level data complement the findings of the ecological analysis and add information about the age and gender characteristics of the partisan groups. PRI partisans were the least educated and the most likely to live in rural areas when compared to PAN or PRD partisans. They were also more likely to be female than the other parties' supporters. PAN partisans lived in urban areas, had the highest levels of education, and generally were the best off in terms of income of the three partisan groups. Compared to PRI partisans, they were more likely to be male. Youth was on the PAN's side—PAN supporters were the youngest of the partisan groups. In contrast, those identifying with the PRD were the oldest of the partisan groups. PRD partisans are also the most likely of the three parties' supporters to be male. The modal PRI partisan, then, was a middle-aged woman of modest means and education, living in a smaller town or village. The modal PAN partisan, in contrast, was a younger, better-educated urban dweller living more comfortably. Finally, the modal PRD supporter was an older male, moderately well educated but poor.[21]

Table 5.7 would suggest that although the PAN has been most identified in Mexican political discourse with the Catholic Church, and although the aggregate data analysis reported above showed areas with greater concentrations of self-reported Catholics to be PAN strongholds, religiosity (as measured by church attendance) does not correlate with PAN partisanship at the individual level any more than with PRI partisanship. PRI supporters at all levels of intensity prove to be quite similar to PAN partisans in terms of religiosity, as measured by church attendance; it is PRD supporters who are notably less religious. The contrast between the findings on religion with aggregate data and these bivariate relationships begs for a multivariate analysis with individual-level data, which I will present later in this chapter.

Thus Mexico's opposition parties had developed local and regional strengths as the opponents to the PRI. The dynamics of contestation between the party of the state (the PRI) and the party of opposition (the PAN in the north and center-west, the PRD in the south) gave each opposition party a strength in its regional bastions beyond what we would have expected given the other bases of that party's support. These regional bases suggest that something beyond just social characteristics accounted for the nature of partisan cleavages in Mexico.

Table 5.7. Social Characteristics of Partisan Groups in Mexico

Party Identification	Education Percent with preparatory or university education	Urban Percent living in cities > 20,000	Income Percent earning 4,000 pesos or less per month	Religiosity Percent attending services never or only occasionally	Age Mean	Sex Percent female
PRI						
Strong PRI	24.9	48.1	66.2	22.7	40.3	56.8
Weak PRI	24.0	66.9	75.7	29.4	37.6	58.2
Lean to PRI	27.6	65.7	71.3	28.6	39.6	56.2
PAN						
Strong PAN	38.9	77.2	69.0	27.2	37.9	42.6
Weak PAN	41.9	82.0	66.2	24.7	35.4	51.1
Lean to PAN	46.9	80.6	65.4	28.2	36.5	51.9
PRD						
Strong PRD	30.8	67.7	80.8	43.0	43.5	41.5
Weak PRD	27.0	68.5	76.2	28.5	42.3	39.2
Lean to PRD	33.3	68.8	82.1	34.4	41.0	45.8
Independent	30.8	68.7	80.9	33.5	39.6	52.0

Source: Mexico 2000 Panel Study, first wave, February 2000.

THE PRO-REGIME/ANTI-REGIME CLEAVAGE

Several observers of Mexican politics in the late 1980s and early 1990s argued that ideological divisions between the parties had been displaced by a pro-regime/anti-regime cleavage. Juan Molinar, for instance, argued that in the 1980s two separate dimensions of party competition had emerged. The first he termed "ideological"; it conformed to the traditional understanding of the left-right spectrum, with those on the left supporting greater state intervention in the economy and those on the right preferring market-based solutions to economic development challenges. The second dimension Molinar called a "tactical and strategic" axis of competition, in which the polls of the axis were defined as pro-system and anti-system. The thrust of Molinar's argument was that because of their proximity on the tactical and strategic axis, the parties of opposition (the PAN and the PRD or its predecessors) were in many ways closer to each other than to the PRI despite their differences on the axis of economic ideology. Indeed, in Molinar's view, during the 1980s the strategic (or pro-system/anti-system) axis became more salient to opposition activists and opposition party leaders than the ideological axis.[22]

Alejandro Moreno extended this argument to mass politics and public opinion by exploring Mexican ideological space in the 1990s. Just as party activists and leaders defined their position in pro-regime and anti-regime terms, the mass public likewise situated itself on the left-right spectrum in noneconomic terms. Using survey data from the 1990s, Moreno concluded: "[L]eft-right orientations in Mexico are defined more by views about democracy and political reform than by the classical economic issues. Consequently, the party electorates differ from each other more on the issues of democracy than on the left-right economic axis."[23] Moreno showed that, contrary to the ruling party's own assertions that it filled the ideological center of Mexican politics, the mass public saw it as the party most to the right among the major contenders.

Molinar's and Moreno's arguments complement Domínguez and McCann's analysis of Mexican voting behavior in the late 1980s and early 1990s. Their two-step model showed that the first and most important decision that a voter had to make was whether he was for or against the PRI—that is, for or against the regime. Once that decision was made, other factors might influence his vote choice (if he were against the PRI, that is).[24] These major studies of Mexican electoral politics agree that the main line of division in the electorate, the main cleavage, had become the pro-regime/anti-regime division, with pro-regime Mexicans favoring the PRI and expressing doubts about the merits of democracy, while regime opponents preferred democracy to all other regime choices and struggled to oust the PRI from power.

One of the main goals of Vicente Fox's campaign was to make this division even more salient and electorally relevant. Fox hammered home the message that Mexicans sought change now, downplaying economic policy issues in order to appeal to former supporters of Cárdenas. As he proselytized for votes to oust the PRI and end the one-party regime, Fox encountered an electorate that was ready for his message.[25]

Feeling thermometers for the major parties provide one means for illustrating the nature of the pro-regime/anti-regime cleavage in the electorate. Figure 5.2 shows the distribution of responses on a zero to ten scale in February 2000, near the beginning of the formal campaign. Several points could be made about these distributions of opinion, but three will suffice here. First, the public's perception of the PRD was quite negative (mean = 4.2 on a scale in which 0 = very bad and 10 = very good), owing perhaps to failures by the Cárdenas administration of Mexico City, to divisive internal squabbles that were openly reported in the press, and to a legacy of hostile television coverage.[26] Second, although the PRI and the PAN had roughly similar mean scores on the feeling thermometer (PRI = 5.7, PAN = 5.8), the way in which those averages were derived differed dramatically. The PAN's distribution as of February showed relatively few respondents reacting in a strongly positive way to the party and relatively few with intensely bad opinions of it. Most respondents clustered in the middle of the spectrum, with only 21 percent choosing the two extreme points (very good = 11 percent, very bad = 10 percent). In contrast, 37 percent of those surveyed chose either very bad (18 percent) or very good (19 percent) to report their opinion of the PRI. Thus the third observation to be made here is that the PRI's scores on the feeling thermometer indicate a bimodal distribution of opinion about the then ruling party, reflecting the pro-regime/anti-regime cleavage discussed above.

Examining the characteristics of those who placed the PRI at either extreme of the feeling thermometer reveals more about this regime-based divide in the electorate. To begin, some significant social differences emerge (see the top four rows of table 5.8). Those strongly supportive of the PRI (and, by inference, of the one-party regime) tended to be disproportionately female. They were also less educated and earned

Figure 5.2. Distribution of Evaluations of the Major Parties

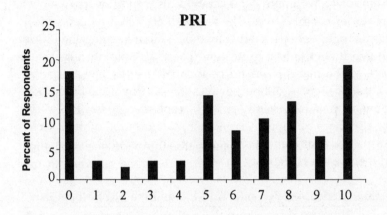

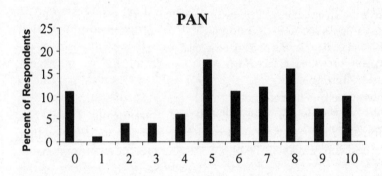

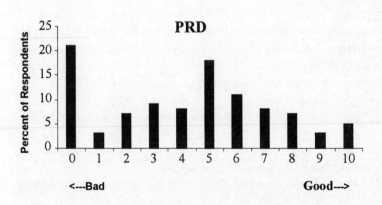

lower incomes than anti-PRI (anti-regime) respondents. These social characteristics fit a widely held view of the PRI's social bases already described above—fervent PRI supporters tended to fall into the social categories in which we might expect to find disproportionate numbers of law-and-order conservatives. The less well educated tended to fear social disorder and were persuaded by the PRI that keeping the PRI in power offered them the best protection. Those at lower income levels were closer to the margin and hence found the PRI's law-and-order message attractive too, as did housewives (the source of the disproportionately female pool of fervently pro-PRI respondents). Pro-PRI Mexicans were also more religious, yet another manifestation of their social conservatism, and more reliant on television. In ideological terms, they identified themselves as rightist.

Table 5.8. Characteristics of Fervently Anti-PRI and Pro-PRI Respondents

Variable	Anti-PRI	Pro-PRI
Sex (% female)	44.6	60.1
Education (% with preparatory/university education)	34.5	15.8
Income (% earning 8,000 pesos/month or less)	67.1	83.9
Religiosity (% attending services never or occasionally)	35.5	26.8
Risk propensity (% willing to take risks)	72.8	47.8
Social trust (% trusting others)	8.6	14.5
Ideology (mean on 0–10 left-right scale)	5.3	8.2
Perception of electoral fraud (% responding that elections will not be clean at all)	36.3	5.7
Perception of regime (% responding that Mexico is not a democracy)	67.4	31.4
Propensity to turn out to vote (% saying they were certain to vote)	70.3	73.7
Presidential vote intention		
Labastida (PRI)	4.7	86.1
Fox (PAN)	50.4	6.6
Cárdenas (PRD)	20.4	1.4
Partisan identity		
PRI	4.4	82.2
PAN	30.8	4.1
PRD	18.5	1.9
None	41.3	8.2
Percent of sample	18.4	17.6

Source: Mexico 2000 Panel Study, first wave, February 2000.

Note: Anti-PRI respondents are those who gave the PRI a 0 on a 0–10 feeling thermometer. Pro-PRI respondents gave the PRI a 10.

Beyond the social variables, however, there emerge some even more interesting differences between pro-PRI and anti-PRI respondents. In terms of general values that may have political salience, one stands out: risk propensity.[27] Several recent studies of Mexican electoral behavior have explored the role of risk aversion in favoring the PRI.[28] Those studies have argued that, given the relative inexperience of opposition parties in positions of executive authority, risk-averse Mexicans tend to choose the PRI on election day to minimize the likelihood of political and policy catastrophes under inexperienced rulers. Confirming these past studies, the evidence provided in table 5.8 suggests that risk takers disproportionately eschewed the PRI while the risk averse flocked to the former ruling party. Somewhat more modest in terms of impact is social trust; those who were more trusting tended to favor the PRI, while those who strongly disliked the PRI did not exhibit much social trust. Oppositionists, in short, seem to have been more cynical about relations with their fellow citizens even while exhibiting greater risk propensity.

Differences in perceptions of the political regime also typify those on either side of the regime-based cleavage. Two-thirds of stridently pro-PRI Mexicans tended to see Mexico as already democratic, compared to only three in ten of the fervently anti-PRI respondents. Perhaps reflecting that view, less than 6 percent of the most strongly pro-PRI respondents expected that the upcoming elections would be a farce, characterized by widespread fraud, while six times as many of the passionately anti-PRI respondents expected the 2000 presidential election to be not at all clean.

My preceding comments suggest that major differences existed in the political cultures of the anti-PRI opposition and the PRI's camp of stalwarts. The pro-PRI camp had all the characteristics of social conservatism—including social bases in the less educated, more rural, and lower income segments of society, especially among housewives—that would lead them to favor the PRI's retention of power. They saw the regime in largely positive terms and as already democratic, and they expressed few doubts about the integrity of the electoral process. Finally, they tended to be risk averse—preferring the devil they knew to the saint they did not. In contrast, those on the anti-PRI side of this most significant political cleavage held the obverse of those social characteristics and views; they lived in urban environments and had higher levels of education and income, allowing them greater latitude to risk a change of regime. Doubtful of the democratic credentials of the PRI-ruled regime, they were more likely to expect electoral fraud and less likely than their pro-PRI countrymen to trust their fellow Mexicans.

Predictably, those who evaluated the PRI most positively planned to vote for Francisco Labastida, the PRI standard-bearer, for president. By contrast, even as early as February, half of those who gave the PRI the lowest score on the feeling thermometer already intended to vote for Vicente Fox. It is also important to note that four in ten of those who gave the PRI zeros on the feeling thermometer considered themselves independents. Among these independent voters, an effective opposition campaign could gain many votes.

BASES OF SUPPORT FOR THE MAJOR PARTIES: A MULTIVARIATE ANALYSIS

Previous sections have shown that there were both social bases and political-attitudinal bases of support for the PRI. In addition, I have argued that there was a dimension of partisanship independent from simple recollection of past voting behavior. How important was partisanship in influencing Mexicans' evaluations of the parties at the outset of the 2000 presidential campaign? Did the pro-regime/anti-regime cleavage outweigh all other factors in determining support for the parties in pre-Fox Mexico?

To sort out the separate effects of the factors just mentioned on Mexicans' views of the parties—a proxy of sorts for their voting intentions—I conducted a multivariate regression analysis to determine which of these factors survive as significant explanatory variables. My dependent variable is each party's score on the feeling thermometer in February 2000. I group the potential independent variables into five blocs: social characteristics, region, attitudes toward politics and the regime, evaluations of the economy, and partisan attachment. The demographic variables are meant to tap any social or religious-based cleavages in the population. Attitudes toward politics and the regime should capture many of the pro-regime/anti-regime sentiments that would reflect that cleavage in the electorate. I include retrospective evaluations—both pocketbook and sociotropic retrospective evaluations of the economy, as well as presidential approval—as controls, because recent studies of Mexican electoral behavior have identified the importance of such evaluations in determining vote choice.[29] Finally, partisanship is incorporated to determine the extent to which those long-term attachments outweigh all other factors in predicting a respondent's evaluation of a party.[30]

Model 1 in table 5.9 incorporates social characteristics, region, political and regime attitudes, and retrospective evaluations into the analysis. Here we see that these variables are of very little help in predicting attitudes toward the PAN and the PRD (note the low R^2 values). People may have felt strongly about the PRD in February (as suggested in figure 5.2), but their social characteristics, region of residence, and views about politics and the regime appear to have had little to do with their feelings.

For the respondents' feelings about the PRI, however, political attitudes and retrospective evaluations add a great deal of explanatory power.[31] In addition to the significant social variables (education, gender, size of community) and region (south), we find significant coefficients for left-right self-placement (those who liked the PRI were to the right), risk propensity (priístas were risk averse), evaluations of the regime (those who felt good about the PRI saw Mexico as being democratic), and expectations of electoral fraud (PRI supporters expected little or no fraud). Also, evaluations of the economy and President Zedillo's approval rating are significant variables: those who thought the national economy was improving and who gave Zedillo a strong performance rating liked the PRI.

These regression results suggest that a relatively strong pro-regime/anti-regime cleavage was operating in Mexico before the 2000 elections, but that it was focused almost entirely on people's views about the PRI. This conclusion, based on the foregoing statistical analysis, conforms to a common-sense understanding of how Mexicans might form their political views and give them direction. Since the PRI was the hegemonic party, with the opposition parties being understood as just that—"opposition" parties, not meant to govern—Mexicans focused their attention on the former ruling party and came out for or against it. The attitudes that yielded strong feelings for or against the PRI came from people's perceptions of the character of the regime in which they lived and of the prospect that their vote would be respected if they tried to oust the PRI. People's willingness to accept the risk of replacing the PRI also shaped their likelihood of being critical of the party then in power. Finally, because the PRI was, in a sense, the party responsible for past economic policy and President Zedillo was from the PRI, those Mexicans critical of the president or of the economic conditions produced under his government evaluated the PRI poorly (note that the scale used on the retrospective evaluation variables is inverse).

Table 5.9. Predictors of Positive/Negative Evaluations of Major Parties

Variable	PRI		PAN		PRD	
	(1)	(2)	(1)	(2)	(1)	(2)
Constant	9.50***	7.60***	5.52***	6.39***	5.38***	5.36***
Social Characteristics						
Church attendance (inverse)	−.01	−.02	−.22***	−.18***	−.06	−.07
Education	−.19**	−.15*	.11	.06	−.03	−.01
Income	−.08	−.06	.10*	.05	−.10*	−.08
Size of town	−.00*	−.00	.00	−.00	−.00**	−.00**
Year of birth	.01	.01	.01	.01	.00	.00
Gender (female = 1)	.27*	.11	−.28*	−.21	−.49***	−.36**
Regions						
North	.45	.36	.65**	.55**	.47	.27
Center-West	.05	.18	1.04***	.81**	.09	−.06
Mexico City metro	−.23	−.20	.03	.12	.48	.23
South	.50*	.45*	.67**	.64**	.84***	.67**
Attitudes about Politics						
Expectation of electoral fraud	−.84***	−.60***	−.33***	−.41***	−.19**	−.21**
Risk propensity	−.92***	−.43***	.59***	.24	.21	.01
Is Mexico a democracy? (yes = 1)	.42**	.21	−.29*	−.15	.17	.21
Ideology	.17***	.11***	.06**	.05**	−.06**	−.02
Retrospective Evaluations						
Pocketbook (inverse)	−.09	−.06	−.09	−.06	.02	−.02
Sociotropic (inverse)	−.20*	−.11	.11	.04	−.03	−.07
Presidential approval (inverse)	−.64***	−.45***	−.09	−.16**	.16**	.04
Partisan Identification						
PRI		2.50***		−.54***		−.34*
PAN		−.53***		2.38***		.25
PRD		−1.02***		−.77***		3.63***
Adjusted R²	.31	.43	.06	.20	.03	.14
N	1398	1398	1398	1398	1398	1398

Source: Mexico 2000 Panel Study, first wave, February 2000.

Notes: † Inverse scale. *** $p < .01$; ** $p < .05$; * $p < .10$. Ordinary least squares estimates, pairwise deletion employed.

Dependent variables are scores on 11-point feeling thermometers for the parties (0 = strongly negative, 10 = strongly positive).

We should also note that in multivariate analysis of attitudes toward the PRI, religiosity decayed into insignificance once attitudinal variables were incorporated. In contrast, for the PAN the frequency of church attendance remains one of the most significant explanatory variables, along with risk propensity (those who like the PAN were risk takers), the expectation of electoral fraud (*panistas* expected fraud), and placement on the left-right scale (*panistas* were also to the right). Yet, for the PAN, adding these attitudinal variables does little to increase the explanatory power of the model. Meanwhile, when the attitudinal variables have been incorporated into the analysis, the regional variables conform to the expectations we developed based on the analysis of aggregate data. The PAN does better in the north and the center-west when controlling for both social variables and respondents' political attitudes. The PRD receives more positive evaluations in the south. Thus, although incorporating attitudinal variables causes some of the social and regional variables to decline to statistical insignificance, some of the main social and regional variables identified to be significant in the aggregate data regressions above emerge as significant with individual-level data too.

Model 2 incorporates partisanship into the analysis. Adding partisanship significantly increases the explanatory power of the models, especially for the PAN and PRD. For the PRD, partisan attachment seems to be almost the only important variable explaining respondents' placements of the party on the feeling thermometer. Frequency of church attendance and expectations about electoral fraud remain important explanatory variables for evaluations of the PAN, but partisanship adds much to the model for the PAN as well. This finding supports the argument made above in that the public's perceptions of the regime focused almost exclusively on the PRI and can be measured in the respondents' placement of the PRI on the feeling thermometer. For the opposition parties, meanwhile, strong feelings seemed to be determined mostly by partisan identity—those who were attached to parties felt strongly about their own and other parties, while those who did not identify with parties could not place the opposition parties on the feeling thermometer on the basis of any factors we can easily identify. Hence the low adjusted R^2 for model 1 for the PAN and the PRD. Adding partisanship to the other variables in order to predict the PRI's placement on the feeling thermometer has an impact similar to that for the other two parties, and it causes few of the previously significant variables to wash out, although it lowers the absolute values of the coefficients in almost all cases. Note that the coefficients for partisanship indicate that being a PRD partisan adds 3.63 points (on an 11-point scale) to a respondent's predicted feeling thermometer rating for the PRD; being a PAN partisan adds 2.38 points to the predicted PAN score; and being a PRI partisan adds 2.5 percent to the predicted PRI rating.

This multivariate analysis lends support to the notion that the major cleavage running through Mexican politics before the 2000 elections revolved around attitudes about the regime. On the anti-regime side of the divide could be found those who considered the regime to be undemocratic and prone to electoral fraud. They showed a willingness to accept risk. People with the opposite characteristics populated the pro-regime side of the divide. Education, gender, and urban or rural residence continued to predict one's evaluation of the PRI, but these factors proved much less important in sorting out views of the opposition parties.

CONCLUSIONS

In seeking to describe the structure of electoral competition and support for the contending parties at the outset of the 2000 Mexican election campaign, several principal factors emerge that could have had important consequences for campaign strategies and their success or failure:

- Electoral competition had increased dramatically in the 1990s. Both the PAN and PRD had eroded the former hegemonic position of the PRI in most districts in the country.

- Competition, however, remained two-party in character in most places outside of Mexico City. This two-party competition tended to concentrate PAN-PRI competition in the north and the center-west and PRD-PRI competition in the south. This two-party contestation also encouraged the evolution of the parties into catchall parties and to turn the elections into contests between ins and outs.

- In the 1990s, partisan dealignment eroded the PRI's once dominant advantage in partisan attachment. Only a quarter of the electorate considered itself strongly attached to a party on the eve of the 2000 presidential campaign.

- The PRI remained strong in its traditional bastions—rural areas populated with less educated Mexicans. The PAN, meanwhile, had developed electoral strengths in urban areas with higher concentrations of better-educated Mexicans, manufacturing-sector employees, and Catholics, especially in the north and center-west. At the individual level, however, the social bases of support for the parties were relatively weak.

• A much stronger cleavage revolved around the regime, pitting those strongly committed to the status quo against those advocating change in the regime.

Because of partisan dealignment and because of the growth of competitiveness in almost all electoral districts around the nation, there were votes to be won away from the PRI in the 2000 election campaign. Clearly there remained enough unattached voters and oppositionists to have made a difference in Fox's campaign to seize the presidency and to end one-party hegemony. Indeed, volatility within the electorate made predicting the outcome of the campaign very difficult for pollsters and pundits. As late as early June 2000, fully 30 percent of respondents to the third wave of the Mexico 2000 Panel Study claimed that they had not decided how they would vote, and large numbers of voters changed their behavior from past elections. Because there was much fluidity in the electorate, effective campaigners who exploited anti-regime sentiment had the opportunity win them over.

Notes

1. Ruth Berins Collier and David Collier, *Shaping the Political Arena: Critical Junctures, the Labor Movement, and Regime Dynamics in Latin America* (Princeton, N.J.: Princeton University Press, 1991).

2. Joseph L. Klesner, "Modernization, Economic Crisis, and Electoral Alignment in Mexico," *Mexican Studies/Estudios Mexicanos* 9, no. 2 (Summer 1993): 187–223.

3. Juan Molinar Horcasitas, "The Future of the Electoral System" in Wayne A. Cornelius, Judith Gentleman, and Peter H. Smith, eds., *Mexico's Alternative Political Futures* (La Jolla: Center for U.S.-Mexican Studies, University of California, San Diego, 1989).

4. Soledad Loaeza, *El Partido Acción Nacional: la larga marcha, 1939–1994, oposición leal y partido de protesta* (Mexico City: Fondo de Cultura Económica, 1999).

5. Juan Molinar, "Counting the Number of Parties: An Alternative Index," *American Political Science Review* 85, no. 4 (December 1991): 1383–92; Guadalupe Pacheco Méndez, "Un caleidoscopio electoral: ciudades y elecciones en México, 1988–1994," *Estudios Sociológicos* 15, no. 44 (1997): 319–50. For further detail, see Joseph L. Klesner, "Dissolving Hegemony: Electoral Competition and the Decline of Mexico's One-Party Dominant Regime," presented at the meeting of the American Political

Science Association, Washington, D.C., August 28–30, 1997; and idem., "Electoral Competition and the New Party System in Mexico," presented at the meeting of the American Political Science Association, San Francisco, August 30–September 2, 2001.

6. The category "two-party" includes both categories listed in table 5.1 (that is, NP ranging from 1.5 to 2.5).

7. These figures come from http://www.elector.com/estados4.htm, last accessed August 15, 1997.

8. Maurice Duverger, *Political Parties* (New York: Wiley, 1954); Anthony Downs, *An Economic Theory of Democracy* (New York: Harper and Row, 1957); Giovanni Sartori, *Parties and Party Systems: A Framework for Analysis* (Cambridge: Cambridge University Press, 1976).

9. Sartori, *Parties and Party Systems*, p. 230.

10. Antonio Gramsci, *Selections from the Prison Notebooks of Antonio Gramsci*, trans. Quintin Hoare and Geoffrey Nowell Smith (London: Lawrence and Wishart, 1971).

11. Angus Campbell, Phillip E. Converse, Warren E. Miller, and Donald E. Stokes, *The American Voter* (New York: Wiley, 1960). See also Michael B. MacKuen, Robert S. Erikson, and James A. Stimson, "Macropartisanship," *American Political Science Review* 83 (1989): 1125–42; Janet Box-Steffensmeier and Reneé Smith, "The Dynamics of Aggregate Partisanship," *American Political Science Review* 90 (1996): 567–80; Warren Miller and J. Merrill Shanks, *The New American Voter* (Cambridge, Mass.: Harvard University Press, 1996).

12. It is important to note that respondents were asked their partisan identity and the strength of that attachment before being asked about their past voting behavior, so questions about past voting behavior could not have primed responses about partisanship.

13. Barry Ames, "Bases of Support for Mexico's Dominant Party," *American Political Science Review* 64, no. 1 (March 1970): 153–67; José Luis Reyna, "An Empirical Analysis of Political Mobilization: The Case of Mexico" (Ph.D. dissertation, Cornell University, 1970); John Walton and Joyce Sween, "Urbanization, Industrialization and Voting in Mexico: A Longitudinal Analysis of Official and Opposition Party Support," *Social Science Quarterly* 52, no. 3 (December 1971): 721–45; Rafael Segovia, "La reforma política: el ejecutivo federal, el PRI y las elecciones de 1973," *Foro Internacional* 14, no. 3 (January–March 1974): 305–30; Rogelio Ramos Oranday, "Oposición y abstencionismo en las elecciones presidenciales, 1964–1982," in Pablo González Casanova, ed., *Las elecciones en México: evolución y perspectivas* (Mexico City: Siglo Veintiuno, 1985); Joseph L. Klesner, "Changing Patterns of Electoral Participation and Official Party Support in Mexico," in Judith Gentleman, ed., *Mexican Politics in Transition* (Boulder, Colo.: Westview, 1987).

14. For state-level analysis, see Ames, "Bases of Support for Mexico's Dominant Party"; Ramos Oranday, "Oposición y abstencionismo en las elecciones presidenciales, 1964–1982"; and Klesner, "Changing Patterns of Electoral Participation and Official Party Support in Mexico." For district-level analyses, see Juan Molinar Horcasitas and Jeffrey A. Weldon, "Elecciones de 1988 en México: crisis del autoritarismo," *Revista Mexicana de Sociología* 52, no. 4 (October–December 1990): 229–62; Klesner, "Modernization, Economic Crisis, and Electoral Alignment in Mexico"; Joseph L. Klesner, "The 1994 Mexican Elections: Manifestation of a Divided Society?" *Mexican Studies/Estudios Mexicanos* 11, no. 1 (Winter 1995): 137–49.

15. Past analyses of Mexican electoral outcomes using aggregate data have never incorporated municipal-level data.

16. Cf. Klesner, "Modernization, Economic Crisis, and Electoral Alignment in Mexico." The statistical results displayed in table 5.5 at the municipal level parallel those obtained with district-level data (N = 300). See Joseph L. Klesner, "The Social Bases of Vicente Fox's Victory: Religion, Race, Region and Other Factors in the Mexican Presidential Election of 2000," prepared for the meeting of the Midwest Political Science Association, Chicago, April 19–22, 2001.

17. Leticia Barraza and Ilán Bizberg, "El Partido Acción Nacional y el régimen político mexicano," *Foro Internacional* 31, no. 3 (January–March 1991).

18. Donald J. Mabry, *Mexico's Acción Nacional: A Catholic Alternative to Revolution* (Syracuse, N.Y.: Syracuse University Press, 1974).

19. The regional distribution of the states used in this chapter is as follows: *north*: Baja California, Baja California Sur, Coahuila, Chihuahua, Durango, Nuevo León, San Luis Potosí, Sinaloa, Sonora, Tamaulipas, Zacatecas; *center-west*: Aguascalientes, Colima, Guanajuato, Jalisco, Michoacán, Nayarit, Querétaro; *center*: Hidalgo, More-los, Puebla, Tlaxcala; *Mexico City area*: Federal District, Estado de México; *south*: Campeche, Chiapas, Guerrero, Oaxaca, Quintana Roo, Tabasco, Veracruz, and Yucatán. These categories are obviously somewhat crude. Much of the territory of México State could be grouped with the center states, but the bulk of the population is located in the greater Mexico City area, so for convenience I have included the whole state with the Mexico City area. Some of Michoacán is in the center-west, while other parts might be usefully grouped with the south, but again I chose not to split the state. As general rules, I have attempted (1) to limit the number of regions to five to simplify the analysis, and (2) not to split states across regions.

20. Klesner, "The 1994 Mexican Elections: Manifestation of a Divided Society?"

21. See also Chappell Lawson, "Why Cárdenas Won: The 1997 Elections in Mexico City," in Jorge I. Domínguez and Alejandro Poiré, eds., *Toward Mexico's Democratization: Parties, Campaigns, Elections, and Public Opinion* (New York: Routledge, 1999).

22. Juan Molinar Horcasitas, *El tiempo de la legitimidad: elecciones, autoritarismo y democracia en México* (Mexico City: Cal y Arena, 1991): 182–200.

23. Alejandro Moreno, "Party Competition and the Issue of Democracy: Ideological Space in Mexican Elections," in Mónica Serrano, ed., *Governing Mexico: Political Parties and Elections* (London: Institute of Latin American Studies, 1998): 38.

24. Jorge I. Domínguez and James A. McCann, "Shaping Mexico's Electoral Arena: The Construction of Partisan Cleavages in the 1988 and 1991 National Elections," *American Political Science Review* 89, no. 1 (March 1995); Jorge I. Domínguez and James A. McCann, *Democratizing Mexico: Public Opinion and Electoral Choices* (Baltimore, Md.: Johns Hopkins University Press, 1996).

25. See contributions by Bruhn, Moreno, and others in this volume.

26. See Bruhn's chapter in this volume.

27. To measure risk aversion, respondents were asked with which of two common aphorisms they most agreed: (1) "Más vale malo por conocido que bueno por conocer," roughly translated as "Better the devil you know than the saint you don't," and (2) "El que no arriesga no gana," roughly the equivalent of "Nothing ventured, nothing gained."

28. Poiré, "Retrospective Voting, Partisanship, and Loyalty in Presidential Elections: 1994," and Alberto Cinta, "Uncertainty and Electoral Behavior in Mexico in the 1997 Congressional Elections," both in Domínguez and Poiré, eds., *Toward Mexico's Democratization*; Scott Morgenstern and Elizabeth Zechmeister, "Better the Devil You Know than the Saint You Don't? Risk Propensity and Vote Choice in Mexico," *Journal of Politics* 63, no. 1 (February 2001): 93–119.

29. Jorge Buendía, "El elector mexicano en los noventa: ¿un nuevo tipo de votante?" *Política y Gobierno* 7, no. 2 (2000): 317–52; Poiré, "Retrospective Voting, Partisanship, and Loyalty in Presidential Elections: 1994"; and Alejandro Poiré, "Un modelo sofisticado de decisión electoral racional: el voto estratégico en México, 1997," *Política y Gobierno* 7, no. 2 (2000): 353–82; Beatriz Magaloni, "Is the PRI Fading? Economic Performance, Electoral Accountability, and Voting Behavior in the 1994 and 1997 Elections," in Domínguez and Poiré, eds., *Toward Mexico's Democratization*.

30. Partisan attachment is operationalized as a dichotomous variable with those reporting to be PRI (or PAN or PRD) supporters scored as 1 and all others scored as 0.

31. A model with social characteristics alone yielded an adjusted R^2 of just .04, while a model with social characteristics and region had an adjusted R^2 of .07.

6

The Making of the Mexican President, 2000: Parties, Candidates, and Campaign Strategy

KATHLEEN BRUHN

This chapter examines the factors that most influenced the key strategic and tactical decisions of the three main Mexican campaigns for the presidency in 2000. Such an analysis can shed light on why any given candidate won or lost, but it cannot provide a full explanation. Even a well-played game can have only one winner. Yet campaign analysis has this virtue: independently of voter response, it provides a glimpse of how parties attempted to discern, shape, and reflect voter preferences. This is a key element in the process of democratic representation. The election results and analysis of polling data may tell us more about why certain options prevailed over others. But campaign analysis provides a window into why these options appeared on the menu to begin with— why voters were faced with a particular set of choices and not others.

This calculation is not a straightforward response to voter prefer-ences, as the early model from Anthony Downs might suggest. Parties are influenced by institutional factors (the rules of the game, both ex-ternal and internal to the parties), party divisions, and the abilities of their respective candidates, in addition to voter preferences. Moreover, parties are limited by their internal competences. Structurally weak parties will have a hard time organizing a grassroots mobilization ef-fort. And party reputation may affect the credibility of campaign prom-ises, even if parties accurately assess voter preferences and respond to them. For example, the PRI had trouble convincing voters that it stood for either "change" or "democracy," though it clearly understood that voters were demanding both.

Finally, parties must target their appeals to different sections of the electorate. Voters do not all want the same thing. Parties must offer different groups enough of what they want to earn their support, but not so much that concessions to one group alienate another important constituency. In this balancing act, parties try to target sections of the electorate that are more likely to listen to their appeal or that are critical swing voters.

Other chapters in this volume analyze the opportunities that Mexico's social and institutional context offered parties and how the decisions that parties made shaped voter responses. My analysis attempts to bridge the gap by looking at the intermediate level, and specifically at the factors that influenced party choices at four key points in the campaign: (1) candidate selection, (2) the development of a campaign message, (3) campaign management, and (4) election-day mobilization. The key actors are the parties themselves (the victorious National Action Party [PAN] and the unsuccessful Institutional Revolutionary Party [PRI] and Party of the Democratic Revolution [PRD]), and their political allies. I agree with the central conclusion of this volume that, indeed, the campaign mattered. However, I seek to show how many of the choices made in the course of the campaign were shaped by party, institutional, and candidate characteristics, as well as by assessments of voter preferences. When these factors all point in the same direction, the party's path is clear. When they do not, as is more commonly the case, then difficult decisions have to be made that imply some trade-offs among the goals that matter to parties, including electoral success, party cohesion, policy coherence, and simple survival.

THE CANDIDATE—OR VICENTE FOX'S EXCELLENT ADVENTURE

Candidate selection provides a good example of how these factors interact dynamically. Since, as Downs noted, parties generally prefer to win, they want to select candidates who have the best chance of winning (responsiveness to voter preferences), all else being equal. Yet parties may be reluctant to support candidates who endanger their internal cohesion or ideological identity (party characteristics). Similarly, selection rules affect which candidates have an advantage in internal selection processes (institutions). Finally, candidate selection is an early test of each candidate's political skills (candidate characteristics). In the 2000 presidential election, there is clear and reassuring evidence that all parties made an effort in their candidate choice to respond to voter preferences. However, in each case, a different additional factor dominated the final decision in ways that had an impact on the fit between the candidate and popular preference.

The PRI: Selection Rules and Institutional Context

For the first time in its long political life, in 2000 the PRI chose its presidential candidate through an open internal primary instead of the mysterious process of *dedazo*—the outgoing president's selection of his successor. The eventual winner competed against three other challengers in a hard-fought campaign. Despite charges that President Ernesto Zedillo (1994–2000) tipped the scales in favor of his preferred candidate by using his influence over local party organizations, most evaluations of the process were positive. Francisco Labastida won in convincing fashion, with about ten million of the eleven million votes cast (by the PRI's official count). The losers accepted defeat, if not entirely graciously, and campaigned for the winner.

Party leaders risked a primary because they had identified "democracy" as a principal demand of the voters, and because past efforts to stake out a pro-democracy stance had failed to convince voters. Even previous electoral reforms passed by PRI-controlled congresses—which had made elections increasingly fair and competitive, as well as dangerous to PRI control—had been attributed by most voters to opposition pressure rather than to genuine PRI commitment to democracy. The PRI's failure to accept internal democracy reinforced the argument that their support of electoral reform had been forced upon them. Thus party leaders staged a risky bit of political theater in order to bolster the PRI's credibility. The primary was the central piece of evidence in the effort to convince voters that the PRI had become, in the words of its slogan, "a new PRI, closer to you."

The presidential primary must be understood in terms of such a strategic response to voters, not as a wholesale conversion to internal democracy. From the 1950s to the mid-1990s, the PRI repeatedly experimented with and largely rejected the use of primaries to select candidates, arguing that they would exacerbate internal divisions and weaken the party in general elections. Although the PRI held seven gubernatorial primaries in 1998–1999, the states were carefully selected and fell short of complete victory by the pro-primary faction. The presidential primary itself was more a splashy publicity effort than evidence of a sea change in general PRI attitudes: none of the PRI's congressional candidates in 2000 was chosen by primary.

However, the specific rules adopted for the primary favored the selection of the candidate who was least objectionable to a broad spectrum of party activists, rather than a candidate with the greatest likelihood of appealing to non-PRI voters. A procedure establishing a national winner-take-all would have favored a centrist candidate. PRI rules went further, requiring the winner to get a majority of the vote in at least two-thirds of the direct-election congressional voting districts. Maverick candidates were considerably disadvantaged by this rule. This was the choice of a party that still viewed itself as the "mainstream"—the party of a Mexican majority, whose most important electoral task is holding its own base together rather than reaching out to new territory.

The winning candidate was—if not the first choice of many groups—perhaps the least objectionable. Labastida's curriculum placed him as a reasonable compromise between the *técnico* and *político* ends of the divide within the ruling party. His technocratic credentials were acceptable if not outstanding. He trained as an economist, but at the National Autonomous University of Mexico (UNAM), alma mater of many *políticos*. He served as undersecretary of programming and budget, but in the administration of the last protectionist president (José López Portillo, 1976–1982) rather than under the neoliberal presidents of the 1980s and 1990s. His biggest "economic" position under Zedillo was as secretary of agriculture. His political credentials were also acceptable. His most important political post was a brief stint (1998–1999) as head of Mexico's powerful Interior Ministry, responsible for political crisis management. But in a largely bureaucratic career, he also had an electoral record: he served as the elected governor of Sinaloa from 1987 to 1992. Thus his nomination ended the long streak of purely technocratic PRI presidential candidates dating back to Luis Echeverría in 1970. PRI strategists hoped that a candidate with balanced political and economic skills would prove more electable than previous candidates while still maintaining sufficient credibility in economic management to reassure investors. Indeed, new party rules stemming from a rebellion by the party's *político* wing required that all presidential candidates have some electoral experience. They were motivated at least in part by concern that the PRI's eroding electoral position reflected its tendency to nominate colorless bureaucrats with little sense of how their actions and policies might be perceived by the public.[1]

Among the eligible candidates, Labastida had made fewer personal enemies within the party, and accumulated less dirty laundry, than the other three aspiring candidates. PRI campaign material later attempted to capitalize on this image, in part to distance Labastida from the PRI's reputation for corruption. His campaign comic book (entitled "An Exemplary Life") made much of Labastida's "real and open struggle against corruption," especially (as governor) against the drug traffickers in Sinaloa. His straight-arrow image would contrast with the more colorful image of his principal rival: PAN candidate Vicente Fox. Labastida was often shown with his wife; the divorced Fox was widely known to have a romantic relationship with his public spokesperson, Martha Sahagún, whom he later married. Similarly, Labastida used the first presidential debate to list Fox's salty language as evidence of character flaws.[2]

However, there is little evidence that voters saw the personal morality issue as a salient one, or that personal morality deflected widespread association of the PRI with corruption. Labastida's prudish ads, far from helping him, probably spared Fox from one common criticism of the PAN: that its governors and mayors have imposed conservative morals on the people (with campaigns against miniskirts, Wonder-bra ads, and condoms, for example). Instead of being tagged as a puritan himself, Fox made merciless fun of Labastida's good-boy image, contrasting his own cowboy persona with Labastida's snappy dressing and impeccably groomed gray hair (la vestida); his finicky manners, associated with suspicions of homosexuality (la mariquita); his allegedly "henpecked" relationship with his (intelligent and omnipresent) wife (mandilón)—in short, portraying his rival as a pretty boy who was not quite manly enough to lead Mexico. These colorful insults, more than Labastida's ineffective rebuttals, stuck in the minds of voters.

Whether or not Labastida's character was a major asset during the internal primary, the fact remains that PRI voters had other options. They could have chosen, among the declared candidates, the effective thuggery of Manuel Bartlett, the establishment-baiting of Roberto Madrazo, or the traditional rural clientelism of negotiator Humberto Roque. Instead, most priístas, especially in the leadership, chose not to rock the boat. Less contented or less risk-averse participants supported other candidates, including the unknown number of opposition voters who probably participated in the primary. In the general election, over half of those who claimed they voted in the internal primary for Roberto Madrazo supported Vicente Fox.[3]

In the end, neither Labastida's strengths as a candidate nor his credentials as the victor in a democratic primary saved him. He won 13.6 million votes in the July 2 general election—only about 4 million more than he supposedly captured in the internal primary. While there is evidence that Labastida's candidacy resulted at least in part from an effort to appeal to voter preferences, the rules of selection reveal underlying assumptions, also evident during the general campaign, that mobilizing the party's base would be sufficient to win the election. These assumptions were ultimately mistaken.

The PAN: Candidate Characteristics

Like the PRI, the major opposition parties identified democracy as a principal demand of the voters. However, simply by virtue of being opposition parties, they had a considerable credibility advantage in claiming that they could represent this popular demand. They had, therefore, more leeway in terms of their selection process; neither party had as much to lose (or gain) by demonstrating internal democracy. By the same token, unlike the PRI, they approached the election with the clear knowledge that mobilizing their core base would *not* be enough to win: they would have to reach out to uncommitted voters and even to voters from the other parties. Thus any candidate would need to appeal to more than party stalwarts.

The PAN's selection of Vicente Fox most clearly follows these criteria. Fox's emergence as the candidate took place not because of, but in spite of, the PAN's internal rules for candidate selection—and against the initial opposition of much of the party's national leadership. Fox was not a mainstream *panista*. A recent entrant into the PAN (in 1987), his political loyalties were questionable, in part because of his friendly contacts with well-known leftist intellectuals and even leaders of the PRD. He was frequently accused within his own party of fiscally irresponsible populism. Despite Fox's undeniable charisma, many PAN leaders preferred to preserve party cohesion by choosing someone with more reliable party credentials.

Fox knew of this opposition. In the 1991 fraud-tainted Guanajuato governor's race, Fox "lost" to a PRI candidate only to see his own party make a deal with the PRI that accepted Fox's defeat in return for the naming of another PAN member as interim governor. Fox's sense of betrayal aggravated an already difficult relationship with the national PAN. Then in 1994 Fox came close to a deal to endorse the PRD's Cuauhtémoc Cárdenas; in the end, while backing away from an endorsement, he preferred to announce his temporary "retirement" from politics rather than campaign actively for the PAN candidate, Diego Fernández de Cevallos. PAN views of Fox as "not a team player" would later come to haunt him—not during the campaign, but certainly during his administration, when his own party's support in the Congress could not always be guaranteed.

Knowing that he could not expect support from key figures in the PAN, Fox created his own organization—the Friends of Fox—to campaign for support at the grassroots. He did so quite deliberately and openly, arguing that, "Something that I have learned from my first political adventures is that in the campaign, it's you, your team, and your preparation, nothing more.... I have tried not to depend on what the National Executive Committee [of the PAN] either does or fails to do."[4] In part, the Friends of Fox was designed to draw in non-*panistas*, people who might support Fox but who remained skeptical of party involvement. However, Fox also poached freely on PAN local committees and even among disgruntled *panistas*. As one former national president of the PAN (and rival of Fox) warned, "in many cases the Friends of Fox have taken in, as an important component in the states, people who have had problems within the PAN, who have been a factor of division in the local PAN, or even who have left the PAN.... If these people achieve, in Friends of Fox, things that they could not achieve within the party and are there with a spirit of revenge against the [party] institution, then Friends of Fox has within it ... an element that can cause problems for the party."[5]

Fox broke with tradition in another important way as well. Customarily in Mexican politics, it was considered bad form to announce one's own political ambitions, and certainly not until one's party had at least opened up registration for potential candidacies. This tradition came from the PRI's own closed process of nomination, where potential presidential candidates knew from experience that visible ambition was the surest way to kill one's hopes for a nomination. As PRI insider Fidel Velázquez once said, "*el que se mueve no sale en la foto*" ("he who moves [promotes his own candidacy/advancement] won't come out in the picture"). This phrase translated as well into opposition politics, where one was expected to be a reluctant candidate.

Fox, in contrast, announced his ambition to become the PAN presidential candidate in July 1997—three years before the presidential election. The timing of his announcement was significant in two ways. First, it came within days of the PAN's disappointing defeats in the July 2, 1997, elections, which had eliminated from serious consideration one of Fox's most dangerous rivals within the PAN up until that point: former PAN president Carlos Castillo Peraza, who suffered an embarrassing loss to Cárdenas in the Mexico City mayoral election. Second, it gave Fox a considerable head start on other PAN rivals. He used the time to build his personal following within the PAN and to increase his national profile. In 1998 he gleefully announced that he had increased his visibility from 18 percent of Mexicans over age sixteen who said in July 1997 that they knew him, to 70 percent by December 1998.[6]

By June 1999, shortly before the opening of the PAN's official registration of presidential pre-candidates, Fox had built up such a personal following that, had the PAN denied him its candidacy, he might have bolted to another party and caused the PAN itself to split, much as the PRI had with the Cárdenas candidacy in 1988. This risk to PAN cohesion was bigger than the risk of accepting Fox's maverick candidacy. In the end, no other candidate registered to oppose him, despite efforts by some PAN leaders to persuade potential candidates to at least make a good show of it. Thus the PAN found itself in the fall of 1999 holding its first-ever presidential primary—with only one candidate. Ironically, it was PAN leaders rather than PRI leaders who in 1999 found themselves proclaiming that "the democratic process does not depend on whether there is one candidate or two, but whether the militant participates expressing his opinion."[7]

Fox's candidacy flouted the established rules of the game to the point that members of his own party accused him of having "kidnapped" the PAN's candidacy, but it also reflected his own ability to reach out beyond traditional party lines to win over groups that initially opposed him. These qualities would stand him in good stead in the general election.

The PRD: Party Characteristics

The PRD's choice of Cuauhtémoc Cárdenas as its candidate followed a more tortuous path in which party characteristics and institutional rules eventually determined the selection of a candidate whose personal characteristics fit uneasily with the goal of reaching out to swing voters.

At one point in time, it was not clear that any trade-off would be involved. While Cárdenas's shortcomings as a candidate had become more than evident in his two previous failed presidential campaigns, he seemed by 1997 to have learned from his mistakes, accepting more advice from political experts in modifying his campaign style. In part as a result, he won the first democratic election for mayor of Mexico City with an impressive margin of victory. His long coattails swept the PRD into second place in federal congressional representation. Moreover, his position as mayor of Mexico City offered certain advantages over his rival Fox, by then governor of Guanajuato. Mexico City is *the* national platform. Over 15 percent of Mexico's population lives in the Federal District and its surrounding suburbs, and national media are concentrated in the capital. Cárdenas was thus in a better situation than Fox to take advantage of a successful term. Moreover, he had a name that few could match; his father, Lázaro Cárdenas, remains one of Mexico's most popular presidents. Fox is the son of a Spanish mother and the grandson of an American.

By 1999, however, as the campaign began to get under way, Cárdenas had largely squandered these initial advantages. His administration as mayor had been more noted for its honesty than for daring reforms, and even in terms of honesty, several top appointments had turned sour, especially in the police and the prosecutor's office. Anxious not to give the PRI any opening for attack, Cárdenas hunkered down and kept his head low to prevent it from getting chopped off. Interviews with his top collaborators in the local government reveal repeated instructions not to rock the boat.[8] In public, his most common reaction to reporters' questions was "I'm not sure, I will have to look into that"—a version of the classic "no comment" that quickly became fodder for political cartoonists and the nightly puppet satires on Televisión Azteca. In short, his lackluster performance as mayor may have limited the damage the PRI could do, but it did quite sufficient damage to his prospects of winning the presidency all by itself.

Why, then, did the PRD once again turn to Cárdenas as its presidential candidate in 2000? We can understand the PRD decision in terms of three key factors: the failure to construct an opposition alliance, the internal structure of the PRD, and Mexican electoral law. The first two factors reflect concerns about party character and unity; the last reflects institutional context.

The idea of a PRD-PAN opposition alliance had come up regularly in local and national elections as the most likely way to beat the PRI. In 2000 the proposal was raised with more insistence than ever. It fell apart in part because of the incompatible ambitions of Cárdenas and Fox. However, this is far from the whole story. The most persistent reason given by PRD and PAN leaders is that ideological differences between the two parties made sustained cooperation impossible. While one must take these justifications with a grain of salt, they do represent the legitimate reservations of many *panistas* as well as *perredistas*. On the PAN side, conservative and pro-business factions distrusted the PRD's populist roots and its alliances with radical leftist organizations. For its part, the PRD had consistently linked the PAN and the PRI by virtue of their common support for neoliberalism. The 2000 campaign followed the same line: "a government of the PAN or a government of the PRI would represent the same step backwards (*retroceso*) for the country."[9] Just as the PAN was founded in large part in reaction against the populist policies of Cárdenas's father (President Lázaro Cárdenas) in the 1930s, Cárdenas's own activism as an independent (non-PRI) politician in the 1990s grew out of his frustrated efforts to stop the advance of neoliberalism within the PRI. And he justified these efforts initially in terms of saving the PRI from the electoral advances of the PAN.

Aggravating these ideological differences was the experience of the previous two presidential terms. As growing numbers of *perredistas* were murdered by factions allegedly tied to the PRI, the PAN's apparent cooperation with the PRI to pass legislation, particularly in the economic area, aroused suspicion and resentment. These experiences could not have reassured the PRD that its policy preferences would get a fair hearing from the PAN in any putative alliance without a PRD candidate at its head.

Only their common desire to get rid of the PRI could have induced these two parties to even consider an alliance for the 2000 election. Parties with such disparate ideological preferences hardly seem a good bet for coalition formation otherwise, particularly considering the nature of the alliance. A "united opposition coalition" would not have been simply a short-term coalition to establish new conditions for competition, like the "Coalition for the No" in Chile or the campaign for direct elections in Brazil, but an alliance to select Mexico's president for six years and probably its legislative majority. The shadow of the future and the potential policy consequences added to the risk. What would such an alliance do with power if it won? Would it hold together over the six years of a presidential term? The coalitions forged between the PRD and the PAN at the state and local levels had produced a disappointing postelectoral record of collaboration in office. Thus the failure of alliance negotiations is in some ways less surprising than the fact that they took place at all.

Nevertheless, their celebration had important consequences, eventually fitting the PAN's campaign strategy better than the PRD's. By declaring an alliance possible, the PAN and PRD signaled to Mexicans that their policy differences mattered less than their common determination to beat the PRI. Having participated in the talks, the PRD would later find it difficult to reverse course and claim that policy differences mattered after all—so much so that people should not join the Fox bandwagon but should support Cárdenas on policy grounds.

In the meantime, the failure of the alliance meant that the claims of the PRD and the PAN to represent the demand for democracy would confront, in the other, a credible opposing claim. The PAN has a much longer record of opposition (since the 1940s), but the party was vulnerable to charges by the PRD that PAN cooperation with the Salinas and Zedillo governments had tainted its once vaunted independence. The PRD's record of pro-democracy sacrifice was more recent and memorable, above all in the shadow of the PRI's shameless abuse of power to defraud Cárdenas of victory in the 1988 presidential election. But the PRD was vulnerable to charges of undemocratic internal practices (in leadership and candidate selection), and the administration of Mayor Cárdenas (1997–1999) gave little evidence of democratic reform in the minds of most citizens.

Yet despite charges of undemocratic behavior from both sides, the battle over the banner of democracy was fought largely on other terms, perhaps *because* both sides were vulnerable to such charges. Instead, it centered around the strengths (and weaknesses) of the candidates themselves. The PAN campaign increasingly identified "democracy" in terms of "change"—meaning alternation in power—and distinguished its candidate as the only one capable of beating the PRI. Hence voters who wanted change/democracy should select Fox. One popular Fox radio ad in the early months of 2000 started with a simple rhythmic message—Mexico now (*ya*), Mexico now (*ya*)—repeated with increasing volume and tempo until the final seconds of the ad, when Fox is identified as the candidate making it possible for Mexico to now, finally, get rid of the PRI. Fox talked openly about the *voto útil* (useful vote), portraying a vote for Cárdenas as a wasted vote since he had no chance of winning. Ads appeared challenging *cardenistas* to consider whether it was better to "vote for Fox to get the PRI out of Los Pinos [the Mexican presidential residence] or vote for Cárdenas to help it stay there." In the weeks before the election, Fox repeatedly called on Cárdenas to resign his candidacy in order to maximize the chances of a PRI defeat, even offering a jointly named cabinet as a reward. Essentially, Fox attempted to reduce the presidential campaign to a referendum on the PRI.

The PRD, in contrast, quickly found itself downplaying alternation per se as the definition of democracy and change. Campaign propaganda took pains to identify "alternation" more in policy than in party terms. Thus one June ad read, "[while] we believe in alternation as the fundamental step to dismantling the political model that has prevailed in Mexico during more than 70 years ... we will vote for real alternation, not for a simple change in figures or personalities," and "real alternation is Cárdenas." True alternation is further explained in terms of policy, as "transform[ing] the economic model that the PRI and the PAN have imposed on the nation," respecting women's choices "without moral impositions or intimidation like the PAN," and favoring the San Andrés accords (for indigenous autonomy in Chiapas).[10] In essence, this strategy assigns a reduced priority to the demand for pure alternation in power.

It also did not work. According to an exit poll conducted by the newspaper *Reforma*, of those who chose their candidate primarily for programmatic reasons, only 17 percent voted for Cárdenas—the same percentage that voted for him overall. Meanwhile, 43 percent of the entire sample identified "change" as their primary reason for picking a candidate. And it was this vote that massively favored Fox: two-thirds of those who wanted change chose the PAN.[11]

These strategic choices, in turn, reflected the changing fortunes of the candidates. At other times and in other elections the PAN relied less on pure alternation as a definition of democracy, and the PRD made alternation a more central goal. In the 2000 election, Cárdenas probably would have pursued a *voto útil* strategy if it had favored him; indeed, the PRD cautiously promoted a version of this strategy in Mexico City when its candidate (Andrés Manuel López Obrador) pulled far ahead—at least in the preelection polls—in the race for mayor.

Once a united candidacy failed, the PRD was thrown back on its own resources. In this context, its specific choice of candidate reflected its internal character: exceptionally fragmented and—in part as a result—exceptionally dependent on the personal leadership of Cárdenas as a factor of internal unity. The diverse groups that compose the PRD converged originally around the 1988 presidential candidacy of Cárdenas, not a recognized party label or a common program. When its various factions threatened to fly apart, the prospect of riding Cárdenas to the presidency kept them together. Although the PRD completed several transitions from one party president to another, these moments were fraught with danger because they exposed the fragility of party unity. The immediate pre-2000 transition was especially difficult. The

March 1999 effort to hold an internal election had been a fiasco: claims of massive fraud eventually led to nullification of the election. Amalia García became president several months later, after extended top-level negotiations and a second election, but the damage was done. Externally, the PRD appeared weak, undemocratic, and corrupt. Internally, the bitterness among factions had deepened; minority factional leaders withheld their cooperation from the García leadership and vice versa. Cárdenas alone could stand above the fray. Thus, despite real opposition within the PRD to choosing Cárdenas as a candidate, his selection seemed to present the least risk of exacerbating these more crippling divisions.

The collapse of communism and state-centered models of development also tended to perpetuate the centrality of Cárdenas. As the PRD's efforts to develop a credible ideological alternative to neoliberalism floundered, it was easy to turn to Cárdenas as a substitute for ideology. "Third Way" movements in Europe and Latin America are often associated with similar dependence on highly popular, at times eminent political figures. But in the PRD, Cárdenas filled this position more as a result of his historical association with *cardenismo* than for his qualities as a candidate. Indeed, one of Cárdenas's most intractable problems was his lack of conventional charisma. His wooden performance in debates and speeches frequently hurt him. And his earnest, even plodding persona—combined with a face etched from stone—constituted a considerable handicap when contrasted to the flamboyant Fox.[12]

Given this situation, it was unfortunate for the PRD's 2000 electoral strategy that Cárdenas won election as mayor of Mexico City in 1997. After two failed attempts to win the presidency, Cárdenas faced an uphill battle to convince voters that he had a better chance of beating the PRI than the untried Fox. Without the 1997 election as continued confirmation that Cárdenas could deliver the vote, even diehard *cardenistas* might have calculated that it was time for him to step aside. And with Cárdenas out of the picture, prospects for an alliance with the PAN might have improved. The greater irony of Cárdenas's 1997 win was that it not only encouraged the PRD's hopes of solo victory, but it also saddled their candidate with the dead weight of his record as mayor of Mexico City.

In addition to party characteristics, institutional rules influenced both the failure of the alliance and subsequent refusals on the part of Cárdenas to resign in favor of Fox. Prior to 1988, Mexican electoral law allowed parties to co-nominate the presidential candidate of another party while running independent congressional slates. In 1988 Cárdenas used this law effectively to build the National Democratic Front (FDN) around several parties, maximizing his resources and political support. Immediately afterwards, and in response to this scare, the PRI added new requirements for the registration of coalitions. Coalitions had to agree on broad slates of candidates, file a common electoral platform, and work as a single party in terms of election monitoring. This required complex zero-sum negotiations to divide up candidacies and money. Following the breakdown of negotiations for a PRD-PAN alliance, both parties separately set out to create "alliances" of their own: the Alliance for Change (dominated by the PAN) and the Alliance for Mexico (dominated by the PRD).[13] In both cases, coalition formation involved excruciating negotiations over candidate slates. In the PRD's case, despite considerable generosity (for example, accepting only 34 percent of the proportional representation candidacies and half of the plurality district candidacies), negotiations dragged on for months. The presidential campaign could not take off because congressional campaigns had not begun and the parties involved could not settle on a price for cooperation. At one point, the second-largest party in the Alliance for Mexico (the Labor Party, or PT) withheld its share of federal electoral funds for the presidential campaign; this delayed the start of the media campaign until February 2000, barely four months before the election. The PAN had similar though less severe problems in its alliance with the Green Party (PVEM). Coalition formation would have presented even more significant problems for two parties of similar size, like the PAN and PRD.

Cárdenas's refusal to resign in favor of Fox even as he fell further and further behind reflected another peculiarity of Mexican electoral law. Once candidates are registered, electoral law discourages their resignation by making future party funding dependent on electoral results. Most parties depend heavily on state funding. If a presidential candidate resigns, the congressional campaigns lose steam. And if the party's overall vote falls, it qualifies for less state funding in the future. In 2000, a late Cárdenas withdrawal would have had devastating implications, a fact recognized by party leaders.[14]

The immediate consequences of the decision to back Cárdenas are more than evident. The PRD lost a million votes between the 1997 congressional election and the 2000 presidential election. In nineteen states, the PRD declined in absolute votes. The big loss leaders, however, were Mexico City (minus nearly half a million votes) and the bedroom communities in adjoining México State (minus 350,000 votes).[15] Despite the victory of the PRD's candidate for mayor of Mexico City, the unexpectedly narrow margin of victory—far lower than preelection polls had led the parties to expect—spoke eloquently of a negative coattail effect. Indeed, a quarter of those who voted for the PRD's candidate (López Obrador) in Mexico City voted for Fox at the national level.[16] The PRD's governmental funding followed its vote share; even worse, some of the funding for which the PRD coalition qualified would go by agreement to other parties in its coalition. And the PRD ended the election with debts contracted in the final months of the campaign. The Alliance for Mexico was—as PRD leaders recognize—a disaster. Adding little in terms of national support, it created havoc in campaign management and cost the PRD time and resources. The PRD could hardly have done worse short of losing its status as a registered party.

I have argued in this section that factors besides responsiveness to voter preferences shaped candidate selection. This is not to say that voter preferences did not matter: all parties clearly attempted to select candidates with popular appeal. In the case of the PRI, however, "popular appeal" was most significant within the PRI itself; internal selection rules suggest that the PRI responded more to concerns about shoring up support among the PRI's core base than to fears that the party might lose the election. In the case of the PRD, efforts to respond to voter preferences conflicted with incentives to preserve party unity and respond to electoral rules. The chosen candidate met, at least partially, both concerns about popularity and these other pressures. Yet by election time this candidate was no longer in an ideal position to compete for the swing voters that both opposition parties had to attract.

THE MESSAGE

The first part of any marketing strategy is the product. As the parties chose their candidates, they tried to guess what Mexican voters wanted and would support, as well as what would meet their internal needs. This is the start of representation. The second aspect of representation is the program—how the product will be packaged and sold.

In marketing their candidates, as well as selecting them, all of the parties attempted to appeal to popular preferences—to promise that they could deliver what they felt the voters wanted. But no party had complete flexibility to design its public appeal. They were limited by party reputation, an ongoing desire to preserve party unity, and the characteristics of the candidates they had selected. If all parties were fully responsive to voter concerns, one might anticipate significant similarities in their electoral platforms. The fact that platforms varied substantially confirms the role of these other factors.

In order to register candidates, Mexican parties file a platform with the Federal Electoral Institute (IFE). They often draw from these platforms in putting together leaflets and brochures summarizing their ideas. Platforms tend to reflect the vision of party elites—particularly the presidential candidates—regarding ideological positioning at the start of the campaign. To analyze platforms, I use a method developed by the Comparative Manifestoes Project (CMP) and applied to the advanced industrial democracies.[17] The data, based on content analysis, are expressed in percentage terms as the relative emphasis for each category with respect to the length of the platform. Individual codes can be summed together to create scales on specific dimensions; thus the left-right scale adds each party's score on thirteen individual items indicating "conservatism" and subtracts thirteen items indicating "leftist" tendencies.[18]

For Mexico, I collected and coded party platforms from the PAN, PRI, and left parties from 1946 to 2000.[19] Raw data were summed together to recreate the left-right scale used in the CMP project. Overall, the CMP left-right scale places the PAN, PRI, and PRD regularly as right, center, and left, respectively. This evaluation matches qualitative assessments of the Mexican party system, enhancing confidence that the data reflect reasonably well the underlying dimension being measured. No left party leapfrogs the PAN or the PRI in any election year for which a left platform existed.

In the 2000 election, however, we see one of only three instances in the entire 1946–2000 period in which the PAN leapfrogs the PRI and locates itself as the center party.[20] Intriguingly, most of this movement occurred not in the PAN platform, which shifts only very slightly to the left compared to 1997, but in the PRI platform, which moves decisively to the right. In both cases, movement was produced not by economic elements of the scale, but by elements reflecting support for issues like political authority, law and order, and state power. Here, the PRI's shift compared to earlier platforms is especially provocative. The 2000 PRI platform was more open to input from the party's bases—at least its governors and local leaders—than any previous platform. And it demonstrates an almost obsessive preoccupation with power and state authority. The PRI's curious campaign slogan—that power should serve the people (*que el poder sirva a la gente*)—may have been a less than brilliant marketing ploy, as I will later argue, but it does reflect the party's internal preoccupation with power. The PAN, in these same social and political elements, moves modestly to the left, while the PRD moves more to the center. The PAN's movement is consistent with the Fox strategy of appealing to the political middle, particularly youth and the middle class, and along the dimension of political rather than economic change.

Thus, overall the parties did draw quite close on multiple issues, suggesting some efforts to adapt their ideological position to perceived voter preferences. Nevertheless, voters continued to make distinctions between the parties in terms of left-right positioning, and to vote accordingly. In the 2000 election, the PRD won 72 percent of the vote among those who identified themselves as "left" and 57 percent of those who identified themselves as "center-left." Among these same groups, the PRI won only 6 and 9 percent, respectively. Of those who identified themselves as center-right, the PAN candidate won 63 percent of the vote. Interestingly, those who identified themselves on the right split nearly evenly between the PAN (40 percent) and the PRI (37 percent).[21]

Also of interest is the curious behavior of the PRD. Though generally moderating on the total left-right scale, the PRD shifted in the opposite direction from the other two parties on a more narrowly constituted economic policy scale. The PAN in 2000 moved slightly to the right, as did the PRI, leaving both very close to one another and on the conservative side of the scale. However, the PRD did exactly the reverse, moving slightly to the left. This platform shift is consistent with the overall strategy of the PRD in 2000: polarization of the election along economic dimensions in order to position the PRD as the real alternative to the PRI and therefore compete with the PAN for protest votes. Once the PRD fell behind in the polls, it had few alternatives to this strategy. Yet the consistent, gradual movement of the PRD toward the left on economic policy over the last four elections suggests that something deeper may be at work—something related to the responsiveness of the PRD to the preferences of its activists and leaders, rather than seeking maximum policy flexibility in order to follow voter preferences.

At the same time, parties understood that few (if any) voters read party platforms. Presentation of the message was primarily accomplished through the use of mass media, public speeches, and the two presidential debates. Some of this discussion properly belongs to the tactical analysis of the campaign, in the next section. Here, I want to highlight some of the key "messages" transmitted by the three candidates' campaigns.

Once again, the desire to present an attractive message is tempered by other factors. Over time, candidate characteristics became increasingly important in all three parties. In addition, the PRI confronted wrenching conflicts between party reputation and the image it wanted to present. Rather than trying to sell the PRI on its merits, such as the record of economic recovery under Zedillo, party strategists attempted the much more difficult task of trying to reduce negative evaluations. In focusing attention on its weaknesses—albeit in the context of promising to change them—the PRI played into the hands of the opposition.

The PRI: Party Reputation versus Voter Preferences

The PRI lost the 2000 presidential election because it *was* the PRI—that is, because its mixed record from seventy-one years of incumbency was successfully exploited by the opposition. But the PRI's campaign helped focus attention on the very issues it should have attempted to downplay.

One illustrative case is its campaign slogan. Slogans should be brief, memorable, and synthesize accurately the main thrust of the candidate's offer to the public. The PRI clearly understood, from focus groups and commissioned opinion polls, that people felt the PRI had become too complacent in power. They wanted a change. The opposition would certainly have raised these issues no matter what the PRI did. Yet in focusing its *own* principal slogans on the same issues, the PRI conceded control over the political agenda of the campaign and agreed to do battle on ground it was less likely to win. The PRI's primary slogan—that power should serve the people—is "a complicated slogan.... Power is a very strong word that in a lot of people provokes rejection, more so if it is linked to the PRI." Or as one PRI campaign insider adds:

> In Mexico, the word power is indissolubly linked to the word authority, and both [words] to a specific form of governing that was precisely what was being questioned; that is, it was like talking about rope in the house of a hanged man. But there was a bigger problem. The spot had a confusing and double reading.... The first impression that the slogan produces is "Damn! so power is NOT serving the people now?"

In the hands of a PRI candidate, running essentially as an incumbent, this slogan had a different reading than in reference to an opposition figure. Labastida tried to portray himself as both incumbent and challenger—in the long tradition of PRI candidates who ran as rebels against the faults of their immediate predecessor. But that worked only when there was no real rival to run against.

Another aspect of Labastida's dilemma was how to promise "change" while coming from the party that had governed for seventy-one years. The slogan of "change with direction" only succeeded in conceding the point that change was needed, without convincing voters that the ruling party was best suited to bring it about. Several of Labastida's efforts to single out specific areas of change backfired, such as his appeal to the middle class by making English and computer classes a central element of education policy. Both the PRD and Fox countered that Labastida's promise was fundamentally elitist; Fox's memorable reply was a devastating ad showing that a typical rural school lacked the electrical connections even to plug in a computer.[22]

Finally, the PRI campaign combined an effort to soften the hard edges of its authoritarian past at the same time as it continued its historically successful tactic of capitalizing on its record of providing public order and arousing vague unease about order under new rulers.[23] The PRI's conservative emphasis on order clashed with its simultaneous efforts to seem more open and democratic, as if the two thrusts were promoted by different factions in the party in a logrolling compromise. Even as Zedillo promised a clean election and respect for results, leaders of the CTM and CT labor unions announced that "if eventually the victory went to Vicente Fox, then the labor sector would run the risk that they would try to reverse its union conquests," and in that situation "we would stage a general strike to force respect for our rights."[24] Some groups in the PRI, if not the party as a whole, discerned correctly what the voters wanted, but they could not credibly offer it. As a PRI campaign insider remarked, even the best marketing ploy "[cannot] sustain a position solidly for more than six months having as a base one truth and ten lies."[25]

Yet it did not have to turn out this way. The PRI had plenty of solid truths on which to base its popular appeal. President Zedillo's approval ratings hit their highest point in 2000, yet the campaign kept its distance from the president. The economy was in relatively good shape. Progress had been made in education, infrastructure, and job creation. To be sure, it would have been difficult after repeated economic crises for the PRI to convince jaded voters that it remained best qualified to manage the economy—but perhaps not as difficult as convincing them that the PRI was best qualified to bring about change. Moreover, the opposition had weaknesses, including inexperience and extravagant promises that could be discredited. The PRI failed to take advantage of these, "going negative" only relatively late in the campaign. In a close election, these two changes might have been enough to eke out a narrow margin of victory.

That the PRI failed to follow this course is perhaps a failure of imagination, an inability to conceive of real electoral loss. The illusion was fostered by a series of commissioned polls that indicated the PRI was ahead of, or at worst tied with, the PAN. Ultimately, however, the PRI campaign message stands as a warning of the consequences of responding to voter preferences without considering the implications of party reputation.

The PAN: Candidate Preferences versus Party Cohesion

The PAN's dilemma was different. On the one hand, they were blessed with a candidate whose unconventional style, political charm, and opposition background positioned him nearly perfectly as the candidate of change. On the other hand, the party had to swallow the unorthodox positions Fox put forward and accept the dilution of its own ideological profile. In the end, the Fox campaign stressed only two themes: Fox (the man) and change (getting rid of the PRI). Fox was change. Change was Fox. Everything else could be filled in by the voter as he or she wished.

Fox's principal slogan offered only two words; "*México, ya*" (Mexico, Now/Already) promised an opportunity to now, already, get rid of the PRI. The letter Y in *ya* was deliberately associated with the V for victory symbol, reinforcing the main message.

In his public appearances, Fox left references to change deliberately vague. He managed to declare himself a center-left candidate one day and attend a mutual admiration banquet with wealthy bankers the next. The name of the PAN-led alliance focuses on the same idea: it is the Alliance for Change, as opposed to the PRD's more nationalistic Alliance for Mexico. The backdrop of the demand for "change" was an unremitting portrayal of the PRI era as one disaster after another, saddling Labastida with the sins of every PRI president from the past seventy years. Indeed, it seems likely that this strategy not only *responded to* popular demands for change but actually *magnified* the strength of these demands.

A similar strategy was used against the PRD: the PAN combated PRD efforts to claim the "change" banner with the "useful vote" theme and with ads that referred to the roots of the PRD in the PRI. For example, one glossy leaflet asks, "Would you like to leave the caveman era?" and responds, "away with the dinosaurs of the PRI and PRD (ex-PRI)."   ·

The PRD: Candidate Characteristics versus Voter Preferences

Whereas the slogan of the PAN matched the qualities of its candidate and the demands of voters, the PRD's slogan was obscure and missed the main thrust of the Cárdenas campaign. "With Mexico, to victory" tried to capture the idea of change as alternation. However, the PRD's strategy was actually much more complex: not only to promise victory over the PRI, but to define alternation in terms of policy distinctions. This idea is completely missing from the PRD's slogan.

The promise of victory itself contrasted with the candidate's most notable résumé entry: two failed attempts at the presidency. It was not immediately credible. The PRD might have done better to choose a slogan focused on its primary advantage: the economic differences between its platform and those of its rivals. At least one attempt was made in the early slogan, "Watching over the country, Watching over you," which quickly faded from view (probably due to its Big Brother-ish overtones). That the PRD did not focus more on economic issues, however, also reflected problems with the strategy itself, including its dubious use in a relatively good economic year and its potential for frightening the middle class.

To the extent that the Fox campaign presented a message beyond the anti-PRI one, it took care to present it as a series of five simple economic commitments.[26] This simplicity contrasts with the more confusing efforts of the PRD to present an economic alternative. Perhaps in part due to its own vague understanding of this alternative, the PRD had trouble putting it into terms the public could understand. Much of the PRD's propaganda was confined to pointing out deficiencies in existing policies.

Together, the candidate and the message constitute the strategic thrust of each party's presidential campaign. Fox bet on a strategy of change, offering vague promises while attempting to polarize the campaign into "the PRI or me." The PRD put its money on a programmatic polarization that relied on economic distinctions, this in a year that boasted reasonable economic growth and contained inflation. And the PRI launched a confused and confusing campaign that half embraced its record (with subtle messages of *après moi, le déluge*) and half rejected it, promising to do better next time.

MANAGING THE CAMPAIGN: MONEY, MEDIA, AND *MÍTINES*

As Joseph Napolitan once noted, "a correct strategy can survive a mediocre campaign, but even a brilliant campaign can fail if the strategy is incorrect."[27] Yet strategy alone often appears correct only in retrospect. Execution matters. Tactical management of the campaign and its resources was handled, in each case, by a campaign team separate from the party hierarchy. Each presidential candidate exercised considerable personal influence over campaign tactics and the selection of voters to target. Only Fox made a significant effort to reach out to groups not traditionally targeted by his party.

Candidate style shows up first in the selection of the campaign team. Fox hired his campaign manager by using a headhunter, finally picking a former regional manager for the Mexican telephone company (TELMEX). Merit, not personal contacts with the candidate, counted most. Cárdenas, in contrast, picked his campaign team from among those individuals he personally trusted. He had known his campaign manager for forty-two years, and for Cárdenas loyalty came first. Labastida's campaign team appears to have been chosen by committee. Initially announcing that he would be his own campaign manager, he later appointed one, then removed him, replaced him, and finally added subcoordinators responsible for different parts of the campaign. The division of campaign responsibilities reflected a drive to balance political factions within the PRI more than a search for either competence or loyalty.

The results in terms of overall campaign management were predictable. Despite a notable amateurishness on the part of the Fox team, it seemed more capable of adapting quickly and learning from its mistakes than its counterparts. The Cárdenas campaign—run essentially by the same person as in 1994—was a virtual repeat of the unsuccessful 1994 effort. As for the PRI campaign, noted one insider:

> The constant rumors and advice about emerging internal friction, the real alignments that by necessity,... loyalties, or opportunism began to appear among leaders, aspirants, bases ... created a true lack of synchronization in the transmission of orders and an unacceptable factionalization of the commanding group. There were areas, for example, that did not know to whom to report ... people who were responsible for an area of operation [that] did not have assured financial backing.... Those in charge of specific tasks were not there because of capacity and experience ... but for other criteria.[28]

In terms of campaign tactics, I focus on three principal decisions: the use of media, the scheduling of campaign trips, and the presidential debates. The Fox campaign chose a strategy of early saturation, emphasis on the mass media, and, within the grassroots campaign, priority for the large urban centers. In the presidential debate, it relied on the verbal virtuosity and charm of its candidate. The Labastida and Cárdenas campaigns both started later in their media campaigns, though Labastida spent more and placed relatively more attention on the mass media. Cárdenas was the master of the grassroots campaign, but he exhibited little sense of priorities in campaign scheduling, often throwing away time and money on areas with low relevance as sources of votes. Labastida spent most of his time at dry official acts that aimed at shoring up his support within the PRI hierarchy. Neither candidate showed particular strength in debates, but Labastida's decision to attack Fox proved unfortunate.[29]

Media

Somewhat unusually for Mexican elections, each of the parties in 2000 had the resources to mount an impressive media campaign. Although parties never feel they have enough money, the 2000 election was the most expensive presidential campaign in Mexican history. The PRI maintained its overall financial advantage, but the disparity was reduced. The PRD and PAN started from fairly level ground in terms of public financing (about 672 million pesos for the PAN and 653 million pesos for the PRD).[30] Once public money ran out, however, the PAN proved it had far deeper pockets than the PRD. Fox's finance coordinator boasted that he had collected about half of campaign expenses from private sources, like thousand-peso-a-plate dinners, raffles, and "hat passing" among businessmen. Meanwhile, the PRD sought commercial loans to cover campaign expenses.[31] Still, the financial situation of the opposition parties had vastly improved over 1994, and opposition access to the media increased. These conditions made more choices available than ever before.

All of the parties spent a lot of time and money on mass media, though the PRI still spent the most. A survey by the Mexican Academy of Human Rights (May 8–26, 2000) found that the PRI placed twice as many political ads as the PAN, and two-and-a-half times as many as the PRD, accounting for over half (50.8 percent) of the total ads shown. The PRI spent at least 5.2 million pesos (over half a million dollars) on advertising fees during this period, compared to 1.9 million pesos for the PAN and 1.8 million for the PRD.[32] A second analysis of ads televised on May 15 found a similar disparity: 1,040 seconds of advertising for the PRI's presidential candidate, 520 seconds for Vicente Fox, and only 270 seconds for Cárdenas.[33] If these figures are representative, the distinction between the media strategies of the PRD and the PAN is less absolute than is often believed, but it is there. Interestingly, the PAN was much more likely to advertise on rival television outlets—39 percent of its spots appeared on TV Azteca and 55 percent on Televisa—while the PRD placed over 81 percent of its spots on Televisa.[34] Fox's campaign thus achieved broader coverage than the PRD campaign.

Although television remained the primary source of information for voters, parties did not neglect more traditional methods of publicizing their message, including banners, posters, bumper stickers, and leaflets. Two campaigns—the PRI's and the PAN's—even produced comic books (a simulation of the popular adult comic books sold in Mexico, mostly to semi-literate people). The PAN version was entitled "Fox del Pueblo" ("Fox of the People," a pun on *voz del pueblo*, or voice of the people). In pictorial form, it tells the story of Fox's life, born "a man of the countryside, lucky enough to shed my umbilical cord in the ranch of San Cristóbal, Guanajuato."[35] Among other amusing episodes, young Vicente plays marbles with the local peasants; ogles the legs of his pretty female classmates at the Iberoamericana; works his way up from the bottom at Coca Cola; adopts four children and starts an orphanage; becomes governor of Guanajuato; and decides to run for president (his divorce is discreetly omitted). For children, there was a Fox coloring book, "Draw Fox Now," handed out to kindergartens and day care centers. Fox appears in fourteen out of sixteen drawings.

In many of the glossy leaflets and pamphlets pushed into mailboxes along with the latest offer of free home delivery from Telepizza, there is an undertone of sex that seems at odds with the PAN's moralistic image. One example, designed to attract the youth vote, was a glossy folded brochure with a young couple embracing on the cover and the question, "Is it your first time?" (with "first time" in bold orange) "If so, do it right." Inside, it explains, "if it is your first time voting ... we invite you to vote for the candidates of the Alliance for Change."

The PAN's rivals seemed to lack the humor and audacity of the PAN propaganda. These characteristics also reflected the images of their principal candidates. Boisterous and loud, Fox is the sort of man to enjoy a portrayal of himself staring at his classmates' legs. The shy and distinguished-looking Labastida could barely be pictured doing such a thing. And Cárdenas dislikes even smiling for the cameras.

While possessed of a dry sense of humor, he does not enjoy poking fun at himself. The PRD produced no comic book.

Campaign Scheduling

A second way of carrying one's message to the voters is personal contact—the classic baby-kissing public appearances—held Mexican-style with a band and banners in the public square. The PRD in particular seemed obsessed with an indiscriminate preference for grassroots campaigning, a style that largely reflected the personal inclinations of its presidential candidate. Cárdenas allegedly "[broke] all records of human concentrations in political rallies," in the last twenty days of the campaign. By mid-May Cárdenas had visited 220 of the 300 electoral districts in a series of marathon tours. The days were fully packed: "never are there fewer than three rallies a day. Generally there are more."[36] It is, note party sources, "part of the *cardenista* philosophy [that] the way to do politics [is] through direct contact with the people."[37] Many of the PRD's "mass media" ads were designed around the image of well-attended rallies to link Cárdenas with "the people" and bolster his status as a contender. Despite negative polls, Cárdenas maintained a touching faith in the ability of rallies to reach people, confiding that, "I trust that the full plazas we are seeing mean full ballot boxes. The poll that matters is that of the second of July."[38]

In contrast, Labastida visited only 66 *municipios* during the first six months of the campaign, compared to 142 for Fox and 158 for Cárdenas.[39] As one commentator noted,

> If the economy is fine, if the image of President Ernesto Zedillo is better than ever, if nobody died—this week, at least— in Chiapas, why take a chance?... Thus they evaluated the campaign for months. It was not the moment to take a risk ... few campaign rallies—at least compared to his adversaries— and a low profile, a discreet presence.[40]

Fox's campaign stops focused more intensely on multiple appearances in major media markets, increasing his name recognition and improving national coverage of his campaign. Fox's logistics secretary claimed to base his candidate's agenda on polls and the location of "the most votes."[41] The PRD, too, claimed to consider the electoral weight of each state. Yet the goal of Cárdenas to visit all three hundred electoral districts left little room for prioritizing. One early April calculation estimated that 73 percent of the districts visited by Cárdenas were classified as "urban," just slightly more than the 68 percent of all electoral sections classified by the Federal Electoral Institute as urban.[42] Indeed, to the extent that favoritism applied, party strategists admitted focusing on the states where the coalition had *more* political force.[43] This strategy minimized the risk that a rally would be sparsely attended and reflect badly on the candidate. But rallies, especially when selected by areas of existing support, rarely reach out to the unconvinced—that is, to the new voters Cárdenas needed to win over. Rather, it emphasized mobilizing the party's core base. This same problem also afflicted Labastida's scheduling, though here the main reason was the need to placate local party elites, rather than the candidate's preferences.

The Presidential Debates

These character distinctions also appeared clearly in the two public confrontations among the candidates: the presidential debates. Cárdenas did well in neither. Whatever his other gifts, he is not a good debater—he speaks poorly and pedantically and usually does worst responding to unexpected questions off the cuff. However, his campaign team knew this from bitter experience in 1994; its debate strategy did not require their candidate to win but simply not to humiliate himself, and in this they largely succeeded.

Most of the humiliation went to Francisco Labastida, particularly in the first debate. Soft-spoken, of modest stature, and handicapped with a slight lisp, he failed to shine next to the large and garrulous Vicente Fox. However, he brought the worst on himself by choosing to bring up the topic of the insults heaped on him by his PAN rival, evidently to present himself as a statesman compared to the crass commonness of Fox. But as a PRI campaign insider noted acerbically, "You cannot, in Mexico, say that the other says that you are a sissy, because ... what you are being in front of Mexicans is precisely a sissy, every time you complain. Still less should you repeat, so that everybody hears them, the whole catalogue of [insults] ... and even less when the other guy is tall and you can't compete with him."[44]

Fox's most potentially costly error came in the run-up to the second presidential debate. Amid controversy over the timing of the debate, Fox insisted on keeping to the original date despite protests by the television networks that they could not put together a production so quickly—and he did it in front of reporters. His childish "today, today" contrasted sharply with Labastida's natural dignity and a seldom seen display of humor by Cárdenas.[45] In the next few days, Fox fell several points in national polls, provoking a corresponding surge by Cárdenas and relief in the PRI, which saw emerging its accustomed scheme of splitting the opposition vote. However, Fox cleverly defused the effect of "Black Tuesday": the childish "today, today" emitted in reference to the debate was converted into a variation on the existing slogan of "now, now"—not "today, the debate" but "today, the transition."[46]

MOBILIZATION STRATEGY: GETTING OUT THE VOTE

Nevertheless, as election day dawned, the outcome remained in doubt. Most of the published polls put Labastida slightly ahead but in a technical tie, with a difference between the candidates of less than the margin of error. The PRI's internal polls promised a solid victory over Fox by 4 to 6 percentage points. Only a handful of polls suggested that Fox would win; one of these was suppressed by incredulous newspaper editors.[47] In such a tight race, the margin of victory is often determined by the undecided or by the rate of turnout. All three campaigns had a strategy to raise turnout among their own supporters. But party characteristics trumped the desire to mobilize supporters in both the PRD and the PRI. Only the PAN benefited from a synergy between its party characteristics and its goal of mobilization.

The PAN: Triumph of a Laissez-Faire Party

The success of the PAN may seem paradoxical since it has rarely distinguished itself as a party with mobilizational capacity. Its biggest advantage in terms of turnout has been its traditional appeal to the educated, urban middle class, which is predisposed to turn out at higher rates without the party having to do much. But the Fox campaign also boasted an organization parallel to the party itself: the Friends of Fox. The Friends of Fox was designed to reach out to "civil society"—those who, though not interested in commitment to a party, supported the presidential aspirations of Fox. Although the Friends of Fox did not view voter mobilization per se as a major priority, they took a prominent role in fund-raising, scheduling campaign swings, even recruiting publicists and helping organize defense of the vote. In part thanks to the efforts of the Friends, the PAN-dominated Alliance for Change managed to accredit poll-watching representatives in 96 percent of all polling places and covered 82 percent of the polls on election day (compared to 66 percent by the PAN in the previous presidential election).[48]

The PRD: A Study in Self-Destruction

In contrast to the PAN, the PRD prides itself on its ability to fill plazas. It is mobilizational to the point that it sometimes acts more like a social movement than a party. Yet in the 2000 campaign, its efforts seemed strangely lackluster. In the 1997 congressional/mayoral campaign, the PRD put into action a comprehensive mobilizational program known as the Sun Brigades (after the party's symbol, the Aztec Sun). A partly volunteer, partly paid staff of thousands began the mobilizational effort months before the election, going house to house in an effort to persuade people to make a commitment to the PRD and carry it out. Observers credited the Brigades with helping demystify the PRD and soften its confrontational image, contributing to its success in Mexico City and the national congressional campaign. In the 2000 campaign, the party proposed to repeat the program.

But this time the Brigades barely left the barracks and had little or no effect. The fault lay mostly within the PRD. In 1997 it went into the election under the leadership of a strong and popular party president, Andrés Manuel López Obrador. His strength came not only from ties to Cárdenas but also from his uncontested victory as party president in an open internal election, as well as successful mobilization efforts in the state of Tabasco. Thus in 1997 the PRD enjoyed relative unity and was riding a wave of local victories. In contrast, the PRD ended 1999 in disarray, under a weak leadership whose legitimacy was challenged by powerful internal factions and amid serious if mostly hidden doubts about the third presidential candidacy of Cárdenas.

To make matters worse, party leaders spent most of their time until nearly the end of February absorbed in difficult negotiations with the other four parties that eventually joined the Alliance for Mexico. Little was done to set in motion the massive organizational effort implied by the Sun Brigades. By the end of May, the Brigades operated only in scattered areas of the country. Even in Mexico City, they began their work so late that their effectiveness was greatly reduced. A sign of the PRD's internal disorganization is the Alliance for Mexico's failure to cover more than 65 percent of the polling places on election day. In 1994—without the help of four allied parties—the PRD covered 67 percent of the polls.[49]

The PRI: Breakdown of the Machine

Given the PAN's traditional ineffectiveness and the PRD's organizational meltdown, one might have expected the PRI to make up lost ground with its famous mobilizational machinery. To be sure, the days were long gone when the unions and popular organizations that make up its sectoral structure could guarantee—as labor leader Fidel Velázquez once put it—120 percent support on election day.[50] Yet what remained was far from worthless. In addition, by 2000 the PRI could draw on a so-called Territorial Movement, based originally on its own efforts to conduct house-to-house canvassing. Labastida, like Fox, also had a personal mobilization network set up initially to support his primary campaign. "Networks 2000" (*Redes 2000*) claimed 5,879,929 members by election day—a "citizen vote" that (with the votes of the PRI) would lift Labastida to victory.[51]

The fact that the PRI lost does not necessarily mean that its mobilization efforts were flawed. Yet given the disarray of the PRD and the organizational weakness of the PAN, it is suggestive that the PRI vote fell so far short of what preelectoral polls anticipated, particularly in the once-strong rural areas, and that overall turnout was lower than expected. Internal analysis of the mobilization effort by the national head of the Territorial Movement has turned up a number of problems. First, there was serious disorganization and lack of communication, essential for mobilization. Second, *Redes 2000* proved ineffective in part because its association with the wife of the candidate converted the movement into a sort of soft nepotism. The majority of local directors of *Redes* were "wives of the leadership, of the delegates, of the mayors, of the candidates."[52] Having been constructed to mobilize support for Labastida in an *internal* primary election, it was ill prepared to reach out to groups beyond the party. Finally, and most important, "the main strategic mistake was utilizing a schema that was created to mobilize sympathizers already identified by the party, when these were enough to win and all that was needed was simply to activate them."[53] There was a house-to-house effort. But the promoters were sent not to convince undecided voters, but with questionnaires to return to party headquarters, a strategy Flores Rico terms "how to waste ten million visits."[54] Thus the internal primary misled the PRI:

> [T]he internal process had already produced almost 10 million votes; we needed 18 million to win, we know who voted in each house and we know how many more live there that did not vote. The task of persuasion consisted, then, in con-

vincing those that did vote to move the rest.... [T]he promotion of the vote was not to convince but to motivate ... the
number of voters per PRI household [to] double.[55]

One might add that seventy-one years of winning could have misled
the PRI as well.

These criticisms probably applied as well to many of the PRI's earlier mobilization campaigns, at least since the late 1980s. The one possible exception lies in increased public scrutiny of the PRI's use of material benefits as an incentive for support, a tactic used to great effect in
earlier campaigns. With material incentives withdrawn, the PRI's mobilization efforts weakened. The PRI's "mobilization machine" was not
designed for such conditions. To some extent this points the finger
away from the parties themselves and their strategies, and back at society. Although its choice of campaign strategy may have been unnecessarily poor, the PRI's mobilizational weakness was largely beyond its
control.

CONCLUSION

There is a scene in the C.S. Lewis novel *The Lion, the Witch, and the
Wardrobe* where the evil queen chases the heroes in a sleigh across a
frozen landscape (always winter, but never Christmas) produced by
her spell. As she travels, the snow and ice begins to melt. Her spell is
breaking. And as spring comes, her sleigh comes to a bumping halt.
The fault lies not with the sleigh but with the surface. As the power of
the queen to control her environment wanes, she becomes ill adapted to
her conditions.

The campaign of Francisco Labastida betrays at many points the
difficulties of a party out of sync with its conditions. The PRI's tortured
efforts to define itself as the party of change and democracy (as well as
order and progress) suffered from a lack of credibility that would have
been hard to overcome in any case. Yet the PRI also paid for mistakes in
strategy that displayed its weaknesses more than its strengths. Could
the PRI have won with a different strategy? Probably—at least for one
more election.

The campaign of Vicente Fox shows many moments of brilliance,
but also many pedestrian ones. It was far from a perfect campaign. Fox
benefited from the polarization of the race into a two-party contest.
Was this polarization inevitable? Probably. But it could also have benefited the candidate of the left opposition.

In this sense, the errors of the PRD loom particularly large. Not only did their candidate selection play into the strategy of Fox to create a two-party race, but their pursuit of internal factional needs tended to facilitate polarization of the campaign. Had the race between the Left and the Right been more equal, the dynamics of the campaign might well have been different. Could the PRD have avoided these errors? Probably.

In each case, however, the strategic development of the three campaigns reflected internal party dynamics as well as the parties' perception of popular preferences. Representation begins at this point, as parties try to balance competing preferences and needs, both internal and external. The menu depended heavily on the chefs: Mexicans had to pick among a limited number of options. Could these options have been different? Probably. But they were not.

Notes

I wish to thank Jorge Domínguez, Chappell Lawson, and the anonymous reviewers of this chapter for their perceptive and helpful comments. I also want to thank the Comparative Manifestoes Project, and especially Dr. Andrea Volkens, for invaluable assistance in coding party platforms (discussed in the second section of this chapter).

1. However, the reform also reflected internal power struggles over control of the party, with the more traditional political managers of the party successfully resisting attempts by the technocratic wing to "modernize" the PRI—at the expense of these traditional political managers.

2. "In the last few weeks, he [Fox] has called me shorty, has called me a little sissy, has called me a stuffed suit, has called me henpecked, has made obscene gestures on television referring to me, and it is not that this offends me personally, but that he is offending Mexican families with such sayings ... gestures and foolishness." Quotes from debate transcript published by *Reforma*, at http://www.reforma.com/nacional/Articulo/004295. For further details, see the contributions by Chappell Lawson and Alejandro Moreno in this volume. Other campaign material followed the same line; one television ad, for example, showed a video of Fox on a campaign stop encouraging a small girl to tell a dirty joke and concluded, "Would you trust your children to this man? We wouldn't."

3. "Gana México urbano y educado," *Reforma*, July 3, 2000. For further details, see James McCann's contribution in this volume.

4. Gerardo Albarrán de Alba, "Fox en su libro: 'La historia de Diego no se repetirá; voy por la Presidencia,'" *Proceso* 1200 (October 31, 1999): 23.

5. Pascal Beltrán del Río, "En la obsesión del triunfo, una derrota panista en el 2000 sería el desplome," *Proceso* 1193 (September 12, 1999): 18–19.

6. Verónica Espinosa, "Fox se dice a la cabeza de la sucesión, pero oculta el origen de sus fondos de campaña," *Proceso* 1156 (December 27, 1998): 18.

7. María Scherer Ibarra, "El PAN construyó su camino al poder y llegó el momento: Bravo Mena," *Proceso* 1193 (September 12, 1999): 17.

8. Confidential interviews by author, September–November 2000.

9. Interview with Cuauhtémoc Cárdenas, in Andrea Becerril and David Carrizales, "Defensa de Cárdenas a la UNAM, en el Tec," *La Jornada*, March 30, 2000.

10. See "La alternancia real es Cárdenas," *La Jornada*, June 26, 2000.

11. "Gana México urbano y educado."

12. In the 1997 Mexico City mayoral race, confronted with equally uninspiring candidates of the PRI and the PAN, Cárdenas managed to humanize his image by simply smiling more often. Interestingly, this was less central in the 2000 campaign, reflecting Cárdenas's aversion to manipulation of his image, as well as his personal reserve and sense of dignity. Thus he selected an advertising firm that suggested an austere image in line with his own self-conception. Interviewed about the "smiling" issue, one of his advisers remarked, "the campaign will be sober, like Cárdenas." Alberto Aguirre M. and Alberto Najar, "Los publicistas: nuevos fabricantes de votos, *La Jornada: Masiosare*, February 13, 2000, p. 11.

13. The Alliance for Change included the PAN and PVEM. The Alliance for Mexico included the PRD, PT (Labor Party), PAS (Social Alliance Party), PSN (Nationalist Society Party), and CD (Democratic Convergence).

14. PRD president Amalia García's comment that the resignation of Cárdenas "would mortgage the future of the party" had a literal as well as a figurative meaning. Lourdes Galaz, "Web@ndo en política," *La Jornada*, February 16, 2000.

15. Claudia Guerrero, "Sale PRD de elección con números rojos," *Reforma*, July 9, 2000.

16. "Le piden combatir pobreza," *Reforma*, July 3, 2000.

17. The Comparative Manifestoes Project graciously sent me its training manuals, and I passed their inter-coder reliability tests prior to coding the Mexico data. My Mexico coding (as well as vote/seat counts from 1946 to 2000) is on deposit with the CMP.

18. The additive list of "conservative items" includes support for the military (104), support for freedom/human rights (201), support for constitutionalism (203), support for strong authority (305), support for free enterprise (401), support for use of economic incentives (402), support for free trade (407), support for economic orthodoxy (414), social services limitation (505), support for national way of life/patriotism (601), support for traditional morality (603), support for law and order (605), and support for social harmony (606). The additive list of "leftist items" includes anti-imperialism/pro-decolonization (103), anti-military statements (105), support for world peace (106), support for internationalism/world government (107), support for democracy (202), support for regulating capitalism (403), support for economic planning (404), support for protectionism (406), support for a controlled economy (412), support for nationalization of industry (413), support for expanding social services (504), support for expanding education spending (506), and support for labor (701).

19. Since 1986 the presentation of an official electoral platform has been a legal requirement for all parties. Prior to this date, only the PAN issued an electoral platform for every election going back to 1946. Following the Comparative Mani-

festoes Project guidelines, I substituted coding of program and principles sections from the Basic Documents of parties in some cases.

20. Since coalitions must act together, a single platform was presented by the PAN-PVEM coalition (the Alliance for Change) as well as by the PRD-PT-CD-PSM-PAS coalition (the Alliance for Mexico).

21. "Apoyan programa contra la pobreza," *Reforma*, July 3, 2000. As discussed elsewhere in this volume, most Mexican voters (as opposed to party elites) have traditionally conceived of "left" and "right" in terms of attitudes toward existing political institutions rather than toward economic policy.

22. While focus groups favored the ad, public ridicule by the opposition had a devastating effect. Similar criticisms came—after the election—from within the PRI itself, noting that focus groups had entirely missed the incongruity of an announcement that "made the servants giggle." See Carlos Flores Rico, *Entre un perro y un poste: cómo perder la presidencia (sin morir en el intento)* (Mexico City: Nuevo Siglo Veintiuno, 2000): 89.

23. One subtle example of this technique is the catchy jingle composed for Labastida by the Mexican *ranchera* singer, Juan Gabriel. The lyrics minimized the leadership qualities of the opposition candidates by using childish nicknames while referring to the PRI candidate with his full first name: "Ni 'Temoc, ni 'Chente, Francisco va a ser el presidente. Ni PRD ni PAN, ni PRD ni PAN, el PRI es el que va a ganar." The defect of this jingle was that it merely reminded voters of their main complaint about the PRI: its history of being the party that was going to win.

24. Rosa Elvira Vargas, "Aún de *panzazo*, el PRI ganará los comicios: Rodríguez Alcaine," *La Jornada*, June 28, 2000.

25. Flores Rico, *Entre un perro y un poste*, p. 70.

26. That is, "support to increase internal savings in the economy," "policies to increase the productivity of economic investment," "programs to increase the level of foreign investment," "programs to reduce the cost of generating formal employment," and "opportunities for everyone."

27. Quoted in Flores Rico, *Entre un perro y un poste*, p. 53.

28. Ibid., pp. 132–33.

29. On the effects on negative campaigning, see Alejandro Moreno's contribution in this volume.

30. This was the result of their even showing in the 1997 congressional election. Alonso Urrutia, "Aprobó el IFE 3 mil millones 912 mil pesos para los partidos," *La Jornada*, January 28, 2000. The exchange rate in 2000 was approximately nine pesos to the dollar.

31. Juan Manuel Venegas, "'Poco más' de 200 millones de pesos ha gastado Fox en tv," *La Jornada*, May 29, 2000, at www.jornada.unam.mx/2000/may00/000529/pol1.html; José Antonio Román, "El PRD gestiona créditos para *apuntalar* la campaña electoral," *La Jornada*, June 6, 2000, at www.jornada.unam.mx/2000/jun00/000606/pol2.html.

32. The disparity diminished when only ads for the presidential candidates were counted. PRI spots publicized its candidates to the Senate nearly as often as its presidential candidate. Elizabeth Velasco, "Más difusión a obras de gobierno que a

publicidad de IFE-IEDF," *La Jornada*, June 7, 2000, at www.jornada.unam.mx/2000/jun00/000607/pol4.html.

33. Juan Antonio Zúñiga, "Muy por abajo de los topes de campaña, los gastos de Cárdenas," *La Jornada*, May 29, 2000, at www.jornada.unam.mx/2000/may00/000529/el.html.

34. Relative advertising costs partly account for this difference—advertising on Televisa was about twice as expensive. However, the local PRD government (and its controversial prosecutor, Samuel del Villar) was also engaged at the time in a vicious confrontation with TV Azteca.

35. The shedding of the umbilical cord was a necessary distinction: Fox was actually born in Mexico City.

36. Blanche Petrich, "El *rancheo*, parte fundamental en la estrategia de Cárdenas," *La Jornada*, May 15, 2000, at www.jornada.unam.mx/2000/may00/000515/pol2.html.

37. María Scherer Ibarra, "Cárdenas afina su estrategia: polarizar las propuestas de cambio," *Proceso* 1226 (April 30, 2000): 25.

38. Daniela Pastrana, "Cuauhtémoc Cárdenas: el ancla y el buen cierre," *La Jornada: Masiosare*, July 2, 2000.

39. Arturo Cano, "Francisco Labastida: el nuevo PRI puede esperar," *La Jornada: Masiosare*, July 2, 2000.

40. Ibid.

41. Francisco Ortiz Pardo, "El 'ejército ciudadano' del PAN avanza," *Proceso* 1219 (March 12, 2000): 12.

42. María Scherer Ibarra, "Oferta de Cárdenas: revertir los efectos del TLC," *Proceso* 1223 (April 9, 2000): 22; Instituto Federal Electoral 1998, p. 224.

43. Scherer Ibarra, "Cárdenas afina su estrategia," 22.

44. *Mariquita* means, literally, a sissy, with connotations of effeminate homosexuals. It is also used in the context of cowardice, overly refined manners, and so on. Flores Rico *Entre un perro y un poste*, p. 115.

45. Cárdenas seemed unusually relaxed and quick thinking, chiding Fox that he was a clever boy and would not forget the answers he had so carefully memorized in only a few more days.

46. For further detail on the "pre-debate" and the second debate, see the contributions by Lawson in this volume.

47. Confidential interview by author, July 2000, Mexico City.

48. See Organización Nacional de Observación Electoral del Magisterio (ONOEM), "Informe de la observación del proceso electoral de la ONOEM" (Mexico City: ONOEM, 1994, mimeo); see also Flores Rico, *Entre un perro y un poste*, p. 129.

49. Ibid.

50. Cristina Martin, "Clase política," *La Jornada*, July 1, 1988.

51. Cano, "Francisco Labastida."

52. Ibid., p. 130.

53. Ibid., p. 121.

54. Ibid., p. 126.

55. Ibid.

7
Primary Priming

James A. McCann

On November 7, 1999, Mexico's ruling Institutional Revolutionary Party (PRI) held an open national primary to choose its presidential nominee. This event was unprecedented in Mexican history and stands as one of the most remarkable features of the recent electoral contest south of the border. Gone was the *dedazo*, the designation of the PRI nominee by the incumbent president and his close circle of advisers. Rather than handpick his likely successor, President Ernesto Zedillo pledged upon taking office "not to interfere, in any way at all, in the process of selection of candidates for the PRI."[1] This promise was not fully kept. Five years after making this pledge, the president barred two potentially strong candidates from running in the primary in an effort to boost the chances of his interior secretary, Francisco Labastida Ochoa.[2] Nevertheless, by the summer of 1999, it was clear that even with the president's support, Labastida would face three significant challengers in his nomination bid: Roberto Madrazo Pintado, governor of Tabasco; Manuel Bartlett Díaz, governor of Puebla; and Humberto Roque Villanueva, a former national head of the PRI.

That the democratic reform process begun in the 1970s would eventually reshape PRI nomination procedures is understandable. In any party system, the rules governing the choices voters face on election day speak volumes about how power is distributed across society. As E.E. Schattschneider observed in his classic work *The Semisovereign People*, "the definition of alternatives is the supreme instrument of power."[3] For generations, the *dedazo* furthered the interests of the PRI by permitting smooth, measured change from one *sexenio* to the next.

Conflict over presidential succession was kept largely under wraps.[4] Amid rising calls for accountability and openness in the 1980s and 1990s, however, this practice was increasingly hard to defend.[5]

Under the new nomination procedures, candidates were compelled to mobilize a mass following in all parts of the country. This incentive stemmed from the PRI's method for counting votes. To clinch the nomination a candidate needed to win at least a plurality in a majority of the three hundred federal legislative districts in Mexico. Roberto Madrazo proved to be especially adept on the campaign trail. Throughout the summer of 1999, polls showed a tight two-man contest between the Tabasco governor and Labastida.[6] As is often the case in a competitive race, the tone of the campaigns became increasingly shrill. According to the PRI's ground rules, nomination seekers were to refrain from voicing "criticisms that could dishonor or discredit any other 'precandidate,' as well as party leaders and bodies responsible for conducting the primary."[7] In practice, such a regulation was unrealistic and unenforceable. In his speeches and in a nationally televised debate, Madrazo labeled Labastida a failure, a liar, and, perhaps worst of all, a puppet of the widely despised former president Carlos Salinas de Gortari.

Francisco Labastida withstood this barrage, fought back in kind, and went on to win the primary decisively with 55 percent of the vote; Madrazo received just 30 percent, while Bartlett and Roque remained in single digits. Labastida was not so fortunate eight months later. On July 2, 2000, he became the first *priísta* to lose a presidential election, thus ending an era of single-party politics that began in the 1920s.

Did the bitter struggle over the PRI nomination play a role in the party's devastating general election loss? This chapter takes up this question. If the open primary left Labastida politically wounded, his example could serve as a cautionary tale for democratic reformers, both in Mexico's two other major political parties—the National Action Party (PAN) and the Party of the Democratic Revolution (PRD)—and in other nations undergoing similar kinds of partisan transitions.[8] Using the freshly minted panel survey described in the opening chapter, I explore the relationship between presidential nomination preferences and general election outcomes. The empirical findings indicate that the primary did indeed influence citizens' beliefs and actions long after nomination decisions were reached. But before moving to these findings, a brief discussion of the scholarly literature on "divisive primaries" is in order.

THEORETICAL OVERVIEW

"[T]he party whose candidate is obliged to fight a hard primary campaign has an important strike against it entering the general election. Common sense, if nothing else, suggests that ... those who backed the primary loser ... may be less than enthusiastic in aiding his vanquisher in the [general election]." These words, written by Andrew Hacker in 1965, offer a clear statement on a party's risk in staging a primary.[9] Austin Ranney's description of nomination politics in five very different political systems where presidential primaries had been conducted—Colombia, Finland, France, Venezuela, and the United States—tends to confirm Hacker's common sense. "[T]he victory of one faction over another is more likely to result in open party splits and secessional candidacies."[10]

In the months leading up to the PRI primary, it appeared that this observation could apply to the Mexican case. As governor of the poor southern state of Tabasco, Roberto Madrazo had cultivated a large and loyal personal following. If threatened, the political machine he controlled could take on national leaders of the party and even the president.[11] When writing for American readers, journalists in Mexico often likened Madrazo to Huey Long, Louisiana's fiery populist governor in the 1930s who became a chronic thorn in the side of Franklin D. Roosevelt. From the beginning of the contest, there was every indication that the "Kingfish" from Tabasco was playing to win and cared little about harmony within the party. Furthermore, his ability to raise funds made him formidable. Over just a six-week period in mid-1999, Madrazo collected nearly US$5 million—a striking amount that was significantly higher than what Francisco Labastida, Manuel Bartlett, and Humberto Roque took in.[12] A war chest this large gave Madrazo the means to set up grassroots organizations in all parts of the country and flood radio and television with professionally produced commercials.

Before long, national polls showed nearly universal name recognition for the candidate and favorability ratings as high or higher than Labastida's. The strategy Madrazo adopted was the kind typically employed by up-and-coming presidential aspirants in established democracies. His prime targets were citizens outside the traditional PRI fold. In Schattschneider's terms, the governor sought to "expand the scope of conflict" within the party. This could only come about by challenging front-runner Labastida and the status quo. A masterful speaker, Roberto Madrazo painted himself as the protector of those who had lost ground through neoliberal restructuring. His media spots featured orphans, widows, and poor workers enduring miserable living conditions, all of whom were said to be ignored by the PRI elite. Labastida was portrayed as a simple yes-man for the president.

The two other contenders, Manuel Bartlett and Humberto Roque, each had many years of experience in party affairs and were already nationally known public figures by 1999. However, neither proved to be as captivating as Madrazo, though both followed somewhat similar campaign strategies. Bartlett latched onto the crime issue, a subject of great concern across Mexico, and took "firmness" as his major theme. President Zedillo—and Francisco Labastida by association—were certainly vulnerable on this issue. But Bartlett's pugnacious manner and shadowy past undoubtedly reminded many of the PRI's authoritarian roots, a legacy that PRI candidates ran away from in the 1990s.[13] Roque raised very few funds and did practically no advertising or grassroots outreach. In his public appearances, he claimed to be the most "economically responsible" candidate, someone who could shrink the country's budget deficit. President Zedillo and the PRI establishment were somewhat vulnerable in this area too. Yet for most citizens, concerns about federal budgeting were much less salient than unemployment, poverty, and public security.

The turbulence Labastida encountered in his run for the presidency was surely more than he envisioned as he contemplated his political future in the first half of the Zedillo administration. Having entered public service in 1962, he had been governor of the northern state of Sinaloa, a secretary of energy in the 1980s, and a member of Zedillo's cabinet (secretary of agriculture and of the interior). Soon after the National Political Council of the PRI met in May 1999 to approve rules for the primary, Labastida picked up endorsements from numerous current and former government officials, and from most PRI governors as well. With connections such as these to draw upon, Labastida mostly ignored the early jabs by Madrazo and his other rivals. After all, the PRI apparatus remained quite solid, particularly in poorer rural areas, where people continued to depend on it for any number of goods and services. Those tied to the ruling party had long become accustomed to backing whichever candidate carried the official stamp. As a party member who headed a union of stall vendors put it, "There are indications that Labastida is the candidate of the president of the republic. That makes him the guy to get behind."[14] Nevertheless, by July conflict between the two leading candidates had escalated to such a level, and the race had become so much closer, that Labastida needed to respond. Following the advice of his political consultants, the front-runner went sharply on the offensive and assailed Madrazo's character. At the same time, he turned somewhat more populist, arguing, among other things, that he alone would protect Mexico's treasured state-owned industries.

After several weeks of charges and countercharges, PRI officials warned that the rancorous sparring might make it impossible for either candidate to be effective in the 2000 general election. A year and a half later, in the wake of President Vicente Fox's inauguration, Labastida echoed this point in an interview with the Mexican newspaper *La Jornada*: "If the party's internal contests are not conducted with a great deal of skill, intelligence, [and] judgment, and if the consequences are not properly gauged, fractures are provoked like the one we [the PRI] are still dragging behind us."[15]

From a theoretical standpoint, social psychological research on *priming* effects can provide a mechanism to account for these potential partisan fractures.[16] Individuals who take part in a nomination contest are called upon very early in the campaign to make a reasonable choice among a potentially diverse set of contenders. This decision may involve sorting through a great deal of complex information about the candidates—their ideological stands, their personality traits, their prior experience in government, and the kinds of people and groups they would bring into an administration if elected. Once a citizen has come up with arguments for or against each of the contestants, these attitudes and the logic of his or her choice may persist long into the post-nomination phase of the election.

In major national elections, citizens are flooded with persuasive messages. Candidates nominated for office invest heavily in preparing political commercials for television, orchestrating mass rallies, and sending party members out into neighborhoods to spread the word. A central premise in the contemporary social psychological literature is that citizens cannot take all of this information in and interpret it in any meaningful way. This would simply be too demanding a job, even for experienced political activists. Instead, individuals pay attention to and remember political messages they have been most primed to accept. An individual's long-standing partisan dispositions, commitments to particular values, and connections to social or economic groups might all become salient as the electoral environment warms up. These attitudes in turn help individuals cut through what writer Walter Lippmann called the "great blooming, buzzing confusion" of politics.[17]

Along similar lines, political choices made early in the election could condition later responses to campaign information and appeals. In the Mexican context, this notion would lead us to expect early supporters of Francisco Labastida to become ever more attached to the PRI nominee throughout the post-nomination campaign and on the day of the election. On the other hand, Madrazo, Bartlett, and Roque's attacks in the primary could have left their followers well primed to accept the arguments made later by the two major opposition leaders, Vicente Fox of the PAN and Cuauhtémoc Cárdenas of the PRD. "The official candidate [Labastida] just wants to continue the same failed policies we have now. And that's logical, because he supports everything you and I want to change," declared Madrazo in a nationally televised debate among all four contenders. Had they been in attendance, Fox and Cárdenas could not have been more blunt or hostile toward Labastida. Come July 2, losing nomination voters might therefore have been more prone to distance themselves from the PRI, either by defecting outright to an opposition party or staying away from the polls. From the standpoint of the party sponsoring the primary election, we might label this a *negative* priming effect.

If the presidential primary caused such an effect, the hand of PRI traditionalists who have counseled over the years against democratic reforms would be considerably strengthened. We should note, however, that some research on divisive nominations in the United States, where relatively open primaries have been the norm for decades, finds that a vigorous battle over candidate selection does not necessarily diminish the party's showing in the general election. Somewhat surprisingly, a protracted fight might even make the party *more competitive* on the day of the election.[18] This could occur because, even in an era of candidate-centered politics, primary elections remain first and foremost party affairs: voters participating in a collective nomination decision are unambiguously acting as partisans. As a consequence of this behavior, their psychological ties to the party might be strengthened, regardless of whether they back a winning or losing candidate.

If partisanship in Mexico were bolstered in this way, the PRI may have emerged from the primary with a stronger mass base, its loss at the polls many months later due to factors not directly connected to squabbles over candidate selection. A primary voter's remark reported by the *Washington Post* speaks to the salutary effect of an open nomination system. "This has never happened before. None of the other parties are doing this. If the party hadn't done this, who knows if I would still be in the PRI."[19] Reformers in the mid-1990s certainly hoped for such a response when the decision was made to do away with the *dedazo*.

Furthermore, Atkeson reminds us that disputes that seem monumental when a party selects candidates for office may shrink or be forgotten once nominations are decided. "[W]hile a nomination campaign encourages intraparty factionalism, a general election campaign provides incentives for party members to unite in support of their party's nominee. It entices individuals back to the party fold by focusing attention on the ... major candidates and the differences between them. These comparisons allow the members of losing factions to examine the nominee in light of his new opponent[s]—the other [parties' candidates]."[20]

Many Mexican citizens may have flocked to Roberto Madrazo thinking he was more likely than Labastida to bring about needed social, legal, or economic changes.[21] These participants were undoubtedly disappointed by Madrazo's loss. In survey interviews conducted at the time, a large number declared they would "stay home or vote against the PRI nominee next July."[22] But when July arrived, Francisco Labastida might have seemed markedly closer to their most preferred choice than either Fox or Cárdenas, who would both transform the Mexican system in ways Madrazo never would. In short, on election day many of the losing voters from the PRI primary might have concluded, as nomination participants in democracies around the world often must, that "half a loaf is better than none." For their part, Madrazo, Bartlett, and Roque essentially took this lesson to heart once the primary votes were tallied. None challenged the validity of the outcome, which had been foretold by many independent survey firms, and they largely refrained from expressing ill will toward Labastida and the party.[23]

As should be clear from this short description, work on divisive presidential primaries, which is based largely on the American experience, offers us opposing sets of hypotheses to consider in the case of Mexico. The negativity sparked by the primary might have worked against the PRI by limiting its ability to mobilize a popular following. Neither Vicente Fox nor Cuauhtémoc Cárdenas faced as significant a challenge for the nomination, and this difference may be one of the factors that contributed to the PRI's loss in 2000. Months after getting beaten by Fox, Francisco Labastida ventured this explanation. However, the negative impact of the primary might have been diluted, and perhaps even reversed, if participants came away with a renewed commitment to the PRI and a deeper appreciation of the stakes involved at the general election stage of the campaign.

DATA, METHODS, AND FINDINGS

Factional Differences

The data for this study are taken from our four-wave national panel study of the Mexican electorate. In the first interview, we asked respondents whether they had taken part in the PRI primary, and, if they had, which candidate had they chosen. Thirty percent of the sample reported turning out, a figure that is somewhat higher than what was published following the November event.[24] Among these self-identified primary voters, the breakdown of candidate support is in keeping with official tallies, though Labastida supporters were slightly overrepresented: 67 percent said they had backed the winning nominee, while Madrazo received 22 percent of the vote, Bartlett 4 percent, and Roque 2 percent.

I begin the analysis of these participants by exploring the differences separating Labastida supporters from rival nomination blocs. As noted above, a central goal of Madrazo and the other challengers was to recruit sympathizers who had not previously backed the PRI. With much of the rank and file behind Labastida, their only hope was to expand the party base. We see in table 7.1 that Labastida's opponents were quite successful in this aim. Less than half of the Madrazo-Bartlett-Roque group had voted for the PRI's Ernesto Zedillo in the 1994 presidential election. In dramatic contrast, over eight out of ten in the Labastida bloc had supported Zedillo five years earlier. Furthermore, those who preferred Madrazo, Bartlett, or Roque in the primary were also slightly more likely to report not participating in the last presidential contest (13 percent versus 9 percent for Labastida voters).

Differences in candidate constituencies are also visible when socioeconomic and demographic traits are assessed. In comparison to the Madrazo-Bartlett-Roque group, primary voters preferring Labastida tended to live in rural areas, which were the traditional strongholds of the ruling party. The typical Labastida backer in the primary was also older, less educated, and less affluent (as measured by asking respondents whether they owned a radio, water heater, oven, television, conventional telephone, or cellular telephone). In short, this constituency fit the classic demographic profile of PRI voters. Not surprisingly, northerners were more likely to rally behind the candidate from Sinaloa as well. No sizable differences were found based on the respondent's religious commitment.

Table 7.1. PRI Nomination Blocs: Political, Social, and Economic Background Characteristics (percents)

	Voted for Labastida	Voted for Madrazo, Bartlett, or Roque
1994 presidential vote		
PRI	82	49
Other party	9	38
Did not vote	9	13
Place of residence		
Rural	30	17
Urban	70	83
Region		
North	36	26
Central	23	27
Metropolitan region	16	20
South	26	27
Age		
18–30	29	41
31–45	36	32
46–64	27	24
65 and above	9	3
Gender#		
Male	48	43
Female	52	57
Education		
Primary or less	55	44
Secondary	22	20
Preparatory or more	23	36
Level of affluence		
Low	13	3
Moderate	57	58
High	30	39
Are you (or spouse) a union member?		
Yes	14	9
No	86	91
Church attendance		
Never/nearly never	10	11
Special occasion/monthly	66	62
Weekly or more often	23	28

Note: # $p < .10$; * $p < .05$; ** $p < .01$. Affluence was measured through a summary index based on whether respondents own a radio, water heater, oven, television, conventional telephone, or cellular telephone. Individuals who own five or six items were placed in the "high" category. Those owning only one or none of the items are in the "low" group. All others fall in the "moderate" group.

Political Dispositions at the Start of the Campaign

The distributions in table 7.1 suggest that the divisive primary might have provided an important service for the PRI despite its acrimonious tone. Individuals who may never have considered themselves sympathetic toward the PRI were mobilized into the party, at least for a day. The negative priming hypothesis holds that a loss at the polls in November would cause participants to abandon the party. Was this the case? Did supporters of Madrazo, Bartlett, and Roque espouse significantly more negative views of the PRI, its presidential nominee, and its record in government as the general election campaign moved forward? Table 7.2 shows the average political tendencies of the two nomination blocs in the first survey wave, as measured by six attitude items. The first reflects attentiveness to the electoral process, three questions indicate more partisan and ideological leanings, and the final three tap into perceptions of governmental performance:

- Level of interest in the campaign, measured through a four-point scale (4 = a great deal, 1 = no interest).

- An evaluation of Labastida's governing skills, a composite measure based on his ability to manage the economy, combat crime, and improve Mexico's educational system (4 = strong leadership abilities, 1 = weak leadership abilities).

- Identification with the PRI, based on a four-point scale (3 = strong PRI identifier, 2 = weak PRI identifier, 1 = leaning PRI identifier, and 0 = does not identify with the party).

- Ideological distance from the PRI, a ten-point scale on which high scores indicate disagreement with the PRI's ideological positions, as perceived by the respondent.

- Approval rating for President Zedillo, based on a five-point scale (5 = strong approval, 1 = strong disapproval).

- Expectations regarding fraud on the day of the election, based on a four-point scale (4 = the election will be totally clean, 1 = the election will not be at all clean).

- An evaluation of Mexican democracy, a three-point scale (1 = Mexico is already a democracy, −1 = Mexico is not yet a democracy, and 0 = not sure whether Mexico is a democracy).

Table 7.2. Political Dispositions within PRI Nomination Blocs Early in the General Election Campaign: Means (and Standard Errors)

	Voted for Labastida	Voted for Madrazo, Bartlett, or Roque	Correlation between Primary Choice and Attitudes
Political engagement			
Interest in campaign	2.18 (.04)	2.19 (.06)	.01
Partisan dispositions			
Evaluation of Labastida's governing skills	3.19 (.04)	2.53 (.07)**	−.35
Level of identification with the PRI	2.02 (.05)	.76 (.08)**	−.47
Ideological distance from the PRI	1.97 (.13)	3.40 (.26)**	.23
Perceptions of governmental performance			
Approval rating for President Zedillo	3.88 (.04)	3.32 (.09)**	−.24
Believe that Mexico is already democratic	2.13 (.04)	1.90 (.06)**	−.11
Believe that the election will be free from fraud	2.98 (.04)	2.62 (.07)**	−.19

Notes: ** Highly significant difference in means ($p < .01$), based on ANOVA multiple comparison tests. The correlation coefficients are computed only for respondents who voted in the primary (Labastida supporters were coded as 1, Madrazo-Bartlett-Roque supporters were coded as 2). Interest in the campaign was coded on a four-point scale (1 = no interest, 2 = little interest, 3 = some interest, 4 = strong interest). Evaluations of Labastida are an average of three judgments: how well the candidate could manage the Mexican economy, reform education, and fight crime (1 = not capable, 2 = slightly capable, 3 = somewhat capable, 4 = very capable). Identification with the PRI was measured through a four-point scale (0 = not an identifier, 1 = leans toward PRI, 2 = identifies with the PRI, but weakly, 3 = strongly identifies with the PRI). Ideological distance from the PRI is the absolute difference between respondent self-placements on an eleven-point left-right scale and perceptions of the PRI's ideological position. Zedillo ratings were gauged through a five-point scale (1 = strong disapproval, 2 = slight disapproval, 3 = neither approve nor disapprove, 4 = slight approval, 5 = strong approval). Beliefs about Mexico's democracy were coded on a three-point scale (1 = Mexico is not yet a democracy, 2 = not sure whether Mexico is a democracy, 3 = Mexico is already a democracy). Beliefs about fraud in the July 2 election were measured on a four-point scale (1 = the election will not be clean at all, 2 = the election will be only somewhat clean, 3 = the election will be more or less clean, 4 = the election will be totally clean).

On average, we find that successful and unsuccessful primary voters alike were equal in their level of interest in the campaign; both groups scored toward the lower end of the scale in the February wave (2.18 and 2.19). There is no indication that supporters of Madrazo, Bartlett, or Roque had become alienated from the electoral process following the November primary.[25] There is much evidence, however, that this bloc was decidedly less friendly toward Labastida and the PRI at the start of the general election campaign. For the remaining attitudes in table 7.2, the differences are consistent and very unlikely to be due to chance ($p < .01$). In the case of the three "partisan disposition" variables, the contrasts are striking. When evaluating Labastida's governing capabilities, the Madrazo-Bartlett-Roque voters rated the PRI standard-bearer on average nearly three-quarters of a point lower on the four-point scale. This translates into a correlation of $-.35$. Even more substantial are the differences in level of identification with the PRI. Individuals who were with Labastida in November averaged 2.02 on the four-point scale, making them a fairly partisan group. For those preferring one of the three losing contestants, the dominant tendency was not even to lean toward the PRI (.76; $r = -.47$ for candidate choice and PRI identification). Moreover, Labastida's supporters from the primary took ideological positions that were markedly closer to the PRI's position. These respondents on average were less than two points away from the party, in absolute terms, while the mean for those backing Madrazo, Bartlett, or Roque was significantly larger at 3.40.

Primary Voting and Attitude Change

Taken together, the results in tables 7.1 and 7.2 would not have been welcome news for the PRI. Individuals who preferred Labastida in the primary appeared well disposed to stick with him come July, but to win the presidency the *priísta* would need to expand his following far beyond the traditional PRI base. This would be no small feat. Soon after the first survey wave was administered, the two leading opposition parties began working tirelessly to pull in voters. PRD and PAN activists fanned out across neighborhoods, and the airwaves quickly became filled with political advertisements. The newspaper *Reforma* tracked the flow of communication throughout this time. According to its report, the Fox and Cárdenas campaigns paid for approximately 83 hours of political advertising on television during the month of February. In March the two campaigns put out a combined total of 155 hours of commercials; in June this figure rose to 179 hours, which averages out to over six hours per day that month. Advertising on Mexican radio stations followed a similar pattern.[26]

In these commercials, and in the literature distributed by opposition activists, the charges raised first by Roberto Madrazo, Manuel Bartlett, and Humberto Roque were again voiced: Labastida lacks the necessary talents and integrity to be a good president; a vote against Labastida is a vote for democracy in Mexico; the PRI is hopelessly out of touch with the concerns of regular people. Were the losing primary participants more receptive to these kinds of arguments, as the negative priming hypothesis posits? Figures 7.1a through 7.1g explore this question by extending the panel into June (the third wave of the survey), just a few weeks before the general election.[27] Levels of interest in electoral politics and beliefs about Labastida, the PRI, and Mexican democracy would almost certainly have changed over this five-month period, and they might have been especially volatile in the earlier stage of the survey (February to May). If the primary left a lasting impression, participants should exhibit more malleable attitude dispositions, given their heightened sensitivity to campaign information.

Looking to figure 7.1a, we discover a high degree of continuity in citizen attentiveness to the campaign. The regression coefficient linking February and May responses is .32, and the path from May to June is .49. With controls for 1994 voting behavior, gender, age, region, education, affluence, union membership, religiosity, and the other political attitudes listed in table 7.2, we also see that primary involvement had significant positive effects on the respondent's level of interest.[28] Between the February and May survey waves, those who had supported one of Labastida's nomination opponents became *more* interested in electoral politics (b = .26, significant at the .10 level). The negative priming hypothesis, which anticipates disengagement by this bloc, picks up no support in this case. In the later stage of the campaign, it appears that Labastida voters from the primary became especially more engaged. At this same period, the losing primary participants also expressed greater interest, though not to the same degree.

Continuing on through this set of figures, the findings for changes in perceptions of Francisco Labastida and personal identification with the PRI likewise show largely positive effects for the ruling party. By May, with the campaigns shifting into high gear, those who had supported Madrazo, Bartlett, or Roque significantly *up*graded their judgments of Labastida ($p < .10$). For the Labastida voters, these significant positive effects were most pronounced in the later stage of the contest. Between

Figures 7.1. The Impact of Primary Choices on Attitude Change in the General Election Campaign: OLS Coefficients (and Standard Errors)

a. Interest in the Election Campaign

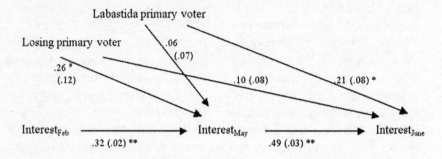

b. Evaluations of Labastida's Governing Competence

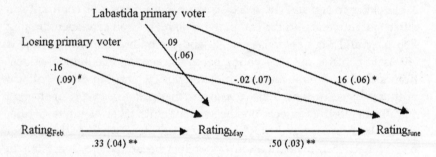

c. Identification with the PRI

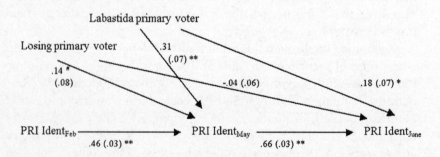

d. Ideological Distance from the PRI

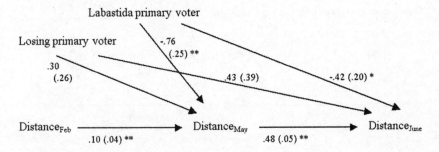

e. President Zedillo's Approval Ratings

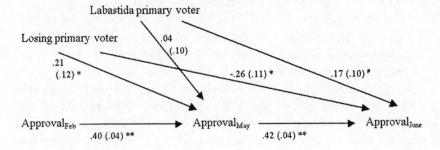

f. Evaluation of Mexican Democracy

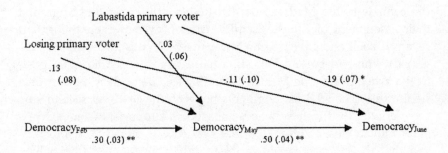

g. Belief That the Election Will be Free from Fraud

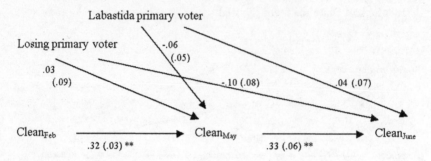

the February and May waves, both sets of primary participants grew significantly more closely identified with the PRI; Labastida backers continued this trend in the later stage of the campaign ($p < .05$).

A slightly different picture is seen in figure 7.1d, where the respondent's ideological distance to the ruling party is modeled. Individuals who had backed Labastida from the start grew nearer to the PRI between the first and second periods. On average, these primary voters moved three-quarters of a point closer on a ten-point ideological scale, a very large shift indeed and highly significant. Between the second and third panel waves, this trend continued. No comparable movement was detected for those who preferred one of Labastida's nomination rivals. These respondents tended to distance themselves from the party as the campaign moved forward, but this effect is not large or significant.

The two voting blocs from the primary also displayed somewhat different tendencies on attitudes toward the Zedillo administration and the question of Mexico's status as a democracy. In the early months of the campaign, the Madrazo-Bartlett-Roque primary voters upgraded their assessment of Ernesto Zedillo. After May, however, this group reversed itself and gave Zedillo lower marks. In this later period, individuals who had backed Labastida tended to rate Zedillo more positively. When evaluating Mexico's standing as a democracy, neither bloc significantly changed its judgments between the first and second survey periods. By the June wave, Labastida's supporters from the primary moved closer to thinking that Mexico was already a democracy and that the election would be clean ($p < .05$). Much of the debate during the final weeks of the campaign focused on the trajectory of democratization. Labastida, along with the president and other leading *priístas*, argued vociferously that the PRI's reform process had in fact transformed the nation into a democracy. Each of the opposition candidates replied that only when the ruling party lost and power was peacefully transferred would Mexico be a genuine democracy. The results in this figure show that those preferring Labastida at the nomination stage were somewhat better primed to accept the PRI's interpretations of democracy. Participants who backed other candidates during the nomination process do not appear to have been significantly susceptible to either set of arguments. Turning to expectations regarding electoral fraud, it appears that respondent beliefs changed a great deal from one wave to the next—continuity scores were only .32 and .33—but the primary had little to do with these changes.

Primary Choices and General Election Preferences

Judging from the results in figures 7.1a to 7.1g, Mexicans who did not get their way at the polls during the primary were not especially prone to drift away from the ruling party and its nominee. To the contrary, we find evidence that the open nomination had a positive effect for the PRI, though this effect is substantially larger for those who had supported Francisco Labastida. In the case of actual voting preferences, does this sanguine conclusion hold?

In the February wave of the survey, it does *not*. The negativity from the primary had clearly spilled over into the general election. Table 7.3 presents the findings from a logistic regression model, where voting preferences at this stage are predicted from the respondent's primary-stage choices, with the background and dispositional variables from tables 7.1 and 7.2 controlled. (In this specification, not having a preference or planning to abstain is treated as the baseline category.) We find in the first model that Labastida's supporters from the primary were significantly more inclined to prefer the candidate than abstain or be undecided. Somewhat surprisingly, however, these respondents also were almost nearly as likely to back someone from the opposition: the regression coefficient is .51 in the former case and .44 in the latter. This suggests that a decision to get behind Labastida in November had a significant mobilizing effect early in the 2000 race, but not substantially in favor of the PRI.[29] The coefficient linking a preference for Madrazo, Bartlett, or Roque to support for Labastida is positive as well, but it is less than half the size of its standard error. More importantly, we see in the second column that this bloc moved slightly in the direction of the opposition (b = .39, s.e. = .26, p = .14).[30]

Table 7.3. A Model of Presidential Preferences in the February Wave: Multinomial Logistic Regression Coefficients (and Standard Errors)

	Model 1		Model 2	
	Labastida	Opposition	Labastida	Opposition
Primary choice				
Labastida primary voter	.51 (.22)*	.44 (.25)#	1.12 (.49)*	1.17 (.50)*
Voted for a Labastida rival	.14 (.31)	.39 (.26)	.39 (.59)	1.00 (.45)*
Background controls				
PRI voter in 1994	.53 (.20)**	.26 (.19)	.56 (.23)*	.43 (.22)*
Opposition voter in 1994	.42 (.27)	.86 (.18)**	.42 (.30)	1.00 (.20)**
Gender (female)	.41 (.16)**	.04 (.14)	.42 (.16)**	.04 (.14)
Age (years)	−.03 (.01)**	−.03 (.01)**	−.03 (.01)**	−.03 (.01)**
Urban resident	.06 (.11)	−.12 (.10)	.06 (.11)	−.12 (.10)
North	.64 (.22)**	.78 (.21)**	.65 (.22)**	.77 (.21)**
South	.38 (.22)#	.12 (.20)	.39 (.23)#	.14 (.21)
Metro region	−.38 (.22)#	−.15 (.18)	−.37 (.22)#	−.15 (.18)
Education level	−.07 (.09)	.14 (.07)#	−.07 (.09)	.14 (.07)#
Level of affluence	−.03 (.08)	.12 (.07)	−.03 (.09)	.12 (.07)#
Religious commitment	.13 (.07)#	.09 (.06)	.13 (.07)#	.09 (.06)
Union membership	.57 (.27)*	.17 (.23)	.57 (.27)*	.17 (.23)
Controls for political dispositions				
Interest in the campaign	−.11 (.09)	.20 (.08)*	−.10 (.09)	.20 (.09)*
Labastida trait differential	.54 (.13)**	−.51 (.12)**	.53 (.14)**	−.51 (.13)**
Identification with the PRI	.58 (.05)**	−.47 (.06)**	.58 (.05)**	−.47 (.06)**
Ideological distance	−.03 (.03)	.04 (.02)#	−.03 (.03)	.04 (.02)#
Zedillo approval rating	−.01 (.08)	.13 (.07)#	−.01 (.08)	.13 (.07) #
Believe Mexico is democracy	.20 (.09)*	.15 (.08)#	.20 (.09)*	.15 (.08)#
Election will be clean	.51 (.10)**	.34 (.09)**	.51 (.10)**	.35 (.09)**
Interaction effects				
PRI voter in 1994 x Labastida primary voter			−.83 (.55)	−1.05 (.60)#
Opposition voter in 1994 x Labastida primary voter			−.08 (.91)	−.71 (.84)
PRI voter in 1994 x voted for a Labastida rival			.96 (.74)	.78 (.65)
Opposition voter in 1994 x voted for a Labastida rival			.28 (.99)	−1.25 (.61)*
Constant term	−17 (.13)	.07 (.12)	−.17 (.14)	.02 (.13)

Notes: # $p < .10$; * $p < .05$; ** $p < .01$. N = 2,355 (multiple imputation used for missing responses). The baseline choice category is planning to abstain or having no preference yet. The political disposition measures are all taken from the February wave.

Though not of central concern to us, it is worth noting that nearly all of the control variables have a significant effect on voting preferences in this period. The citizens' voting choices in 1994 figured prominently in their political calculus. Individuals who had supported one of the opposition presidential candidates in the previous election were over twice as likely to prefer someone from the opposition in the February wave; on the other hand, those voting for Zedillo in 1994 were over one and a half times more likely to stick with the PRI. (These figures are calculated by taking the inverse of the natural log for the logit coefficients.) In keeping with earlier research on Mexican electoral behavior, women, older citizens, and southerners tended to back the PRI.[31] Not surprisingly, the most significant predictors in the model were the attitude dispositions measured in February. Perceptions of the major contestants' governing capabilities and the respondent's party identification played a particularly large part in structuring candidate preferences.[32]

If those who did not get their way in the primary tended to move away from the PRI during the general election, we might expect people without a history of backing the party to be considerably more prone to defect. Some studies of party members in other democracies hold that participants with a long-term commitment to their party can take disappointment in stride. Not getting one's first choice in candidate selection may not lessen one's party attachments.[33] To test this possibility, a set of interaction terms was added to the model (primary choice x voting behavior in 1994). These effects were statistically significant, fairly sizable, and in the expected direction, with newcomers evidencing greater sensitivity to decisions at the nomination stage. To clarify these complex relationships, table 7.4 shows the predicted probabilities of candidate preferences in February, broken down by choices in the primary and the 1994 presidential election. These probabilities were derived from the second model in table 7.3, with all control variables set to their mean values.

For those who turned out for the ruling party in 1994, what little effect there was for the primary boosted the PRI. According to the model, the probability that an early supporter of Labastida would stick by him in February was .41, as compared to a probability of .38 for turning to one of the PRI's opponents. Interestingly, the Madrazo-Bartlett-Roque supporters in this group were somewhat *more* inclined to prefer Labastida over a rival: .47 versus .35. PRI voters from 1994 who did not take part in the primary were slightly less inclined to back Labastida (a probability of .36) and more likely to say that they were abstaining or had no preference (a 25 percent chance). Staging a divisive primary seems not to have "provoked fissures" within the preexisting base of the PRI, as Labastida argued following the 2000 general election. To the contrary, winners and losers alike came away more committed to the standard-bearer.

Table 7.4. Political Choices from 1994, PRI Nomination Preferences, and Expected Presidential Preferences Early in the General Election Campaign: Assessing Interaction Effects

General Election Preferences, February 2000	Primary Election Choice		
	Labastida	Madrazo, Bartlett, or Roque	Did Not Vote in Primary
PRI voters in 1994			
Francisco Labastida	.41	.47	.36
Opposition candidate	.38	.35	.39
Not sure/Plan to abstain	.21	.18	.25
Opposition voters in 1994			
Francisco Labastida	.40	.17	.25
Opposition candidate	.49	.56	.55
Not sure/Plan to abstain	.11	.26	.20
Did not vote in 1994			
Francisco Labastida	.38	.13	.30
Opposition candidate	.48	.64	.35
Not sure/Plan to abstain	.15	.23	.35

Note: These probabilities were derived from the multinomial logistic regression coefficients presented in table 7.3. All control variables were set to their mean value.

Among those who had voted for an opposition candidate or stayed away from the polls in 1994, the regression model makes very different predictions. In comparison to individuals who did not take part in the primary, supporters of Madrazo, Bartlett, or Roque were *less* inclined to back Labastida. The pattern for abstainers in 1994 is particularly dramatic. In this case, a vote for the Sinaloan in November translates into a 38 percent chance of backing him in the first survey wave, a 48 percent chance of preferring a nominee from the opposition, and a 15 percent chance of being undecided or planning to abstain. In stark contrast,

Mexicans who did not participate in 1994 but voted for one of Labastida's nomination challengers preferred one of the opposition candidates over the *priísta* by a ratio of nearly five to one (.64 versus .13). Respondents who did not take part in the 1994 election or the primary were evenly split, with a probability of .30 for supporting Labastida, .35 for backing someone from the opposition, and .35 for abstaining or not having a preference.

On the whole, the forecasts in the middle and bottom of table 7.4 plainly illustrate the risk a party takes in staging a primary. The Madrazo-Bartlett-Roque bloc was very different from the traditional PRI base, in terms of both socioeconomic characteristics and political orientations. This diversity speaks to the success of the party in reaching out to new potential supporters; it is what the reformers hoped for. Yet the regression findings also highlight the possibility of backfire. Participants who are not regular supporters of the party and do not get their way in the primary may turn especially hard against the party during the general election.

Voting Preferences in the Later Stages of the Campaign

Perhaps this interpretation is warranted as we investigate decision making in the later stages of the campaign. However, the path diagrams in figures 7.1a through 7.1g report a fair amount of fluctuation in attitudes between February and June, with the dispositions of primary voters generally tilting to the PRI as the campaign progressed. We might therefore suspect that the negative priming effects in tables 7.3 and 7.4 were short lived. Table 7.5 shows this to be the case. When presidential choices made in the July 2 election are modeled via multinomial logistic regression, the debilitating impact of the PRI primary vanishes. (No significant interaction effects between nomination choices and control variables were found in this case.)

Between February and July, the probability of casting a vote for Labastida dropped precipitously, even among those who supported his nomination. In the first wave, nearly four out of ten survey respondents voiced their support for the PRI leader. By July, just over 30 percent of the sample reported voting for him. Each of the authors in this volume wrestles with the question of why this drop occurred. Whatever the causes, the primary appears to have had little to do with the PRI loss. Quite to the contrary, mobilization behind Labastida during the primary offered a large and lasting bump up in the polls, even when personal evaluations of the candidate, identification with the ruling party, and a host of other potentially important variables are controlled. The results in this table imply that the odds of voting for Labastida rather than abstaining were nearly three times as high for the candidate's followers from the nomination stage. More importantly, supporting one of Labastida's rivals for the nomination no longer pushed respondents toward the opposition at this stage. Table 7.6, which maps the expected probabilities of candidate choice, clarifies this point.

Table 7.5. A Model of Voting Choices in the February Wave: Multinomial Logistic Regression Coefficients (and Standard Errors)

	Labastida	Opposition
Primary choice		
Labastida primary voter	1.06 (.20)**	.68 (.23)**
Voted for a Labastida rival	.50 (.34)	.45 (.26)#
Background controls		
PRI voter in 1994	.41 (.19)*	.22 (.21)
Opposition voter in 1994	.67 (.27)*	.79 (.22)**
Gender (female)	.38 (.17)*	.22 (.14)
Age (years)	.01 (.01)	.01 (.01)
Urban resident	−.23 (.11)#	−.13 (.10)
North	−.01 (.20)	.08 (.19)
South	.29 (.22)	.34 (.21)
Metro region	.07 (.21)	.13 (.19)
Education level	.13 (.13)	.21 (.09)*
Level of affluence	.06 (.06)	.12 (.05)*
Religious commitment	−.01 (.07)	−.01 (.07)
Union membership	.43 (.28)	.06 (.26)
Controls for political dispositions		
Interest in the campaign	.06 (.09)	.15 (.08)#
Labastida trait differential	.28 (.12)*	−.15 (.08)#
Identification with the PRI	.15 (.05)**	−.16 (.07)*
Ideological distance	−.02 (.02)	.02 (.02)
Zedillo approval rating	−.02 (.08)	.01 (.09)
Believe Mexico is democracy	.10 (.08)	.07 (.07)
Election will be clean	.09 (.13)	.08 (.11)
Constant term	−.27 (.17)	.53 (.13)**

Notes: # $p < .10$; * $p < .05$; ** $p < .01$. N = 2,355 (multiple imputation used for missing responses). The baseline choice category is planning to abstain or having no preference yet. The political disposition measures all come from the first (February) wave; vote choice was measured in the final (July) wave. No significant interactions were found between choices in the primary election and voting behavior from the 1994 presidential election.

Table 7.6. PRI Nomination Preferences and Expected Voting Behavior in the July 2000 Presidential Election

Voting Behavior on July 2, 2000	Primary Election Choice		
	Labastida	Madrazo, Bartlett, or Roque	Did Not Vote in Primary
Francisco Labastida	.36	.28	.25
Opposition candidate	.52	.56	.52
Did not vote	.12	.16	.23

Note: These probabilities were derived from the multinomial logistic regression coefficients in table 7.5. All control variables were set to their mean value.

According to the regression model, the probability that a Labastida primary voter would stick with the PRI on July 2 was .36, after controlling for all of the background and dispositional predictors. This is lower than the probability of support for the candidate in February (table 7.4, first column) but significantly higher than the 25 percent chance that is predicted among those who did not take part in the primary. Those who turned out in November to back Madrazo, Bartlett, or Roque were more inclined to vote on July 2, but they were not funneled into the opposition. The predicted ratio of opposition to PRI support for these respondents is 2.00 (that is, .56/.28). For citizens who did not take part in the primary, this ratio is slightly higher, at 2.08. In short, the long general election campaign helped heal the divisions that were so apparent in February.[34]

CONCLUSION

Political parties across the world all face the fundamental challenge of designing candidate recruitment rules that are fair but efficient, and ultimately edifying for the party. In democratizing nations undergoing rapid institutional and cultural changes, this can be a daunting task. There are many sound reasons for party leaders to conduct primaries: well-fought nomination contests can extend the potential base of support for the party; a primary can convey information about citizen preferences and judgments, which in turn can be useful as the party fashions policy positions and strategies; ambitious office seekers who do not receive the nomination may be less tempted to wage an independent insurgent campaign, as Cuauhtémoc Cárdenas did in 1988, if they were rejected by voters rather than by elites meeting behind closed doors; and by competing in open primaries, candidates may acquire campaigning skills and resources they otherwise would not have. None of this matters, however, if conflicts over candidate selection tarnish the image of the eventual nominee and alienate voters to such an extent that an election is lost.

For *priístas* striving to explain the party's defeat in July 2000, this latter possibility could have an air of plausibility. Many party officials criticized Ernesto Zedillo for a democratic reform process that went too far too quickly, with Francisco Labastida paying the heavy ultimate cost. The survey results described here offer an alternative picture.

Many within the PRI may wish to turn the clock back to a more authoritarian era in Mexican politics, when mass-level participation was carefully managed and party elders made the key decisions on candidate nominations. Such a thing might not be possible in an age of rising democratic sentiments. But even if it were, this analysis implies that it would not be electorally wise. In the final analysis, the PRI was not penalized for its open nomination system. Had the *dedazo* been retained in 1999, many Mexicans would have doubted the party's loudly trumpeted commitment to democratization. Under this scenario, one can easily imagine Labastida's standings in the polls sinking much more quickly and deeply.

Notes

I thank Jorge Domínguez, Chappell Lawson, Brandon Rottinghaus, Lee Wilson, Marcus Kurtz, Alejandro Poiré, and Federico Estévez for helpful comments.

1. Damian Fraser, "Survey of Mexico," *Financial Times*, November 23, 1994.

2. George W. Grayson, "A Guide to the November 7, 1999, PRI Presidential Primary," *Western Hemisphere Election Study Series* 17, study 4 (Washington, D.C.: CSIS Americas Program).

3. E.E. Schattschneider, *The Semisovereign People* (Hinsdale, Ill.: Dryden, 1960): 66.

4. On this point, see Frank Brandenburg, *The Making of Modern Mexico* (Englewood Cliffs, N.J.: Prentice-Hall, 1964).

5. On the eve of the 1988 election, for example, Gallup pollsters asked a representative sample of Mexican citizens whether the PRI should choose its presidential nominees through the *dedazo*, through a national assembly of the party, or through a vote by rank-and-file party members. Only 4 percent preferred leaving nomination decisions up to the president; 24 percent wanted a national assembly to be held, and six out of ten respondents supported a primary system. See Jorge I. Domínguez and James A. McCann, *Democratizing Mexico: Public Opinion and Electoral Choices* (Baltimore, Md.: Johns Hopkins University Press, 1996): 46. Even the

most ardent *priístas* had misgivings about the *dedazo*. Just 6 percent of those who rated the party at "10" on a ten-point evaluation scale believed that the president should continue selecting nominees; 62 percent favored primaries.

6. Federico Estévez and Alejandro Moreno, "Campaign Effects and Issue-Voting in the PRI Primary," presented at the meeting of the Latin American Studies Association, Miami, March 16–18, 2000.

7. Grayson, "A Guide," p. 5.

8. In recent years, major parties in many other transitional presidentialist democracies—Uruguay, Chile, Argentina, the Dominican Republic, Bulgaria, and South Korea, to name only a few—have experimented with direct primaries to select presidential candidates. Very little is known about how such reforms influence public opinion, partisan cohesiveness, and voting behavior in general elections.

9. Andrew Hacker, "Does a Divisive Primary Harm a Candidate's Election Chances?" *American Political Science Review* 59 (1965): 105–10.

10. Austin Ranney, "Candidate Selection," in David Butler, Howard R. Penniman, and Austin Ranney, eds., *Democracy at the Polls: A Comparative Study of National Elections* (Washington, D.C.: AEI, 1981): 97. On this point, see also Michael Gallagher, "Conclusion," in Michael Gallagher and Michael Walsh, eds., *Candidate Selection in Comparative Perspective* (Beverly Hills, Calif.: Sage, 1988), which deals with candidate selection procedures in European democracies; and Nelson W. Polsby, *Consequences of Party Reform* (Oxford: Oxford University Press, 1983), a critique of U.S. presidential primary elections in the wake of the McGovern-Fraser reforms.

11. This was most apparent in 1995, when President Zedillo moved to replace Madrazo. In state elections the previous year, *priístas* in Tabasco had grossly violated campaign finance regulations, and the governor's administration was widely viewed as among the most corrupt in the nation. Getting rid of Madrazo would be an early signal that the new president was serious about bringing integrity to Mexican politics. However, when news of Zedillo's intentions surfaced, Madrazo supporters took to the streets. The capital city was shut down, and opposition party activists who had been protesting electoral fraud were attacked. In response, the president backed down.

12. Grayson, "A Guide."

13. Mexican voters with long memories would recall that Bartlett oversaw the counting of votes in 1988, an election marked by widespread political harassment and fraud; see Domínguez and McCann, *Democratizing Mexico*, p. 151.

14. Michael Riley, "Many Uncertain about Mexico's First Presidential Primary," *Houston Chronicle*, September 19, 1999.

15. This quote appears in Federico Estévez and Alejandro Poiré, "Early Campaign Dynamics in the 2000 Mexican Presidential Election," presented at the meeting of the Midwest Political Science Association, Chicago, April 19–22, 2001.

16. On priming effects, see Dietram A. Scheufele, "Agenda-Setting, Priming, and Framing Revisited: Another Look at Cognitive Effects of Political Communication," *Mass Communication and Society* 3 (2000): 297–316.

17. Walter Lippmann, *Public Opinion* (New York: The Free Press, 1965 [1922]): 55.

18. On the potential positive effect of conflict during primaries, see Lonna Rae Atkeson, "From the Primaries to the General Election: Does a Divisive Nomination Race Affect a Candidate's Fortunes?" in William G. Mayer, ed., *In Pursuit of the White House, 2000* (New York: Chatham House, 2000); James A. McCann, "Nomination Politics and Ideological Polarization: Assessing the Attitudinal Effects of Campaign Involvement," *Journal of Politics* 57 (1995): 101–20; Walter J. Stone, Lonna Rae Atkeson, and Ronald B. Rapoport, "Turning On or Turning Off? Mobilization and Demobilization Effects of Participation in Presidential Nomination Campaigns," *American Journal of Political Science* 36 (1992): 665–91; and Emmett H. Buell, Jr., "Divisive Primaries and Participation in Presidential Campaigns: A Study of the 1984 New Hampshire Primary Activists," *American Politics Quarterly* 14 (1986): 376–90.

19. Quoted in John Ward and Molly Moore, "Fantastic Four Take to the Air; Mexican Ruling Party Sets Precedent with TV Debate in Presidential Race," *Washington Post*, September 9, 1999.

20. Atkeson, "From the Primaries," p. 292.

21. Estévez and Moreno, "Campaign Effects."

22. Estévez and Poiré, "Early Campaign Dynamics."

23. As we might expect, Madrazo's actions were most closely scrutinized for signs that he planned to exit the PRI. With many eyes on him, the second-place finisher declared his loyalty to the party on November 9. Over the next few days, the Tabasco governor took part in several joint appearances with Labastida. These gestures led many in the party to jump with joy. "I don't think anybody thought it was going to come out this well," declared a PRI pollster. "There's a clear victor ... and a humble loser. Does the world get any better than this?" (These sentiments are noted in Dudley Althaus and Michael Rile, "Primary Provides Boost for Mexico's Ruling Party," *Houston Chronicle*, November 9, 1999.) Such optimism was well founded, since public opinion polls at this juncture recorded a bounce for the party comparable to what U.S. parties typically experience after wrapping up their presidential nominations.

24. It was widely reported that approximately ten million citizens—or about one-sixth of the eligible electorate—participated in the primary, though estimates made by independent pollsters at the time varied; see Sam Dillon, "Mexican Pollsters Challenge Size of Turnout in the Primary," *New York Times*, November 16, 1999. The higher turnout rate gauged here is probably due to some combination of response bias—that is, primary voters being slightly more willing to be interviewed—and overreporting. The tendency for some citizens to say they took part in an election when in fact they did not is a troubling problem affecting research on political behavior in many countries.

25. This conclusion holds for two other markers of political engagement: general interest in politics and tendency to discuss politics with family and friends.

26. I thank Alejandro Moreno for sharing the *Reforma* report with me.

27. To retain all possible cases for this analysis, I made use of King et al.'s "multiple imputation" approach for missing survey responses. See Gary King, James Honaker, Anne Joseph, and Kenneth Scheve, "Analyzing Incomplete Political Sci-

ence Data: An Alternative Algorithm for Multiple Imputation," *American Political Science Review* 95 (2001): 49–69.

28. It is important to include these many control variables so that we can arrive at a good estimate of the unique effect of the primary on political attitudes during the general election campaign.

29. If the control variables are omitted from this model, a vote for Labastida in the primary has a much more pronounced effect on preferring the *priísta* over an opposition nominee in February.

30. These results substantiate the claim of Federico Estévez and Alejandro Poiré that, judging from survey responses in October 1999, intraparty conflict would take a heavy toll on the PRI in the 2000 election. See their "Early Campaign Dynamics."

31. Domínguez and McCann, *Democratizing Mexico*, chapters 4 and 5.

32. In this and subsequent models, trait ratings were measured in terms of candidate differentials—that is, the evaluation of Francisco Labastida minus the evaluation of the most highly rated major opposition candidate (Fox or Cárdenas). Along similar lines, party identification was cast as a differential. Individuals who strongly identified with one of the opposition parties were coded as –3; weak opposition identifiers were –2; leaning identifiers were –1; and those not espousing any party identification were set to zero. On the positive side of the scale, strong PRI identifiers were coded as 3; weak PRI identifiers were 2; and people leaning toward the PRI were set to 1. In the case of ideological distance away from the parties, a comparable scale was created: absolute distance away from the PRI, as measured on an eleven-point left-right scale, minus the absolute distance away from the opposition party closest to the respondent (either the PAN or PRD). The coding for the four other dispositional controls—interest in the campaign, presidential approval ratings, judgments about the Mexican political system, and expectations of fraud—was the same as in table 7.2.

33. See, for example, James A. McCann, Randall W. Partin, Ronald B. Rapoport, and Walter J. Stone, "Presidential Nomination Campaigns and Party Mobilization," *American Journal of Political Science* 40 (1996): 756–67; and Stone, Atkeson, and Rapoport, "Turning On or Turning Off?"

34. This verdict can be extended to more demanding neighborhood activism for the PRI. In our surveys, we asked respondents if they had attended local meetings on behalf of any political party. Approximately 10 percent reported doing so for the PRI. A regression model similar to the one in table 7.5 indicates that individuals who backed Madrazo, Bartlett, or Roque in the primary were as likely as Labastida's supporters to attend such functions; conflict over candidate selection *did not* lead to a breakdown in grassroots party mobilization.

PART III

Campaign Messages and Voter Responses

8

Television Coverage, Vote Choice, and the 2000 Campaign

CHAPPELL LAWSON

It is difficult to overstate the potential influence of television on Mexican political life. Over two-thirds of Mexicans get their information about politics primarily from the small screen, and even among the most affluent and educated segments of the population, television remains the dominant medium. Moreover, despite its traditional biases, television news is viewed as more credible than any other form of political communication in Mexico: print, radio, campaign advertisements, candidate speeches, conversations with friends and family, and the like.[1]

Of particular importance are Mexico's two main nightly newscasts, one on each of the country's commercial networks. Sandwiched between evening soap operas (*telenovelas*), they command some of the highest audience ratings for news programs in the world. At least seven times as many Mexicans rely on these two programs for information about politics as rely on all print media combined, and ten times as many rely on them as rely on conversations with relatives and acquaintances.[2] From the official beginning of the 2000 presidential campaign in mid-January until the end of June, these two programs devoted more than twenty-four hours of free airtime to the three main presidential candidates.[3]

In dramatic contrast to past elections, opposition candidate Vicente Fox received at least as much of this time as the ruling party's standard-bearer, Francisco Labastida. The 2000 race was thus Mexico's first presidential campaign in which opposition candidates were able to present themselves on a roughly equal footing with the Institutional Revolutionary Party (PRI). Crafting clever campaign messages may have mattered less for opposition figures when those messages never reached television audiences—that is, when the PRI was able to frame the contest unilaterally and to count on systematically favorable coverage. In 2000, however, voters were in a better position to evaluate political alternatives.

Other chapters in this volume discuss the content of campaign messages in greater detail, analyzing the development of candidate strategies and how these strategies found expression in debates and political advertisements. This chapter focuses on how the campaign was reported on Mexico's dominant medium—in other words, the extent to which the main presidential contenders were able to project the images they had crafted through regular media coverage. It also assesses the effect of this coverage on how Mexicans cast their ballots in July 2000.

The first section evaluates television news coverage in 2000, drawing on data from the Federal Electoral Institute (IFE), *Reforma* newspaper, the Mexican Academy of Human Rights, and a separate, detailed content analysis of the two leading nightly news programs. These data demonstrate that television coverage of the main presidential candidates was much more even-handed than in previous presidential races. Consequently, Fox was able to convey his message of "change" to voters, and Labastida was unable to rely on previously loyal allies in broadcasting to spin campaign events in a favorable way. Nevertheless, important differences persisted in the tone of campaign coverage on Mexico's two main networks: the country's largest broadcaster, Televisa, remained substantially more sympathetic toward the ruling party than its newer rival, Televisión Azteca.

The second section analyzes the effects of television coverage on voters' choices in 2000. This analysis demonstrates that exposure to television news exercised a powerful influence over voter choices in Mexico, with Televisión Azteca viewers switching toward the main opposition candidate. Ultimately, television coverage worked to Fox's advantage, helping to determine the outcome of the election.

TELEVISION COVERAGE

For over a decade, bias in favor of the PRI has made Mexico's leading broadcasters the object of ritual criticism by opposition and civic groups. In the presidential election of 1988, for instance, the quasi-monopolistic Televisa network devoted perhaps 80 percent of all air-time to the PRI, and even the limited coverage granted to opposition contenders was often nasty. Bias was so notorious that it became a campaign issue in its own right, with National Action Party (PAN) candidate Manuel Clouthier leading a crusade against Televisa anchorman Jacobo Zabludovsky and the program that he hosted (*24 Horas*).

Despite the emergence of a second private network, Televisión Azteca, in the early 1990s, bias persisted in the 1994 presidential campaign. PRI candidates received over half of all airtime in that race, while opposition parties had to make do with relatively scanty and hostile coverage.[4] Although coverage had changed profoundly by the midterm elections of 1997, many observers feared that the high stakes of a tight presidential race might trigger a return to the bad old days of collusion and censorship. Despite the protestations of network executives, accusations of media bias began to fly as the contest heated up.[5]

Volume of Coverage

How exactly did coverage on Mexico's principal news networks stack up in 2000? Measurements of the volume of coverage are remarkably consistent and generally supportive of the networks' claims of balance. Table 8.1 presents four aggregate measurements of television news coverage for the three major candidates from the official beginning of the campaign in February 2000 to the end of June that same year.[6]

Table 8.1. Volume of Coverage for Major Candidates

	Column 1	Column 2	Column 3	Column 4
Candidate (party/ coalition)	IFE (all news programming)	IFE (two main news shows)	*Reforma* (two networks)	MIT (two main news shows)
Labastida (PRI)	47%	34%	34%	33%
Fox (Alliance for Change)	31	39	36	36
Cárdenas (Alliance for Mexico)	23	28	29	30
Total	100%	100%	100%	100%

Data in column 1 of the table summarize coverage by all television news broadcasts across the country, as measured by the IFE. These figures suggest that the PRI's standard-bearer received a disproportionate share of news coverage, and critics of Mexican television were quick to point out these discrepancies as the campaign unfolded.[7] In an important sense, however, these figures are deeply misleading. The overall IFE data represent a mechanical summation of coverage across ninety different news programs, from the widely watched nightly news broadcasts on Televisión Azteca and Televisa to afternoon shows on small provincial stations. Some of these broadcasts, of course, commanded a vastly greater share of the audience than others. Among respondents in the Mexico 2000 Panel Study, for instance, approximately 93 percent of those who watched television news relied on one of the two major networks, and approximately two-thirds relied on one of two major nightly news programs (*Noticiero* of Televisa and *Hechos* of Televisión Azteca).[8] Only a tiny fraction of viewers reported watching any of the dozens of pro-government provincial news programs, each of which received equal weight with the main news broadcasts in the aggregate IFE sample. Thus, although the data in column 1 presumably represent an accurate count of what was broadcast during the campaign, they bear little relation to what Mexican viewers actually saw.

The next three columns focus on television coverage on the two national networks (Televisa and Televisión Azteca) that dominate Mexican broadcasting. Column 2 shows IFE figures for the two major news programs alone; column 3 shows summary data from *Reforma* newspaper's monitoring of the two major networks; and column 4 summarizes the results of a separate content analysis from a random sample of *Hechos* and *Noticiero* programming during the campaign. Because the methodologies and programs analyzed varied somewhat, the figures are not identical.[9] All three, though, reveal the same basic tendency: major-party candidates received roughly equivalent shares of airtime. Fox received the most coverage, followed by Labastida (PRI) and Cuauhtémoc Cárdenas (Alliance for Mexico). According to all measurements, Labastida's share of the coverage was substantially below his party's share of the vote in past elections, while Cárdenas's was consistently higher than a nonpartisan observer might expect.

Aggregate measures of time, of course, can be a misleading indicator of the bias in the volume of coverage. It may be, for example, that the distribution of time over the course of the campaign indirectly favored one candidate. For instance, heavy coverage of one opposition candidate in the beginning of the campaign might have helped establish him as the front-runner among the PRI's main rivals, thus creating a bandwagon among those voters whose principal objective was to defeat the ruling party. Similarly, scanty coverage at key periods of the campaign (such as during the closing rallies, for example) might have proved problematic for any of the major candidates. To the extent that Labastida received disproportionate airtime during the last few weeks of the campaign, as some observers charged, there could still be important biases in the volume of coverage.

Figure 8.1 shows coverage of each major-party candidate as a percentage of the airtime devoted to those three candidates on the main networks by week from January to July, according to the *Reforma* data. The top layer represents Labastida; the middle layer, Cárdenas's Alliance for Mexico; and the bottom layer, Fox's Alliance for Change. With the exception of a slight expansion in Cárdenas's share toward the end of the campaign, there are no obvious secular trends in the data. In terms of quantity of coverage, then, Mexico's major networks appear to have behaved themselves rather well.

Figure 8.1. Breakdown of Network News Coverage of Main Candidates by Week

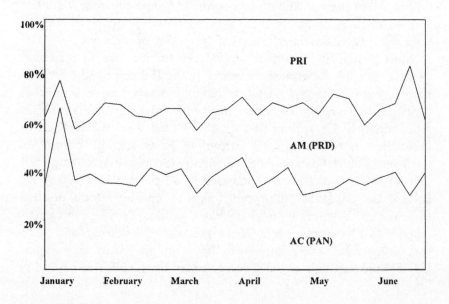

Tone of Coverage

Focusing exclusively on the quantity of time devoted to each candidate, of course, may obscure striking differences in the quality of coverage. Unfortunately, tone of coverage is more difficult to measure than volume. These measurement problems are compounded by the fact that, to an even greater degree than volume, tone often reflects the actions of the candidates themselves. At the beginning of the campaign, for instance, Fox was given to inflammatory statements that seemed calculated to attract media attention, despite the reputation they gave him for antics and negative campaigning. Accusing the PRI of institutionalized involvement in drug trafficking (a charge that led the ruling party to file suit with electoral authorities), poking fun at his opponent's stature, using crass language and gestures, and other outrageous tactics all played an important role in building up Fox's image as a forceful leader and aggressive opponent of the regime, despite the fact that such tactics were often criticized. By contrast, Labastida went out of his way to cultivate a refined, presidential image. He made fewer gaffes than Fox, even at the risk of appearing bland and colorless. This approach was a classic front-runner's strategy, designed to maintain an early lead and to avoid alienating undecided voters. The flip side of Labastida's low-testosterone style, however, was that it aroused less intense support from PRI loyalists. His refined demeanor also sometimes left him looking, at least by comparison to the more *macho* Fox, a bit fey. All of these qualities came across in media coverage, both live and scripted. As a result, there was anecdotal evidence to support widely divergent characterizations of the quality of coverage.

More systematic, quantitative evidence on the tone of television news is mixed. Global measurements by the IFE across all television news programs suggest that Mexican broadcasters were somewhat gentler with Francisco Labastida than with either of his main rivals. Approximately 2.8 percent of Labastida's time was characterized as "positive," in contrast to 2.3 percent of Fox's and 1.7 percent of Cárdenas's. Labastida also received slightly less negative coverage (2.1 percent of his total airtime), compared to 4.5 percent for Fox and 2.3 percent for Cárdenas. Subtracting negative coverage from positive coverage and dividing by total coverage, Labastida's net positive coverage was 0.7 percent, while Cárdenas's was −0.6 percent, and Fox's was −2.2 percent. These differences, however, are hardly overwhelming, and the vast bulk of the coverage coded by the IFE was neutral in tone.

References to the main candidates on television news programs (that is, aural cues) show more or less the same trend. What slight differences did exist tended to work in favor of Labastida, who had a net positive score of 0.9 percent (compared to −1.8 percent for Fox and 0.0 percent for Cárdenas).[10] The overwhelming majority of references (over 93 percent for all three candidates), however, were coded as neutral in tone.

As with volume of coverage, global assessments of the tone of coverage mask striking differences between provincial broadcasters (generally more sympathetic to Labastida) and the main networks based in the Federal District (which treated Fox quite well). According to the IFE data, Fox scored well on the news programs that really mattered. He garnered 82 percent of all the coverage on programs broadcast from the Federal District that the IFE considered "positive," while Labastida received only 8 percent. Subtracting negative coverage from positive coverage and dividing by total coverage, we find that Fox did the best of the three candidates on programs broadcast from the capital (a net positive rating of 0.8 percent, compared to −0.9 percent for Cárdenas and −1.5 percent for Labastida).[11] Thus, when the behavior of provincial broadcasters is taken into account, the IFE data offer little evidence to support the notion that Mexico's major networks were biased in favor of Labastida. On the contrary, coverage of Fox on the major networks was more favorable than coverage of either Labastida or Cárdenas.

Data from *Reforma* newspaper's monitoring efforts tell a somewhat different story. Compared to the IFE, *Reforma* was less circumspect in coding the tone of news stories. About half of all time in the *Reforma* data set is classified as either positive or negative, in contrast to about 5 percent of airtime in the IFE coding. Although potentially more subjective, this coding offers a much larger stock of qualified coverage to analyze. Figure 8.2 summarizes net positive coverage of the three major candidates on the two main networks, according to the *Reforma* data.

As the figure shows, *Reforma*'s coding strongly suggests bias in favor of Labastida. Overall, Labastida's net positive rating from January to June was 36 percent; Cárdenas's was 26 percent, and Fox's was 12 percent. Although differences between the two leading candidates diminished as the campaign picked up steam, Labastida's coverage remained noticeably more positive than Fox's and equivalent to Cárdenas's. In June, for instance, Labastida's net positive rating was 44 percent, compared to 42 percent for Cárdenas and 21 percent for Fox.

Figure 8.2. Tone of Network Coverage of Major-Party Candidates
(*Reforma* data)

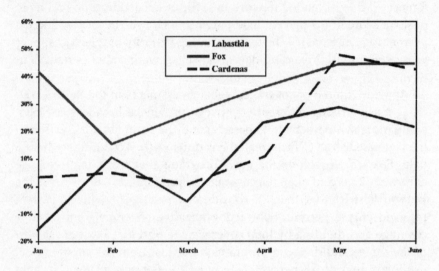

Interestingly, and contrary to impressionistic claims reported in the popular press, the *Reforma* data do not suggest that coverage became more biased toward Labastida in the course of the campaign. *Reforma's* figures suggest that coverage in fact became more favorable for the opposition.[12] Although Fox's coverage ranged from 17 percent net positive to 10 percent net positive in the first three months of the campaign, during April–June it rose to between 21 and 28 percent. The change in Cárdenas's net positive rating was even more dramatic—from single digits in the first three months of the campaign to 48 percent in May.

MIT Analysis of Tone

To address the issue of tone in a more systematic way, we conducted a detailed examination of the two main nightly news programs—*Hechos* on Televisión Azteca and *Noticiero* on Televisa. This analysis, conducted at the Massachusetts Institute of Technology (MIT), drew on a randomly selected sample of forty news broadcasts (twenty from each program) during the period February 18 to June 30—a period timed to coincide with the Mexico 2000 Panel Study.[13] To facilitate comparison with IFE and *Reforma* data, we included measurements of the total time in the program, the total time assigned to the presidential campaigns, the time assigned to each of the three major-party candidates, and the time assigned to the three main political parties.[14] (As shown in table 8.1, sample data are similar to those collected by *Reforma* and the IFE.) Rather than replicate the more comprehensive counts of time done by *Reforma* or the IFE, however, our goal was to examine a representative sample of programming in greater detail. To this end, we included some fifty separate measures of television coverage. For instance, we recorded the average length of the sound bite (in seconds) that each candidate received, the order of campaign stories (that is, which candidate appeared first and which last in the campaign segment of the broadcast), and a range of related metrics.

Coding of stories by the IFE and *Reforma*, like most traditional content analysis, focused on narration and aural cues. To capture these sorts of cues, we recorded the number of references to each major candidate, as well as the type of reference (to the candidate's honesty or character, competence, chances of winning, or other); the tone of the reference (positive or negative); and the source of the reference (anchor or reporter, other party, government official, or other). For instance, aspersions cast by Fox on Labastida's manhood were coded as negative references to the PRI candidate's character by another party. A poll by an independent survey research firm showing Cárdenas in first place among voters in the Federal District was coded as a positive reference to the PRD's chances of winning from an "other" source.

In addition to these traditional measures, however, we devoted substantial attention to the coding of images. We counted each shot as a separate image, so that a new image was recorded and evaluated every time the camera angle changed.[15] We then recorded the total number of images devoted to each candidate, from which we calculated the average number of shots per story.[16] We also recorded whether the images presented in each story were real-time (that is, from events addressed in the story, typically that day), file (from previously recorded events), or static (photographs of the candidate or party symbols).[17] Third, we recorded the type of aural cues that accompanied each image in the story. These cues were divided into four types: (1) voice-and-image, in which a candidate's own voice could be heard while his image also appeared on the screen; (2) quote-and-image, in which the anchor or reporter paraphrased the candidate while the candidate's image appeared on the screen; (3) image-only, in which the anchor or reporter presented the story with footage of the candidate but without any direct citations; and (4) voice-only, in which only the candidate's voice was heard, with no image of him on the screen (as in a telephone interview with the candidate).[18]

Finally, each image was coded into one of thirteen categories: (1) pan or aerial shots of a large supportive crowd; (2) shots of the candidate with a supportive crowd; (3) the candidate accompanied by a popular personality, such as an entertainer, clergyman, or athlete; (4) an interview of the candidate with an agreeable interviewer; (5) an interview with a supporter of the candidate; (6) the candidate surrounded by reporters; (7) the candidate alone; (8) the candidate speaking to a passive audience, typically in a formal setting; (9) shots of a disturbance at the candidate's event; (10) the candidate with an unsupportive crowd or heckler; (11) an interview of the candidate with an aggressive or hostile interviewer; (12) an interview with a critic of the candidate; and (13) other shots during the story.[19] As a final, composite measure of tone, these types of images were then combined into positive, negative, and neutral categories. Pan or aerial shots of a large supportive crowd, shots of the candidate with supporters, images of the candidate accompanied by a popular personality, interviews of the candidate by an agreeable interviewer, and interviews with a supporter of the candidate were coded as positive images. The opposite categories were coded as negative images (with the exception that there were no images of candidates with generally detested or unpopular figures). Finally, images of the candidate alone, the candidate surrounded by reporters, or passive audiences listening to the candidate's speech were coded as neutral, as were "other" images. The measure of "net positive images" represented positive images minus negative images, divided by total images.

Overall results from this analysis are startlingly consistent. Combining Televisión Azteca and Televisa broadcasts, there are very few detectable differences in the quality of coverage across the three major candidates. As table 8.2 shows, all three candidates received roughly equally negative aural cues.[20] All three also received about the same number of shots of the candidate with supporters, as well as close to the same number of coveted pan/aerial shots of the large crowds attending their respective rallies. And net positive images, perhaps the best summary measure of visual tone, were similar across the three candidates.

Certain other metrics suggest that coverage actually favored Fox. For instance, Fox was more likely than the other two main candidates to appear first or last in the campaign segment of the broadcast. Coverage of Fox was also visually richer than coverage of Labastida or Cárdenas, with a somewhat greater number of images per story and a substantially greater number of images overall. Images of Fox were also more likely to be accompanied by voice, allowing him to speak directly to the audience more frequently than either of his rivals.

Table 8.2. Tone of Network News Coverage of the Main Candidates

	Labastida	Fox	Cárdenas
Percent of times appearing first or last	33%	37%	30%
Net positive characterizations	−80%	−72%	−79%
Average length of sound bite (seconds)[a]	25.6	23.6	26.7
Total images in sample	442	500	426
Total number of stories in sample	81	82	74
Average number of images per story	5.5	6.1	5.8
Percent voice-and-image	20%	27%	23%
Percent real-time images	84%	77%	82%
Pan/aerial shots of supporting crowd	43	37	32
Shots of candidate with supporters	106	94	104
Net positive images	38%	35%	36%

[a] Excluding April 25 (which showed cuts from the first debate) and June 28 (after the end of the campaign).

Even many of the subtle differences in coverage that appeared to favor Labastida are attributable to innocent reasons. For instance, campaign coverage of Fox was moderately less likely to include real-time footage. The reason appears to be that Fox habitually took one business day off from campaigning each week during the early phases of the campaign, retiring to his farm in Guanajuato. Reporters who wished to include stories about Fox in their daily coverage were thus forced to substitute stock footage. Similarly, Fox's sound bites were on average slightly shorter than those of his main rivals. The reason appears to be that Fox obligingly summarized his main points for the cameras in pithy, punchy, and sometimes crass phases—a quality that definitely did *not* damage his electoral prospects.

Beyond these aggregate figures, however, there does appear to have been a significant shift in tone during the second half of the sample. Cárdenas and Labastida both did better in the May–June period; Fox did correspondingly worse. Like the *Reforma* data, these figures reveal a surge in positive coverage of Cárdenas in the second half of the campaign. Unlike both the *Reforma* and IFE data, however, data from our sample corroborate anecdotal impressions about shifts in coverage of the other two candidates. Although visuals of the Alliance for Change remained positive on balance, the tone of coverage shifted sharply against Fox. Fox's net positive score was just under 38 percent in the first half of the campaign, dropping to slightly over 32 percent net positive in May–June (a change of about −5 percent). By contrast, Cárdenas's net positive score jumped from 16 to 53 percent, and Labastida's increased from 25 to 48 percent. Fox thus went from being the candidate with the most favorable coverage to the one with the worst.

The turning point in the sample appears to have been late April, a period that coincides with the aftermath of the first presidential debate. This timing is manifestly suspicious, as the first debate was widely considered a victory for Fox and was followed by a decline in Labastida's lead in most polls. In the wake of the debate, senior figures in the PRI (such as Labastida adviser and former deputy interior minister Emilio Gamboa) applied intense pressure on broadcasters to grant more favorable coverage to Labastida and undercut his principal adversary. It is also possible that the ruling party consciously encouraged the networks (in particular, Televisa) to improve coverage of Cárdenas in the hope that more favorable coverage of the Left would erode part of Fox's support.

In addition to these changes over time, there were important differences in coverage between the two networks. The bulk of the visuals that supported Labastida, it turns out, actually came from Televisa. Televisión Azteca coverage, by contrast, was slightly more favorable toward Fox than it was toward the PRI candidate. On that network, Fox's net positive images rating was 37 percent, about the same as Cárdenas's and 5 percent higher than Labastida's. On Televisa, by contrast, Fox's net positive score was 31 percent, in contrast to 34 percent for Cárdenas and 49 percent for Labastida. Overall, then, Fox received balanced coverage from Televisión Azteca over the course of the campaign. Coverage on Televisa, by contrast, was somewhat biased in favor of Labastida.

MEDIA EFFECTS IN 2000

Content analysis suggests that overall coverage of the 2000 race on Mexico's primary medium was relatively balanced. Even on Televisa, where visuals were least kind to Fox, the main opposition candidate received generally favorable coverage. All three candidates clearly had the chance to get their messages out to voters. Under the circumstances, the overall impact of television news on voters' attitudes and behavior is not immediately obvious.

On the other hand, different segments of the Mexican electorate were clearly exposed to different messages over the course of the campaign. Despite the similarity in volume, the tone of coverage on Televisión Azteca was substantially more sympathetic to Fox than was reporting on Televisa. Consequently, we might expect viewership of Televisa to be associated with increased support for Labastida, while Televisión Azteca viewership ought to favor Fox.

To test this hypothesis, we employ data from the first and fourth waves of the Mexico 2000 Panel Study (conducted, respectively, in February and July). Our analysis relies on multinomial logistic regression on voter choice in July, in which partisan preferences were coded into one of four categories: (1) Labastida, (2) Fox, (3) Cárdenas, and (4) all other responses, including undecideds, supporters of the minor parties, and nonvoters. Our analysis attempts to control for other influences that were correlated both with voters' choices and with media exposure—in other words, those variables that could potentially exercise a confounding effect. To a certain extent, the panel nature of the data effectively takes into account some of these confounding variables, as it allows us to consider changes in the opinions of individual citizens. Nevertheless, it may be that certain background factors not only encouraged voters to favor Fox at the beginning of the race but also made voters more likely to switch to him over the course of the campaign. For instance, if more educated voters relied disproportionately on Televisión Azteca (as they in fact do), and if they were more likely to switch toward Fox during the campaign for reasons that had nothing to do with the television cues they received, omitting education from the analysis would make the effect of Televisión Azteca coverage appear greater than it actually was.

In order to control for such potentially confounding factors, we included a range of variables in the analysis. Table 8.3 divides these variables into three categories—demographic factors, prior attitudes, and campaign influences—which together constitute a fairly comprehensive set of controls.

Note that this model includes two variables dealing with network news: (1) which network the respondent preferred for news coverage,[21] and (2) the amount of news programming the respondent reported watching on both of the main networks.[22] The first variable serves as an additional control for political attitudes. In Mexico, preferences for one network over another sometimes reflect opinions about politics, with opposition voters favoring Televisión Azteca and pro-government viewers preferring Televisa. It is theoretically possible that network preference indicated underlying propensities to change one's vote during the campaign that were not fully captured by measures of ideology, vote preference in February, and attitudes toward the main presidential candidates, or by the panel nature of the data.[23]

Table 8.3. Variables Included in Analysis of Media Effects

Demographics	Prior Attitudes	Campaign Influences
Age	Vote preference in February	Radio listenership
Gender	Rating of Labastida in February	Newspaper readership
Education	Rating of Fox in February	Frequency respondent talked about politics
Income proxy (index of household items)	Rating of Cárdenas in February	Self-reported exposure to Labastida advertisements
Ethnicity (skin color)	Ideological self-identification in February	Self-reported exposure to Fox advertisements
Region (north, center, Mexico City/México State, or south)	Television network preference in February	Self-reported exposure to Cárdenas advertisements
Urban/rural		Weekly Televisa viewership
Union membership (respondent or spouse)		Weekly Azteca viewership
Beneficiary of a federal welfare program (e.g., Progresa)		
Church attendance		

The results suggest that exposure to network news exercised a statistically significant influence on voting behavior in the 2000 election, controlling for other factors.[24] Of the variables included in the model, only the following were statistically significant predictors of voting for Fox over Labastida: age, voting intention in February, ratings of Fox and Labastida in February, ideology, union membership, and viewership of Televisión Azteca. All of these variables operated in the expected direction; voters who were younger, liked Fox, disliked Labastida, intended to vote for Fox in February, considered themselves centrists or leftists, did not belong to a union, and watched Televisión Azteca news turned to Fox. By contrast, most demographic variables had little effect once preferences at the start of the campaign were taken into account.

To give a sense of the relative magnitudes of these effects, table 8.4 shows the marginal impacts of these statistically significant variables on the probability of voting for one of the two main candidates (with other variables held at their mean values).[25]

Table 8.4. Results of Multinomial Logistic Regression Analysis on Voting Intention

Variable	Marginal Influence on Likelihood of Voting for:		Net Change in Chance of Supporting Fox over Labastida
	Labastida	Fox	
Age*	2%	−15%	−17%
Vote for Labastida in February**	28	−6	−34
Vote for Fox in February**	−10	32	42
Opinion of Labastida in February**	28	−14	−42
Opinion of Fox in February**	−17	18	35
Ideology (higher is political right)*	9	−4	−12
Union membership†	8	−6	−14
Weekly TV Azteca viewership*	−4	11	15
N = 953			
Chi-square statistic = 725			
Cox and Snell statistic = .53			

†$p < .10$; *$p < .05$; **$p < .01$.

As the data indicate, the effect of television coverage was substantial. This remains true even when television is placed in comparison with other familiar influences (age, union membership, ideology, and so on).

Figures 8.3a and 8.3b present the results for television exposure in graphic terms. They show the effects of Televisa and Televisión Azteca viewership on the chance of voting for Fox and Labastida, with other variables held at their mean values.[26] As the figures indicate, Televisión Azteca viewership was associated with dramatic increases in support for Fox and a corresponding decrease in support for Labastida. The effects from Televisa were more ambiguous and not statistically significant for either candidate; the principal effect of exposure to Televisa news coverage, in fact, was increased support for both major candidates at the expense of undecided voters.[27]

At first glance, these results might seem somewhat puzzling. After all, Televisa was more biased than Televisión Azteca, but only Televisión Azteca coverage had a statistically significant effect. In addition, Televisa coverage appears to have helped Fox as much as Labastida (although neither effect is statistically significant). Why did television coverage have the effect it did?

The most likely answer lies in the nature of media influence in Mexico. Traditionally, exposure to information about politics has been a powerful predictor of support for the opposition. In a society where one party had controlled the executive branch for seventy-one years, many citizens lacked enough knowledge about the political opposition to feel comfortable voting for a change.[28] Access to virtually any kind of information—whether from newspapers, radio, television, political advertisements, opposition party activists, or simply conversations about politics with friends and family—typically worked to the advantage of Mexico's opposition parties.[29]

In the absence of pronounced bias, exposure to television news should benefit Fox. Because Televisa coverage was biased against Fox, however, this normally pronounced effect was attenuated. Bias on Televisa also erased the normally negative influence of exposure to political information on attitudes toward the PRI. Televisión Azteca viewers, on the other hand, were exposed to relatively balanced coverage. Therefore, Televisión Azteca viewership worked powerfully in favor of Fox and against Labastida.

Figure 8.3a. Marginal Effects of Exposure to Network Television on Probability of Voting for Vicente Fox

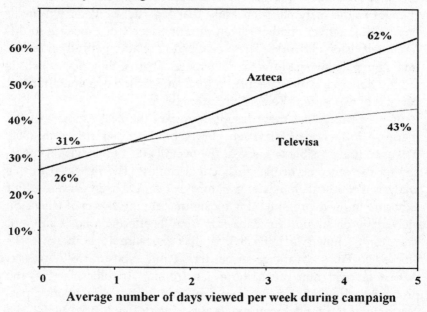

Average number of days viewed per week during campaign

Figure 8.3b. Marginal Effects of Exposure to Network Television on Probability of Voting for Francisco Labastida

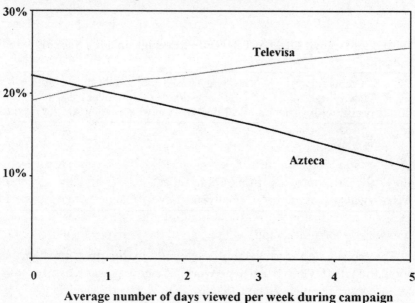

Average number of days viewed per week during campaign

Estimating Aggregate Media Effects

The data presented in table 8.4 and figures 8.3a and 8.3b represent changes in the marginal probability that a particular voter will favor one candidate over another, given differing levels of exposure to different television networks. These results do not automatically translate into aggregate swings in voter preference. That is, they do not tell us exactly how many more people, in total, appear to have voted for Fox because of exposure to Televisión Azteca news.

If we assume that these results represent the best estimate of the marginal influence of television viewership on voter choice in 2000, however, it is possible to guess at the overall effect of television coverage on the outcome of the presidential contest. The first step in this analysis is to calculate the net gain for Fox over Labastida as a result of exposure to news programming by subtracting the effects of television viewership on support for Labastida from its effects on Fox's support. The result, shown in table 8.5, is that exposure to both networks worked to Fox's advantage in net terms, but exposure to Televisión Azteca favored him much more. Controlling for other factors, the probability of voting for Fox over Labastida increased by about 5 percent among those who watched Televisa every day.[30] By contrast, the net gain for Fox associated with Azteca viewership reached as high as 47 percent for those who were most exposed.

Table 8.5. Marginal Effect of Television Coverage on Fox's Support over Labastida

Self-reported Viewership (days per week)	Net Change for Fox over Labastida (Televisa)	Net Change for Fox over Labastida (TV Azteca)
1	0%	8%
2	2	17
3	3	27
4	4	37
5 or more	5	47

The second step is to weight these effects by the proportion of the population that viewed each network. Weighting is necessary both because more people watched Televisa than watched Televisión Azteca and because more people watched the news occasionally rather than every day. Thus, although the effects of heavy exposure to Televisión Azteca news may have been devastating for Labastida, only a small fraction of the population received such heavy exposure.

About 62 percent of respondents in the first (nationally representative) round of the Mexico 2000 Panel Study reported watching Televisa news at least occasionally, the bulk of them watching one or two days per week.[31] Approximately 46 percent of the sample reported watching some news on Televisión Azteca; about three-quarters of them watched only once or twice a week. One-quarter of respondents reported watching some news programming on both networks, and approximately 18 percent of the sample reported never watching either. Self-reported exposure to television news is shown in table 8.6.

Table 8.6. Television News Viewership in Mexico 2000 Panel Study

Days per Week	Percent of Sample (Televisa news)	Percent of Sample (TV Azteca news)
1	26%	20%
2	19	13
3	13	9
4	2	2
5 or more	2	1

Weighting the effects of exposure to television news by the proportion of respondents so exposed yields a striking result. Overall, exposure to Televisa had very little influence on Fox's margin of victory; the net effect of Televisa news was to raise Fox's lead over Labastida by about 1.0 percent. By contrast, Televisión Azteca coverage was responsible for a swing toward Fox of 7.6 percent—slightly more than Fox's actual margin of victory. Extrapolating from the marginal influences of television coverage on voting behavior that were found in the panel sample, then, the effects of Televisión Azteca coverage were large enough to change the outcome of the election.

This swing of 7.6 percent, of course, captures the difference between watching Televisión Azteca and watching nothing at all—that is, not being exposed to the information and images contained in Televisión Azteca's broadcasts. A more plausible scenario is to consider what would have happened if Televisión Azteca's treatment of the presidential contenders had resembled Televisa's. In that case, television coverage of the campaign would still have worked marginally to Fox's advantage, but the effects would have been substantially attenuated. Instead of a 7 to 8 percent net gain, Fox could have expected a net gain over Labastida of approximately 1 percent. All else equal, he would have lost the election.

These extrapolations are necessarily speculative. They depend upon the validity of the model developed from panel data and its generalizability to the bulk of the population. Perhaps most importantly, they rely on self-reported viewership rates, which yield substantially higher estimates of audience size than actual ratings data. Nevertheless, the magnitude of the effects noted here are impressive, and it seems clear that television news coverage of the campaign exercised a powerful effect on voters' choices.

This point is all the more trenchant when we recall that even Televisa coverage was strikingly more balanced in 2000 than it had been in any previous presidential contest. Unlike 1988 and 1994, biases were relatively constrained and subtle. At the very least, then, these findings suggest that old-style television coverage would have made opposition victory in the 2000 election exceedingly difficult. Vicente Fox would have been unable to present his messages and image to the electorate— or at least to present them in such a compelling and attractive fashion. Unable to get a fair hearing on Mexico's dominant medium, he might never have converted political opportunity into electoral success.

Notes

Measurements of television coverage presented here are drawn in part from a content analysis supervised by the author and conducted primarily by Mariana Sanz. I am grateful to *Reforma* newspaper, the Federal Electoral Institute, and Edmundo Berumen for providing data from their analyses of Mexican television coverage, as well as to the Mexican Academy of Human Rights for providing recordings of the news programs with which to conduct the more detailed content analysis reported here. An examination of television influences across various stages of the 2000 campaign is provided in Chappell Lawson and James McCann, "Television Coverage, Media Effects, and Mexico's 2000 Elections" (manuscript under review), which supports the main findings in this chapter.

1. Mexico 2000 Panel Study, first wave (February).

2. Data taken from the Mexico 2000 Panel Study (first wave), which included a battery of questions on the credibility of different sources.

3. Author's analysis of data from the Federal Electoral Institute's media monitoring effort, described further below. Monitoring by *Reforma* newspaper (also described further below) indicates that total coverage of the three main candidates on

the two networks from January 1 to June 28 exceeded seventy-three hours. Paid advertising on the networks during the same time period reached twenty-five hours; for details, see Alejandro Moreno's contribution to this volume.

4. Data for 1988 are from Pablo Arredondo Ramírez, Gilberto Fregoso Peralta, and Raúl Trejo Delarbre, *Así se calló el sistema: comunicación y elecciones en 1988* (Guadalajara: Universidad de Guadalajara, 1991) and from the author's interviews with Ricardo Alemán of *La Jornada* newspaper, who undertook a similar study of the 1988 campaign (Mexico City, September 1996). Data from 1994 are from the Mexican Academy of Human Rights and the Civic Alliance. See also Chappell Lawson, *Building the Fourth Estate: Democratization and the Rise of a Free Press in Mexico* (Berkeley: University of California Press, 2002): 52–55, 159–61.

5. See Mony de Swaan, "Altibajos en la difusión," *Milenio Diario*, May 21, 2000; Mony de Swaan, "Crece la disparidad" (manuscript, May 2000); Mony de Swaan, Carolina Gómez, and Juan Molinar Horcasitas, "Medios y objetividad," *Milenio Diario*, June 25, 2000; Juan Molinar Horcasitas, "Medios de información," in "Cinco temas vistos por consejeros electorales," *Milenio Semanal*, June 11, 2000; Mark Stevenson, "Pressure Increases on Mexican Media," Associated Press, June 20, 2000; Julia Preston, "Mexican TV, Unshackled by Reform, Fights for Viewers," *New York Times*, June 7, 2000; Guadalupe Irízar, "Es equidad tema central en Televisa," *Reforma*, May 9, 2000; Ramón Sevilla Turcios, "Alertan sobre favoritismo en televisoras," *Reforma*, April 27, 2000.

6. Data for the three minor candidates are excluded.

7. See de Swaan, Gómez, and Molinar Horcasitas, "Medios y objetividad."

8. The figure was 92.9 percent in the first (nationally representative) wave of the panel, in February 2000 (N = 2,398). In the second (nationally representative) cross-sectional survey in July 2000 (N = 1,199) the figure was 93.3 percent. In the February sample, 63 percent reported watching primarily one of the two nightly news programs; in the July cross-section, that figure was 69 percent. Up to two news programs were recorded for each respondent; figures here are for the first news program mentioned.

9. The IFE's monitoring was conducted by Berumen and Associates; it relied on a comprehensive count of time for each show monitored. *Reforma's* monitoring was conducted for twelve hours every day in three different times: early morning (6 through 10 a.m.), early afternoon (1 through 4 p.m.), and evening prime time (7 through 11 p.m.); every type of program broadcast in the corresponding time and channels was monitored: news programs, sports, soap operas, entertainment shows, and so on. The MIT content analysis is described further below.

10. That is, 2.8 percent of references to Fox were positive (compared to 1.7 percent for Cárdenas and 3.0 percent for Labastida), while 4.0 percent of references to Fox were negative (compared to 1.7 percent for Cárdenas and 2.1 percent for Labastida).

11. For Labastida, 0.3 percent of time was coded as positive and 1.8 percent was coded as negative; for Fox, 3.3 percent of time was coded as positive and 2.4 percent as negative; for Cárdenas, 0.6 percent of time was coded as positive and 1.4 percent as negative.

12. This trend is also visible, though to a lesser extent, in the IFE data.

13. Days selected were: February 25, March 3, March 13, March 17, March 20, March 22, March 27, April 13, April 17, April 25, May 2, May 4, May 8, May 12, June 1, June 7, June 13, June 14, June 28, and June 30; collectively, this represented approximately 20 percent of the total coverage. To maximize the validity and reliability of the data, the coding scheme was piloted three times—and tweaked each time to amend the categories or clarify coding criteria—on news broadcasts not included in the sample. Inter-coder reliability varied somewhat by category but was uniformly high. For time, it was over 90 percent; for coding of images (described below), it was over 75 percent.

14. In the last case, only stories that specifically mentioned the party were counted. For instance, a story on a local government would be counted toward a party's total only if the partisan affiliation of the administration in question were named (for example, the PAN administration in Jalisco or the PRD government of the Federal District).

15. In the sample we analyzed, the number of different images per story ranged from one to forty.

16. This metric was designed to speak directly to a finding by investigators from the Mexican Academy of Human Rights that coverage of the PRI during the 1994 presidential campaign tended to employ a larger number of shots—and thus to be more visually appealing—than coverage of the opposition parties. See Patricia Cruz, "Cómo ver las campañas electorales por televisión" (Mexico City: Mexican Academy of Human Rights, 1997); Patricia Cruz, "La práctica de la ética en los medios de comunicación" (Mexico City: Mexican Academy of Human Rights, 1997).

17. One criticism of Mexican television in the past was its excessive reliance on file footage of opposition figures, especially Cárdenas. See Cruz, "Cómo ver las campañas electorales por televisión" and Cruz, "La práctica de la ética en los medios de comunicación."

18. These measures were designed to get at earlier types of media bias that might not be picked up by other codings. Throughout the Salinas administration (1988–1994), for instance, Televisa virtually never presented voice-and-image shots of Cárdenas.

19. Other images included shots of a landscape, an unknown speaker, or the president (not with the candidate). Collectively, "other" images accounted for approximately 16 percent of the total, most of which were sui generis.

20. The bulk of these references were simply media reports of candidates or their proxies attacking each other. Only thirty-seven (20 percent) qualified references were made by anchors or reporters. Of these thirty-seven, twelve referred to Labastida (of which two were positive), twelve to Fox (of which five were positive), and thirteen to Cárdenas (all of which were negative).

21. Respondents were asked whether they watched any particular news program and which news program that was. They were then asked if they also watched any other news program and, if so, which one. For those respondents who named programs on more than one network, network preference was measured by the news show they named first.

22. For each news program they mentioned, respondents were asked how many days per week they watched it.

23. The results are virtually identical when only the second of these variables is included for each network.

24. Alternative statistical models, such as using a simultaneous equations approach to correct for potential switching from one network to another over the course of the campaign, reveal the same results. For details, see Lawson and McCann, "Television Coverage, Media Effects, and Mexico's 2000 Elections." The model presented here was chosen for ease of interpretation.

25. The base case from which these marginal probabilities are derived is the mean of all continuous variables and the mode of all categorical variables. In the base case, 25 percent of voters supported Labastida, 24 percent supported Fox, 6 percent supported Cárdenas, and 44 percent were undecided, did not vote, or supported one of the minor parties.

26. Categorical variables were held at their modal values.

27. Neither network had a significant effect on support for Cárdenas.

28. See Beatriz Magaloni, "A Bayesian Retrospective Model of Electoral Choice in Dominant Party Systems," presented at the meeting of the American Political Science Association, Washington, D.C., August 28–31, 1997; Jorge I. Domínguez and Alejandro Poiré, eds., *Toward Mexico's Democratization: Parties, Campaigns, Elections, and Public Opinion* (New York: Routledge, 1999).

29. Lawson, *Building the Fourth Estate*, pp. 163–69; Domínguez and Poiré, *Toward Mexico's Democratization*; Jorge I. Domínguez and James A. McCann, *Democratizing Mexico: Public Opinion and Electoral Choices* (Baltimore, Md.: Johns Hopkins University Press, 1996); and James A. McCann, "The Changing Mexican Electorate: Political Interest, Expertise, and Party Support in the 1980s and 1990s," in Mónica Serrano, ed., *Governing Mexico: Political Parties and Elections* (London: Institute of Latin American Studies, 1998).

30. That is, the probability of voting for Fox is 12 percent higher in that group than among those who have no exposure to Televisa news, and the probability of voting for Labastida is 7 percent higher—a net gain of 5 percent for Fox.

31. For those respondents interviewed in more than one wave of the Mexico 2000 Panel Study, exposure data represent the average of reported television viewership over the course of the campaign. Respondents whose average self-reported use was less than one day per week were treated as nonviewers.

9

Mexico's Great Debates: The Televised Candidate Encounters of 2000 and Their Electoral Consequences

CHAPPELL LAWSON

Paralleling the broader opening in television coverage of Mexican campaigns has been the emergence of televised candidate debates. Although the first such duel was not held until 1994, debates soon spread to the Mexico City mayoral races of 1997 and 2000, as well as to the Institutional Revolutionary Party's (PRI) 1999 presidential primary. In the 2000 presidential race, Mexican campaigning moved beyond even these encounters. Not only did the race feature two formal debates, it also treated Mexicans to the political equivalent of "reality television" when the three leading candidates met to discuss logistics for the second encounter. Their impromptu negotiations were broadcast live on both major networks, producing some of the most memorable exchanges of the entire campaign. Although the two formal debates probably proved more influential in shaping public opinion, the "pre-debate" epitomized Mexico's transition from heavily scripted electioneering to a livelier campaign context.

This chapter first describes the main candidate encounters of 2000, discussing in detail how the candidates presented themselves and how their presentations shaped the dynamics of the campaign. It then analyzes how debate exposure affected citizens' attitudes toward the main candidates, including their voting preferences. It concludes that Mexico's "great debates" had important consequences for the 2000 campaign. Most obviously, they contributed to the erosion of Francisco

Labastida's support and thus to the eventual defeat of this PRI candidate. But the debates also had important indirect consequences for voting behavior—framing the election as a referendum on PRI rule, highlighting Vicente Fox's role as the leading opposition contender, and shaping strategic decisions by the candidates. Ultimately, these indirect effects probably exercised as great an influence on the outcome of the race as any direct effect of the debates on voting behavior.

MEXICO'S "GREAT DEBATES"

The 2000 campaign produced three televised encounters between the rival contenders for the presidency: the April 25 debate between all six contenders, including the three minor-party candidates; the May 23 "pre-debate" between Francisco Labastida, Vicente Fox, and Cuauhtémoc Cárdenas; and the three-way debate between the major-party contenders on May 26. All three debates proved to be major campaign events. Not only did they command the attention of the candidates and their staffs, they also dominated news coverage. Figure 9.1 shows seconds of television time devoted to the three main candidates on Mexico's two main national networks each week over the course of the campaign.[1] The top layer in the figure represents coverage of Francisco Labastida; the middle layer, Cuauhtémoc Cárdenas; and the bottom layer, Vicente Fox. As the graph shows, the debates produced spikes in news coverage that dwarfed even the closing rallies of the campaign.

Figure 9.1. Seconds of TV Coverage of the Three Main Candidates, by Week

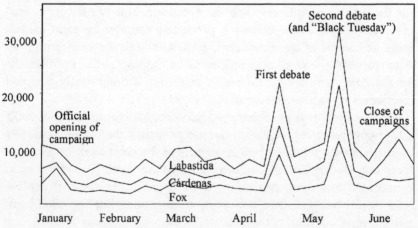

Among respondents in the second wave of the Mexico 2000 Panel Study, approximately 14 percent reported seeing the entire first debate, and an additional 27 percent reported seeing part of it.[2] Some 58 percent heard commentary about the debate on television, and 40 percent discussed the event with friends or family members. Exposure to the second debate (which may have included recall of the "pre-debate") was even more pronounced, with 51 percent of respondents in the third wave of the panel watching at least part of the second debate, 60 percent hearing commentary about it on television, and 72 percent discussing it with friends or family members.[3] In all, approximately 60 percent of respondents interviewed in July reported having seen at least part of one of the two formal encounters.[4] There was thus clear potential for the debates to affect voters' attitudes, and the presidential candidates took that potential seriously.

The April Debate

By comparison to what would come later, the first debate was a highly scripted affair. The six contenders stood at separate lecterns and delivered prepared remarks according to a prearranged order. Aside from opening and closing statements, the "debate" addressed three very broad topics (politics, economics, and social issues), to which each of the candidates spoke in varying order. The role of the moderator, who sat at a separate table, was limited to perfunctorily thanking each candidate after his remarks and recognizing the next candidate. This extreme version of the "joint press conference" format left little room for give-and-take among the candidates themselves, and none at all between the candidates and journalists or audience members.

Nevertheless, the event retained a certain debate-like flavor. Despite its extreme formality, candidates tended to respond as much to their rivals' remarks as to the broader topics they were supposed to address. Furthermore, the prominence of the issue of political change made the candidates' remarks seem like an extended dialogue on a common theme.

That dialogue did not reflect well on the PRI. In general, the opposition politicians ganged up on the ruling party and criticized its candidate. Although several issues surfaced that were not directly related to political change, including potentially uncomfortable ones for Fox, corruption and alternation in power dominated the discussion. The principal themes of the debate thus dovetailed nicely with Fox's overall campaign message.

Opening statements set the tone for the event, with all six candidates emphasizing the need for change. Minor-party candidate Porfirio Muñoz Ledo, the first to speak, devoted the bulk of his address to urging support for the opposition (conceived collectively) against the ruling party. Cárdenas, who followed, accused the PRI of corruption and links to drug trafficking. Cárdenas also criticized the National Action Party (PAN) for its past collusion with the ruling party, its reactionary stance on cultural issues, and its position on Mexico's massive bank bailout plan (which was identical to the PRI's). Nevertheless, his emphasis on the need for change indirectly supported Fox's framing of the race.

Fox made this framing explicit, emphasizing the need to replace the ruling party with an ideologically plural opposition government. He also claimed to be leading in the polls, a contention he subsequently repeated twice. This contention went unchallenged by the other candidates, making it clear that Fox was the main opposition contender.

Fox's opening statement was followed by that of Manuel Camacho, who stressed the graft and repression that characterized PRI rule. Among other things, Camacho referred explicitly to the recent massacre of peasants in Acteal (in the state of Chiapas), the slaughter of leftist activists by Guerrero state police in 1995, and corruption surrounding the banking crisis. Throughout the debate, Camacho played the role of opposition pit bull, attacking Labastida's claims to represent meaningful change.

The last opposition candidate to speak, Gilberto Rincón Gallardo, presented himself as a longtime crusader against "the authoritarianism of the PRI." He pointed out, for instance, that he was the only opposition candidate to have suffered personally from official repression, having been arrested repeatedly during several decades of civic activism. All five opposition candidates returned to these themes of PRI authoritarianism repeatedly over the course of the evening.

Perhaps surprisingly, the main target of their attacks declined to offer an alternative framing of the 2000 campaign. For instance, Labastida did not describe the election as a contest between Left and Right, with the PRI comfortably in the center. He emphasized neither recent economic trends (which were strongly favorable) nor his proposals for reducing crime (widely considered one of the most important problems in the country). Instead, the PRI's nominee presented himself as an authentic agent of change, who alone had the experience and qualifications necessary to govern the country. His opening statement used the word "change" or some variant thereof eight times—more than all the other candidates combined. His closing statement included no fewer than ten such references, again the most of any candidate. And during his topical presentations, Labastida elaborated at length on the campaign slogan, "Government should serve the people" (*Que el poder sirva a la gente*). Consequently, Fox's framing of the election as a referendum on change went largely unchallenged.

Perhaps the most memorable moment of the encounter came during the discussion of social issues, when Labastida took Fox to task for aspersions he had cast on Labastida's manhood during the campaign. Reciting the inventory of insults (shorty, pansy, skirt, and so on), Labastida argued that Fox lacked the necessary character and seriousness to be president. After interventions by Camacho and Muñoz Ledo, Fox delivered the most memorable retort of the evening:

> My dear Mr. Labastida, you may take away my antics, but they can never take away from you [in the PRI] your deceitfulness, your poor record of governance, and your corruption—never.[5]

In the end, it was Fox who had the last word—quite literally, in the sense that his closing statement came after those of the other five candidates. Mexicans, he told the audience, had heard two opposing visions that evening: the vision of Francisco Labastida (which represented corruption, poverty, and unemployment), and "our" project (which represented a new future for Mexico). Together, Fox concluded as he made his trademark V sign for victory, Mexicans could finally "break the chains" of authoritarianism and change their government.

Fox's personal style made his message all the more compelling and credible. Throughout the debate, he came across as animated and forceful, with frequent cadence changes and vigorous gestures that punctuated his main points. In his three-minute opening statement, for instance, his hands were visible over fifty-five separate times. Although he looked down at his notes frequently at the beginning, he managed to maintain reasonable eye contact. He also appeared confident, without swaying motions, sideways glances, or other indications of insecurity and discomfort. He thus projected the image of someone ready, willing, and able to take on the ruling party.

By comparison, Fox's chief rival within the opposition came across as simply dull. In his opening statement, Cárdenas maintained the best eye contact of all six candidates, almost never shifting his glance or looking down. But his cadence barely changed over the course of his remarks, and he never gestured with his hands. During the rest of the debate, the better-crafted elements of his presentation tended to fade, while their flat quality remained. Cárdenas also appeared uncomfortable in later rounds, when comments by other candidates forced him to diverge from his prepared remarks.

Labastida proved to be the most polished of the candidates, but not the most forceful. His gestures were restrained—his hands were visible only five times in his opening statement, for instance; he rarely blinked; and he maintained excellent eye contact throughout the encounter. His principal weakness was to sway at the lectern occasionally, a symptom of nervousness that increased somewhat as the evening wore on and criticism from his opponents mounted.

The two contenders with the worst standing in the polls, Manuel Camacho and Porfirio Muñoz Ledo, delivered the weakest presentations. Muñoz Ledo spent most of his opening statement looking into the wrong camera or down at the lectern; he gestured exactly zero times. Camacho gestured frequently (twenty-eight times in his opening statement), maintained good eye contact, and changed his cadence at appropriate moments, but he was also visibly nervous. The former regent of Mexico City fidgeted uncomfortably at the podium and—in a classic symptom of insecurity—blinked almost incessantly. In his 180-second opening statement, for instance, Camacho blinked over 150 times—in contrast to approximately 130 times for Cárdenas, about half that many for Fox, and only six for a clearly well coached Labastida. In the end, neither Camacho nor Muñoz Ledo seemed quite ready for prime time.

Among the three minor-party candidates, Rincón Gallardo acquitted himself by far the best. Although he seemed to slouch at the lectern in his opening statement, it soon became apparent that his posture represented an effort to accommodate his physical disability (including a deformed arm and hand). Rincón Gallardo's presentation was not particularly dramatic or rousing, and he obviously lacked Fox's physical charisma. Nevertheless, he projected an abiding, personal commitment to the cause of democracy and social justice. He was also able to back up his rhetoric with substance—in the form of both his handicap and his activist past. Consequently, his appeal for better treatment of the traditionally abused or marginalized segments of Mexican society resonated powerfully.

In terms of issue content, then, the candidates did not differ markedly. All six emphasized the theme of change—in Labastida's case, through better administration and leadership; in the case of the opposition candidates, through defeat of the PRI. All six also linked political change with economic outcomes, implying that electoral choices would shape the performance of the national economy and the distribution of material benefits. In terms of presentation and background, however, there were substantial differences between the candidates. Among the opposition contenders, Fox and Rincón Gallardo delivered the best presentations and proved most effective at tying their remarks to their personal experiences and qualifications. For Rincón Gallardo, creating this linkage was a matter of stressing his personal disability and his record as an activist. For Fox, it was a matter of projecting a forceful style that indicated his conviction about kicking out the PRI, as well as emphasizing his lead in the polls.

By contrast, Francisco Labastida came across as serious but not passionate or vigorous. Combined with his position as the candidate of the ruling party, Labastida's relatively restrained personal style rendered his rhetoric of change less credible. There was thus a notable disjuncture between the content of his remarks, on the one hand, and his background, personality, and style, on the other.

THE AFTERMATH OF THE APRIL DEBATE

Not surprisingly, Fox came out of the first debate on top. Despite the fact that a plurality of respondents in the second wave of the panel favored Labastida (by a margin of 8 percent), a decisive plurality (48 percent) of those who saw the debate found Fox to be the winner. Moreover, 56 percent agreed that, regardless of which candidate they personally felt had won, the debate represented a victory for Fox.

The fact that Fox and Labastida were clearly the principal contestants appears to have influenced respondent perceptions of the candidates' performances. Post-debate judgments of trailing candidates, especially Rincón Gallardo, fell substantially among those who had not personally seen the debate. As a result, Fox emerged even stronger in relative terms. These results are shown in table 9.1.

The decisive nature of Fox's victory becomes even clearer when we break down post-debate judgments by partisan affiliation. As table 9.2 shows, respondents tended to see the debate in terms more favorable to their preferred candidate. PAN identifiers and leaners were the most likely of all groups to view it as a Fox win; PRI partisans, the most likely to see it as a victory for Labastida; and leftists, the most likely to claim a triumph for either Cárdenas or Rincón Gallardo. Nevertheless, virtually every category of voter found Fox to be the winner. Even PRI partisans were almost as likely to judge the debate as a victory for Fox.

Table 9.1. Fox Won the First Debate

	Who Won the Debate? (respondents' personal view)	Who Fared Best from the Debate? (regardless of respondents' view)
Fox	48%	56%
Labastida	26%	29%
Rincón G.	17%	9%
All others	9%	6%
Total	100%	100%
N	282	539

Note: Undecided responses and "no answer" omitted.

Table 9.2. Perceived Winner of First Debate by Respondents' Partisan Affiliation

Partisan Self-ID (February)	Who Was Generally Perceived Winner of the First Debate?					
	Labastida	Fox	Cárdenas /other	Rincón Gallardo	Total	N
PRI	47%	42%	5%	6%	100%	213
PAN	14%	73%	4%	10%	100%	172
PRD/other	17%	51%	15%	17%	100%	69
None	24%	62%	6%	8%	100%	85
N	303	157	31	48	100%	539

Note: Undecided responses and "no answer" omitted.

Fox's victory appeared to reinforce trends favorable to his candidacy. In the weeks after the encounter, Labastida's already shrinking lead disappeared, and published surveys during the rest of the campaign would show the two contenders neck and neck. According to Fox's internal tracking poll, for instance, his support grew by 4 percent in the week following the first debate, definitively surpassing that of Labastida for the first time.[6] The April debate thus came to represent a natural break point in the campaign, separating a period of comfortable

Labastida leads from a much tighter race. Whatever its true influence on voters, therefore, Fox's victory in the debate was perceived to have had an impact. And that perception had significant consequences for campaign strategy and tactics.

For the Labastida camp, the debate triggered a shift from the restrained approach of a front-runner to a much dirtier, more aggressive campaign.[7] New tactics included a series of harshly negative television spots directed at Fox, stepped-up pressure on the mass media to back the ruling party, and a growing reliance on heavy-handed clientelism to secure the PRI's traditional base. In the week after the debate, Labastida and his top aides met with various state-level leaders to ensure that the ruling party's famous "machinery" was working properly for the official candidate. Following these meetings, reports of vote buying and coercion increased dramatically. Meanwhile, coverage of Labastida on provincial broadcast media and the Televisa network, both of which were traditionally linked to the ruling party, turned conspicuously more favorable. Despite Labastida's change-oriented rhetoric, his tactics became increasingly reminiscent of the "old PRI" he had criticized in the first half of the race.

Predictably, the debate had almost the opposite effect on the Fox campaign. While not totally abandoning his folksy, freewheeling ways, Fox projected a more serious image during the second half of the campaign. To be sure, personal jabs at Labastida persisted, as did assaults against the political system he represented. Nevertheless, with his status as opposition leader assured and his standing in the polls rivaling Labastida's, Fox made an effort to look more presidential.

For Cárdenas, meanwhile, the debate virtually ensured that his role would remain limited to that of a spoiler. Although he opted to stay in the race in order to preserve his party (which depended on its 2000 vote share for future funding), the debate cost him the chance to convert the contest into a true three-man race. Indeed, it appeared that his Party of the Democratic Revolution (PRD) now faced a new threat from the left, in the form of Rincón Gallardo. Only by reconnecting with his core base and continuing to emphasize a leftist message did Cárdenas manage to retain his natural constituency.

Finally, for the trailing candidates, the debate informed decisions about their prospects. Unable to grow beyond a sliver of the electorate in the aftermath of the debate, Muñoz Ledo withdrew less than three weeks later and endorsed Fox. Camacho also flirted with the idea of abandoning the race in favor of Fox (though he ultimately chose to continue his doomed independent campaign). So did Rincón Gallardo, whose campaign was temporarily energized by the debate. In the end, his Social Democratic Party failed to reach the minimum threshold necessary for parliamentary representation, but based on his performance in the first debate, remaining in the race made sense at the time.

"Black Tuesday"

Less than one month after they first confronted each other, Mexico's three main presidential candidates were scheduled to debate a second time. As the appointed day—Tuesday, May 23—drew near, however, it became clear that they could not agree on the format of the contest. When last-minute negotiations between representatives of the three camps failed to produce an accord, Cárdenas invited Fox and Labastida to join him at his campaign house on Tuesday afternoon to discuss the arrangements in person. Television news crews soon gained entrance to the courtyard of the home and broadcast the candidates' ensuing discussions live. Across the country, ratings for popular afternoon shows plummeted as Mexicans tuned in to watch the men who would be president posture, joke, and casually insult one another on national television.[8]

Perhaps surprisingly, Fox got the worst of it in the ensuing exchanges. He came across as stubborn and prone to overstatement, demanding that the debate be held that same night over the apparently reasonable objections of his opponents. (At one point he banged his fist on the table and repeated the word "today"—*hoy*—four times in less than forty seconds.) Fox also insisted that the country's major television and radio networks were prepared to broadcast the debate that same evening and that he expected to receive written confirmation by fax to that effect at any moment. The implausibility of these claims later appeared to be confirmed when Joaquín Vargas, the representative of the broadcasting industry at the negotiations, reported that Televisa was not prepared to broadcast any debate on such short notice.[9] Although Fox delivered a convincing peroration toward the end of the encounter—lambasting the PRI, lamenting Cárdenas's willingness to join forces with Labastida, and calling again for political change—his stubbornness and hubris made him look foolish.

Fox's two rivals were quick to reproach him for his antics. Cárdenas characterized Fox's insistence on holding the debate that same night as "absurd" and "capricious"; he also dismissed Fox's claim to have confirmation from the networks that the debate could still be held on

Tuesday as mere asseveration, which in Fox's case could not be believed. Labastida echoed many of Cárdenas's criticisms; as he put it
toward the end of the impromptu negotiation:

> If you would allow me to add something, Mr. Cárdenas. We
> have to send a signal through the seriousness with which we
> behave. It seems to me that the signal we are sending to the
> people ... with all this frivolousness and nonsense is very
> negative about the way we handle the affairs of state. Both
> the campaign and the affairs of state require seriousness; the
> people demand that we treat them with seriousness and re-
> spect. And with all respect to Mr. Fox, I think that this is not
> the best way to manage a debate.

If anything, Labastida was too polite. He seemed to be taking his
cues from Cárdenas, and he failed to exploit the spontaneous nature of
the broadcast to pounce more aggressively on Fox's mistakes or to
advance his own message. Although serious and well spoken, he again
failed to come across as inspiring or forceful.

Consequently, it was Cárdenas who emerged from the encounter
looking the best. Comfortable and relaxed, he displayed the more human
and even humorous side of his personality that almost never surfaced
in public appearances. He also enjoyed something of a home-field advantage, with most of his supporters off-camera but conveniently
within earshot. In contrast to the hoots and laughter that followed
some of Fox's statements, television audiences could occasionally hear
shouts of support for "Cuauh."

Predictably, media reports in the aftermath of the "pre-debate"
were not kind to Fox. Both television networks gave saturation coverage to the event over the following twenty-four hours, playing repeated clips of Fox insisting "*hoy.*" Although the main nightly news
anchors behaved themselves in a relatively restrained fashion, several
broadcast journalists editorialized against the main opposition candidate.[10] Meanwhile, newspaper columnists pilloried Fox's character, and
talk radio programs on May 24 were inundated with callers who insisted that, after witnessing Fox's performance, they simply could not
imagine voting for him. Among Fox's supporters, May 23 soon became
known as "Black Tuesday."

The main consolation for Fox's campaign was that public opinion
surveys failed to register a dramatic decline in his support. According
to internal campaign tracking polls, Fox dropped only one point in the

three days after Black Tuesday, while Labastida's and Cárdenas's support edged up only slightly.[11] Thus it appears that those most put off by Fox's behavior were either already opposed to his candidacy or were uncomfortable with their other options.

Nevertheless, Black Tuesday was a trying episode for Fox. Among other things, it represented the first incident to which his storied campaign machine had no immediate or adequate response. Although the Azteca network gave "response time" to Fox's director of communications (and future wife), Martha Sahagún, later that night, Black Tuesday proved a difficult episode to spin. Viewers had seen the candidate for themselves, live and unedited. They had also watched Cárdenas, normally wooden and soporific, come across as personable and statesmanlike. And although Labastida had not managed to appear particularly forceful, the contrast between his demeanor and Fox's apparent silliness was obvious. Any effective response to the debacle would have to come from the candidate himself. Fortunately for Fox, it came that same week.

The May Debate

In keeping with Fox's insistence on format changes, the second debate proved substantially more interactive than the first. Instead of standing at separate lecterns, the three main contenders sat around a single table together with the moderator (well-regarded television journalist Ricardo Rocha). Like the first encounter, the May debate began with three-minute opening statements by the candidates and ended with three-minute closing remarks, with the body of the event concentrating on three separate themes. Unlike the first debate, however, these themes were substantially more focused on particular policy areas raised by the main candidates in their campaigns: (1) social equality, education, and culture; (2) public safety, corruption, and impunity; and (3) employment and income distribution. Even more importantly, the debate allowed for up to twelve minutes of "free discussion" among the candidates on each policy area after their opening remarks.[12] There was thus ample room for actual debate and a fair amount of spontaneity to the candidates' exchanges.

By luck of the draw, Fox was the first to speak that evening. This gave him the opportunity to engage in a bit of damage control by responding directly to the week's events. And by that time, his campaign team had discovered an appropriately clever spin. Fox began his opening statement on Friday evening thus:

My friends, thanks to all of you who have invited us into your homes tonight. I am glad that we are finally able to hold this debate, so that you and I can discuss the great change that is already [ya] under way. When I insisted this week on having an open debate, there were some who thought that I was a bit stubborn. Even my mother told me so. But ending seventy years of corruption, poverty, and desperation requires character, firmness, and true leadership. I believe firmly that the problems of the country must be resolved today [hoy]. Do you think that a weak and gray figure could have confronted the PRI and its allies? Do you believe that a person without emotions could move the conscience of the Mexican people and bring about change? To end seventy years of authoritarian rule requires character and firmness.

Fox then proceeded to invoke the entire pantheon of Mexican political crusaders who also had opposed one-party rule with "character, firmness, and a little stubbornness." He concluded with a plea for change, a message of thanks to his supporters, and a promise not to let them down.

Cárdenas indirectly contributed to Fox's efforts at spin control. In contrast to his quips in the pre-debate, he devoted virtually all of his energy in the second debate to criticizing the regime. He led off by enumerating the economic failings of the PRI, focusing in particular on poverty and returning to the issue of official corruption he had emphasized in April. This trend continued throughout the evening, with Cárdenas expending the bulk of his ordnance on Labastida rather than on Fox.

By comparison to the first debate, Labastida stressed the theme of change less systematically. Moreover, the "changes" he did mention were linked to policy measures—improving education, guaranteeing universal access to health care, combating corruption, reducing street crime and impunity, and advancing women's rights—rather than to political reform. Although perhaps wiser than his previous emphasis on change, this approach still left him without a clear alternative framing of the contest.

The interactive sessions of the debate produced several lively exchanges among the candidates, and these exchanges grew even livelier as the event went on. In addition to the formal topics they were supposed to cover, the candidates focused on their opponents' character flaws, records in office, and campaign gaffes. During the discussion of education, for instance, Cárdenas lambasted the PAN for culturally retrograde measures in the states it controlled. Fox in turn denounced

Cárdenas's record as governor of Michoacán and mayor of the Federal District (which prompted Cárdenas to wonder aloud why anyone would believe yet another of Fox's falsehoods). Later, Cárdenas and Labastida traded remarks about Labastida's capacity to manage the nation's economy, with Cárdenas expressing amazement that the same people who had provoked so many earlier crises should now be expected to do a bang-up job.

Black Tuesday raised its head several times in the debate. Fox himself brought up the incident during the free discussion period on corruption, expressing satisfaction that Cárdenas was making amends for having collaborated with Labastida against the "forces of change" three days before. Cárdenas, having none of it, replied that what had happened in the pre-debate was nothing more than Fox's "being caught in his own lies." In a subsequent exchange with Labastida, Fox insisted that the confirmation from Televisa he had been awaiting at Cárdenas's house did finally arrive and that it revealed what he had claimed all along. Labastida responded that Fox was continuing to misrepresent and distort the information in the fax he had allegedly received, and he challenged Fox to respond directly to that charge.

In general, however, Fox's adroit reframing of the incident prevented Black Tuesday from dominating the debate. Labastida could not dwell on the pre-debate without turning Fox's performance into a purely partisan matter. Meanwhile, Cárdenas could not raise it himself without appearing to side with Labastida against a fellow opposition candidate. As a result, Fox was able to use the second debate to turn viewers' attention away from Black Tuesday and toward other campaign issues.

As in April, these issues tended to reflect badly on the PRI. In terms of content, therefore, Labastida once more got the worst of the encounter. Fox dismissed Labastida's promises on education by pointing out that his tenure as education minister had produced little in the way of results; Cárdenas made the same point about progress on indigenous rights during Labastida's tenure as interior minister. And both opposition candidates tagged the ruling party with corruption, which Fox characterized as "synonymous" with the PRI. In fact, Fox and Cárdenas competed primarily by attempting to link each other to the old regime while presenting themselves as the authentic voice of Mexico's opposition. Labastida once again found himself in the unenviable position of either defending the old regime he had previously criticized or claiming implausibly to be an agent of change.

In terms of style and presentation, Fox was clearly more comfortable than his opponents with the interactive format of the May debate. His remarks were more fluent, his interventions more to the point, and his criticisms of his rivals more mordant. And as in his other public addresses, Fox accompanied his remarks with appropriate facial expressions, convincing changes of cadence, and forceful gestures. Fox also won the prize for cleverest gimmick of the evening, following Cárdenas's criticism of the PAN's position on the bank bailout. In response, Fox handed Cárdenas the computer codes that would make public key information about the bank bailout, information that the PAN's delegation in Congress had previously refused to release. Fox was afraid, he said, to entrust them to Labastida.[13]

In stylistic terms, Fox's rivals suffered by comparison. Cárdenas came across as sincerely committed to advancing leftist positions that his rivals had rejected, but his presentations remained rather halting and dull. Meanwhile, Labastida appeared much as he had in previous encounters—polished and serious, but bland. Unlike in the first debate, each of the participants in the second looked like a potential president. Nevertheless, it was Fox who clearly delivered the most impressive performance.

The Aftermath of the May Debate

Public reactions soon ratified Fox's victory. Although Fox continued to trail Labastida among respondents in the third round of the panel (34 percent to 36 percent, with 12 percent undecided), 56 percent named him as the winner (against only 27 percent for Labastida and 17 percent for Cárdenas). Moreover, 60 percent of those who felt that the debate had advantaged one candidate over the others, regardless of their own personal reactions, considered it a victory for Fox. These results are shown in table 9.3.

Cárdenas appears to have done somewhat better than in the first contest. Although he failed to attract voters beyond a relatively narrow constituency, he nevertheless succeeded in rallying that constituency. Unlike the first debate, when PRD partisans judged Fox to be the winner, in the second debate they preferred Cárdenas. Equally important, Cárdenas finished ahead of Labastida among those not affiliated with any party. Table 9.4 documents these findings, grouping respondents' beliefs about who won the debate according to their partisan identification at the beginning of the campaign.

Table 9.3. Fox Won the Second Debate

	Respondents' Winner (according to debate viewers)	Generally Perceived Winner (according to what respondents heard)
Fox	56%	60%
Labastida	27%	28%
Cárdenas	17%	12%
Total	100%	100%
N	497	659

Note: Undecided and "don't know" responses are omitted.

Table 9.4. Who Won the Second Debate, by Respondents' Partisan Affiliation

Partisan affiliation (February)	Candidate Respondents Felt Won the Second Debate				
	Labastida	Fox	Cárdenas	Total	N
PRI	49%	41%	10%	100%	197
PAN	8%	87%	5%	100%	158
PRD/other	35%	9%	56%	100%	66
None	21%	51%	28%	100%	76
N	132	279	86	100%	497

Note: Undecided and "don't know" responses are omitted.

The clear loser in the debate was Francisco Labastida. As in April, the PRI's candidate barely managed to convince a plurality of his fellow *priístas* that he had done best. The scope of Labastida's defeat becomes even clearer when we consider respondents' perceptions of which candidate benefited most from the debate (regardless of which candidate they personally believed had won). As table 9.5 shows, a plurality of those who sympathized with the PRI in February acknowledged that Fox had benefited most from the May encounter.

Fox's success in the debate proved crucial in repairing the damage from Black Tuesday. Although his opponents continued their attempts to exploit the incident, opinion rapidly divided along partisan lines. In fact, criticism of Fox's character produced something of a boomerang effect among his supporters. Seizing on their candidate's message in the second debate, they converted *hoy* into a new campaign chant that promised immediate, decisive action. By election day, *Hoy!* had joined *Ya!*, *Adiós* (to the PRI), *Vicente Presidente*, and other memorable slogans in the Fox repertoire. As a result, any ardor lost on Black Tuesday was restored by the second debate.

Table 9.5. Perceived Winner of Second Debate by Respondents' Partisan Affiliation

Partisan Self-ID (February)	Generally Perceived as the Winner of the Second Debate				
	Labastida	Fox	Cárdenas	Total	N
PRI	44%	47%	9%	100%	269
PAN	13%	83%	4%	100%	201
PRD/other	11%	44%	44%	100%	72
None	28%	59%	13%	100%	117
N	186	394	79	100%	659

Note: Undecided responses are omitted.

Black Tuesday and the second debate also proved useful for Cárdenas by demonstrating that he was more than a "spent cartridge" (as aging revolutionaries in Mexico were once known). By differentiating himself from the other candidates on both policy positions and image, Cárdenas was in a better position to reject Fox's pleas for a unified opposition ticket and to continue his independent campaign on behalf of Mexico's Left. Despite repeated polls showing that he could not hope to win, Cárdenas's vote share crept upward during the last month of the campaign.

In the end, then, the events of late May reinforced the candidates' previous campaign strategies. Labastida continued to launch assaults on Fox's character, relying, among other things, on negative advertisements. Fox continued to emphasize the need for change over all other potential topics. And Cárdenas continued to distance himself from both camps, agreeing with Labastida about Fox's personal deficiencies and with Fox about the need for alternation in power. These strategies characterized the remainder of the race.

DEBATES, TRAITS, AND CANDIDATES' FATES

At first glance, the evidence suggests that the main effect of Mexico's 2000 debates was to reinforce viewers' existing preferences. Some 14 percent of respondents in the second wave of the Mexico 2000 Panel Study reported that the first debate strengthened their preferences, while less than 3 percent reported that the debate had weakened their attachment to their preferred candidate, and only 4 percent of respondents reported that it had led them to change their vote. Most respondents (54 percent) reported not being influenced by the first debate at all, and an additional 26 percent could not say whether the debate had any effect on their vote choice. Responses for the second debate appear somewhat greater, with 27 percent of people reporting some type of debate effect. (These responses may have included reactions to the "pre-debate," about which respondents were not separately questioned.)[14] But reinforcement effects still dominated; only 10 percent of respondents reported that the debate had changed or weakened their preference, while 17 percent reported that it had strengthened their choice of candidate.

Many respondents, of course, did not see the debates. To assess the effect by level of exposure, table 9.6 groups respondents into tiers.[15] As the table indicates, debate effects were substantially greater among those with higher levels of exposure. Thirty-nine percent of high-exposure respondents reported some type of effect from the first debate, in contrast to less than 8 percent of those with low exposure; for the second debate, the same figures were 41 percent and 15 percent.

Table 9.6. Effects of Debates by Level of Exposure

	Low Exposure	Medium Exposure	High Exposure	N
First Debate				
Changed preference	1%	3%	5%	34
Weakened preference	1%	6%	4%	25
Strengthened preference	5%	16%	30%	134
No influence/Don't know	92%	75%	61%	766
Total	100%	100%	100%	959
N	441	313	205	959
Second Debate				
Changed preference	5%	7%	7%	59
Weakened preference	3%	4%	5%	37
Strengthened preference	7%	20%	29%	170
No influence/Don't know	85%	69%	60%	710
Total	100%	100%	100%	976
N	378	324	274	976

Nevertheless, the increased influence of the debate among more heavily exposed respondents came almost entirely in the form of strengthening existing preferences. High-exposure respondents were scarcely more likely than medium-exposure respondents to alter or weaken their electoral preferences, but they were significantly more likely to reinforce their prior views. This finding makes sense if we assume that the individuals most exposed to the debate were also more exposed to other cues and were thus more resistant to persuasive appeals.

The debates, then, do not seem to have triggered large-scale shifts in voter preferences. In aggregate terms they appear to have mainly confirmed existing trends in favor of Fox. These findings are supported by cross-sectional polls, which showed relatively modest or short-lived changes in voter preferences.[16]

Nevertheless, it may be that debate exposure had consequences at the individual level that are not readily apparent in aggregate-level data. For instance, debate exposure may have been correlated with exposure to other campaign influences that had the opposite effect on attitude change. Controlling for these confounding factors should yield a clearer sense of debate effects.

To measure the impact of the debate on individual-level attitudes toward the three main candidates, we examine three items: an index of candidate trait evaluations (honesty and competence in addressing different problems);[17] candidate feeling thermometer ratings; and voting intention. In addition to debate exposure, independent variables include a standard set of demographic and attitudinal controls: age, gender, education, socioeconomic status, region, urban residency, church attendance, union membership, partisan identification in February, and voting preference in February. To isolate the effects of the debate from other campaign stimuli, the analysis also includes a general index of political engagement, comprising interest in politics, attention to the campaign, frequency of interpersonal communication about politics, exposure to television news, and exposure to televised political advertisements.[18] Table 9.7 reports the results of this analysis for candidate trait ratings and feeling thermometers across both debates, using the second wave of the Mexico 2000 Panel Study for analysis of the first debate, and the third wave for analysis of the second debate. For economy of presentation, table 9.7 reports only the standardized coefficients for debate exposure; full results are provided in tables 9.10 through 9.13 in the appendix to this chapter.

Table 9.7. Effects of Debate Exposure on Opinion of the Main Candidates

	Labastida	Fox	Cárdenas
First Debate			
Candidate trait evaluations	.051	.068†	−.026
Candidate feeling thermometer rating	−.072*	.040	.013
Second Debate			
Candidate trait evaluations	−.078*	.026	.046
Candidate feeling thermometer rating	−.096**	−.020	−.001

Notes: Cell entries are standardized OLS regression coefficients. Full results from the twelve regressions summarized here are available upon request. Control variables include age, gender, education, socioeconomic status, region, urban residency, church attendance, union membership, partisan identification in February, voting preference in February, and an index of political engagement (comprising interest in politics, attention to the campaign, frequency of interpersonal communication about politics, exposure to television news, and exposure to televised political advertisements).

† $p < .10$; * $p < .05$; ** $p < .01$.

As table 9.7 shows, the debates were clearly liabilities for Francisco Labastida. Although debate exposure had only limited effects on attitudes toward the two opposition candidates, it was highly negative for the PRI's nominee. Labastida's feeling thermometer ratings fell significantly as a result of both contests, and in the second debate, candidate trait evaluations also dropped. Although his trait evaluations appear to have improved somewhat after the first debate, Fox's improved still more. Consequently, the net effects for Labastida vis-à-vis his main rival were consistently damaging.

The discrepancy between the effects of the first debate on Labastida's feeling thermometer and its effects on perceptions of his honesty and competence merits further comment. Normally, feeling thermometer ratings and candidate trait evaluations track neatly, with factors that diminish one of them tending to diminish the other. One explanation for this result is that voters, though satisfied with Labastida's honesty and competence, were simply uninspired or unimpressed by him as an individual. In other words, the PRI candidate's lack of vigor and charisma hurt his overall feeling thermometer ratings. An alternative explanation lies in the content of the debate itself. Although Labastida's polished performance and emphasis on change reassured audiences about his personal abilities, criticism by his opponents also likely led viewers to associate him with the old regime. If so, both Labastida and the opposition could be said to have succeeded in their debate presentations: Labastida in convincing voters about his capacity to conduct the affairs of state, and his opponents in characterizing him as a spokesman for the ruling party.

Table 9.8 presents the results of a multinomial logistic regression on candidate preference in April (after the first debate). A vote for Labastida is treated as the base case, so that the coefficients in table 9.8 represent the effects of a variable on the relative likelihood of favoring another option (undecided, Fox, or another opposition candidate) over the PRI's nominee. Thus the first set of columns in table 9.8 indicates whether a particular factor led respondents to favor Fox over Labastida, while the second set of columns reports whether that same factor led them to favor another opposition candidate (typically Cárdenas) over the PRI nominee.

This model controls for the usual battery of demographic and attitudinal variables, including both vote preference and party identification in February. As the data show, the April debate clearly hurt Labastida vis-à-vis the opposition candidates, especially Fox.

These effects were quite powerful—much larger than the effects of general political engagement. The impact of exposure to the April debate is illustrated graphically in figure 9.2. The vertical axis in the figure represents the probability of voting for a particular candidate, based on the multinomial logistic regression model shown above, holding constant all variables except for debate exposure.[19] The horizontal axis indicates level of debate exposure, based on whether respondents had seen the debate, heard commentary about it, and discussed it with others.[20] As the figure indicates, the likelihood of supporting Labastida declined substantially with debate exposure, while the probability of casting a ballot for Fox grew by roughly the same amount. For example, increasing debate exposure from a moderately low level (one) to a moderately high level (four) raised the odds of voting for Fox by more than 30 percent.

It must be noted, however, that this effect diminished over time. Among respondents in subsequent rounds of the panel, debate exposure did not exercise a significant effect on vote preference. Nor was viewership of the first debate a significant predictor of partisan attitudes or vote choice among respondents in the postelectoral cross-section (July) once other factors were taken into account. Thus debate effects appear to have been at least partially reversed by subsequent campaign stimuli. Rather than fundamentally and permanently altering

Table 9.8. Effects of Exposure to the First Debate on Candidate Preference

Variable	Fox		Other Opposition		Undecided/None	
	Beta	Stan. Error	Beta	Stan. Error	Beta	Stan. Error
Index of debate exposure	2.18**	.481	1.52**	.529	.944	.615
Index of campaign exposure	-.175	.275	-.082	.312	-1.05**	.356
Undecided/none (February)	1.30**	.388	1.38**	.427	2.57**	.401
Favors Fox (February)	3.29**	.391	2.27**	.475	1.73**	.545
Favors other party (February)	.914†	.555	2.38**	.484	1.86**	.629
PRI partisan (February)	-.670†	.351	-.827*	.394	-1.51**	.385
PAN partisan (February)	1.23**	.433	-.136	.518	-.297	.529
PRD partisan (February)	.642	.535	1.93**	.479	-1.58*	.753
North	.007	.341	-.436	.400	.160	.432
Center	.315	.336	.120	.405	-.217	.467
Metro	-.091	.324	.055	.353	.066	.379
Year of birth	-.009	.009	-.014	.010	-.029**	.011
Gender (male)	-.384	.248	.080	.277	-.083	.304
Urban residency	.525†	.274	.736*	.323	.468	.341
Education	.148	.133	.237	.154	.515**	.166
Church attendance	-.053	.105	-.076	.117	.077	.126
Union membership	-.426	.358	.381	.415	-.686	.487
Socioeconomic status	-.079	.311	.263	.347	-.341	.376
Constant	-.218**	.740	-2.51**	.847	-2.02*	.879
Valid N	939					
Cox and Snell statistic	.644					
Chi-squared statistic	971					

Note: Results are based on multinomial logistic regression, with coefficients in the first column and standard errors in the second for each category. Base case is a vote for Labastida.

† $p < .10$; * $p < .05$; ** $p < .01$

Table 9.9. Effects of Exposure to the Second Debate on Candidate Preference in June

Variable	Fox		Other Opposition		Undecided/None	
	Beta	Stan. Error	Beta	Stan. Error	Beta	Stan. Error
Index of debate exposure	.598	.410	.572	.458	-.041	.485
Index of campaign exposure	.223	.212	-.001	.236	-.436	.248
Undecided/none (February)	.849*	.366	1.10**	.381	2.05**	.365
Favors Fox (February)	3.00**	.356	1.41**	.450	1.64**	.461
Favors other opposition (February)	.649	.521	1.85**	.455	1.21*	.552
PRI partisan (February)	-.665†	.341	-1.60**	.359	-1.32**	.353
PAN partisan (February)	.688†	.390	-.643	.460	-.384	.449
PRD partisan (February)	1.00†	.547	1.37**	.481	-.342	.591
North	.082	.320	.221	.375	.725†	.378
Center	.434	.289	-.175	.359	-.508	.403
Metro	.116	.297	.451	.317	.498	.330
Year of birth	.007	.008	-.004	.010	-.013	.010
Gender (male)	-.145	.222	-.221	.253	-.366	.265
Urban residency	.444†	.257	.531†	.304	.681*	.323
Education	.089	.123	.246†	.141	.242	.150
Church attendance	.074	.098	-.058	.108	.002	.112
Union membership	.151	.336	.088	.383	-.042	.417
Socioeconomic status	-.014	.254	.182	.289	-.143	.301
Constant	-2.66**	.717	-1.89*	.784	-1.63*	.801
Valid N	958					
Cox and Snell statistic	.571					
Chi-squared statistic	812					

Note: Results are based on multinomial logistic regression, with coefficients in the first column and standard errors in the second for each category. Base case is a vote for Labastida.

† $p < .10$; * $p < .05$; ** $p < .01$

citizen preferences, then, the first debate proved to be one of several events that helped to erode Labastida's lead.

The impact of the second debate was more muted, even in the short run. The results of multinomial logistic regression analysis, using the same vote model as for the first debate, are reported in table 9.9. Although the debate again appears to have hurt Labastida vis-à-vis the opposition candidates, this result does not reach statistical significance.

Figure 9.2. Effects of First Debate on Support for Fox and Labastida

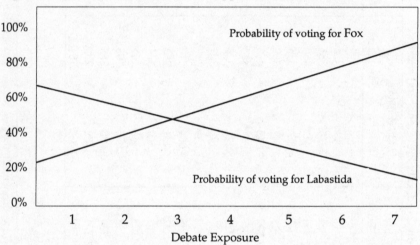

These findings suggest that voting intentions were less malleable by the time of the second debate. Most voters who would abandon Labastida during the campaign had already done so, and the debate merely confirmed their distaste for him. Consequently, although Labastida's image and reputation suffered as a result of the encounter, it had less of an effect on vote choice.

CONCLUSIONS

All told, Mexico's 2000 debates tended to undermine support for Francisco Labastida. In side-by-side comparison with his main rivals, especially Vicente Fox, the PRI's candidate fared badly. His unconvincing performance and Fox's more compelling presentation—especially in the first debate—thus contributed to Fox's July victory.

The effects of exposure to the first debate on vote choice faded over time in the wake of Black Tuesday, the second debate, and other campaign events. Consequently, none of these episodes, by itself, had a decisive or irrevocable effect on public opinion. It would thus be wrong to conclude that Labastida's loss in the first debate cost him the election. Rather, the April encounter was one of several factors that eroded his early advantage over Vicente Fox.

Audience reactions to that debate suggest the deeper flaws in Labastida's initial campaign strategy. By emphasizing change, Labastida clearly hoped to neutralize Fox's main rhetorical weapon and to protect himself against opposition criticism. Labastida's message was probably more than just a campaign gimmick; presumably, it also reflected the kind of president he hoped to be. Regardless of the calculus behind his decision, however, Labastida's emphasis on change went far beyond standard inoculation tactics. Instead, the issue of change dominated his prepared remarks in the first debate, as well as his campaign messages more generally. In one-way, one-sided communication (such as spot advertisements or speeches to undecided voters), references to change might have played well, reassuring some independent voters that the PRI had finally rejected authoritarianism. In a side-by-side comparison with opposition candidates, however, making change a focus was unlikely to pay off. Although such a strategy may have helped Labastida's personal trait ratings with some opposition voters, these same voters remained perfectly capable of identifying the more efficacious instruments of change. As a result, they were not inclined to switch to Labastida. At the same time, Labastida's emphasis on change failed to rally his natural base. The April debacle underscored all these facts and prompted Labastida to alter his strategy. By then, however, it was too late. Fox had established himself as the focal point for opposition sentiment, and Labastida's initial lead in the polls had disappeared. It was an open race.

Labastida did not lose as much support from the second debate, despite the fact that audiences were no kinder in their assessments of his performance. Presumably, voters' preferences were firmer by late May, and reinforcement effects thus dominated to an even greater degree than in the first debate. It is also possible that Labastida's change in message alienated opposition voters but prevented further deterioration in his support among PRI voters. In any case, the second debate failed to recoup Labastida's earlier losses.

The effect of the debates on campaign strategy calls attention to the *indirect* influence that these encounters had on the 2000 contest. The 2000 debates dominated news coverage, provided fodder for political discussion, and absorbed the energies of the main contenders and their staffs. Even when the reactions of the mass public to the debates were relatively modest or short lived, then, the reactions of opinion elites were not. As a result, the debates came to serve as focal points for crucial decisions about campaign strategy, which themselves shaped the rest of the contest. The first debate, for instance, confirmed Fox as the main opposition challenger, led another opposition contender to withdraw, and encouraged Cárdenas to refocus on his core base. Black Tuesday had an equally profound effect, helping (among other things) to rehabilitate Cárdenas in the minds of some opposition voters. Finally, the second debate helped to repair the damage from Fox's pre-debate performance and revitalize his campaign. In both April and May, then, candidate encounters exercised an important influence on the election. Even beyond their direct impact on public opinion, the candidate encounters of 2000 constituted crucial campaign events.

Notes

1. Data are taken from a daily content analysis by *Reforma* newspaper, which was conducted for twelve hours every day in three different times: early morning (6 through 10 a.m.), early afternoon (1 through 4 p.m.), and evening prime time (7 through 11 p.m.) for every type of program broadcast in the corresponding time on the two national networks. Data from the Federal Electoral Institute's media monitoring effort show virtually identical results.

2. Among respondents in the fourth round of the panel, approximately 40 percent reported seeing all or part of the first debate—almost exactly the same amount.

3. Unfortunately, the third wave of the panel included no questions on the (unexpected) "pre-debate," which took place after the questionnaire for the third round had already been prepared. Fifty percent of the postelectoral cross-section and 48 percent of those in the fourth wave of the panel (July) reported having seen the "pre-debate."

4. The exact figures were 57 percent in the fourth wave of the panel and 62 percent in the postelectoral cross-section.

5. In Spanish: "Mi estimado Señor Labastida, a mí tal vez se me quite lo majadero, pero a ustedes, lo mañosos, lo malos para gobernar, y lo corruptos no se les va a quitar nunca."

6. When surveys by *Reforma* are weighted by the demographics of the exit polls, thus making them more comparable to the actual electorate, the debate marks the first time that Fox definitively took the lead (author's correspondence with Alejandro Moreno).

7. Author's interviews with Labastida campaign staff, Mexico City, June 2000.

8. See *Reforma*, May 24, 2000, p. 1. In the Mexico 2000 Panel Study, 50 percent of the postelectoral cross-section and 48 percent of those in the fourth wave of the panel reported having seen at least part of the event.

9. Televisión Azteca, on the other hand, announced that it was ready to hold the debate whenever the candidates were ready.

10. Mony de Swaan, Carolina Gómez, and Juan Molinar Horcasitas, "Medios y objetividad," *Milenio Diario*, June 25, 2000.

11. Author's interview with Rafael Giménez, director of ARCOP and pollster for the Fox campaign, Mexico City, May 2000.

12. According to the ground rules (enforced by the moderator), none of the candidates' interventions during the free discussion period could be more than a minute long, and no candidate could have more than four interventions during each period.

13. Cárdenas declined to take the document, but Rocha gallantly accepted it in his place. In a humiliation for Fox, it later transpired that the password he had delivered did not work.

14. See note 3.

15. Debate exposure was measured according to whether respondents had watched all, part, or none of the debate (with watching the entire event counting as two exposures and watching part counting as one exposure), whether they had seen commentary about the debate on television, whether they had heard commentary about the debate on the radio, whether they had read commentary about it in a newspaper or magazine, and whether they had discussed the debate with friends and family members (with one exposure for each). In table 9.6, respondents with zero or one exposure were categorized as "low exposure"; those with two or three exposures were treated as "medium exposure"; and those with four or more exposures were considered "high exposure."

16. Author's interview with Rafael Giménez, Mexico City, May 2000.

17. Items in the index included: candidates' perceived capacity to manage the economy, candidates' perceived capacity to control crime, candidates' perceived capacity to improve the educational system, and candidates' perceived honesty. The index for the third wave was constructed the same way, with the exception that the third wave of the panel lacked the question on honesty. Fortunately, this item was included in the fourth wave of the panel, and responses to this item were included in the index for those respondents who participated in both the third and fourth waves (about three-quarters of third-wave participants). Replicating the analysis for both debates without the item on honesty did not substantially change the results.

18. All items were weighted equally, and the index included responses to all these items for all waves of the panel in which the respondent participated.

19. Continuous variables were held at the mean values; categorical variables were held at their modal values. Thus the base case in this model was a PRI identifier or leaner who planned to vote for Labastida in February.

20. For further detail, see note 15. Distributions for the first debate were as follows: no exposures, 25 percent; one exposure, 21 percent; two exposures, 18 percent; three exposures, 15 percent; four exposures, 11 percent; and five or more exposures, 12 percent.

Chapter 9 Appendix

Table 9.10. Effects of Exposure to First Debate on Candidate Trait Ratings

Variable	Labastida		Fox		Cárdenas	
	Coefficient	Stan. Error	Coefficient	Stan. Error	Coefficient	Stan. Error
Constant	.691**	.139	.857**	.139	.675**	.144
North	.162*	.066	-.074	.067	-.047	.069
Center	-.047	.066	-.024	.068	-.179*	.071
Metro	-.095	.064	-.172**	.065	-.097	.068
Year of birth	.004*	.002	-.001	.002	-.000	.002
Gender (male)	.009	.048	-.042	.049	.091†	.051
Urban residency	-.009	.055	.033	.056	-.043	.058
Education	-.025	.026	.073**	.027	.051†	.028
Church attendance	.002	.020	.018	.020	.023	.021
Union membership	.019	.069	.002	.070	.106	.073
Socioeconomic status	-.020	.061	-.012	.062	-.042	.065
Debate exposure	.145	.094	.176†	.094	-.072	.098
Campaign index	-.037	.054	.000	.055	.125*	.057
Labastida rating (February)	.376**	.029	—		—	
PRI ID (February)	.458**	.053	—		—	
Fox rating (February)	—		.370**	.030	—	
PAN ID (February)	—		.203**	.057	—	
Cárdenas rating (February)	—		—		.445**	.031
PRD ID (February)	—		—		.280**	.076
N	831		800		795	
F-statistic	37.9		21.8		25.0	
Adjusted R-squared	.38		.27		.30	

Note: † $p < .10$; * $p < .05$; ** $p < .01$

Table 9.11. Effects of Exposure to First Debate on Candidate Feeling Thermometers

Variable	Labastida		Fox		Cárdenas	
	Coefficient	Stan. Error	Coefficient	Stan. Error	Coefficient	Stan. Error
Constant	5.68**	.588	7.00**	.587	4.39**	.617
North	.225	.272	.257	.275	-.055	.278
Center	-.048	.276	.126	.283	-.201	.282
Metro	-.393	.259	-.301	.263	-.198	.266
Year of birth	.011	.008	-.017*	.008	-.013†	.008
Gender (male)	-.061	.199	-.151	.202	.063	.206
Urban residency	-.581*	.227	-.393†	.230	-.402†	.234
Education	-.189†	.108	-.004	.110	.008	.110
Church attendance	.047	.084	-.017	.086	.024	.088
Union membership	.561†	.288	-.523†	.295	.062	.297
Socioeconomic status	-.366	.250	.336	.256	-.102	.259
Debate exposure	-.768*	.386	.397	.392	.128	.396
Campaign index	-.097	.225	.126	.229	.016	.232
Labastida rating (February)	.002	.003	—	—	—	—
PRI ID (February)	2.56**	.199	—	—	—	—
Fox rating (February)	—	—	.004	.003	—	—
PAN ID (February)	—	—	2.13**	.219	—	—
Cárdenas rating (February)	—	—	—	—	.320**	.035
PRD ID (February)	—	—	—	—	1.58**	.309
N	850		841		732	
F-statistic	19.9		8.2		13.6	
Adjusted R-squared	.24		.11		.20	

Note: † $p < .10$; * $p < .05$; ** $p < .01$

Table 9.12. Effects of Exposure to Second Debate on Candidate Trait Ratings

Variable	Labastida		Fox		Cárdenas	
	Coefficient	Stan. Error	Coefficient	Stan. Error	Coefficient	Stan. Error
Constant	.797**	.146	.928**	.146	.838**	.148
North	.032	.069	.158*	.072	.087	.072
Center	.079	.065	.186**	.068	-.025	.067
Metro	-.045	.064	-.104	.066	-.019	.065
Year of birth	.003†	.002	.001	.002	.002	.002
Gender (male)	.006	.049	-.003	.050	.124	.050
Urban residency	-.035	.059	.091	.061	-.035	.060
Education	.009	.027	.043	.027	.005	.027
Church attendance	.016	.021	-.011	.022	.009	.022
Union membership	.049	.074	-.018	.076	.059	.075
Socioeconomic status	-.033	.055	.002	.056	-.001	.056
Debate exposure	-.205*	.091	.066	.093	.113	.092
Campaign index	.044	.047	.036	.048	.037	.048
Labastida rating (Feb.)	.373**	.030	—	—	—	—
PRI ID (Feb.)	.347**	.056	—	—	—	—
Fox rating (Feb.)	—	—	.240**	.032	—	—
PAN ID (Feb.)	—	—	.405**	.060	—	—
Cárdenas rating (Feb.)	—	—	—	—	.317**	.030
PRD ID (Feb.)	—	—	—	—	.388**	.077
N	856		845		844	
F-statistic	30.7		19.9		16.2	
Adjusted R-squared	.33		.24		.20	

Note: † $p < .10$; * $p < .05$; ** $p < .01$

Table 9.13. Effects of Exposure to Second Debate on Candidate Feeling Thermometers

Variable	Labastida		Fox		Cárdenas	
	Coefficient	Stan. Error	Coefficient	Stan. Error	Coefficient	Stan. Error
Constant	5.93**	.593	5.30**	.577	2.30**	.567
North	-.122	.285	.302	.282	.204	.266
Center	.185	.266	.313	.265	-.037	.248
Metro	-.181	.255	-.654**	.253	.153	.240
Year of birth	.007	.007	-.001	.007	.006	.007
Gender (male)	-.082	.197	.158	.195	.092	.185
Urban residency	-.439*	.242	.205	.239	.051	.226
Education	-.220*	.109	.081	.108	.083	.100
Church attendance	.009	.084	-.011	.084	.086	.081
Union membership	.455	.299	-.477	.299	-.044	.279
Socioeconomic status	.021	.221	-.162	.219	-.116	.210
Debate exposure	-.979**	.364	-.194	.363	-.012	.342
Campaign index	-.214	.189	-.042	.187	-.162	.176
Labastida rating (February)	.004	.004	—	—	—	—
PRI ID (February)	2.67**	.201	—	—	—	—
Fox rating (February)	—	—	.006†	.003	—	—
PAN ID (February)	—	—	2.47**	.213	—	—
Cárdenas rating (February)	—	—	—	—	-.298**	.031
PRD ID (February)	—	—	—	—	1.47**	.290
N	893		890		796	
F-statistic	20.9		12.2		12.6	
Adjusted R-squared	.24		.15		.17	

† $p < .10$; * $p < .05$; ** $p < .01$

10

The Effects of Negative Campaigns on Mexican Voters

ALEJANDRO MORENO

When President Ernesto Zedillo appeared on television in the evening of July 2, 2000, Mexicans witnessed what no one had seen in their country for seventy-one years. The president conceded his party's loss in the presidential election and acknowledged Vicente Fox's victory. "For the well-being of our beloved country, I wish success to the next government, which will be led by Mr. Fox," Zedillo declared in an live television announcement.[1] Ruling party candidate Francisco Labastida, who had served as governor of Sinaloa and as interior minister in Zedillo's administration, conceded defeat around midnight. The once invincible Institutional Revolutionary Party (PRI) had lost the presidency.

In the following hours and days, politicians, journalists, and political analysts provided several immediate yet plausible explanations for the PRI's defeat. Interpretations included the memorable effects of the 1994–1995 peso crisis; an apparently divisive PRI primary; a weak PRI candidate facing a charismatic opposition contender; substantial differences in campaign messages, strategies, and tactics; media coverage; a great deal of strategic voting; and an unusually low participation of PRI loyalists—in addition to the fact that the PRI's vote share had been in decline election after election. For most political actors, there was no single explanation for the historical event, but rather a set of causes that ultimately led to political change.

Like other contributors to this volume, I argue that the 2000 campaign had significant effects on the outcome of the race. Voting intentions

Table 10.1. The Mexican Horse Race: Candidate Preferences in 2000 (subsamples of likely voters)

"If the presidential election were held today, for whom would you vote?"

	January 2000	February 2000	March 2000	April 2000	May 2001	May 2002	June 2002
	%	%	%	%	%	%	%
Francisco Labastida/PRI	50	44	44	42	37	39	39
Vicente Fox/PAN-PVEM	35	42	42	45	43	43	43
Cuauhtémoc Cárdenas/ PRD-Others	14	13	12	12	17	15	15

Source: Reforma, national preelection polls, N = 1,500 average for the total sample each month.

Note: The official election results were: Fox, 43 percent; Labastida, 38 percent; and Cárdenas, 17 percent.

changed substantially from the time Francisco Labastida won the PRI nomination in November 1999—when he was leading in most polls by as much as 20 percentage points among the general public—to the day he lost the presidential race by 6.5 percentage points. As the data in table 10.1 show, Labastida lost about 11 points from January to June, while support for Fox grew by about 8 points over that same period.

Unlike other presidential contests in Mexico, when the government's record was relatively poor but the PRI still won, in 2000 both the government and the economy were performing relatively well, according to most political and financial analysts. Media polls indicated that President Zedillo enjoyed an approval rating of 67 percent just a few weeks prior to the election.[2] Clearly, something other than current conditions convinced voters that it was time for a change. Part of the reason, I argue, lay in Fox's relentless attacks on Mexico's long-ruling party. In 1992, pundits captured the sentiment of the U.S. election and its motto, "It's the economy, stupid!" It seems that many Mexicans who supported Fox at the polls were driven by a parallel reasoning: "It's the PRI, stupid!"

Studying attitude change in an evolving political environment poses serious challenges; most of the theoretical frameworks that might be of use were developed under very different, more stable circumstances. My inquiry into what happened in Mexicans' minds as they watched the political campaigns on their televisions or discussed the campaigns with friends and family members seems justified by the fact that most of the information and campaign dynamic was absolutely new in Mexico. The degree of visible criticism and negativity had no precedent in the country's electoral history. I attempt to make a case for the careful study of campaign effects in Mexico by focusing on how voters received and processed negative campaign messages.

Specifically, I argue that the once impossible task of defeating the PRI in a presidential race was facilitated by negative campaigning. I first review the literature on negative campaigning, developing a model of "negativity reception gaps."[3] I then describe the content of the 2000 campaign and illustrate its negative character. Third, I analyze the effects of negativity reception gaps on political attitudes and voting behavior. Finally, I discuss the implications of these findings for the outcome of the 2000 race. Overall, I show that "going negative" worked for Vicente Fox, not by attracting new voters but by influencing many of his main opponent's partisans to abandon their candidate. At the same time, Francisco Labastida's own negativity had an unexpected result: it hurt his image among some of his early supporters.

THE EFFECTS OF NEGATIVE CAMPAIGNS ON THE ELECTORATE

Going negative is an old campaign practice. Reverend Timothy Dwight, once president of Yale, said: "If [Thomas] Jefferson is elected, the Bible will be burned, the French 'Marseillaise' will be sung in Christian churches, [and] we will see our wives and daughters the victims of legal prostitution; soberly dishonored; [and] speciously polluted."[4]

As in the preceding example, candidates are common targets of accusations and criticism in political campaigns. The 1876 U.S. presidential race illustrates some of the negativity in campaign messages. "Despite their personal standing, the election was exceptionally dirty. [Samuel J.] Tilden was called a syphilitic swindler and [Rutherford B.] Hayes was accused of murdering his mother in a fit of insanity—an impressive double calumny."[5]

Examples of negative campaigns abound, both from the "good old days" and from more recent media-dominated electoral contests. Nonetheless, scholarly efforts to theorize on the effects of negativity are rather scarce. Most of the literature on negative campaigns reports findings from specific races at different levels of public office, but still lacking is a relatively consistent body of theory.

Both rational choice and social psychological approaches conclude that negative campaigning works, though these perspectives disagree on the exact mechanisms that are operating. Negative ads are processed and remembered more easily than positive or advocacy ads, and they appear to be potentially more persuasive. Negative ads also seem to increase the public's level of information, thereby producing learning effects. In fact, people learn more about candidates and issues through negative ads than through positive ones. Despite the fact that voters do not like negative messages and attacks, negative ads provide voters with valuable information about the potential costs of their voting decisions.

Some of the effects of negativity act, directly or indirectly, on candidate image and voting intentions. For example, negative ads generally improve their sponsor's image and weaken his or her opponent's. Consequently, negative ads increase electoral support for their sponsor.

Several caveats apply to these conclusions. First, negativity may only help candidates in general elections and not in primary elections, suggesting that different types of electorates react differently to negative messages and criticisms. Second, the degree to which negative ads decrease the probability of voting for the attacked candidate depends on several factors; for example, going negative increases the challenger's chances of winning but decreases the incumbent's chances, according to district-level studies. Finally, credibility also plays a role: negative ads that are perceived as true are favorable for their sponsor and unfavorable for the target.

Since the publication of Ansolabehere and Iyengar's *Going Negative* in 1995, studies about the effects of negativity have focused heavily on turnout. Ansolabehere and Iyengar concluded that negative messages activate voters with a stronger partisan predisposition and demobilize less partisan and more independent voters, decreasing turnout and polarizing the electorate. Nonetheless, subsequent findings have been somewhat inconsistent, providing contradictory evidence of the demobilizing effects of negativity. Some analysts argue that negativity reduces turnout, some that it increases it, and some that it has no effect whatsoever on turnout. Moreover, there may be a double effect: negative ads may reduce turnout in districts with a high proportion of independent voters but increase it in highly partisan ones. All of these findings provide useful information for political consultants, but they fall far short of providing a solid theoretical framework for scholarly work.

In his study of the campaign to ratify the American Constitution, William Riker provides an adequate theoretical foundation for analyzing negativity.[6] Riker conceives of campaigns in terms of framing—as an attempt to persuade voters to see what is at stake in an election in a way the candidate wants them to see it. More specifically, Riker thinks of campaign rhetoric as *heresthetic*, the art of presenting a structure of choices in such a way that even those who would not support a position would end up doing so. In this sense, going negative exposes the dangers of electing one's opponents in a world where voters are generally risk averse. If effective, negative messages lead voters to minimize their maximum regret from their vote, following what Riker calls a "minimax regret strategy." In other words, negative messages attempt to persuade voters that certain choices could lead to maximum regret.

Negativity "Gaps" and Persuasion

In most campaigns, negative messages do not go in one direction only; the sponsor of an attack may be the target of an attack by another sponsor at the same time. The potential for such campaign effects to cancel each other out adds to the difficulty of assessing these effects. However, the potential for persuasion may increase if some messages are more intensely perceived—or received—than others. This idea echoes that of "receptions gaps," originally developed by John Zaller.[7]

Research on public opinion has consistently found that individuals vary significantly in their levels of attention to political information. In the presence of competing political messages, other things being equal, individuals who are more likely to receive a message from one source are as likely to receive a message from another source. Likewise, those who are less likely to receive a message from one source are also less likely to receive a message from another. This factor also adds to the difficulty of assessing the effects.

Zaller proposes a way to surmount this difficulty.[8] If the intensity of opposing messages is the same, he argues, the effects of one or the other are hard to observe and seldom make a difference in the aggregate, since they cancel one another out. However, if the relative intensity of messages varies, it should be possible to determine which individuals receive the dominating message. The difference between receiving a more intense message and receiving a less intense one constitutes what Zaller calls a "reception gap." According to this approach, the effects of the dominating message should be stronger among those who report a higher reception gap—that is, among those who "get" one message but not the other. These individuals are usually characterized by holding middle to low levels of political attention. Zaller notes, however, that the group most affected by campaigns might vary depending on the intensity of the campaign: the lower the intensity, the higher the effects on the most attentive; the higher the intensity, the higher the effects on the least attentive.

Borrowing Zaller's concepts, I assume that negative opposing messages (like any other type of political communication) compete with each other and that some negative messages have a greater degree of reception than others. I also assume that reception of negative messages may lead to persuasion and, therefore, to observable impacts of negative campaigns. Although the Mexico 2000 Panel Study does not offer a way to control for specific negative messages, as in an experimental situation, it nevertheless offers an excellent way to observe the effects of negativity gaps and determine which potential voters are more likely to be influenced by them. To supplement the panel data, I also draw on other information sources to develop my argument; these include national cross-section polls, a national exit poll, and media monitoring data that help demonstrate the tone and magnitude of the campaign messages.

NEGATIVE CAMPAIGNS AND POLITICAL PREFERENCES IN THE 2000 MEXICAN PRESIDENTIAL RACE

There are many types of negative campaigns—candidate centered, party centered, policy centered, and so on.[9] Mexican election campaigns, especially negative campaigns, have been heavily regime centered, with attacks and criticism aimed at the very fundamentals of the PRI regime. Many of Vicente Fox's messages, for example, focused on his opponents, and several ads used candidate-centered messages and images that emphasized the other candidates' characters, usually as response tactics at specific moments in the campaign. In general, though, the Fox campaign's strategy was twofold. First, Fox had to expose the PRI regime as corrupt and inefficient, and thus convince voters that it was time for a change. The word "change" (*cambio*) was of central importance as a rhetorical weapon, and in order to make change appealing to voters the status quo had to be harshly criticized in a credible way. Second, Fox had to present himself to the electorate not as the best but as the only alternative for change. Otherwise, the anti-PRI vote might split, allowing the ruling party to win in a three-way race. Accomplishing both tasks would rally voters to oppose the PRI and dissuade some of them from voting for Cuauhtémoc Cárdenas, a three-time presidential candidate nominated by the leftist Alliance for Mexico.

Jorge G. Castañeda, a Fox campaign adviser and later foreign minister in the Fox cabinet, argued that Fox "transformed the election from a beauty contest into a referendum on change, challenging Mexicans to vote for or against perpetuating the PRI's hold on power."[10] Although this message was more visible than in the past, it was not new. Regime-centered negative messages were not an invention of the Fox campaign; they had been around for some time. What is puzzling is the way in which voters reacted to them in 2000.

Political campaigns in Mexico have been charged with negativity. Opposition parties typically blamed the PRI regime for corruption and perennial economic crises. The PRI traditionally appealed to voters' fears of change, arguing that things could be worse if inexperienced opposition figures came to power. So many competing messages discrediting the other's opponents can be expected to obscure the effects of negativity. However, the PRI's messages have usually been more salient than the opposition's, simply because the ruling party enjoyed more access to the media than did its competitors. It was not until the 1997 congressional elections, when financial resources became more balanced and opposition parties were able to advertise intensely on television, that the opposition's negative messages began to reach a wider electorate.[11] News coverage was generally more balanced in that contest, and the amount of information that voters received during the 1997 campaign was negatively associated with attitudes toward the PRI.[12] It is reasonable to expect, then, that campaign information—negativity included—played a role in 2000 as well.

Negative messages could be found in speeches, debates, news coverage, and political advertising. The televised presidential debates were the perfect arena for direct confrontation and attacks. "[Fox] has called me shorty, fairy, drag queen, suck-up," complained Labastida in the April presidential debate, trying to expose Fox as a vulgar man. Fox replied: "Mr. Labastida, I may stop being vulgar, but you and you party will never stop being deceitful and corrupt."[13] Some of these exchanges were aired repeatedly in nightly news broadcasts and, of course, in televised political ads. News coverage sometimes portrayed the candidates and their parties as attack dogs, and the media themselves occasionally engaged in attack journalism, adding to a highly negative environment.

In 2000, the amount of coverage (in minutes) given to the three main presidential candidates was relatively balanced.[14] According to the Federal Electoral Institute's (IFE) monitoring of the media, the amount of coverage was not biased toward any of the major candidates, as it had been in the past. However, the IFE's monitoring, which covered national and local news broadcasts, lacked two important elements for understanding the tone of the campaign. First, it was limited to radio and television news programs while ignoring other types of programming popular with Mexican audiences. Second, its measures of the tone coverage were qualitatively inadequate, offering little evidence about the nature of news coverage. Based on its monitoring, IFE concluded that most of the information provided in the news was "candidate neutral." Since tone matters for the study of negativity, it is crucial to determine not only the amount of time devoted to political coverage by candidate but also the quality of this information.

An alternative though more modest monitoring of electronic media conducted by the newspaper *Reforma* illustrates some central features of the campaign's information flow. Table 10.2 shows total airtime for each of the three main presidential candidates on the major radio and television networks based in Mexico City but with a national reach. The monitoring was conducted for twelve hours every day in three different times: early morning (6 through 10 a.m.), early afternoon (1 through 4 p.m.), and evening prime time (7 through 11 p.m.). Every type of program broadcast on the selected channels in the corresponding time slots was monitored, including news programs, sports coverage, soap operas, and entertainment programming. One media innovation in the 2000 campaign was the inclusion of the presidential candidates on talk shows, where the tone was less policy oriented and more prone to criticism and attacks advanced with a degree of humor. Because *Reforma*'s monitoring recorded both the time and tone of media messages, it offers useful data about candidate coverage on radio and television.

Table 10.2. Candidate Coverage on Radio and Television, January 1–June 28, 2000 (paid advertising not included)

	Cárdenas	Fox	Labastida	Total
Total number of seconds	483,962	758,914	628,016	1,870,892
(percent)	(25.9%)	(40.6%)	(33.6%)	(100.0%)
Radio	409,693	660,563	536,378	1,606,634
	(25.5)	(41.1)	(33.4)	(100.0)
Favorable	140891	314,306	225,471	680,668
	(34.4)	(47.6)	(42.0)	
Neutral	197939	208,289	199,349	605,577
	(48.3)	(31.5)	(37.2)	
Unfavorable	70863	137,968	111,558	320,389
	(17.3)	(20.9)	(20.8)	
Television	74,269	98,351	91,638	264,258
	(28.1)	(37.2)	(34.7)	(100.0)
Favorable	27,019	33,159	41,325	101,503
	(36.4)	(33.7)	(45.1)	
Neutral	39,458	43,682	42,084	125,224
	(53.1)	(44.4)	(45.9)	
Unfavorable	7,792	21,510	8,229	37,531
	(10.5)	(21.9)	(9.0)	

Source: *Reforma*, daily monitoring. Entries are the total number of seconds registered for each candidate. Percentages are shown in parentheses and should be read horizontally for the totals and vertically for the favorable, neutral, and unfavorable categories.

According to the data in table 10.2, Vicente Fox had more free airtime, on both network television and radio, than any other candidate. Forty-one percent of the 1.8 million seconds dedicated to the three main presidential candidates between January 1 and June 28, 2000, when the campaign ended, was dedicated to Fox. Thirty-four percent focused on Labastida, and 26 percent on Cárdenas. The fact that an opposition presidential candidate had more airtime than a PRI candidate was unprecedented. Most of Fox's coverage was on radio, but television networks also assigned slightly more time to him than to his rivals: 37 percent of the 264,000 seconds monitored, as opposed to 35 percent for Labastida and 28 percent for Cárdenas.

Reforma classified coverage as "favorable," "neutral," and "unfavorable" depending on the source's tone and position at the time of the transmission. On radio, of all seconds of coverage centered on Fox, 48 percent was favorable, 31 percent neutral, and 21 percent unfavorable. Labastida's time coverage was 42 percent favorable, 37 percent neutral, and 21 percent unfavorable. The balance tipped toward Fox, who had a net favorable coverage (percent favorable minus percent unfavorable) on radio of 27 percentage points, versus Labastida's 21 points. Television time, however, was less favorable for Fox. In balance (favorable minus unfavorable time), Labastida had 36 points of net favorable coverage, whereas Fox had only 12 points. These numbers suggest that, although candidates had similar amounts of airtime, the tone of television coverage was biased toward the PRI candidate.

What about political advertising? According to *Reforma*'s monitoring, the Labastida campaign had more paid advertising time than Fox's or Cárdenas's, and sometimes even more than both of them together. This was this case even without taking into consideration government-sponsored ads, which accounted for more airtime during the campaign than the ads of all three major candidates combined.[15] Figure 10.1, which shows the weekly patterns of televised advertising from January to June, reveals the three campaigns' different strategies.

Without going into detail, the trends visible in the upper portion of the figure show that the Labastida and Fox campaigns increased their TV advertising as the election drew nearer. The Cárdenas campaign decreased its paid TV time at a moment when the other two candidates were advertising most heavily. Labastida's advertising peak in late May seems to be a response to the candidate's weak performance in the two televised presidential debates.

Figure 10.1. Total Time of Political Advertising and Time of Negative Advertising on Television by Presidential Candidate, January–June 2000

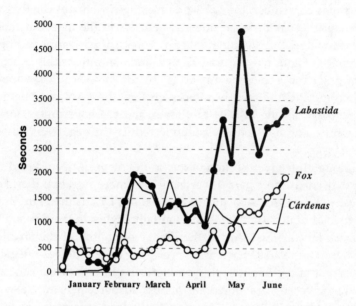

Political ads aired weekly on TV by candidate

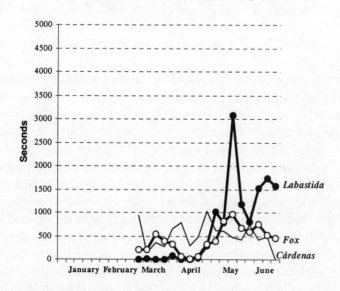

Negative political ads aired weekly on TV by candidate

Source: *Reforma*, daily monitoring.

The lower part of figure 10.1 shows the weekly airtime for advertisements coded as negative or attack ads by *Reforma*. It is evident that by mid-May the Labastida campaign had dramatically increased its television ads, most of them targeting Fox. As the data show and observers may remember, the Labastida messages were not charged with negativity until after the presidential debates. In the first four months of his campaign, the PRI candidate ran advocacy ads, emphasizing the importance of children learning English and computer skills in schools and of pregnant women having access to adequate health services. By the time the PRI initiated its attacks on Fox, the PAN candidate had already criticized the PRI, its candidate, and the government for several months, and had actually begun to reduce the negative tone of his rhetoric.

Although the lower portion of the figure, by itself, would lead us to think that Labastida's paid advertising was more negative than Fox's, this was not the case. Labastida did have more TV ads than Fox, but the relative load of negativity was substantially higher in the Fox ads than in Labastida's, at least during the first five months of the six-month campaign. Figure 10.2 shows the advertising time coded as "negative" as a percent of the total television advertising time for each candidate. Fox's negative ads accounted for almost 90 percent of his television advertising in mid-March. This negativity load was reduced to less than 10 percent by mid-April, but it then rose to over 90 percent by mid-May. In June, the last month of campaign, the electorate became less and less exposed to negative messages from Fox but increasingly exposed to those from Labastida, who started his attack strategy fairly late.

Fox had targeted the PRI regime in general, eventually adding ads that focused on Labastida; the PRI-sponsored ads, in contrast, emphasized Fox's character and personality: "a mendacious person with no principles whatsoever." One ad accused Fox of "exporting" gardeners to the United States when he served as a governor of Guanajuato, meaning that he failed to create the new jobs in his state that would have halted out-migration. In addition, Fox was generally portrayed as crass, with PRI ads asking voters whether they wanted to place their children's education in his hands. An all-time favorite ad used scenes from the so-called Black Tuesday, when Fox appeared on live television stubbornly arguing with Cárdenas and Labastida over the timing of the imminent presidential debate, with Fox insisting on "today." That incident made the phrase "today, today, today" famously Fox's.[16]

Figure 10.2. Negative Advertising as a Percent of Total Time of Political Advertising on Television by Presidential Candidate, March–June 2000

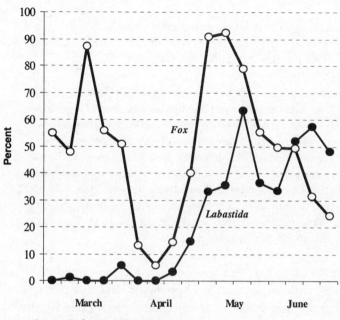

Source: *Reforma*, daily monitoring.

Unlike the PRI's advertising spots, of course, many of Fox's ads were regime centered. In November 1999, a PAN ad showed black and white images of the Mexican presidents since the 1970s while an off-screen voice asked, "Do they really think we don't remember? Do they really think we will swallow for another six years the same swill that has caused us so much suffering in the past?" This was just the beginning of a negative collection of campaign advertisements. Although images are difficult to reproduce here, the following transcripts of televised ads illustrate the sort of criticism leveled against the PRI regime:

> We don't forget that those who are responsible for [the student massacre in] 1968, for peso devaluations in 1976 and 1982, for the "system breakdown" [electoral fraud] in 1988, and for the "Errors of December" [the 1994 peso devaluation] are the same cynical people who are asking us to trust them

yet again. They have not changed, nor will they change. We, the majority of Mexicans, are the ones who have changed. We'll see you on July 2. We've already [ya] won. Vote for the Alliance for Change. Fox for President.

Imagine a country where government officials serve the public instead of serving themselves. Imagine Mexico without the PRI. Imagine it and it's done. Fox, now [ya].

[A man with his back to the camera speaks]: Hello. My name is Juan, and I'm portrayed like this because, well, I must look like a fool. If not, how can you explain that after seventy years of governing, they claim to represent change? This is my wife, María, who also must look like a fool. And now they are going to end the corruption, crime, and poverty that they themselves created. They think we are fools, but we aren't. On July 2, we are going to look to the future in Mexico. We are the majority, and we know the truth. There are more and more of us every day.

During the campaign, Fox was perceived as the candidate who levied the most criticism against his opponents, and this perception became even more widespread as the election neared. Table 10.3 provides some evidence of this. In March, 51 percent of respondents to a *Reforma* national poll said Fox spent most of his campaign criticizing other candidates, while 23 percent said he devoted most of his campaign to communicating his policy proposals. The proportion of respondents who said Fox was criticizing his opponents rose to 62 percent by June in the *Reforma* series of national polls, compared to about 47 percent for Labastida and Cárdenas, for a gap of 15 percentage points in perceived negativity between Fox and either of his two main opponents.

According to the lower part of table 10.3, Fox's perceived negativity emphasized his opponents' personalities and characters (48 percent) and, to a lesser extent, their political parties (42 percent), their record in office (41 percent), and their policy proposals (39 percent). These data suggest that direct personal attacks may have had the strongest impact on voters, though criticism of parties and the administration was also strong. I referred to some of Fox's attacks on Labastida above, but the PRI candidate was not always the target. Fox also accused Cárdenas of "returning" to the PRI, a party he had abandoned in 1987, by not joining the wave of change that Fox claimed to represent.

Table 10.3. Perceived Negativity and the Presidential Candidates

	March	May 14	May 28	June
"In your opinion, what is [CANDIDATE] mostly doing in his campaign—communicating policy proposals or criticizing other candidates?"	(%)	(%)	(%)	(%)
Fox				
Communicating proposals	23	26	22	22
Criticizing other candidates	51	51	59	62
Labastida				
Communicating proposals	42	38	45	36
Criticizing other candidates	35	41	38	47
Cárdenas				
Communicating proposals	27	30	31	32
Criticizing other candidates	41	43	46	47
"Which candidate is the one that has [ACTIVITY] the most?"				
Criticized other candidates' character				
Fox	—	—	—	48
Labastida	—	—	—	21
Cárdenas	—	—	—	11
Criticized other candidates' parties				
Fox	—	—	—	42
Labastida	—	—	—	17
Cárdenas	—	—	—	15
Criticized other candidates' record in office				
Fox	—	—	—	41
Labastida	—	—	—	18
Cárdenas	—	—	—	14
Criticized other candidates' proposals				
Fox	—	—	—	39
Labastida	—	—	—	21
Cárdenas	—	—	—	17
Sample sizes	1,533	1,547	1,543	1,545

Source: *Reforma*, national preelection polls.

The data in table 10.3 corroborate a perceived negativity gap: Fox was indeed the most negative candidate. Exit poll data confirm this: 51 percent of the 3,380 respondents in *Reforma*'s national exit poll said that Fox was the candidate who criticized his opponents the most, in contrast to 25 percent who named Labastida and 11 percent, Cárdenas. Since the Mexico 2000 Panel Study provides the main evidence for the rest of the argument, it is important to note that panel participants in the third wave also perceived Fox as the most negative candidate.

MODELING THE EFFECTS OF NEGATIVITY RECEPTION GAPS

Using the panel data, I calculate the negativity gaps for the two main candidates (Fox and Labastida) and then use them as variables in the rest of the analysis. Figure 10.3 shows a matrix with the proportion of panel respondents in the third wave of the Mexico 2000 Panel Study— conducted in June, a few weeks before the election—that are classified into one of four categories: (a) respondents who perceived Labastida and Fox more or less equally negative[17] (35 percent of respondents fall into this category); (b) respondents who perceived Labastida as criticizing others, but not Fox, which I will call a "Labastida negativity gap" (13 percent of respondents); (c) respondents who perceived Fox as criticizing others, but not Labastida—a "Fox negativity gap" (27 percent of respondents); and (d) neither candidate was perceived as negative, and thus there is no negativity gap (25 percent of respondents). The Fox negativity gap is 27 percent versus Labastida's 13 percent, resulting in a two-to-one negativity ratio, a finding consistent with the national polls and the exit poll mentioned earlier.

Who was more likely to perceive a negativity gap? Table 10.4 shows the results from a logistic regression model designed to answer this question. The model explains each of the four categories of perceived negativity separately. The explanatory variables are campaign awareness (based on recognition of candidate slogans),[18] perceptions of unfavorable news coverage for the candidates, and partisan identification. Both awareness and news coverage are variables from the third wave of the panel study; party identification was measured in the first wave.

The coefficients in table 10.4 indicate that measures of awareness and perceived coverage are strongly and negatively correlated with lack of negativity (first column): the higher the awareness and the more the perceived negative coverage, the lower the probability of perceiving no negativity. Awareness does not explain the Labastida negativity gap (column 2) nor the candidates being equally negative (column 4), but it does explain a Fox negativity gap (column 3)—the higher the campaign awareness, the more likely the perception of Fox's negativity. The coefficients in columns 2 through 4 for these variables indicate that perceptions of unfavorable coverage for Labastida increase the probabilities of a Labastida negativity gap and an equal negativity, but they decrease the probabilities of a Fox negativity gap. In contrast, perceptions of unfavorable coverage for Fox increase the probabilities of a Fox negativity gap but have no influence on a Labastida gap.

Figure 10.3. Negativity Gaps: Fox and Labastida

Fox

		Attack	No attack	
Labastida	Attack	35% (n=343) *(a) NO GAP*	13% (n=128) *(b) LABASTIDA GAP*	48% (n=471)
	No attack	27% (n=261) *(c) FOX GAP*	25% (n=251) *(d) NO GAP*	52% (n=512)
		61% (n=604)	39% (n=379)	100% (n=983)

Why is there such a divergence between these two variables? The answer appears to be that partisanship mediates perceptions of negative campaigns. Strong and weak PRI and PAN partisanship do not explain the lack of negativity gaps, but they do explain a portion of the Fox and Labastida gaps. For example, strong and weak PAN identifiers were more likely to perceive a Labastida gap, while strong PRI identifiers were less likely to do so. In other words, PAN partisans were more likely than PRI partisans to be aware of Labastida's attacks. By the same token, Fox's negativity gap was more likely to be perceived by strong and weak PRI identifiers and less likely to be seen by strong and weak PAN identifiers: PRI partisans were more aware than PAN partisans of Fox's attacks. In sum, party loyalists of a candidate's opponents were more likely to be cognizant of that candidate's negativity gap.

Table 10.4. A Model of Perceived Negativity (logistic regression coefficients)

	No Negativity	Significance Level	Labastida Negativity Gap	Significance Level	Fox Negativity Gap	Significance Level	Equally Negative	Significance Level
Campaign awareness	−0.200	0.000	0.038	0.534	**0.195**	0.000	0.014	0.740
Labastida unfavorable news coverage	−0.796	0.002	**0.735**	0.003	−0.944	0.000	**0.694**	0.000
Fox unfavorable news coverage	−0.488	0.010	−0.244	0.302	**0.541**	0.002	0.059	0.716
Strong PRI identification	−0.085	0.695	−1.267	0.004	**1.540**	0.000	−1.198	0.000
Weak PRI identification	0.105	0.606	−0.252	0.399	**0.563**	0.006	−0.441	0.019
Weak PAN identification	0.042	0.856	**1.070**	0.000	−0.875	0.004	−0.243	0.229
Strong PAN identification	0.316	0.320	**0.946**	0.005	−1.023	0.025	−0.308	0.286
Constant	−0.350	0.033	−2.212	0.000	−1.944	0.000	−0.473	0.003
−2 log likelihood	1066.555		697.898		992.907		1217.218	
Model chi-square	47.650	0.000	62.257	0.000	144.289	0.000	53.498	0.000
Percent correctly predicted	74.54%		86.97%		77.70%		67.11%	
Number of cases in the analysis	982		982		982		982	

Source: Mexico 2000 Panel Study, author's calculations.

Note: In order to facilitate the table reading, statistically significant coefficients, at least at 0.1, are bold (except for constant).

Figure 10.4 illustrates the previous argument graphically. Based on the model shown in table 10.4, the lines represent the estimated probabilities of Fox and Labastida negativity gaps by campaign awareness and party identification. This figure confirms that a Fox negativity gap was more likely among PRI identifiers and less likely among PAN identifiers. (Similarly, the Labastida gap was more likely among PAN identifiers.) This figure indicates that awareness made a significant difference in explaining the Fox gap but not the Labastida gap—that is, the higher the individual awareness, the higher the likelihood of a Fox negativity gap. But awareness, as mentioned earlier, does not explain the Labastida gap. To elaborate further, the Fox gap was strong among PRI identifiers generally, but it grew even stronger among highly aware PRI identifiers.

Were PRI identifiers more responsive to negative campaigns, especially Fox's? The answer is yes. Table 10.5 shows a dynamic model of candidate image based on eleven-point opinion thermometer differentials, using OLS regression. (Columns 2 and 3 are dynamic, since they assess within-candidate differentials from February to June, but column 1 is static and represents, for illustration purposes, between-candidate differentials in June.) In the first column, positive values represent Fox's favorable image, while negative values refer to Labastida's favorable image. Values close to zero represent indifference toward the candidates.[19] As the data show, campaign awareness is significantly and positively related to a favorable image of Fox. Those who perceived Fox's negativity gap (mostly PRI identifiers) were more likely to have a better opinion about Labastida. Those who perceived Labastida's gap (mostly PAN identifiers) were more likely to have a better opinion of Fox. Everything, then, is as expected.

Nonetheless, the story appears more striking when we look at changes over time. Let us look at Labastida's feeling thermometer differential. Positive values indicate an improvement in the opinion scale from February to June, while negative values represent deterioration of his image. According to the coefficients, Labastida's negativity gap hurt his image. Since we already know that Labastida's gap was more likely among PAN identifiers, we should expect to have a negative coefficient for them. However, PRI identifiers are the ones who have a negative and significant coefficient. In other words, Labastida's image was hurt by his own negativity among his own party loyalists.

Changes in Fox's image reveal a somewhat different story. Although a deteriorating Fox image was more likely among those who

Figure 10.4. Fox and Labastida Negativity Gaps by Campaign Awareness
(predicted probabilities from model in table 10.4)

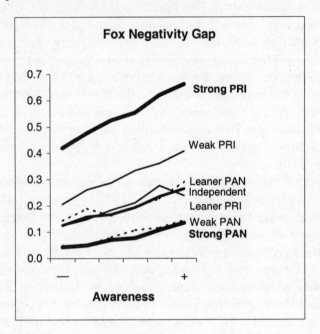

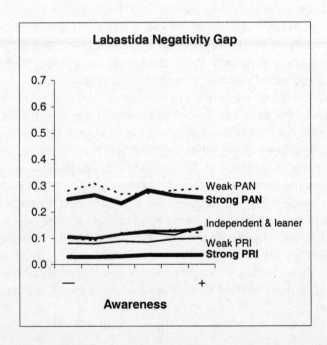

registered a Fox negativity gap, such deterioration was only significant among PRI identifiers. In sum, Fox's negative campaign did not hurt his image among PAN identifiers, even as Labastida's negativity did hurt his image among PRI identifiers.

Since the coefficients for equal negativity are significant for both candidates, perceiving both negative messages may not have any important impact on either candidate; they may simply have canceled each other out, as expected. In summary, negative campaigns hurt Labastida's image but not Fox's, since those who lowered their opinions of both candidates during the campaign were PRI identifiers. This did not hurt Fox, only Labastida. Negativity worked for the PAN's candidate but not for the PRI's.

Let us now turn to change in vote preference. Table 10.6 shows the same set of explanatory variables used in the previous discussion, but employed here to explain change in voting intention. The dependent variables are indicators of potential voters who stayed with either of the two main candidates (columns 1 and 2), switched from Fox to Labastida or from Labastida to Fox (columns 3 and 4), or simply abandoned either Fox or Labastida. These combinations are coded as dichotomous variables using responses to the questions on voting intention in February and June.

What determines loyalty to the candidates? What prompted respondents to stay with their preferred candidate from February to June? Overall, respondents who perceived Labastida's negativity gap, who identified with the PAN, and who were more aware of the campaign tended to stick with Fox. Labastida loyalists, on the other hand, were PRI partisans and those who perceived Fox's negativity gap. So far, the correlates of loyalty do not reveal anything striking, unless we accept a reinforcing role for negativity. The model of change in preferences, however, is a bit more revealing.

Negativity gaps had different impacts on respondents who switched from Labastida to Fox and vice versa. The Labastida negativity gap increased the chances of changing from Labastida to Fox, especially among PRI partisans, and it decreased the chances of changing from Fox to Labastida, mainly among PAN partisans. In contrast, the Fox negativity gap seems not to have influenced changes in preferences. In sum, Labastida's negativity hurt the PRI candidate by influencing some PRI partisans to switch to Fox.

This does not mean that Fox's negativity did not work at all to change preferences. Looking at columns 5 and 6 in table 10.6, which

Table 10.5. A Model of Changing Candidate Image and Negativity Gaps, February–June 2000 (ordinary least squares regression coefficients)

	Opinion Thermometer Differential—Fox minus Labastida in June		Opinion Thermometer Differential—Labastida in June minus Labastida in February		Opinion Thermometer Differential—Fox in June minus Fox in February	
	b[a]	Significance Level	b	Significance Level	b	Significance Level
Campaign awareness	**0.213**	0.005	0.008	0.910	0.025	0.733
Fox negativity gap	**−3.050**	0.000	0.467	0.164	**−1.821**	0.000
Labastida negativity gap	**2.880**	0.000	**−1.241**	0.002	0.320	0.403
Equally negative	0.306	0.336	**−0.810**	0.009	**−0.848**	0.006
Strong PRI identification	**−2.992**	0.000	**−0.979**	0.005	**−0.745**	0.030
Weak PRI identification	**−1.759**	0.000	**−1.070**	0.001	−0.244	0.433
Weak PAN identification	**1.311**	0.000	0.015	0.965	−0.549	0.101
Strong PAN identification	**2.401**	0.000	0.308	0.513	−0.170	0.711
Constant	0.502	0.149	0.737	0.033	1.131	0.001
Multiple R²	0.63				0.26	
Adjusted R²	0.39				0.06	

Source: Mexico 2000 Panel Study, author's calculations.

Note: In order to facilitate the table reading, statistically significant coefficients, at least at 0.1, are bold (except for constant).

[a] b = OLS regression coefficient.

Table 10.6. A Model of Changing Voting Intentions and Negativity Gaps, February–June 2000 (logistic regression coefficients)

	Fox Supporter Stays with Fox		Labastida Supporter Stays with Labastida		Fox Supporter Switches to Labastida		Labastida Supporter Switches to Fox		Fox Supporter Defects		Labastida Supporter Defects	
	b[a]	Sig[a]	b	Sig	b	Sig	b	Sig	b	Sig	b	Sig
Campaign awareness	0.223	0.000	−0.157	0.014	0.021	0.873	0.095	0.304	0.1422	0.110	−0.041	0.623
Fox negativity gap	−1.823	0.000	1.122	0.000	0.727	0.158	−0.461	0.333	−0.0296	0.940	1.153	0.011
Labastida negativity gap	1.232	0.000	−2.432	0.002	−1.989	0.065	2.252	0.000	0.2397	0.681	0.625	0.161
Equally negative	0.212	0.375	−0.368	0.154	−0.897	0.126	0.540	0.199	−0.1464	0.686	0.243	0.501
Strong PRI identification	−1.040	0.014	3.399	0.000	−1.497	0.172	1.758	0.000	−3.0625	0.003	3.137	0.000
Weak PRI identification	−1.066	0.002	2.096	0.000	0.140	0.831	2.372	0.000	−1.0183	0.018	3.431	0.000
Weak PAN identification	2.326	0.000	−0.816	0.073	1.938	0.000	−7.039	0.587	2.5445	0.000	−2.472	0.016
Strong PAN identification	2.895	0.000	−1.738	0.091	1.515	0.041	−1.002	0.348	3.3574	0.000	−1.630	0.115
Constant	−2.278	0.000	−1.660	0.000	−4.106	0.000	−4.638	0.000	−2.3308	0.000	−2.648	0.000
-2 log likelihood	684.430		641.511		196.263		339.005		347.725		354.687	
Model chi-square	409.998		494.456		29.300		96.126		129.021		252.163	
Percent correctly predicted	85.34%	0.000	86.49%	0.000	97.56%	0.000	94.70%	0.000	90.60%	0.000	89.49%	0.000
Number of cases analyzed	982		925		982		982		649		628	

Source: Mexico 2000 Panel Study, author's calculations.

Note: In order to facilitate the table reading, statistically significant coefficients, at least at 0.1, are bold (except for constant).

[a] b = logistic regression coefficient; sig = significance level.

present coefficients for abandoning either of the two candidates, we see that negativity gaps did not influence voters who abandoned Fox during the campaign, but the Fox negativity gap influenced some voters to abandon Labastida. In other words, Fox's negative messages worked, not necessarily by attracting voters to him but by influencing some early Labastida supporters to abandon the PRI candidate. This is the single most important piece of evidence about the persuasion effects of negative campaigns: Fox's negative messages prevented some PRI partisans from voting for Labastida. In other words, it seems likely that negativity had some demobilizing effect among initial PRI supporters.

In summary, negative messages are mediated by partisanship, and high campaign awareness makes individuals in general more likely to receive negativity gaps. The Fox negativity gap influenced PRI partisans, especially the most highly aware ones, to abandon Labastida. The data analyzed here thus provide evidence that negative campaigns in the 2000 Mexican presidential election had significant effects on voters' opinions and preferences.

CONCLUSION

The July 2000 presidential election is now regarded as a historic event for Mexicans. To public opinion researchers and political scientists, it offers a good opportunity to understand the dynamics of information and the effects of negative campaigns. The winning candidate had been perceived as the most negative competitor in most surveys, and with good reason: he was indeed the most negative according to content analysis of television advertisements and news coverage. Analysis of panel data demonstrates that Fox's negativity worked, but it was not as effective in buying him more supporters as it was in influencing his opponents' supporters to defect. At the same time, Labastida's own negativity brought unexpected results for his campaign: it weakened his image among many of his own party. The combined effects may have accounted for a great deal of the 19 percent difference in support that switched from Labastida's favor to Fox's between the beginning of the campaign in January and its conclusion in June.

One lesson from 2000 is that, in a competitive election, negative campaigns work for a challenger who goes negative early on, but not for a candidate of the incumbent party who begins running a negative campaign late in the game, especially among his own followers. Independent voters are, in general, less attentive to negative messages than to partisan ones, and therefore the negative effects among nonpartisans may have been weaker than among partisans. According to the data presented in this chapter, negative messages, measured as reception gaps, are more highly received by supporters of the target candidate. This may lead partisans to perceive their preferred candidate's negative messages as less negative. This was true for Fox but not for Labastida. Although Fox's negativity had little impact on changing his own supporters' minds (unless we acknowledge a reinforcing effect on them), it had a significant effect on changing some PRI partisans' voting intentions. Likewise, Labastida's negativity had little impact on changing PAN partisans' preferences, but it had a significant effect on worsening his own followers' opinion of him. In conclusion, PRI partisans were more likely to be influenced by negative campaigns.

This chapter leaves open the question of what happened to Labastida supporters who defected as a result of exposure to negative campaigning. They did not go to Fox in significant numbers. Some surely went to Cárdenas, but many simply did not vote. Analysis of the effects of negative campaigning thus lends further support to conclusions in other chapters in this volume about changes in the partisan composition of turnout over the course of the 2000 presidential race.

Notes

1. *Reforma*, July 3, 2000.

2. *Reforma*, June 1, 2000.

3. I borrowed the concept of "reception gaps" from Zaller's effort to isolate the effects of competing messages in the process of political communication. See John Zaller, "The Myth of Massive Media Impact Revived: New Support for a Discredited Idea," in Diana C. Mutz, Paul M. Sniderman, and Richard A. Brody, eds., *Political Persuasion and Attitude Change* (Ann Arbor: University of Michigan Press, 1996). I elaborate more on this concept later in the chapter.

4. Kathleen Hall Jamieson, Paul Waldman, and Susan Sherr, "Eliminate the Negative? Categories of Analysis for Political Advertisements," in James A. Thurber, Candice J. Nelson, and David A. Dulio, eds., *Crowded Airwaves: Campaign Advertising in Elections* (Washington, D.C.: Brookings Institution Press, 2000).

5. *The Economist*, November 25, 2000.

6. William Riker, *The Strategy of Rhetoric: Campaigning for the American Constitution* (New Haven, Conn.: Yale University Press 1996).

7. Zaller, "The Myth of Massive Media Impact Revived."

8. Ibid.

9. See, for example, John H. Aldrich, "Presidential Campaigns in Party and Candidate-Centered Eras," in Matthew D. McCubbins, ed., *Under the Watchful Eye: Managing Presidential Campaigns in the Television Era* (Washington, D.C.: Congres-

sional Quarterly Press, 1992). See also Jamieson, Waldman, and Sherr, "Eliminate the Negative?"

10. See Jorge G. Castañeda, "A Historic Vote for Change," *Newsweek*, July 17, 2000.

11. See Chappell Lawson's contributions in this volume.

12. See Alejandro Moreno, "Campaign Awareness and Voting in the 1997 Mexican Congressional Elections," in Jorge I. Domínguez and Alejandro Poiré, eds., *Toward Mexico's Democratization: Parties, Campaigns, Elections, and Public Opinion* (New York: Routledge, 1999).

13. The original wording in Spanish is: Labastida: "*Me ha llamado chaparrito, mariquita, la vestida, mandilón.*" Fox: "*Señor Labastida, a mí tal vez se me quite lo majadero, pero a ustedes lo mañosos, lo corruptos ... no se les va a quitar nunca.*" For further discussion on the role of the debates, see the contributions by Lawson in this volume.

14. For further detail on the nature of television coverage, see the chapters by Lawson in this volume.

15. According to *Reforma*'s monitoring, from February 25 to May 25, 2000, government-sponsored ads outnumbered Fox's ads three to one and Cárdenas's ads four to one (*Reforma*, June 1, 2000).

16. For more on "Black Tuesday," see Lawson's chapter on the "great debates," in this volume.

17. The question is the same as that shown at the top of table 10.3.

18. This measure of campaign awareness was used in Moreno, "Campaign Awareness and Voting in the 1997 Mexican Congressional Elections," and is an additive index of slogan recognition. The third wave of the panel study included six candidate slogans, five of which were included in the index. Reliability analysis indicates a Cronbach's alpha of .74.

19. See Federico Estévez and Alejandro Moreno, "Campaign Effects and Issue-Voting in the PRI Primary," presented at the international congress of the Latin American Studies Association, Miami, 2000.

11

Strategic Coordination in the 2000 Mexican Presidential Race

BEATRIZ MAGALONI AND ALEJANDRO POIRÉ

Divisions within Mexico's opposition played a major role in sustaining the long-lasting dominance of the Institutional Revolutionary Party (PRI). Patterns in local elections during the last twenty years demonstrate that the PRI tended to prevail more often where the opposition stood divided and where a tripartisan mode of competition existed. By contrast, the PRI tended more often to lose where there was a bipartisan mode of party competition or an opposition coalition.[1] In 1999, opposition leaders from the National Action Party (PAN) and the Party of the Democratic Revolution (PRD) considered forging an all-encompassing opposition alliance for the 2000 presidential race. Although both the PRD's Cuauhtémoc Cárdenas and the PAN's Vicente Fox expressed interest in the idea, each wanted to lead the alliance. Eventually, both entered instead into alliances with minor parties, making it clear that there would be no coalition of left and right. As it turned out, such an alliance was not necessary; Fox defeated the PRI without the support of PRD party elites.

In this chapter we seek to assess the extent to which opposition co-ordination at the mass level contributed to the PRI's defeat. To what extent did PRD voters contribute to Fox's victory? Our findings indicate that Fox received support from strategic voters, but Cárdenas's dismal showing also demonstrates his failure to convince his supporters that he was the better opposition option. Mexicans who were more likely to cast a strategic vote saw Cárdenas as a sure loser and less competent than Fox. Strategic voters also tended to come disproportionately from those whose identification with the PRD was weak, leaving Cárdenas only those voters who had a strong attachment to his party.

Despite evidence of strategic voting, we conclude that a larger proportion of Fox votes came from sources other than the PRD—first, people who had traditionally voted for the PAN or reported identifying with this party; second, independent voters who did not lean toward any party but were attracted by Fox's candidacy; and third, PRI partisans dissatisfied with their party's candidate, most of whom probably had supported Roberto Madrazo in the PRI's primary.

In the first section below, we explain why a PAN-PRD alliance failed at the elite level. We then present evidence of strategic voting and calculate how much it contributed to Fox's victory. The third section presents a model of strategic voting. What led *perredistas* (PRD partisans) to remain loyal to Cárdenas? What considerations did PRD supporters take into account when deciding whether to defect to Fox or Labastida? To what extent were these defections driven by strategic considerations? Our concluding section discusses the implications of this analysis for Mexico's electorate and for the literature on strategic voting.

COORDINATION DILEMMAS AND A FAILED ALLIANCE

Coordination dilemmas among opposition forces play a major role in sustaining dominant parties.[2] During the years of PRI rule, both institutional and ideological factors helped to divide the opposition.[3] One rule that seriously discourages coordination is the prohibition on cross-endorsement of presidential candidates, established in the 1993 electoral reform. Opposition parties interested in endorsing a common presidential candidate must also craft alliances for all 628 legislative races for federal deputy and senator.[4] Coalitions must produce a joint electoral platform, notwithstanding ideological differences among the partners. Finally, the current electoral code awards an alliance the amount of public funding that its largest constituent party would have received, rather than the sum of the financing that each party in the alliance would have received if it fielded a separate candidate.

When PAN and PRD leaders discussed the possibility of forging an alliance for the 2000 presidential election, they tried to reverse the ban on cross-endorsements, which they viewed as a major impediment. The PRI, however, enjoyed a comfortable majority in the Senate and was able to block the proposed reform. Nevertheless, the fact that both the

PAN and PRD ultimately did form electoral coalitions indicates that this ban did not pose an insurmountable obstacle to coordination. If parties were committed to forging broad and lasting electoral alliances, they could cross-endorse a presidential candidate.

What accounts, then, for the willingness of the PAN and PRD to forge alliances with other minor parties but not between themselves? The key impediment was the choice of a presidential candidate: both parties saw themselves as the natural leader of the alliance, and neither Fox nor Cárdenas was prepared to yield the top spot.

There were also ideological obstacles to a PAN-PRD alliance that were not present in the Alliance for Change or the Alliance for Mexico. On economic issues, the PAN and PRD stand to the right and the left, respectively, of the PRI. Differences over economic issues have had a deeper effect on elite behavior than on mass behavior. For example, in the 57th Legislature, elected in 1997 (the first legislative session in which the PRI did not command a majority), the least frequent alliance was between the PAN and PRD. The PAN tended to vote with the PRI more often than with any other party.[5]

As coalition theory suggests, it is easier to coordinate legislative parties that share similar ideologies or that are "connected" in some ideological space.[6] The same dynamics seem to apply for electoral coalitions. At the local level, successful coordination among opposition parties has generally included ideologically connected parties, usually on the left. In only a handful of states (such as Nayarit and Chiapas) have the PAN and PRD successfully crafted electoral alliances.

Ideological cleavages also divided opposition voters. Over half of PAN and PRD voters were reluctant to support any such alliance, partly because they saw the large ideological incompatibilities between these two parties and partly because they did not want the alliance to be headed by the "wrong" candidate. In December 1998, 48 percent of those intending to vote for the PAN said they would support an alliance of the two parties, 41 percent opposed the proposed alliance, and 11 percent were in agreement only if the candidate heading the alliance was from the PAN. A similar division was found among PRD partisans: 48 percent reported being in favor of the alliance, 35 percent against, and 17 percent in support only if the candidate to the presidency was from the PRD.[7] Thus less than half of PAN and PRD supporters gave unconditional backing to the potential alliance. The majority either opposed the alliance or supported it only if it were headed by the "right" candidate.

Those who objected to the alliance did so primarily on ideological grounds, perceiving larger incompatibilities between the PAN and PRD than between either of the opposition parties and the PRI. Mexico's landscape has at least two dimensions.[8] On the economic dimension, the PAN and PRD stand apart, with the PRI positioned in the middle. On the political dimension, however, the PAN and PRD have generally stood together, sharing the goal of establishing a democracy and defeating the PRI. Opposition voters who are likely to coordinate, or might support, an all-encompassing opposition alliance must give a higher salience to the political than to the economic dimension. As Magaloni has argued, the relative salience of these two dimensions is clearly reflected in the voters' preference profiles among the three major parties.[9]

In Magaloni's national survey, respondents were asked which party they would vote for if they had to choose between two alternatives.[10] Using these binary comparisons, we construct voter preference orders among the three major parties. Following Magaloni, we classify opposition voters into three categories (in the formulas, > indicates a strong preference and ≥ indicates a weak preference). The first are *radical opposition voters*, who rank the PRI third.[11] Preference profiles such as PAN > PRD > PRI or PRD > PAN > PRI fit this characterization. The second category is *ideological opposition voters*, who rank the PRI second. Preference profiles such as PAN > PRI > PRD or PRD > PRI > PAN fall into this category. The last category is *rigid opposition voters*, who, unable to rank the three parties, only report a first preference. The preference profiles of rigid voters are PAN > PRI ≥ PRD or PRD > PRI ≥ PAN. These voters can be regarded as a party's base, voters who were highly unlikely to cast a vote for any party other than their own.

Preference profiles reflect whether a voter perceives the economic-ideological dimension or the political dimension as the more salient. Ideological opposition voters perceive larger incompatibilities between opposition parties than between either the PAN or PRD and the PRI, indicating a higher saliency for the economic dimension in voters' utility functions. *Radical opposition voters*, in contrast, see more commonalities among the opposition. These voters want to defeat the PRI regardless of party or economic platform. Finally, rigid opposition voters seem to place the highest value on party loyalty and dislike any alternative to their own party.

In Table 11.1 we report opposition voter types by preference profiles obtained from the Reforma national poll in December 1998, when a possible PAN-PRD alliance was first debated in the media. Among

PAN supporters, 29 percent were "ideological," 40 percent were "radical" and potentially strategic, and 31 percent were "rigid." There were more potentially strategic voters among PRD supporters (20 percent ideological, 45 percent radical, and 35 percent rigid).

Table 11.1. Opposition Types Derived from Preference Rankings, December 1998

Ranking	Percent	Ranking	Percent
PAN Ideological	30	PRD Ideological	20
PAN > PRI > PRD		PRD > PRI > PAN	
PAN Radical	40	PRD Radical	45
PAN > PRD >PRI		PRD > PAN > PRI	
PAN Rigid	31	PRD Rigid	35
PAN > PRI ≥ PRD		PRD > PAN ≥ PRI	
Total	100		100

Source: National Reforma poll, December 1998. Party types are derived from preference rankings among the three major parties. Rankings are constructed from binary comparisons among these parties. Classification of voter types is taken from Magaloni, "Dominio de partido y dilemas duvergerianos en las elecciones federales de 1994," *Política y Gobierno* 3, no. 2 (1996).

Hence there were ideological obstacles to the alliance because not all of PAN and PRD partisans gave higher salience to the political dimension over the economic. Had the PAN and PRD attempted to forge an alliance, they would have risked alienating their ideological supporters. At the outset of the campaign, PAN supporters appear to have been slightly more ideological and hence more reluctant to support a right-left electoral alliance, especially one headed by the PRD candidate.

We can further support this claim by looking at the opinions these voters had of Vicente Fox and Cuauhtémoc Cárdenas, already perceived as the most likely opposition presidential candidates by the time this poll was implemented (see table 11.2). Fifty-four percent of the PAN's ideological supporters and 67 percent of its rigid supporters had an unfavorable opinion of Cárdenas. This contrasts with the PAN's radical voters, only 34 percent of whom had unfavorable opinions of the PRD candidate. Because there were fewer radical voters among PAN supporters, these data indicate that an opposition alliance headed by Cárdenas would have had little success.

Table 11.2. Voters' Opinions of the Candidates by Voter Types, December 1998

	Opinion of Cárdenas			Opinion of Fox	
	Favorable	Unfavorable		Favorable	Unfavorable
PAN ideological voter	47%	54%	PRD ideological	80%	20%
PAN radical voter	66	34	PRD radical	76	24
PAN rigid voter	51	49	PRD rigid	52	48
Total PAN	51	49	Total PRD	68	32

Source: National Reforma poll, December 1998. Party types are derived from preference rankings among the three major parties. Rankings are constructed from binary comparisons among these parties. Classification of voter types is taken from Magaloni, "Dominio de partido y dilemas duvergerianos en las elecciones federales de 1994," *Política y Gobierno* 3, no. 2 (1996).

By contrast, PRD partisans had relatively favorable evaluations of Fox: 76 and 80 percent of PRD ideological and radical electors, respectively, had favorable opinions of Fox. Only the PRD's rigid voters held less favorable evaluations, and 50 percent of them actively disliked Fox. Hence a left-right electoral alliance would have been attractive to the electorate only if it were headed by Fox, an alternative the PRD elites never seriously considered.[12]

Despite the failure of the alliance at the elite level, many PRD partisans understood that Fox was the most serious opposition challenger, and they were willing to support him. In fact, Fox's support increased dramatically between December 1998 and February 2000, when the first wave of the panel was collected. By then, it seems, it had become clear to many opposition voters that Fox was the only serious contender and that Cárdenas was trailing.

Table 11.3 presents preference rankings among the three main political parties using data from the first wave of the panel, based on eleven-point feeling thermometer ratings of the three parties and their candidates. We compare these responses to construct complete voter preference profiles.

Table 11.3. Preference Rankings, First Wave of the Panel (percentages)

Type of Opposition Voter	PRD Ranked First	PAN Ranked First	Type of PRI Voter	PRI Ranked First
Rigid	0.17	0.17	Rigid	0.23
(PAN > PRD ≥ PRI)				
(PRD > PAN ≥ PRI)				
Ideological			PAN leaner	
(PAN > PRI > PRD)	0.12	0.30	(PRI > PAN > PRD)	0.42
(PRD > PRI > PAN)				
(PAN ≥ PRI > PRD)	0.07	0.13	(PRI ≥ PAN > PRD)	0.14
(PRD ≥ PRI > PAN)				
Subtotal	0.19	0.43		0.56
Radical			PRD leaner	
(PAN > PRD > PRI)	0.36	0.30	(PRI > PRD > PAN)	0.18
(PRD > PAN > PRI)				
(PAN ≥ PRD > PRI)	0.28	0.10	(PRI ≥ PRD > PAN)	0.03
(PRD ≥ PAN > PRI)				
Subtotal	0.64	0.40		0.21
Total	100.00	100.00		100.00

Comparisons between tables 11.2 and 11.3 provide a sense of how incentives to coordinate evolved. The contents of these tables should be viewed cautiously, given that preference rankings are constructed from questions that differ in their wording—the first come from binary comparisons, and the second from feeling thermometers. However, it appears that the willingness of PRD supporters to coordinate to support the PAN increased dramatically between December 1998 and February 2000, with PRD radical supporters jumping from 45 to 64 percent. An important finding is that the increase in radical or potentially strategic supporters did not come at the expense of ideological types; in both surveys, 20 percent of PRD supporters ranked the PRI second and the PAN third. The increase in potentially strategic supporters came at the expense of rigid PRD voters.

Information is the most likely source of this shift. Fox became much more visible and well known over this period. As more information on his candidacy became available, voters were increasingly capable of ranking him. Thus conditions were ripe for opposition coordination in the 2000 presidential race. At the outset of the campaign, the overwhelming majority of those who ranked the trailing opposition candidate first were able to rank the three alternatives, placing the PRI last.

STRATEGIC COORDINATION AT THE MASS LEVEL

Even without elite coordination between the main opposition candidates, voters have often been able to coordinate on their own. To identify strategic voters, one needs a way to measure voters' sincere preferences, which can then be contrasted with actual voting choices. Here we define strategic voters as those who abandon their sincere choice—a trailing candidate—for one of the front-runners in order not to waste their vote.

The evidence suggests that Mexican voters are highly disposed to behave strategically. Jorge Domínguez and James McCann found that a substantial portion of voters with "right-wing predispositions" (presumably PAN supporters) voted strategically for Cuauhtémoc Cárdenas, the candidate of the left-wing coalition, in the contested 1988 presidential election.[13] These authors also found, in the 1991 midterm elections, that electors with left-wing predispositions (presumably PRD supporters) voted for the PAN. They obtained these results through a simulation of their multinomial logit voting model, where they compute probabilities of voting for each of the three alternatives by setting the values of their sociodemographic variables and some issue positions to represent a "typical" right-wing or left-wing voter. However, most of these sociodemographic variables and issue positions were not statistically significant in the voting model, indicating that they might not be the best way to identify voters' real preferences.

Alejandro Poiré has employed a different approach to measure strategic voting in the crucial 1997 elections.[14] Following Alvarez and Nadler, Poiré models voters' utility functions for the three major parties through a conditional logit vote model. From this model he infers voters' "sincere" preference.[15] Strategic voters are defined as those who did not cast their votes for the party that the model predicts yields the highest utility.

This strategy of estimation, however, also presents some problems: it might lead us to falsely predict strategic voting (a voter not choosing the party that gives the highest utility) when what is actually happening is that the model fails to predict voting choices correctly. Lacking panel data, both of these approaches face a common difficulty: namely, that voters' sincere preferences must be inferred from vote choice, which might in itself be the product of strategic considerations. The Mexico 2000 Panel Study allows us to follow a different approach, one that resolves this difficulty: we can use information from previous rounds of the panel to separate the voters' sincere preferences from their vote choices.

We take party identification in the first wave of the panel as a measure of voters' sincere preferences. We justify our choice of this variable on two grounds. First, we know that in the Mexican context, reported party identification is very highly correlated with the vote but slightly less changeable and thus not contaminated by strategic considerations or campaign-specific events. Second, we take reported party identification in the first wave because we want to identify sincere preference at a point before campaign-specific issues, such as candidate traits or media coverage, start to influence voter choice. Defectors are defined as those who in subsequent rounds of the panel voted for a party other than the one with which they identified in the first round. Not all defectors are strategic voters. For us, strategic voters are only those who abandon a trailing candidate for a front-runner.

In table 11.4 we report the correlation between voting intentions in the course of the campaign and "exogenous" party identification (that is, self-reported partisanship in the first round of the panel). The first thing to note is that the correlation between reported party identification and voting intentions in the first wave of the panel is very high, which underscores the endogeneity problem of party identification.

This correlation is almost perfect for the PRI and PAN; 92 percent and 94 percent, respectively, of those who identified with these parties reported that they intended to vote for their party's candidate. The correlation is much lower for the PRD: close to 20 percent of those who reported identifying with the PRD did not intend to vote for Cárdenas. This means that at the start of the campaign, many *perredistas* had already abandoned Cárdenas for a stronger contender, with 9 percent switching to Labastida and 10 percent to Fox. As the campaign progressed, Fox captured increasing shares of PRD defectors, a point explored in greater detail below.

Table 11.4. Change in Vote Preference by "Exogenous Party ID"

	Voted for ... (percentages)			
Party Self-Identification	PRI	PAN	PRD	Total
PRI partisan				
February	92	7	1	100
April–May	82	14	4	100
June	75	19	6	100
Campaign average	*83*	*13*	*4*	
July (postelectoral)	71	24	4	100
PRD partisan				
February	9	10	81	100
April–May	11	14	75	100
June	10	17	73	100
Campaign average	*10*	*13*	*77*	
July (postelectoral)	14	22	64	100
PAN partisan				
February	4	94	2	100
April–May	7	88	5	100
June	10	85	5	100
Campaign average	*7*	*89*	*4*	
July (postelectoral)	8	87	5	100
Independents				
February	34	52	14	100
April–May	36	49	15	100
June	30	45	25	100
Campaign average	*33*	*49*	*18*	
July (postelectoral)	25	60	15	100

Note: Exogenous party identification is reported party identification in the first wave.

The second observation to note from table 11.4 is that the correlation between party identification and voting intention falls systematically for the three parties over the course of the campaign. The fall is particularly acute for the PRI and PRD, and relatively milder for PAN. In fact, the PAN was highly successful in retaining the support of its core voters. Of those who self-identified as *panistas* at the start of the campaign, near the end of the campaign (third wave of the panel), 85 percent still said they would vote for Vicente Fox. Fox ultimately received the support of 87 percent of the *panistas* (as captured in the postelection wave).

By contrast, the PRI lost 30 percent of its core supporters, of whom 24 percent went to Fox and 4 percent to Cárdenas. Strategic voting implies abandoning a trailing candidate for a front-runner to avoid throwing one's vote away. Unless these voters wrongly perceived that Labastida was the trailing candidate, their behavior cannot be attributed to conventional strategic voting. More likely, these PRI partisans abandoned Labastida because they were not convinced that he was the best candidate.

The PRD was the party that lost the largest share of its core vote. Approximately 40 percent of its initial supporters defected over the course of the campaign—22 percent to Fox and 14 percent to Labastida.[16] Cárdenas seems to have lost his core supporters for two reasons: he failed to convince his supporters that he was the best option, and his previous election losses caused many voters to perceive him as a sure loser from the very beginning of the campaign.

As the calculus of voting makes explicit, strategic voting depends on relative utility comparisons for the parties and a voter's perception that his/her vote can make a difference in causing a party to win or lose. Let us suppose that there are three parties—A, B, and C—and this is the voter's ordering of his party preferences. "The likelihood of voting for the second-choice candidate (party) increases as the voter evaluates A and B more similarly and as B is increasingly preferred to C. It also increases as the chances that one's vote would help B win grow and as the chances of A's winning decline."[17] Thus the "wasted vote logic" is compatible with the theory of calculus of voting, which is based on expected utility maximization.[18]

Table 11.5 reports the relative utility comparisons of PRD identifiers according to whether they deserted Cárdenas at the polls or remained loyal. Utility comparisons are derived from feeling thermometers. Those who remained loyal to Cárdenas derived, on average, higher utility (8.22) from this candidate than did those who defected to Fox (6.33) or to Labastida (5.33). Those who deserted to the PRI's candidate derived, on average, a much smaller utility differential from Cárdenas and Labastida (1.75) than those who remained loyal to Cárdenas (5.33). The same is true for those who defected to Fox, although the difference is less notable. On average, those who identified with the PRD in the first wave of the panel displayed a closer utility measure for Cárdenas/Fox than for Cárdenas/Labastida. Utility differentials help explain why most PRD defections went to Fox.

Table 11.5. Utility Differentials among PRD Loyalists and Defectors

PRD Identifiers in First Round Who:	Mean Utility Cárdenas	Mean Utility Differential Cárdenas-Labastida	Mean Utility Differential Cárdenas-Fox
Deserted to Labastida	5.33	1.75	2.00
Deserted to Fox	6.33	3.04	2.23
Loyal to Cárdenas	8.22	5.33	3.21
Mean	7.44	4.37	2.65

Strategic voting is more prevalent when there is a clear loser but the election remains very close between other candidates, as happened in Mexico in 2000. Table 11.6 reports the mean expected probabilities of victory and mean vote share calculations for each of the three major candidates.[19] The data are from the second and third waves of the panel. (Unfortunately, we cannot determine how voters calculated these probabilities at the outset of the campaigns because the first wave of the panel did not contain comparable questions.)

Table 11.6. Expected Probabilities of Victory and Vote Share Calculations

	Mean Probability of Victory		Mean Vote Share Calculations	
Candidate	April–May	June	April–May	June
Labastida	0.42	0.39	39.7	40.0
Fox	0.35	0.36	36.4	40.5
Cárdenas	0.23	0.25	22.0	26.4

It is clear that the public perceived the race to be very competitive, and it knew which candidate was trailing. According to the mean public perception, the race was between Labastida and Fox, with Cárdenas trailing by at least 10 percentage points. In May, the mean perceived probability of a Labastida victory was 42 percent; it dropped to 39 percent in June when the margin between Labastida and Fox narrowed to only three percentage points. Note that vote share calculations for June show the leading candidates in a tie, with Cárdenas trailing by about 20 percentage points.

Voters do not like to back trailing candidates. Table 11.7 shows that voters' balloting intentions reflect their perceptions of a candidate's probability of winning. Most voters supported one of the two candidates they felt had a high probability of victory. Sixty-three percent of Fox supporters and 81 percent of Labastida supporters thought their candidate had the greatest chance of winning. This contrasts sharply with the situation for Cárdenas: only 43 percent of his supporters thought he could actually win. The remainder supported him even though they felt they were wasting their votes. More *cardenistas* thought Labastida was going to win (28 percent) than Fox (10 percent). Only 19 percent of those who cast votes for Fox thought that Labastida would win, and PRI voters were virtually sure of a Labastida victory. It is this last group that turned out to have overly optimistic expectations.

Table 11.7. Candidate with Highest Perceived Probability of Victory by Vote Intention (percentages)

Perceived Probability of Outcome	Vote for Fox	Vote for Labastida	Vote for Cárdenas	Total
Fox	**63.2%**	8.4%	10.0%	31.3%
Labastida	19.1	**80.9**	28.6	46.9
Cárdenas	2.5	2.6	**46.3**	9.7
Tie: Fox-Labastida	12.2	5.3	2.2	7.6
Tie: Fox-Cárdenas	1.0	0.3	6.9	1.7
Tie: Labastida-Cárdenas	0.0	0.5	3.9	0.8
All candidates tie	2.0	2.0	2.2	2.0

In 2000, for the first time in Mexico's recent history, voters had a real opportunity to defeat the PRI. In previous contests, the average voter thought that the PRI was undefeatable, either because it really would attract the most votes or because it would rig the outcome to make it look as if it had.[20] It was not until 2000 that strategic voting was viewed as able to make a difference.

Figure 11.1. Composition of Candidates' Final Vote Shares by "Exogenous Party ID"

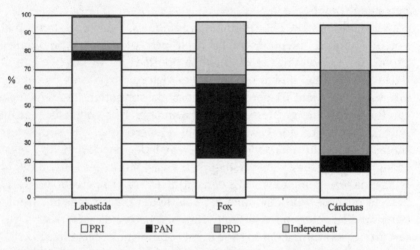

Note: "Exogenous party identification" is reported party ID in the first round. Candidates' vote comes from the fourth round. Columns do not add to 100 percent because "other" and "do now knows" are not reported.

Figure 11.1 reports final vote shares by respondent's party identification in the first wave of the panel. Fox's votes came mainly from core PAN supporters (41 percent), followed by independents (29 percent) and defectors from the PRI (21 percent). Strategic opposition voters contributed only 5 percent to Fox's victory. However, these results presumably underestimate the amount of strategic coordination by the opposition, much of which may have taken place before February.

A MODEL OF STRATEGIC VOTING

One final task in this chapter is to estimate the determinants of strategic voting. Here we define strategic voting as abandoning the trailing candidate for one of the front-runners. Thus, only voters who deserted Cárdenas for Fox or for Labastida are included. We estimate a multinomial logit of defections to either of these candidates, employing PRD loyalists as the base category. As in the preceding section, we define loyalists as those who reported identifying with the PRD in the first round and reported voting for Cárdenas in the last round. Defectors are PRD identifiers who voted for a non-PRD candidate. Since we are modeling a behavior that normally takes place only at the margins, we have a relatively small number of observations.

If defections correspond to strategic voting, they should be driven by some of the variables included in the calculus of voting model. A voter might defect for strategic considerations—not wanting to waste a vote—but that voter might also defect because he/she sincerely changes preferences. A voter might change his/her preference if a different candidate ranks higher in terms of perceived competence, issue position, or personal traits.

The most important independent variable for testing for strategic considerations in defections is probabilistic assessments. Since we are exploring voters' propensity not to waste their votes on trailing candidates, we employ as probabilistic assessments a voter's evaluation of Cárdenas's chances of winning. The lower his chances, the more likely a voter will perceive that he is wasting his vote and the higher the probability that the voter will cast a strategic vote. The sign of the coefficient for the variable "Cárdenas's likelihood" should thus be negative.[21]

Another independent variable is strength of partisanship, which we expect to hinder strategic voting. The less attached a voter is to a party, the higher his propensity to abandon the party for strategic reasons. Hence those who strongly identify with a political party are less likely to cast a strategic vote. We create a variable of strength of partisanship from the question, "Do you regard yourself as 'very' or 'not very' 'panista,' 'priísta,' 'perredista,' or 'other,'" where 1 indicates that the respondent is "very" partisan. We expect this variable to have a negative effect on strategic voting.

We also include as an independent variable the voter's assessment of democracy. We hypothesize that those who abandoned Cárdenas did so because they believed that by defeating the PRI they were building democracy. We have created a "new democracy" variable that reflects whether a voter changed his/her assessment of democracy after deserting the PRD. The variable equals 1 when a voter in the third wave of the panel answered "no" to the question, "Is Mexico a democracy?" and subsequently answered "yes" to this question in the fourth wave. We expect this variable to have a positive sign for defections to

Fox and to Labastida, but for quite different reasons: strategic voters who abandoned Cárdenas for Fox attempted to defeat the PRI in order to bring about democratic change, while strategic deserters to Labastida might have rationalized their vote for the ruling party by changing their assessment of Mexico's political system.

We also include specific campaign events that might have triggered strategic defections. In particular, we include a variable that reflects whether the voter saw the first presidential debate, although we are uncertain of this variable's effect. The debate might have shaped a perception that Cárdenas was not a strong contender and that Fox was. In this case, the debate should have a positive effect on strategic defections to Fox, but not necessarily to Labastida. Another possibility is that the debate simply reinforced preexisting preferences, in which case the variable would have a negative effect for desertions to both Fox and Labastida. Another campaign event that we include is "Black Tuesday"; we anticipate that people who saw the candidates debating about when to hold the second debate would be less likely to defect to Fox.[22]

The last set of independent variables involves voter evaluations of each candidate's competence in handling different problems—the economy, crime, and education. We add these three items and employ mean candidate competence in our model. We expect defectors to come from the ranks of voters who were not convinced by Cárdenas's candidacy and were attracted by one of the other candidates. Candidate-centered considerations do not necessarily reflect strategic evaluations for abandoning a political party. Thus we can view these variables as controls. If the other independent variables are statistically significant, we can conclude that, holding candidate-centered considerations constant, strategic considerations did play a role in PRD defections. The results of this analysis appear in table 11.8.

Strategic considerations clearly played a role in party defections. Those who attributed a low likelihood of victory to Cárdenas were more likely to defect. The coefficient is negative and statistically significant for desertions to both Labastida and Fox. We also tested for the effect of two other variables that attempt to capture probabilistic assessments and information about whether the voter was aware of the candidates' relative standing. These variables are: (1) whether a voter had heard or read poll results, and (2) the absolute difference between the probabilities of victory of the two front-runners. Both of these measures are taken from the third wave. The first of these variables also gave a positive, statistically significant result for defections to Fox but not for Labastida.[23]

Table 11.8. Multinomial Logit Analysis of PRD Strategic Desertions

Independent Variable	Desertions to Labastida		Desertions to Fox	
	Coefficient	Standard Error	Coefficient	Standard Error
Presidential debate (3)	0.59	1.43	−2.37*	1.36
Black Tuesday	−0.51	0.41	−4.14**	1.88
Cárdenas likely to win	−0.56*	0.30	−0.86**	0.39
Strong party identification	−2.88*	1.74	−4.38**	2.00
High competence grade for Cárdenas (3)	−1.96**	1.01	−3.62***	1.25
High competence grade for Fox (3)	0.70	1.05	2.63***	1.11
High competence grade for Labastida (3)	0.06	0.74	−0.25	0.68
New democracy	3.05**	1.60	1.39	1.62
Constant	6.00	4.18	17.23	6.73

N = 51; LR chi^2(16) = 47.17; Prob > chi^2 = 0.0001;
Log likelihood = −22.8; Pseudo R^2 = 0.51

As expected, strength of partisanship had a negative effect on strategic defections. Those who reported being very attached to the PRD were less likely to defect. The coefficient is negative and significant for defections to Labastida and Fox, but the magnitude of the coefficient is almost twice as large for defections to Fox.

The "new democracy" variable had a positive effect on party defections, but the coefficient reaches statistical significance only for the case of Labastida. The presidential debate did not trigger further strategic defections to Vicente Fox in this model; if anything, it seems to have reinforced PRD voters' preexisting preferences. The "Black Tuesday" variable performs as expected: those who watched the debate about the debate were less likely to defect to Fox.

Perceived competence produced an interesting effect. The higher Cárdenas's perceived competence, the less likely a voter is to defect to either of the other candidates. The magnitude of the coefficient is stronger for Fox. Another important result is that evaluations of Labastida did not matter in explaining strategic defections to the PRI. Those PRD supporters who defected to Labastida did so not because of his candidacy, but because they did not like Fox. Desertions to Fox, however, were significantly shaped by his candidacy: if a PRD identifier evaluated Fox highly, there was a high chance that he would defect.

To get a sense of the range of effects, we evaluate the multinomial logit model at different values of the independent variables, holding the rest of the variables at their mean values. Figure 11.2 plots the probabilities of defecting according to different values of the variable of Cárdenas's likelihood of victory. The data show that strategic calculations were a key consideration for *perredistas* who defected to Fox, but they had almost no impact on defections to Labastida. As a voter's assessments of Cárdenas declined, her likelihood of defecting to Fox increased significantly. To retain the support of *perredistas*, Cárdenas had to be perceived as a sure winner. If his perceived chances of winning fell below 80 percent, the probability of defecting to Fox was above 50 percent. The mean value of this variable was 0.47, indicating that one crucial reason why nearly 40 percent of *perredistas* abandoned Cárdenas is that they perceived him to be a sure loser.

Figure 11.2. Effects of Probabilistic Assessments on Defections

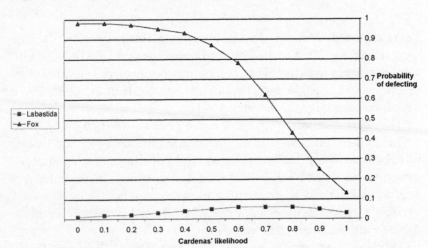

The effects of some of the other independent variables are reported in table 11.9. First consider strength of partisanship. This variable significantly shaped defections to Fox but had minimal impact on defections to Labastida. A respondent who reported being "very" *perredista* had a 0.23 chance of defecting to Fox and a .04 chance of defecting to

Labastida. If the respondent did not report being strongly attached to the PRD, his chances of defecting to Fox increased to 0.93 and measured the same for Labastida. Hence Cárdenas was crucially dependent on strong party attachments to deter *perredistas* from defecting to Fox. Those with weak partisan attachments abandoned him in droves.

Table 11.9. Effects of Partisanship, Candidates, and the Debate on Defections

Variable		Defect to Fox	Defect to Labastida
Partisanship			
Strong	1	.23	.04
Weak	0	.93	.04
Candidates			
Cárdenas	.84	.99	.004
	2.35	.89	.05
	3.86	.05	.03
Fox	1.08	.12	.16
	2.54	.89	.05
	4.00	.99	.003
Labastida	1.07	.92	.03
	2.53	.89	.05
	3.99	.84	.07
Viewed the debate?			
Yes	1	.49	.28
No	0	.93	.03
New democracy in Mexico?			
Yes	1	.89	.27
No	0	.79	.04

Other rows in the table report the probabilities of defecting depending on candidacy variables. Consider the effects of voters' perceptions of Cárdenas's competence in handling various economic problems. The average voter gave him a score of 2.35. As evaluations increased one standard deviation (1.51), the chances of defecting to Fox decreased from 0.89 to 0.05. Thus an obvious way for Cárdenas to retain the support of his party's followers would have been to convince them of his strength as a candidate and, in particular, his competence. Note that this variable barely affects defections to Labastida.

Perceptions of Fox also had a strong impact. If a voter rated his competence one standard deviation below the mean score (2.54), the chances of defecting to Fox decreased from 0.89 to 0.12. If evaluations of Fox increased by one standard deviation above the mean, the likelihood of defecting approached 100 percent. Thus Cárdenas lost a very large percentage of his party's supporters because of Fox's greater strength as a candidate. Note that Fox's candidacy also shaped defections to Labastida but in the reverse direction: the chances of defecting to the PRI increased significantly as voters' evaluations of Fox declined. In fact, Fox's candidacy was one of the strongest variables for explaining defections to Labastida, indicating that those who defected to the PRI candidate did so mainly because they disliked Fox. Labastida's candidacy had little impact on defections, despite the fact that he and Fox were perceived to be equally competent. When scores increase one standard deviation above the mean, the likelihood of defecting to Labastida increases marginally, from 0.03 to 0.05. Thus defections to Labastida cannot be attributed to the strengths of his candidacy.

The presidential debate appears to have had a strong impact on the decision we are modeling. Contrary to what one might expect, however, the debate did not increase Fox's chances among *perredistas*; it significantly *decreased* the likelihood of voters defecting to him, from 0.93 to 0.49. The presidential debate had the opposite outcome for Labastida, increasing his chances of attracting defectors from 0.03 to 0.28. Instead of encouraging the impression among *perredistas* that Fox was a worthwhile, viable opposition candidate, the debate seems to have generated a negative image of Fox among PRD partisans. As Fox's image worsened, so did PRD voters' propensity to strategically defect to Labastida.

The last variable presented in the table addresses voters' assessments of democracy. Those who believed that a new democracy had been established in Mexico—viewing the political system as authoritarian in June and as democratic in July—were more likely to defect. This variable is positive for both candidates, though twice as strong for Labastida. We interpret this result as follows: *perredistas* who voted for Labastida changed their assessments of Mexico's political system in order to justify their choice of the ruling party candidate. By contrast, *perredistas* who voted for Fox appear to have changed their evaluations of the political system; by helping defeat the PRI, they would further the cause of democracy.

CONCLUSION

This chapter analyzed strategic coordination in Mexico's 2000 presidential race. At the beginning of the campaign, many analysts (including the authors) anticipated that a divided opposition would lead to a PRI victory. Ultimately, an opposition coalition was not necessary because voters coordinated in a decentralized manner. Several factors were key elements for opposition coordination, including the high salience of the political change issue; the strength of candidate Fox vis-à-vis the PRD and PRI candidates; the weakness of partisan attachments; and, most notably, the unprecedented dissemination of information about candidates' relative standings in the polls.

Ideological differences divided the opposition. On economic policy, the PAN and PRD stood to the right and the left of the PRI, respectively. But there was also another dimension of competition—the political-regime dimension—where the two opposition parties stood together against the PRI. We have argued that the prevalence of strategic voting against the PRI depended on the relative saliency of these dimensions. At the campaign's outset, the majority of the opposition electorate, and PRD supporters in particular, preferred both opposition parties to the PRI. From these relative rankings we can infer that the issue of political change clearly dominated over other ideological concerns. Conditions thus were ripe for strategic voting to take place. Our data demonstrate that the trailing opposition party, the PRD, lost about 40 percent of its supporters over the course of the campaign, with most of them ultimately voting for Fox.

Despite the magnitude of strategic defections, Fox's victory cannot be attributed to strategic coordination alone. Our analysis shows that a larger share of his support came from PAN identifiers, independent voters, and, surprisingly, *priístas* who defected from the ruling party, apparently because they were lukewarm toward Labastida's candidacy.

The propensity of opposition voters to coordinate against the PRI was not unique to the 2000 presidential election. But coordination was more likely in 2000 because the public was aware of the relative standing of the two front-runners and saw a unique opportunity to defeat the PRI. Those who were cognizant of Cárdenas's poor prospects and the poll results tended to cast a strategic vote. Our results indicate that Cárdenas lost a sizable portion of his supporters largely because he was perceived as a sure loser. This contrasts to previous presidential races, especially the 1994 race, in which most PRD partisans believed

Cárdenas's claim that private polls gave him the lead.[24] Even if Cárdenas had attempted to mislead his supporters about his relative standing in 2000, the publicly available information would have precluded this as a successful strategy. Thus our analysis supports Gary Cox's claim that strategic coordination depends crucially on the dissemination of accurate information about candidates' relative positions and the competitiveness of the race.[25] The greater the voters' access to accurate information from reliable polls, the easier it is for them to coordinate.

The candidates themselves also played a significant role in the election's outcome and in the dynamics of strategic voting. The PRD lost a large proportion of its electorate because of the weakness of the Cárdenas candidacy and the strength of the Fox candidacy. Deserters from the PRD tended overwhelmingly to be voters who did not perceive Cárdenas as competent in handling the economy, crime, and education, or who perceived Fox as highly competent. Fox's impact was so important for the dynamics of strategic voting that it even explains the small proportion of PRD partisans who defected to Labastida; in fact, Fox's candidacy was the only variable among all those tested that shows a substantial impact on defections to Labastida. These voters defected to the PRI mainly because they disliked Fox and they voted to keep him from victory.

Another variable that had a significant effect on the dynamics of opposition coordination was the weakness of partisan attachments. *Perredistas* who were weakly attached to the PRD were significantly more likely to cast a strategic vote. The Left's support came overwhelmingly from voters with strong partisan attachments to the PRD. Most scholarly research on strategic voting assumes that voters are free to switch their votes according to utility differentials and probability assessments. These models predict that, in equilibrium, a trailing candidate should garner virtually no support because of strategic defections, leading to the consolidation of a two-party system for elections taking place in single-member plurality districts, such as is the case with Mexico's presidential contests.[26] Our results indicate that partisanship makes this equilibrium highly unlikely: voters who hold strong party identifications are not likely to cast strategic votes.

As Joseph Klesner makes clear in his chapter in this volume, attachments to opposition parties appear to be relatively weak. Nonetheless, both the PRD and the PAN seem to have a group of core supporters who were willing to waste their votes in order to invest in their respective party's future. This demonstrates that the Left is not likely to disappear in Mexico. Instead, Mexico's electorate will be characterized by a combination of a small core of stable constituencies with a larger, more fluid group of voters. This context encourages various types of campaign effects, including strategic coordination.

Notes

The authors wish to thank Alberto Díaz-Cayeros, Federico Estévez, Jorge I. Domínguez, and Chappell Lawson for helpful suggestions at various stages of this research. Poiré wishes to acknowledge research support from the Asociación Mexicana de Cultura, through ITAM, as well as a grant from the Fundación México en Harvard and assistance from Harvard's Weatherhead Center for International Affairs. Gaëlle Brachet collaborated with valuable research assistance.

1. See Alberto Díaz-Cayeros and Beatriz Magaloni, "Party Dominance and the Logic of Electoral Design in Mexico's Transition to Democracy," *Journal of Theoretical Politics* 13, no. 3 (2001).

2. Gary W. Cox, *Making Votes Count* (Cambridge: Cambridge University Press, 1997).

3. Díaz-Cayeros and Magaloni, "Party Dominance and the Logic of Electoral Design."

4. Ibid.

5. See María Amparo Casar, "Coaliciones y cohesión partidista en un congreso sin mayoría: la Cámara de Diputados de México," *Política y Gobierno* 7, no. 1 (2000).

6. See Robert M. Axelrod, *The Evolution of Cooperation* (New York: Basic Books, 1984).

7. Reforma national poll, December 1998.

8. See Juan Molinar Horcasitas, *El tiempo de la legitimidad: elecciones, autoritarismo y democracia en México* (Mexico City: Cal y Arena, 1991); Jorge I. Domínguez and James A. McCann, "Shaping Mexico's Electoral Arena: The Construction of Partisan Cleavages in the 1988 and 1991 National Elections," *American Political Science Review* 89, no. 1 (1995); Beatriz Magaloni, "Dominio de partido y dilemas duvergerianos en las elecciones federales de 1994," *Política y Gobierno* 3, no. 2 (1996); Beatriz Magaloni, "Transition in a Single Party System: Economic Reforms and the Emergence of Partisan Politics in Mexico" (Ph.D. dissertation, Duke University, 1998); Alejandro Moreno, *Political Cleavages: Issues, Parties, and the Consolidation of Democracy* (Boulder, Colo.: Westview, 1999); Alejandro Poiré, "Un modelo sofisticado de decisión electoral racional: el voto estratégico en México, 1997," *Política y Gobierno* 7, no. 2 (2000).

9. Magaloni, "Dominio de partido y dilemas duvergerianos."

10. The actual question was, "If you were to choose between the PRI and the PAN, for which party would you vote: PAN, PRI, none, don't know?"

11. Magaloni, "Dominio de partido y dilemas duvergerianos."

12. For further discussion of the failure of the negotiations, see Kathleen Bruhn's contribution in this volume.

13. Domínguez and McCann, "Shaping Mexico's Electoral Arena."

14. Poiré, "Un modelo sofisticado de decisión electoral racional."

15. R. Michael Alvarez and Jonathan Nagler, "A New Approach for Modelling Strategic Voting in Multiparty Elections," British Journal of Political Science 30, no. 1 (2000).

16. Percentages from the postelectoral fourth wave of the panel tend to be slightly misleading, as there was strong overreporting of votes for Fox.

17. Paul R. Abramson et al., "'Sophisticated' Voting in the 1988 Presidential Primaries," American Political Science Review 86, no. 1 (1992).

18. Anthony Downs, An Economic Theory of Democracy (New York: Harper, 1957); William H. Riker and Peter C. Ordeshook, "A Theory of the Calculus of Voting," American Political Science Review 62, no. 1 (1968); William H. Riker, "The Two-Party System and Duverger's Law: An Essay on the History of Political Science," American Political Science Review 76, no. 4 (1982).

19. We corrected voters' probabilistic assessments and vote share calculations such that they would total 100. Thus if the elector answered, for example, that Fox had a 0.80 chance of winning, Labastida had 0.80, and Cárdenas had 0.4, we divided these numbers by the sum of these probabilities (2.0), changing these probabilities to 0.4, 0.4, and 0.2, respectively.

20. See Magaloni, "Transition in a Single Party System."

21. Unfortunately, voters' probabilistic assessments about the parties' chances of winning were not included in the first wave of the panel, where most strategic decisions seem to have been made. We thus lose many observations (the first panel plus data from the postelectoral survey) when adding this variable to the models.

22. For a discussion of the debates and Black Tuesday, see Chappell Lawson's contribution on the "great debates" in this volume.

23. Results from these models are available from the authors upon request.

24. See Adolfo Aguilar Zinser, ¡Vamos a ganar! La pugna de Cuauhtémoc Cárdenas por el poder (Mexico City: Océano, 1995).

25. Cox, Making Votes Count.

26. Maurice Duverger, "Duverger's Law: Forty Years Later," in Bernard Grofman and Arend Lijphart, eds., Electoral Laws and their Political Consequences (New York: Agathon, 1986); Cox, Making Votes Count.

12

The Issues, the Vote, and the Mandate for Change

BEATRIZ MAGALONI AND ALEJANDRO POIRÉ

Despite the historic nature of Vicente Fox's victory in 2000, the meaning of that victory is not immediately apparent. Fox's campaign was centered around the notion of change, and large numbers of Mexicans listed change as the primary reason they supported his candidacy. But electoral support for "change" could be interpreted in at least two ways: it could be a mandate to alter certain governmental policies, or it could simply demonstrate that the electorate is fed up with the long-governing Institutional Revolutionary Party (PRI)—and have no clear prospective interpretation.

This chapter explores the role that issue voting played in Mexico's 2000 presidential election. On what key issues did the electorate focus when choosing the first non-PRI president in Mexico's contemporary history? Why did the PRI fail to take advantage of the country's outstanding economic performance in the two years prior to the election? Was issue voting strong enough or specific enough to warrant speaking of a clear-cut mandate for Fox? Finally, were Mexican voters swayed by their overall like and dislike of candidates, or were there more sophisticated evaluations lurking beneath what appeared to be a marketing-dominated event?

We seek to address these questions by evaluating the impact of three types of broadly defined categories of issue voting. First, we analyze voters' and candidates' positions on a set of specific policy proposals and political predispositions. Second, we study voters' opinions on a set of valence issues, as indicated by the differential abilities of candidates at handling key problems faced by the nation. Finally, we deal with voters' performance evaluations of the incumbent president, his government, and the economy.

Our findings suggest that if the Mexican electorate gave a mandate in 2000, it did not include thorough political reform. Fox's victory, like his campaign, had a very broad meaning, anchored in the typical Mexican voter's hard-learned distrust of official promises about economic stability and prosperity. Voters' economic expectations were an essential ingredient in Fox's efforts to create a broad-based coalition against the PRI. Issue voting was certainly present, but in its least specific sense—that is, in terms of voters' evaluations of the candidates' abilities to tackle certain challenges. Only with regard to privatization of the electric power industry did the electorate respond to more specific policy concerns. Even the broad-ranging left-right dimension faded in electoral importance once the central economic concerns are taken into account. The mandate Vicente Fox received was one to do better than the PRI at running the country. That was the powerful, unromantic, unpretentious message delivered by Mexican voters on July 2, 2000.

This chapter is organized as follows. We first discuss some key issues in the 2000 presidential campaign. We then consider the potential implications of the issue context in 2000 for presidential vote choice, testing the impact of different issues on voting preference. We conclude with an overall interpretation of the evidence.

THE ISSUES IN MEXICO'S 2000 RACE

To be sure, Mexico's 2000 presidential campaign will be remembered as one dominated by "change." The very name of Vicente Fox's electoral coalition (the Alliance for Change) highlighted this fact, as did most of his campaign slogans and propaganda. But in the Mexican context, change could have very different meanings. Mexico's pre-2000 party system encompassed two main dimensions. The first was a political-institutional one, where at the right-most extreme lay staunch conservatives, accepting all features of the political status quo, and thereby of the existing style of authoritarian rule by the PRI, and with the left-most extreme anchored by rapid and thorough political transformers, often lingering with anti-systemic strategies. Political reformists of different degrees lay in between. The second dimension was the conventional left-right divide, with neoclassical economic perspectives on the right and Keynesian ones on the left.[1] While past evidence has underscored the prevalence of the PRI-versus-opposition divide in the Mexican electorate, other studies have found more significant cleavages in the Mexican party system, with economic and moral issues increasingly playing some role.[2]

As in previous elections, the issues that relate to the PRI-versus-opposition cleavage played the most significant role in the campaign. But in 2000, candidates also campaigned on other, less salient issues (such as education and the privatization of the electric power industry, to name the most important ones), and different waves of the panel included indicators for several of those issues. Our findings suggest that the relevance of the political-institutional dimension of the Mexican party system (especially in its *political reform* component) was overcome by more "politics as usual" evaluations of the incumbent party and its candidate.[3]

At first glance, the 2000 presidential race does not seem to have been significantly shaped by retrospective evaluations. Economic performance in the two years prior to the elections was particularly outstanding. The public's approval of the president was at one of its peaks, with an overwhelming majority of the electorate approving of Ernesto Zedillo's handling of various economic issues. The puzzle, then, is how the PRI could lose an election when economic evaluations should have favored the incumbent. Our results indicate that Mexican voters stopped perceiving the PRI and its candidate as the most competent in handling the national economy.[4] In this sense, voters' perceptions of candidate traits played a particularly strong role.

Ideology and Policy Positions

The Mexican electorate started the 2000 campaign somewhat less divided along ideological lines than it had been in the recent past.[5] Figure 12.1 shows the distribution of voters on the left-right dimension, with a large majority tilted to the right (the median voter was located at 7 on a 10-point scale) and a mode at the extreme right of the scale.

Moreno has convincingly argued that this left-right dimension in Mexican politics encompasses both economic and political concerns, with economic liberalism and political conservatism toward the right and state-led economics plus political reformism to the left.[6] It is clear, however, that the content of these dimensions can be altered by the political context. In particular, at least since 1997 Mexico had witnessed substantial political transformations, accompanied by a greater degree of consensus on some of the country's main institutional features. Also,

the economic crisis of 1994–95 and its aftermath had remained hot political topics, with Zedillo's government struggling to pass bills essential to economic recovery throughout his term. It could thus be the case
that, by 2000, economic matters dominated this left-right indicator.

Figure 12.1. Ideological Distribution of the Mexican Electorate

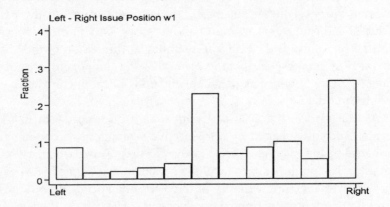

A typical way to explore this hypothesis is through factor analysis,
analyzing which issues correlate most closely with overall measures of
ideology. This procedure did not yield satisfactory results when performed on the available data.[7] Clearly, the left-right dimension captures
information beyond that related to electric power industry privatization,
political reform, and crime policy.[8] The overall ideological distribution
of the electorate, however, was divided along partisan lines. Figure 12.2
shows the distribution of partisans in the panel's first wave, with me-
dians and inter-quartile ranges (the thicker bars) for each party.[9]

The PRI confirmed its "rightist" character with its median partisan
at 8 on the scale and only 10 percent of its constituency to the left of 4.
This party's followers were also the least dispersed, with a standard
deviation of 2.73 (compared to 2.99 for *panistas* and 3.61 for *perredistas*).
The PAN's electorate was also firmly on the center-right side of the
spectrum, with the median partisan at 6 and less than 25 percent of its
partisans beyond 5. Nevertheless, there remained a sizable minority
(about 9 percent) on the left-most extreme. The PRD began the 2000
campaign ideologically divided. Approximately 17 percent of *perredistas* located themselves at the left-most extreme, while 18 percent located themselves at the far right, with the median PRD partisan at a 5.

Figure 12.2. Ideological Distribution by Party Identification, February

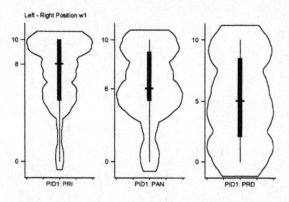

Figure 12.3. Campaign Effects on Ideological Position, Change from February to June

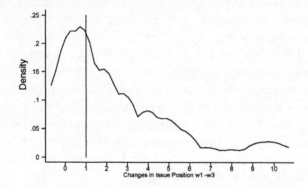

Although the campaigns produced some ideological polarization, changes in the overall shape of the electorate were minimal. Most voters changed their issue positions only slightly in the course of the campaign. Figure 12.3 shows the distribution of ideological shifts between February and June, with the median position marked at 1.[10]

To be sure, most voters moved in the expected direction during the campaign. PAN and PRI constituents shifted farther from the center and closer to the right, but the PRD coalition remained in ideological disarray. Figure 12.4 shows the placement of partisans in the third wave of the panel study, with the PRI median at its most extreme (9.5) and the PAN further to the right than at the beginning of the contest (its median now at 7); the PRD's median remained at 5.[11]

Figure 12.4. Ideological Distribution by Party Identification, June

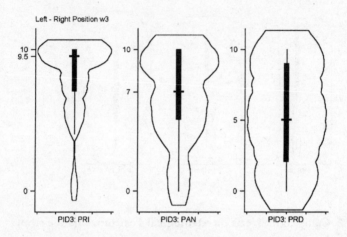

Left - Right Position w3

What of more specific issues, such as political reform, crime policy, and privatization? We expected political reform to be an issue that pitted most opposition voters against *priístas*.[12] But although the electorate looked somewhat divided on this issue, it did not seem to have the same clear-cut partisan correspondence as the left-right dimension. Figure 12.5 shows the partisan distribution of opinions on the political reform scale. As expected, the median partisan from the PRD was most in favor of reform, at 8, with the median for the PAN at 7 and the PRI at 5. However, the dispersion of partisans across this dimension is substantial. Distributions for crime policy, shown in figure 12.6, reveal even greater dispersion across partisan lines.

In general, for issue positions to be significant vote predictors, at least one of the two following conditions should be met: voters are significantly divided in their own positioning across partisan lines and will thus reflect their differing ideal points in vote choices;[13] or voters are not distinguishable by partisanship in the dimension, but candidates' positions clearly are.

Neither of these conditions was met in the case of crime policy. As table 12.1 shows, voters perceived all candidates to be very close. Even in the case of political reform, where parties in the electorate were somewhat more divided, the candidates were still seen as relatively tightly grouped.

Candidate and party positions, however, were more dispersed in terms of ideology and privatization. In particular, the issue of the electric power industry pushed Fox to the extreme right of the distribution, along with some of his party loyalists. *Panistas* remained dispersed across the scale, but their median was quite far from both the PRD and PRI bases. Approximately 75 percent of PRI and PRD partisans located themselves at 5 or below, with over 50 percent of supporters of both parties at 1.

Figure 12.5. Issue Positions on Political Reform by Party Identification, June

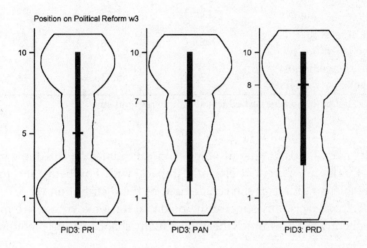

Figure 12.6. Issue Positions on Crime Policy by Party Identification, June

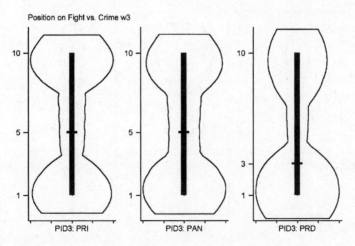

Table 12.1. Candidates' Ratings on Issue Scales

	Candidate Locations on Issue Scales[a]		
	Cárdenas/PRD	Fox/PAN	Labastida/PRI
Left-right dimension			
(candidate, February)	3.07	**6.06**	6.89
(party, February)	3.24	**5.69**	6.87
(candidate, June)	3.71	**5.89**	7.06
(party, June)	3.51	**5.89**	7.14
Crime policy (left–right, June)	4.66	**5.15**	5.66
Political reform (enough–more, June)	5.17	5.66	**5.29**
Electric power industry (public–private, June)	3.69	6.33	**4.48**

[a] As located by 40 percent best-educated sample respondents.

The overall positioning of voters and candidates on this topic suggests the issue's potential electoral impact, with Fox being the most vulnerable candidate at the center-right of the distribution (at 6.3). Of course, these facts only suggest the potential for issue voting; we must subsequently test how much the issue actually shaped voting preference.

Figure 12.7. Issue Positions on Electric Power Industry by Party Identification, June

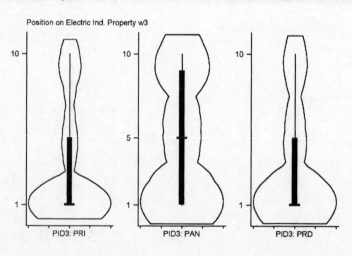

Most Important Problem and Candidate Evaluations

Generally speaking, policy-consensual campaigns are the fertile soil for valence issues. Where all agree on what is the right thing to do, candidates with high competency ratings stand to gain. While we can hardly portray the Mexico 2000 campaign as policy-consensual, it is true that certain topics (such as macroeconomic policy and trade) were not highly contested. Table 12.2 shows the issues that Mexicans perceived as the country's most important problems during the four waves of the panel. Economic concerns clearly topped the list, even though inflation was no longer a substantial threat and economic growth in recent years had been very robust. Crime and public safety also played an important role, being consistently designated the most important problem by at least a quarter of the electorate, while political and development issues trailed far behind in voters' eyes.

Table 12.2. Voter Perceptions of the Salience of Key Issues

Most Important Problem Facing the Country	Panel Wave			
	February	April/May	June	July
Economic	**51.5%**	**48.6%**	**51.6%**	**45.2%**
Political	10.1	10.6	12.5	10.9
Development	7.8	6.3	7.0	6.5
Crime	24.5	29.2	24.5	31.5
Other	6.1	5.3	4.5	5.9
N	2,170	880	920	1,174

Note: Economic problems include unemployment (9% in February), "the economy" (19%), inflation (3%), wages (2%), lack of support for the countryside (2%), and poverty (12%). Political problems include government corruption (7%) and lack of good public servants (2%). Development includes education (2%), health (<1%), pollution (1%), and social problems (5 %).

Table 12.3. Best Candidate by Type of Attribute, February

Attributes	Candidates			
	Labastida	Fox	Cárdenas	None
Able to handle economy	**24.77%**	20.87%	6.07%	48.29%
Most honest	21.20	**23.58**	6.66	48.56
Able to fight crime	**22.77**	18.95	5.72	52.56
Able to improve education	**24.27**	18.66	4.90	52.18
Average	23.26	20.50	5.83	50.40

More telling than overall perceptions of the country's most important problems are voters' perceptions of the abilities that candidates might bring to bear in solving those problems. Table 12.3 shows the percentage of voters who gave one of the three major candidates the highest rating on each of four attributes: competence in handling the economy, honesty, competence in controlling crime, and competence in improving education.[14] It shows that Labastida was rated highest in ability to improve education and to control crime, and also in terms of economic expertise, while Fox was the victor in terms of honesty.

Although Labastida was the candidate with the best rating in economic expertise, Fox did not lag far behind. In other words, voters perceived little difference in these candidates' relative abilities to manage the economy, an area where the PRI had long remained the undisputed leader. Although this result could be the product of Labastida's campaign style, which did not tout the Zedillo administration's recent economic record, it could also result from voters being wary of the likelihood of a recurring crisis.

Performance Evaluations

As it turns out, Mexico's recent economic performance was not that highly regarded by the public, strongly related to Zedillo's personal characteristics, and in all likelihood not terribly fungible for the candidate of the PRI, given voters' memories of past economic crises. Ratings of Ernesto Zedillo illustrate this point. At first glance, Zedillo enjoyed high approval ratings throughout the campaign. Subtracting disapprovers from approvers and leaving out those who expressed neutral opinions, we find that Zedillo's net positive rating was 34 percent in February, 34 percent in April/May, and 30 percent in June. After his famous admission of the PRI's defeat on election night, these soared to 59 percent. But Zedillo's positives turn to gray once we look at typical retrospective indicators, especially sociotropic economic evaluations. These results are shown in table 12.4.

The only two subjects on which the electorate reported net positive numbers were pocketbook economic considerations—for which voters can credit themselves[15]—and public safety—which voters evaluated at the local level, not the national one. Sociotropic economic evaluations, while at almost their highest level in President Zedillo's term,[16] were still on the negative side. And for every voter who thought corruption had diminished, there were almost three who thought it had worsened.

Table 12.4. Retrospective Performance Evaluations, February

Evaluation	Area of Concern			
	National Economy	Personal Economy	Public Safety[a]	Fighting Corruption
Worsened somewhat, a lot	29.13%	20.69%	20.07%	33.44%
About the same	53.37	56.79	54.78	53.48
Improved somewhat, a lot	17.50	22.53	25.15	13.08
Net opinion	−11.63	1.84	5.08	−20.36

[a] Indicates opinion with regard to local public safety.

Apart from these not so optimistic figures for the PRI's candidate, Mexico's wicked economic cycles from the mid-1970s until 1995 had produced a voter distrustful of government promises and accustomed to a boom-and-bust economy.[17] Zedillo's government successfully averted investors' and analysts' expectations of an end-of-term crisis, but the Mexican electorate as a whole remained skeptical. A full 75.7 percent of panel respondents in April/May expected an end-of-term crisis, and the same was true of 76.2 percent of respondents in June.

In short, the 2000 election presented clear opportunities for issue voting. There were important, readily identifiable problems on which voters focused, and voters evaluated the candidates' abilities to address these problems differently. Meanwhile, the classic cleavages of the Mexican party system remained relevant for both voters and parties. There were even specific positional issues (such as industry privatization) on which voters and candidates differed enough to make a difference. We now single out those effects that had a real impact on voter choice from those that served as a simple background.

THE VOTE

In analyzing vote choice, two important methodological points require clarification. The first concerns the relatively low response rates to issue questions in public opinion questionnaires. While not excessive,[18] missing data in each of these indicators eventually add up, since logistic regression models require that each observation included in the model have valid information for all of the variables analyzed. Thus it might quickly become very difficult to make confident statistical assessments based on list-wise deleted data.[19] Moreover, King and colleagues have convincingly argued that statistical analyses performed on multiply imputed data should generally produce estimates that are more reliable than those obtained from list-wise deleted data, unless certain restrictive conditions apply.[20] We therefore performed all analyses for this chapter on multiply imputed data.[21]

A second methodological issue concerns the panel waves to be analyzed. The model we present here is based on the first and third waves of the panel, for several reasons. First, a two-wave design allows us to control for the potential endogeneity that PID and candidate evaluation variables might have with vote choice: that is, for the fact that respondents may change their partisan affiliation to accord with their candidate preference, and vice versa. Second, using the first wave of the panel alone does not allow us to take into account changes during the campaign. The one drawback from using the third wave (June) is that the dependent variable is not vote choice but voting intention; thus shifts during the last weeks of the campaign are simply not accounted for by the model. However, we believe this is preferable to using the fourth (postelectoral) wave, which did not include a question on the prospects for economic crisis and which was contaminated by a surge in Zedillo's approval rating among opposition voters.[22] This surge is not surprising, given the statesmanlike way in which Zedillo conducted himself on and after election day. But it prevents us from obtaining an accurate measurement of what the effect of such evaluations might be on voters' decisions.

Our model includes six categories of explanatory variables.[23] First, we control for social and economic indicators, as well as political sophistication (an index of voter interest and knowledge of politics). Second, we include voters' partisan identification in February. Third, we use a set of indicators of retrospective and prospective evaluations. Because not all of these indicators were available for the third panel wave,[24] as a second-best strategy we tested the impact of the variables from the first time period when these were not available for the third. These indicators address economic and noneconomic concerns, as well as presidential approval. Fourth, we include respondents' stated positions on each issue; we here also include first- and third-wave indicators, where available, to control for potential campaign effects.[25] Fifth, we include valence issues—namely, perceptions of the most important problem and which candidate was best able to manage the economy. And finally, we included an indicator of disposition toward risk. Table 12.5 presents the multinomial model's results; a second version of the model excludes partisan identification to test the robustness of other indicators.[26]

Table 12.5. Multinomial Logit Models of Party Choice

	Model 1		Model 2	
	Labastida	Cárdenas	Labastida	Cárdenas
Size of town or locality (x1000)	−0.0005*	0.0000	−0.0005**	−0.0001
Income	−0.0753	−0.1336*	−0.0621	−0.1240*
Formal education	−0.1391	0.1616	−0.2036[†]	0.1071
Age	0.0014	0.0108	−0.0043	0.0112
Sophistication index[a], w 1	0.0177	−0.0153	0.0184	0.1348
PRI ID, wave 1	0.3858**	−0.2805[†]		
PAN ID, wave 1	−0.8364**	−1.1825**		
PRD ID, wave 1	−0.3462	0.6100**		
Presidential approval, w 1	0.0812	−0.1685	0.2124	−0.2391[†]
Presidential approval, w 3	0.6753**	0.0257	0.7142**	−0.0306
Nat'l economic evals, w 1	−0.3263[†]	−0.2535	−0.1817	−0.2451
Fight corruption, wave 1	−0.2081	−0.0489	−0.1410	0.0867
Public safety, wave 1	0.2430	0.3928[†]	0.1783	0.3255[†]
Risk averse, wave 1	0.5271[†]	0.3234	0.8200**	0.3998
Left-right position, wave 1	−0.0009	−0.0428	0.0202	−0.0766[†]
Left-right position, wave 3	0.0950	−0.0190	0.1035	−0.0285
Political reform,[b] wave 3	0.0063	0.0243	0.0103	0.0075
Electric. industry property, wave 3	−0.0396	−0.0743[†]	−0.0608*	−0.0832*
Crime policy, wave 3	0.0182	0.0272	−0.0005	−0.0181
Expect end-of-term crisis, wave 3	−0.5137[†]	0.3650	−0.6014*	0.1858
Labastida best for economy, wave 1	0.6119*	−0.2425	1.1452**	−0.2682
Fox best for economy, w 1	−0.7975*	−0.4727	−1.4623**	−1.3436**
Cárdenas best for economy, wave 1	0.4575	1.0025	0.1956	1.8706**
Most important problem is economic, wave 1	−0.6288[†]	−0.0581	−0.5820*	−0.1237
Most important problem is political, wave 1	−0.7078	0.4467	−0.6793	0.3080
Most important problem is crime, wave 1	−0.6848[†]	0.3104	−0.7174*	0.1816
Model constant	1.2895	0.0360	0.7071	−0.6986

Coefficients obtained from multinomial logit estimation on 924 observations from 5 imputed datasets. Vote intention for Vicente Fox is base category.

[a] Inverse scale, higher value indicates less sophistication.

[b] Higher value indicates demand for more reform.

**p < .01; *p < .05; [†]p < .10.

Five general points are to be made from the evidence presented in table 12.5. First, valence issues were consistently good predictors of vote choice, in terms of both the problems identified and the candidates' relative abilities at solving *the* key problem. In particular, Fox's economic competence seemed to have a slightly stronger salience than Labastida's, as indicated by the magnitude of the corresponding coefficients. Second, issue positions were only marginally important in determining the outcome of the election, although the one most salient during the campaign—privatization of the electric power industry—did play a minor yet significant role. Third, Cárdenas's vote was almost solely explained by partisan identification; in other words, almost no one other than PRD partisans voted for him. Although attitudes toward privatization appear to have exercised an impact over and above that of partisan affiliation, a comparison of models 1 and 2 reveals that broader ideological self-identification fades into insignificance once partisanship is taken into account. Fourth, and perhaps most important, the results suggest a complex relationship between retrospective and prospective economic evaluations. Although most of the coefficients show the expected sign, Fox obtained an advantage over the incumbent party's candidate among those who thought the economy had improved in the country's recent past. Finally, some tepid social cleavages remained lurking beneath voter behavior, with Fox benefiting from urban, better-educated, and higher-income segments of society. We now turn to a more specific discussion of the substantive implications of these and other findings.

Substantive Effects of Selected Variables

Although the raw coefficients presented in table 12.5 are essential in determining the accuracy of particular hypotheses, they are quite difficult to interpret in nonlinear specifications (especially when the dependent variable is trichotomous, as in our case). Moreover, simple calculations of the effect of changes in the variables disregard the fact that point estimates of the parameters in the model are subject to the uncertainty captured by their standard error, as well as the underlying uncertainty generated by the statistical procedure.[27] To address these problems and highlight our substantive findings, we present results of simulations based on the model specified above, using the software package *Clarify*.[28]

Table 12.6 presents the estimated probabilities of supporting one of the three main candidates for a PAN leaner, with all other variables in the model at their means. Confidence intervals reflect the uncertainty captured by the simulation procedure. We will use this as a benchmark from which to gauge the magnitude of a particular shift in any of the explanatory variables, and thus to compare their relative weight in voters' decisions. The results are shown in table 12.7.

Table 12.6. Simulated Voting Probabilities (baseline model)

	Mean	95 Percent Confidence Interval	
P (vote Labastida)	0.3812	0.215	0.568
P (vote Fox)	0.4246	0.248	0.594
P (vote Cárdenas)	0.1942	0.159	0.231

Note: Simulated probabilities obtained from 1,000 random draws of the coefficients estimated in model 1, table 12.5. All variables held at their means, except PID, where we use a PAN leaner.

Table 12.7. Impact of Selected Explanatory Variables on Vote Choice

	Probability Change by Candidate		
	Labastida	Fox	Cárdenas
Labastida best for economy, Feb.	**0.158**	*−0.078*	−0.080
Fox best for economy, Feb.	−0.141	**0.162**	*−0.021*
Cárdenas best for economy, Feb.	*0.009*	−0.140	**0.130**
Economy is most important, Feb.	**−0.142**	0.105	0.038
Politics is most important, Feb.	**−0.175**	0.044	0.131
Crime is most important, Feb.	**−0.171**	0.069	0.102
Left-right position, June[a]	**0.118**	*−0.069*	*−0.049*
Electric industry property, June[a]	*−0.025*	**0.085**	*−0.060*
Risk aversion, February	0.096	**−0.105**	*0.009*
PRI ID, February	**0.318**	−0.173	−0.144
PAN ID, February	−0.304	**0.594**	−0.290
PRD ID, February	−0.305	−0.184	**0.489**
Zedillo approval, June	**0.280**	−0.197	−0.083
National economic evaluation, February	*−0.115*	**0.146**	−0.030
End-of-term crisis expected, Feb.	**−0.147**	*0.060*	0.088

Note: Simulated changes in probability obtained by shifting each explanatory variable from its minimum to its maximum value. Values in bold face indicate statistical significance at the 5 percent level. Probabilities in italics are not distinguishable from zero with 90 percent confidence.
[a] Variables shifted from their 20th to their 80th percentile.

The results suggest that valence issues played an important albeit uneven role in the election. Whenever voters considered the economy, politics, or crime to be the most important problem facing the nation, they punished the incumbent party's candidate. It is worth noting that this effect was strongest among those who thought the most important problem was political. This is perhaps the most direct indicator we have about any *political-institutional* content the concept of "change" might have had in the campaign, and it is here where the direction of the PRI candidate's loss acquires importance. Those who thought politics was the most important problem facing Mexico certainly abandoned the PRI. But these voters did not turn to Vicente Fox; they turned to Cuauhtémoc Cárdenas.

This finding, added to the null effect of the political reform issue, runs directly against the notion that the 2000 election constituted a mandate for thorough political reform. Since Fox did not benefit from a political-institutional reformist impulse, claims that his mandate for change includes sweeping political revision are, to say the least, exaggerated. To be sure, the mandate for change is at its heart political, but we contend that it was more closely aligned with the performance-oriented "throw-the-rascals-out" mandate typical of normal democracies, rather than the more elaborate "let's-transform-our-polity" notion of a "foundational" election.

This interpretation is strengthened by the effect of the "economy as the most important problem" on voting choices; Labastida remains the loser among this group, and Fox made substantial gains. Of every fourteen votes Labastida lost to those who thought that the economy was Mexico's most important problem, about ten would have gone to Fox and only four to Cárdenas.[29] This finding is complemented by voter opinions about the candidates' ability to manage the economy: the strongest effect seems to be the one favoring Fox. In other words, the extent to which Fox could credibly claim that he was the most capable with regard to the economy mattered more for Fox backers than other candidates' claims to macroeconomic competence.

The sources of Fox's gains on this issue are revealing. The fact that a voter who thought Cárdenas was best at managing the economy was no less likely to vote for Labastida implies that she had already decided not to vote for the PRI, and was only thinking about whom to back in the opposition field. However, if a voter were to think that Fox was the most capable of handling the economy, this gain would come almost entirely at Labastida's expense. This finding—along with the relatively similar proportions of the electorate who thought these two were the most able candidates on this issue—indicates that the PRI stood to lose more on economics in this particular election than in any prior contest. Conversely, Labastida's gains came equally from both opposition candidates, and not exclusively from Fox. Even though slightly more voters saw Labastida as most apt at handling the economy, Fox's initial supporters would reward him and punish Labastida more than the latter's voters would do the opposite, allowing Fox to gain from the salience of economic issues.

The effect of valence issues was thus considerable. Candidates transmitted cues indicating their competence (or lack thereof) on economic matters, and voters reacted in distinguishable patterns. Fox made gains on the economics issue, due to the greater salience of this topic to his voters and to his opponent's inability to credibly claim greater expertise.

With regard to issue-position voting, the results suggest that the left-right dimension played little role once partisanship and valence issues were taken into account. However, voters did respond to a much more specific issue: as a respondent moved from the right to the left on the privatization of the electric power industry (from 8 to 1 in the scale), her probability of favoring Cárdenas over Fox increased by about 8.5 percent. Thus, while moderate, this particular issue clearly mattered in the campaign, and candidates were well advised to spend some of their television advertising money on it.

Propensity toward risk played a familiar role, helping the PRI and hindering the opposition. Even after controlling for partisanship, voters who were risk averse (a minority of 35 percent in February) were less willing to vote for the opposition. This finding has a double-edged quality that allows for interesting speculations. While risk-averse voters tend to favor the PRI, giving it an overall advantage of 9.6 percent in an individual's probability of voting for it, their conservative character will make them more prone to punish a party that is seen as unreliable.[30] This effect, in turn, implies that risk-acceptant voters (a majority of 65 percent in February) will be more likely to vote for Fox (by about 10 percent), but they will *also* be much more tolerant of candidates' ambiguities and contradictions. In fact, although voter uncertainty about candidate positions did not seem to be substantially different among candidates or issues,[31] risk aversion is diversely distributed among the electorate. This finding might explain both the relative ease with which Fox would get out of seemingly irreconcilable contradictions during the campaign, as well as the higher cost paid by Labastida for his campaign's changes in focus.[32] In short, what for the PRI had been a blessing in the recent past came back to haunt it with a vengeance once voters learned to distrust the party's economic promises. Risk aversion put the incumbent candidate in a straightjacket, utterly unable to re-invent himself, and it gave Vicente Fox a free ride, turning him into a prototypical Teflon candidate.

The effects of partisanship differed across candidates. Fox was the candidate who received the highest level of support among sympathizers from his own party. The probability that an independent voter favored him in the election went up by 59 percent if this voter became a strong PAN identifier. This number is higher than what Labastida got from PRI identifiers (only 32 percent) and what Cárdenas got from his party's core constituents (49 percent). In Vicente Fox the PAN found a leader who was able to solidify its core constituency and to build bridges to a plurality coalition.[33] By contrast, Labastida's partisan bonus was the weakest of the three candidates, signaling an important vulnerability at the PRI's core. This evidence is consistent with an interpretation of the PRI's primary as a divisive experiment, driving strong PRI identifiers aligned with losing candidate Roberto Madrazo away from the polling booth on election day.

Change came to mean defeating the incumbent party, regardless of how good its performance had been in the past few years and how much voters liked the current president himself. The crisis of 1995 was fresh in voters' minds, casting the PRI's economic competence in doubt. Finally, presidential approval had an important effect in the 2000 election. The difference between approving or disapproving of Zedillo's performance translated into almost a 28 percent slide in the probability of voting for Labastida. Regardless of how much his campaign tried to de-emphasize the continuity between his platform and that of his former boss, Labastida certainly benefited from Zedillo's high approval ratings. These ratings, however, seemed to have less to do with the PRI's future economic performance than with Zedillo's perceived honesty and other personal characteristics, as we will show below.

This becomes clear when we look into voters' economic expectations. Recent research has suggested increasing voter skepticism of PRI promises regarding economic stability, especially after the 1995 crisis.[34] In February, approximately three of every four Mexican voters were pessimistic about Mexico's near-term economic future, and these pessimistic expectations weighed heavily against Francisco Labastida, lowering by as much as 14 percent his likelihood of obtaining a vote.

The models presented in table 12.7 do produce one surprising result. Challenging conventional wisdom, voters who thought that the economy had improved in the last year were more likely to "take the gift" and vote for Fox. This effect was not negligible in magnitude, with a shift in retrospective sociotropic evaluations producing an increase of 14 percent in the odds of voting for Fox.[35] However, given the impact of voters' expectations shown above, this result is less surprising.

The 1994–1995 crisis had a very strong homegrown character, with clear signs of political and economic mismanagement. It was an important catalyst in bringing about rapid political change, as local elections in 1995 and the congressional elections of 1997 showed. Its effect was that of altering voters' prospective evaluations of the PRI. In this sense, short-term gains made by PRI governments did not necessarily enhance voters' expected utility from the PRI. What the evidence shows conclusively is that, all else equal, voters who thought the country was better off in the last year were more likely to vote for Fox.

This finding suggests further examination of the interaction between retrospective and prospective evaluations and vote choice. Table 12.8 shows the proportion of respondents who expected, according to their combined retrospective evaluations of President Zedillo and the national economy, that an end-of-term crisis would ensue.

Table 12.8. Economic Expectations by Retrospective Evaluations

National Economy, wave 1	Presidential Approval Ratings (June)			
	Disapprove	Indifferent	Approve	Total
Worse	0.857	0.889	0.732	0.803
	(12.0)	(3.0)	(14.4)	(29.4)
Unchanged	0.868	0.886	0.755	0.803
	(15.8)	(5.1)	(31.9)	(52.7)
Better	0.833	0.900	**0.505**	0.586
	(2.8)	(1.3)	**(13.8)**	(17.9)
	0.860	0.889	0.691	0.764
Total	(30.6)	(9.4)	(60.1)	(100)

Note: Figures indicate the proportion of respondents expecting an end-of-term crisis in June. Figures in parentheses show the percentage of the sample for each cell.

The first thing to be noted is the overall independent effect of these two variables on what is on average a very high expectation of a crisis (76 percent of the sample). Among those who approved of Zedillo's performance, 69 percent thought there would be a crisis, versus over 86 percent for the rest of the sample. Similarly, only 59 percent of those who thought the economy had improved believed that a crisis would strike, against 80 percent of those who thought otherwise. What is perhaps most compelling is the fact that, unless a voter thought that the economy had improved and had a high opinion of Zedillo, she would most certainly be expecting yet another end-of-*sexenio* economic disaster. Only among the small minority of the electorate who liked Zedillo and believed the economy had improved was there a roughly even chance (51 percent) of being an optimist or a pessimist. For all other cells in table 12.8, the proportion of pessimistic voters was at least 73 percent, very close to the sample mean of 76 percent.

In this context, it is no wonder that Labastida had a hard time benefiting from recent economic indicators. Even among those who approved of President Zedillo's performance in office and felt the economy had improved, at least half disbelieved Labastida's promises of future economic improvements.

In order to illustrate how this configuration of opinions influenced voter choice, we turn to figure 12.8. Figure 12.8 displays the four most extreme scenarios for the interaction between retrospective and prospective evaluations, along with the corresponding simulated election outcomes for each of them.[36] Triplots on the top row indicate bad perceptions of the president and the national economy, while those in the bottom row show good evaluations. The left column of triplots implies that an economic crisis is expected, and the right one that no crisis is expected. The corresponding mean probabilities for each of these scenarios are shown in table 12.9.

The best scenario by far for Fox was that in which retrospective evaluations and future expectations were bleak, with a 48 percent probability of voting in his favor. But it is surprising to show how little his lead shrunk (to 44 percent) when voters' retrospective evaluations changed to the exact opposite and prospective evaluations remained bad. As figure 12.8 vividly shows, the effect of this shift was mostly to drive voters away from Cárdenas and into a head-to-head competition between Labastida and Fox, yet one in which the Guanajuato businessman still prevailed. The same effect is apparent, although in a smaller magnitude, for the tiny minority of voters (2 percent of the

Figure 12.8. Effect of Economic Evaluations on Vote Choice

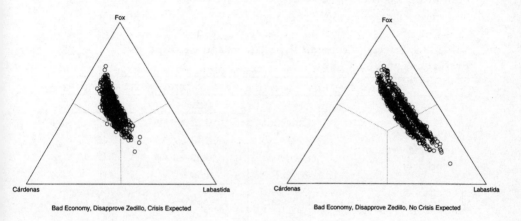

Bad Economy, Disapprove Zedillo, Crisis Expected

Bad Economy, Disapprove Zedillo, No Crisis Expected

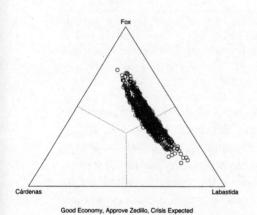

Good Economy, Approve Zedillo, Crisis Expected

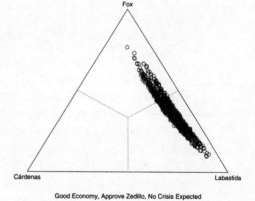

Good Economy, Approve Zedillo, No Crisis Expected

electorate) who did not expect a crisis, despite having bad evaluations of both the president and the economy. It was only when voters did not expect a crisis that good economic evaluations effectively put Labastida in a position to win more votes than his opponent, as shown in the bottom-right corners of table 12.9 and figure 12.8.

Table 12.9. Effect of Economic Expectations and Retrospective Evaluations on Vote Choice

		End-of-Term Crisis Expected?	
		Yes	No
Disapprove Zedillo (June) Bad national economy (February)	Labastida	0.22	0.35
	Fox	**0.48**	0.46
	Cárdenas	0.30	0.19
	Percent	*11.0*	*1.8*
Approve Zedillo (June) Good national economy (February)	Labastida	0.39	**0.54**
	Fox	0.44	0.37
	Cárdenas	0.17	0.10
	Percent	*6.9*	*6.8*

Note: Figures in roman are mean probabilities of vote choice for each scenario (June). Figures in italics denote the overall percentage of respondents in each of these scenarios. Values in bold face indicate statistical significance at the 5 percent level.

The bitter lessons that Mexicans learned during 1995 were not wasted—at least from the opposition's perspective. The PRI and its candidate faced an uphill battle at the beginning of the 2000 campaign. Labastida was unable to capitalize on his party's loyalty and the president's popularity. He failed at mending the wedge created by his party's presidential primary, and he could not turn out his constituencies to vote or strengthen his prospects with the high approval ratings of President Zedillo. This was, at least in part, the result of voters' reluctance to buy his promises of economic stability. The irony lies in the fact that this time voters were again wrong in their expectations about Mexico's near economic future: despite a U.S. recession and the failure of the Fox administration to pass a much-needed fiscal reform program, Mexico has managed to avert the dramatic setbacks of the recent past.

Ernesto Zedillo's government was thus ultimately successful at attaining what was perhaps his presidency's deepest aspiration. For his party, no doubt, this goal was accomplished just a bit too late. In the years between 1982 and 2000, different PRI administrations got more than their fair share of chances at competing for voters' loyalties under carefully managed but increasingly democratic rules. Over and over again, they squandered them, hurting the country and hurting themselves. By 2000 the Mexican voter had had enough.

THE MANDATE AND THE FUTURE

This chapter has argued that the election of Vicente Fox was indeed the expression of a desire for change. Change, however, was based mostly on the expectation of greater competence in managing the economy, fighting crime, and reducing corruption. That kind of change does not necessarily imply major political reforms or substantial policy shifts, though better governmental results could be conditional on such reforms. Change for the Mexican voter meant, above all, more effective government, not a new political system. Nor did Fox's mandate include major economic reform along *panista* lines. The fact that the majority of the electorate demanded that the electric power industry remain in public hands is at odds with the fact that the candidate who won was seen as the most prone to privatize it.

The 2000 elections also highlight the renewed theoretical importance of risk aversion. This is not a measure that belongs to the semi-authoritarian past. On the contrary, its close correspondence with partisan affiliation and its putative effect on voters' behavior suggest it lies at the heart of speculations about the future shape of the Mexican party system. The mere possibility of an electorate dominated by risk seekers eager to take at face value the demagogical, ambiguous, and irresponsible offers of anti-establishment, media-savvy candidates who dismiss "politics-as-usual" solutions for the country's problems means that risk aversion remains crucial for contemporary electoral analysis in Mexico.

Luckily, this grim scenario seems far from occurring, with partisan attachments strongly influencing voter opinions. Yet not all parties have the same ties with voters, and internal party politics complicates the process of realignment. With both the PRI and the PRD undergoing considerable organizational and leadership struggles, these ties could loosen as much as they could strengthen in the near future.

Finally, there is an important theoretical lesson to be drawn from voter behavior in Mexico 2000. Almost every model of retrospective voting assumes that voters use these obvious, low-cost evaluations to substitute for informationally costly and inherently uncertain prospective evaluations.[37] Yet these are ultimately the ones that should count, to the extent that the act of voting is construed as the collective feat of choosing a government.[38] After witnessing a series of end-of-term crises for over almost a quarter-century, Mexican voters did not need informational shortcuts to see what was in store for them in the near term. Only those who did not think a crisis was coming rewarded Labastida for the economy's retrospective performance. Once voters are pleasantly surprised by economic outcomes, we should expect the electorate to return to a more standard use of retrospective evaluations. In the meantime, Mexico's recent macroeconomic history worked to the PRI's disadvantage.

Notes

The authors wish to thank Alberto Díaz-Cayeros, Federico Estévez, Jorge I. Domínguez, and Chappell Lawson for helpful suggestions at various stages of this research. Poiré wishes to acknowledge support from the Asociación Mexicana de Cultura, through ITAM, as well as a grant from the Fundación México en Harvard and other support provided by Harvard's Weatherhead Center for International Affairs. Gaëlle Brachet provided valuable research assistance.

1. Juan Molinar Horcasitas, *El tiempo de la legitimidad: elecciones, autoritarismo y democracia en México* (Mexico City: Cal y Arena, 1991).

2. Chappell Lawson, "Why Cárdenas Won: The 1997 Elections in Mexico City," in Jorge I. Domínguez and Alejandro Poiré, eds., *Toward Mexico's Democratization: Campaigns, Elections and Public Opinion* (New York: Routledge, 1999); Beatriz Magaloni, "From Hegemony to Multipartism: Issue-voting and the Emergence of Partisan Cleavages in Mexico," ITAM Working Papers in Political Science (Mexico City: ITAM, 2000); Alejandro Moreno, "Party Competition and the Issue of Democracy: Ideological Space in Mexican Elections," in Mónica Serrano, ed., *Governing Mexico: Political Parties and Elections* (London: University of London, 1998); Alejandro Moreno, "Campaign Awareness and Voting in the 1997 Mexican Congressional Elections," in Domínguez and Poiré, *Toward Mexico's Democratization*; Alejandro Poiré, "Un modelo sofisticado de decisión electoral racional: el voto estratégico en México, 1997," *Política y Gobierno* 7, no. 2 (2000).

3. V.O. Key, *The Responsible Electorate: Rationality in Presidential Voting, 1936–1960* (Cambridge, Mass.: Belknap, 1966).

4. Jorge I. Domínguez and James A. McCann, "Shaping Mexico's Electoral Arena: The Construction of Partisan Cleavages in the 1988 and 1991 National Elections," *American Political Science Review* 89, no. 1 (1995); Beatriz Magaloni, "Is the PRI Fading? Economic Performance, Electoral Accountability and Voting Behavior," in Domínguez and Poiré, *Toward Mexico's Democratization*.

5. Alejandro Moreno, "Ideología y voto: dimensiones de competencia política en México en los noventa," *Política y Gobierno* 6, no. 1 (1999).

6. Moreno, "Party Competition and the Issue of Democracy."

7. The correlations among the available issue positions and the left-right dimension were minute and not always distinguishable from zero. In the third wave of the panel (June), the partial correlation coefficients (holding other variables at their means) between the left-right dimension and the issues of privatization of the electric power industry and the political reform were not distinguishable from zero; the correlation with the crime policy issue was only 0.14.

8. The first wave of the panel also included an additional item on economic policy, which yielded unsatisfactory results as well.

9. The violin plots were constructed using Thomas J. Steichen's Stata 7.0 © ado-file. They draw a symmetric density line on the sides of a box-plot and show the distribution of voters for each category of the x-axis variable, keeping these of the same size. For the first wave, however, the following is the distribution of partisanship as used here: PRI, 39 percent; PAN, 23 percent; PRD, 9 percent; independents, 29 percent. This measure does not include "leaners" (coded here as independents) but only weak and strong partisans. Fourteen percent of the sample were leaners, with more than half of them leaning toward the PAN, a third toward the PRI, and the rest toward the PRD.

10. We use the third wave here to minimize the potential impact of the honeymoon effect on issue positions. Even so, the distribution of position shifts between the first and fourth waves looks very similar, albeit less concentrated toward zero (with 41 percent at 1 or below and 66 percent at 3 or below).

11. Moreno, "Party Competition and the Issue of Democracy"; Moreno, "Ideología y voto."

12. The way the question was worded, political reformers would be at the right-most extreme and conservatives would be at the left-most one.

13. Except for the fairly unrealistic case in which candidates are on opposite sides of the dimension from their partisans, this condition should hold.

14. This variable was created by combining voter ratings of each of the three candidates as "very," "somewhat," "a little," or "not at all" on every issue. Candidates were coded as "the best" only when their rating was strictly better than those of the other two candidates; that is, a voter rating Labastida as "very" honest, Fox as "somewhat" honest, and Cárdenas as "very" honest would be coded as "none" on the question regarding the most honest candidate.

15. D. Roderick Kiewiet, *Macroeconomics and Micropolitics: The Electoral Effects of Economic Issues* (Chicago: University of Chicago Press, 1983).

16. Authors' calculations based on *Reforma*'s published series of quarterly presidential evaluation polls.

17. Beatriz Magaloni, "Institutions, Political Opportunism and Macroeconomics Cycles: Mexico 1970–1998," presented at the ITAM Research Workshop in Political Science (Mexico City, 2000).

18. For the third wave of the panel, for example, while we had 862 valid responses to the vote choice question (88 percent), we obtained only 755 (77 percent) for the left-right positioning and 820 (84 percent) for the electric power industry privatization question.

19. For the models we run in this chapter, the maximum N using list-wise deletion was 337, or 34 percent of the June sample.

20. Gary King et al., "Analyzing Incomplete Political Science Data: An Alternative Algorithm for Multiple Imputation," *American Political Science Review* 95, no. 1 (2001).

21. Estimation was performed using James Honaker et al., "AMELIA: A Program for Missing Data (Windows version)," (Cambridge, Mass.: Harvard University, 2000).

22. We also conducted very similar models on the panel's first and fourth waves. In general, the signs of the coefficients were the same and in most cases equally significant. The fourth wave, however, did not include an indicator for expectation of economic crisis, and thus the model was by design under-specified. This, along with the measurement problems discussed below, produced coefficients for retrospective evaluations and valence issues that were, unsurprisingly, small and sometimes insignificant.

23. Our analysis employed multinomial logit for all available respondents from the panel's third wave. It was performed on five multiply imputed datasets, and thus the coefficients reported are the weighted average of the same model being estimated on each of these sets. Gary King, Michael Tomz, and Jason Wittenberg, "Making the Most of Statistical Analyses: Improving Interpretation and Presentation," *American Journal of Political Science* 44, no. 2 (2000).

24. The ideal situation would have been to have all indicators available for the third wave since they represent voters' current evaluations exogenous to voter choice. See Morris P. Fiorina, *Retrospective Voting in American National Elections* (New Haven, Conn.: Yale University Press, 1981).

25. Admittedly, this departs from a standard expected utility framework, where issue distances are used instead of simple issue positions (see, for example, Poiré, "Un modelo sofisticado de decisión electoral racional"). However, recent research (Ana Lorena De la O Torres, "Aversión al riesgo en política: un supuesto insostenible para el electorado mexicano de 1997" [Bachelor's thesis, Instituto Tecnológico Autónomo de México, 2001]; Ana Lorena De la O Torres and Alejandro Poiré, "La agenda de investigación en torno a la aversión al riesgo," *Gaceta de Ciencia Política, ITAM* 1 [2000]) leads us to believe that such measurement of issue positions is in better accordance with Mexican voters' underlying dispositions toward risk; see R. Michael Alvarez, *Information and Elections* (Ann Arbor: University of Michigan Press, 1997). In short, PRD partisans do not seem to discount uncertain offers from their candidates, while PAN and especially PRI partisans seem much less willing to forgive ambiguity on behalf of their candidates (Kenneth A. Shepsle, "The Strategy of Ambiguity," *American Political Science Review* 66 [1972]). This would suggest that using a model based on issue distances, which estimates one parameter for each of the issues involved, might be unrealistic since each party might be judged differently by voters. This latter assumption is the one behind a model that only incorporates voter issue positions and estimates one parameter for each of the candidates, as we here do.

26. Alternative model specifications were tested for robustness. We selected these models for their theoretical and statistical appeal.

27. King, Tomz, and Wittenberg, "Making the Most of Statistical Analyses."

28. Ibid.; Michael Tomz, Jason Wittenberg, and Gary King, "CLARIFY: Software for Interpreting and Presenting Statistical Results" (2001). Simulations are performed in the following fashion (assuming they are based on a single estimation procedure from a single database): the underlying distribution of the estimated coefficients is used to generate 1,000 random draws of coefficients from it. Each of these drawn coefficients is combined with the explanatory variables at the levels they are set, in order to estimate the quantities of interest (in this case the probabilities of vote choice). We thus obtain a distribution of 1,000 simulated quantities of interest, from which we can calculate a number of statistical measures (mean, standard deviation, and so on), instead of reporting point estimates that do not take into account the standard error of the coefficients nor their interrelationships in the statistical model. When we have multiple databases and statistical models, as a result of multiple imputation, this process is accordingly repeated across each of the models and data, its results being averaged and weighted as other analyses performed on multiply imputed data.

29. Although the estimated probability increase is not conclusively different from 0 for either Cárdenas or Fox, the loss from Labastida is certainly positive.

30. Alvarez, *Information and Elections*.

31. As measured by the standard deviation of voters' locations of candidate positions on each of the issues in June.

32. For instance, Fox issued contradictory statements on Mexican workers in the United States, the bank bailout plan, and other issues. Labastida began his campaign with a focus on political empowerment, then turned to education, then went negative against Fox, and ended with a generally positive message that lacked specific content.

33. See Alejandro Poiré, "Turnout in Mexico's Presidential Election: Evidence from the Mexico 2000 Panel Study," ITAM Working Papers in Political Science (Mexico City, 2001).

34. Magaloni, "Institutions, Political Opportunism and Macroeconomics Cycles: Mexico 1970–1998."

35. The relative impacts of moving from neutral to positive or to negative are about symmetrical—that is, a change of about 0.07 in probability against/for Fox.

36. Triangle plots were elaborated using Nicholas J. Cox's Triplot.ado programming code for Stata 7.0©. Observations within the triangle indicate the 1,000 simulations of a respondent's probabilities of voting for each candidate, according to the coefficients obtained in Model 1 and the selected levels of explanatory variables.

37. Anthony Downs, *An Economic Theory of Democracy* (New York: Harper, 1957); Key, *The Responsible Electorate*; Fiorina, *Retrospective Voting in American National Elections*; John Ferejohn, "Incumbent Performance and Electoral Control," *Public Choice*. 50 nos. 1–3 (1986).

38. Downs, *An Economic Theory of Democracy*.

13

Conclusion: Why and How Did Mexico's 2000 Presidential Election Campaign Matter?

Jorge I. Domínguez

Democratic citizens "fly to the assemblies," in Jean-Jacques Rousseau's famous phrase from the *Social Contract*.[1] They ponder, argue, and decide. Disagreement and decision are as fundamental for democratic politics in large countries as in Rousseau's Geneva.[2] In our times, the principal opportunity for citizens to deliberate, disagree, and decide the fate of politics in their countries is during election campaigns. Election campaigns matter normatively for the quality of democracies; empirically, they shape the circumstances of governance.

Yet why and how do presidential campaigns matter?[3] How do they shape the views, values, and behavior of voters? Do they matter more in new democracies such as Mexico's than in consolidated democracies such as those in North America and Western Europe? Politicians and their backers everywhere think that campaigns matter, and they spend vast amounts of time and money on campaigns. Research on political campaigns has been most extensive in the United States. In general, as Steven Finkel summarizes the state of scholarship, the U.S. findings "show that the overwhelming majority of individual voters could be predicted from attitudes such as party identification and presidential approval that were measured before the political party conventions. Changes in orientations during the general election period had little impact on vote choices at both the individual and aggregate levels." For the U.S. 1980 presidential election, three variables unrelated to the campaign itself (race, party identification, and presidential approval) predicted 81 percent of the votes. In elections as different as 1940, 1948, and 1980, only about 5 percent of the voters "converted" during the campaign, switching support from one candidate to the other.[4]

Scholars who emphasize the significance of economic factors in shaping the vote come to similar conclusions. Gregory Markus has studied the impact of the economy on U.S. voting behavior across time, using individual-level data, to predict election results taking into account just party identification, race, and sociotropic economic assessments (that is, assessments about the nation's economy, not about one's own pocketbook). Markus ignored the possible impact on the vote from campaign-related variables such as candidate assessments, issue positions, the nature of campaigns, the results of presidential candidate debates, and so on. He found only a 3 percent margin of error in his predictions of election results that might be attributed to omitted variables, such as campaign effects.[5]

Election outcomes in Western Europe can also be predicted without taking the campaign into account. Michael Lewis-Beck's research on economic voting in Britain, France, Germany, Italy, and Spain shows that social class, religiosity, ideology, and economic factors thoroughly explain variation in voting behavior across several elections in each of these countries. Economic voting is not short-sighted, moreover; it is a slower-moving, more stable variable than just the economic results in the run-up to the election.[6]

This book allows us to assess the impact of the 2000 presidential campaign. On July 2, 2000, for the first time since its founding (under a different name) in 1929, Mexico's ruling party, the Institutional Revolutionary Party (PRI), lost the presidency and accepted the loss.[7] The five months before the July 2000 election saw a shift of between 12 and 15 percent of the votes away from the PRI's Francisco Labastida in favor of the candidate of the lead opposition party, the National Action Party (PAN), Vicente Fox—a shift larger than Fox's 6.5 percent margin of victory or than comparisons to the United States and Western Europe might lead us to expect. Altogether, one out of every three Mexican voters changed their voting intention at some point between February and July 2000. Many did so just from "don't know" to one of the candidates, or from one of the candidates to abstention on election day. Yet there were also defections from, and shifts toward, each of the three main presidential candidates, the third being Cuauhtémoc Cárdenas, candidate of the Party of the Democratic Revolution (PRD).

In 2000, the prospects for a Labastida victory were good. There were four key reasons. First, both the PAN and the PRD had fielded presidential candidates, thus dividing the opposition vote. The PRI had not claimed a majority of the votes cast since the 1991 nationwide congressional election; a divided opposition made a PRI presidential victory possible. Second, the PRI retained a strong partisan base. Third, the PRI had won past elections by drawing support even from voters who held negative short-term retrospective assessments of its economic stewardship but who were averse to turning the government over to uncertain alternatives.[8] The economy had performed quite well in each year but the first of President Ernesto Zedillo's six-year term, making it possible for the PRI to gather even greater electoral support. Fourth, in the months preceding the election, the public had a high assessment of Zedillo's performance as president. Not surprisingly, therefore, as the chapters by Chappell Lawson and Alejandro Moreno show, Labastida held a strong lead in the polls at the start of 2000. Indeed, a standard "North Atlantic democracy" voting behavior model (positive sociotropic retrospective economic voting, high regard for presidential performance, and strong PRI partisanship) would forecast Labastida's election as president of Mexico in a divided field under first-past-the-post election rules. As the election campaign started, most Mexican politicians, journalists, pollsters, and pundits expected a PRI victory. That did not happen.

Why did the unexpected opposition victory come about? I argue that the campaign informed and influenced enough Mexicans to have a significant impact on the election's outcome, even if most Mexicans voted according to preferences set before the campaign began. Longer-standing factors such as party identification strongly mediated campaign effects. The campaign had strong effects on core partisans, and it informed and sorted out the politics of the opposition. Political communications were pertinent, therefore.[9] Were it not for the campaign, the PRI's Labastida might have become president instead of the PAN's Fox.

The 2000 election and the campaign do not, of course, explain Mexico's slow-moving transition to democracy, though they are a part of it. Later in this chapter, I show how the transition, begun years earlier by many Mexicans from all walks of life, created the structural circumstances, reshaped aspects of political culture, and induced changes in laws and institutions to make the 2000 election opposition victory thinkable and possible. The steps taken before the 2000 elections to found an independent Federal Electoral Institute (IFE), to reduce electoral fraud, to create greater freedom for intellectuals, the mass media, and public opinion pollsters, and to provide public funding for political parties, along with the leadership of social movements and opposition political parties are key elements—prior to the 2000 campaign—in Mexico's democratization.

Campaigns are less likely to matter if:

1. There are strong political attachments based on salient social cleavages. Voters whose behavior is determined by their residence, religiosity, or social class are less likely to be influenced by transient campaign events. Examples abound. Many Catalans, Scots, and Bavarians vote for regionally rooted parties. Many Dutch or Chilean Sunday-mass Roman Catholics vote Christian Democrat. There is strong working-class voting for the British Labour Party and the Scandinavian Social Democrats.[10]

2. Partisan attachments are strong. Party identification results from long processes of political socialization, confirmed repeatedly during adulthood. Parties of the Left often create partisan subcultures with networks of labor unions, community associations, women's groups, soccer clubs, and so on. Parties of the Right often buttress their support through overlapping memberships with religious organizations. The vote choice of strong partisans is less affected by campaigns. An electorate of strong partisans has few independents to swing elections depending on campaign events, and few strategic voters because citizens vote sincerely just for their party of long affiliation.[11]

3. Judgments about the economy's past shape the behavior of voters, that is, retrospective economic voting. Retrospective voting focuses on known facts, namely, how the economy has affected the country and my family's and my own economic circumstances. For this purpose, it does not matter whether citizens vote their "pocketbook"; that is, they focus on their personal or family economic situations, or are sociotropic. The key point is that retrospective economic voting behavior is less susceptible to the manipulations and promises of politicians during the campaign. Research in the United States and Europe shows, moreover, that economically oriented voters are not fools; they take a longer view of economic performance than just the few weeks or months during the campaign.[12]

4. The election is a vote on the political regime and specifically on its democratic qualities and potential. Is the political regime authoritarian? Do citizens vote against the incumbent in order to bring about democratization or to deepen trends toward political opening already under way? Such judgments are likely to be standing preferences relatively unaffected by the conduct of an election campaign.

Campaigns are more likely to matter if:

1. Voter perceptions of presidential candidates have an impact on voters. Voters may be attracted to, or repelled by, a candidate. Candidates may effectively mobilize their voters as a function of their appeal. Voters are, however, not detached or uncaring about the characteristics of candidates. Modern electoral campaigns feature the "personalization of politics," most so in presidentialist political systems.[13]

2. Issues shape the behavior of voters. Issues become salient during the campaign and help to modify the attitudes of voters. (Arguments about the predictability of U.S. and Western European elections characteristically exclude issue variables.)

3. Judgments about the economy's future shape the behavior of voters: prospective economic voting. Judgments about an economy's future are influenced in part by judgments about its past, of course, but also by the promises that candidates and parties make and by political reporting and mass media advertising. Prospective economic voting suggests that the campaign had an impact on voting. "Future expectations about what economic performance the government will deliver emerge as a decisive individual vote determinant in Western European electorates.... [T]hese future expectations," Lewis-Beck concludes, "appear to edge out the direct impact of traditional retrospective evaluations."[14] Politicians shape expectations about the economic future.

4. Constitutional and legal structures create opportunities to maximize campaign effects. Party primaries do so because party identification is assumed while the focus is on the choice of candidates; candidates differentiate themselves through personality traits and, occasionally, appeal to issues. Party conventions have somewhat similar effects. Constitutional requirements for two-round presi-

dential elections, if no candidate receives a majority in the first round, increase campaign effects between the two rounds: If my preferred candidate loses, whom do I support in the second round?

5. Major events mark the campaign, and these events modify voter preferences. Presidential debates exemplify events that might swing some voters, most likely those previously uncommitted but possibly those who had preferred a different candidate. Campaign processes could also matter, such as the effects of the mass media, candidate debates, and "negative" campaigning, that is, attempts to discredit one's opponents.

6. The vote of citizens can be bought or coerced. Parties, their electoral machineries, and candidates pay voters for their votes or engage in intimidating campaign practices to nullify prior voter preferences. Such mobilization may also override the impact of other campaign stimuli.

DID THE 2000 MEXICAN PRESIDENTIAL CAMPAIGN MATTER?

The attachment of Mexicans to social cleavages was relatively weak, and, as a consequence, campaign effects could be larger than in the United States or Western Europe.[15] Joseph Klesner's study of the structure of the electorate explored this question. His analysis shows that social attachments have a statistically significant effect in explaining positive or negative evaluations of the three major political parties in Mexico. Those who hold the PAN in high regard are much more likely to attend church and are more likely to live outside the Mexico City metropolitan region. Those who think highly of the PRI are generally less well educated and somewhat more likely to be female and live in rural southern Mexico. Those who have high esteem for the PRD are much more likely to be males who live in southern Mexico and more likely also to live in rural areas. The explanatory significance of all the combined social attachments on the evaluations of political parties, however, is very modest (the adjusted R^2 is at most .07 for any one of the three parties). Other variables, such as approval of the incumbent president, propensity toward risk, and attitudes toward the political regime, are much more important explanations of the relative evaluations of the political parties.

In his chapter, James McCann finds that region of residence, age, gender, and, to a lesser extent, social class, religiosity, and union membership had a significant effect early on in the campaign. It helped to distinguish between supporters of establishment-backed Labastida and his opponents in the November 1999 primary election contest for the PRI presidential nomination, which Labastida won. It also helped to explain citizen preferences early on in the campaign (February 2000). But the impact of all sociodemographic factors had weakened markedly by election day on July 2, 2000, when such variables proved much less important than others.

Chappell Lawson's chapter on mass media effects on voting behavior shows that sociodemographic variables had little impact, with the modest exception of union membership. Beatriz Magaloni and Alejandro Poiré's chapter on the issues and the mandate for change in the election finds "some tepid social cleavages" affecting voter behavior, with Fox benefiting from urban, better-educated, and higher-income segments of society, but these factors added little explanatory punch. Nor did demographic variables play a significant role in fostering strategic coordination among voters.

On the other hand, Wayne Cornelius finds that certain demographic factors have a greater impact on the voting choice than campaign gifts to voters or party representative home visits. Chappell Lawson and Joseph Klesner's chapter on the likelihood of turnout shows that the findings vary by level. At the level of districts, the extent of literacy in a community had no discernible impact on the likelihood of voting before the mid-1990s, but high-literacy communities became a significant fountain of votes in the second half of the 1990s. Higher levels of religiosity were also found in high-turnout communities on election day. On the other hand, at the individual level, few of the variables were significant predictors of change in the likelihood of voting, including education, socioeconomic status, gender, and other demographic variables. Only residence in central and northern Mexico was a factor affecting the likelihood of turnout among the social cleavage variables. Equally or more important were other variables.

Mexican politicians, the mass media, and many scholars have long attributed significance to social cleavage explanations of Mexican voting behavior. Social class, religiosity, education, and region supposedly account for differences in the choice of party and for election turnout. For the most part, this was not true in the 2000 presidential election. Variables tapping social cleavage effects had no impact on electoral results or were weak or inconsistent in their explanatory utility. Nor have social cleavage variables explained voting outcomes in any election since 1988, when Mexican elections became reasonably meaningful.[16] Social cleavage–based identities pose no bar to campaign effects in Mexico.

In contrast, partisan attachments are very strong. Not surprisingly, Klesner shows that partisanship is a strong explanation for how voters evaluate the political parties. Lawson and Klesner's study of electoral turnout shows that partisanship was at least as important as other variables in explaining turnout patterns. Turnout was greater in districts where the PAN was strong than in those where the PRI was strong. In addition, a legacy of PRI voting loyalty explains much of the support for Labastida in the November 1999 PRI primary, according to McCann. McCann also shows that PRI primary-election participants who had voted for the PRI in the 1994 elections were much more likely to vote for Labastida in 2000 regardless of their choice during the PRI primary.

Alejandro Moreno's chapter on the impact of negative campaigning shows the importance of partisanship in explaining how negativity is perceived. For the most part, PRI partisans did not see their candidate, Labastida, as engaging in negative campaigning, whereas PAN partisans did see him that way. Similarly, most PAN partisans did not perceive Fox as a negative campaigner, whereas most PRI partisans did. Partisans are more likely to believe that their preferred candidate's negative campaigning simply provides accurate information that justifies their own partisanship. Party identification is also the most powerful explanation for the voting choice examined by Magaloni and Poiré. PRI, PAN, and PRD partisans were strongly likely to vote, respectively, for the PRI, PAN, and PRD presidential candidates. Partisanship is unrivaled in its capacity to explain voting behavior in Mexico.[17]

The explanatory impact of partisanship had changed, however, by the 2000 election. In the late 1980s, Mexico began a process of partisan realignment and dealignment. In the 1988 presidential election, Cuauhtémoc Cárdenas drew a very large proportion of the electorate and established the basis for what would become the PRD. The PRD gathered voters who had once supported small left-wing parties, as well as former supporters of the PRI. The Cárdenas 1988 campaign also drew some voters who had typically supported the PAN in the belief that Cárdenas had the best chance of defeating the PRI—that is, strategic voters.[18] During the 1990s, as Klesner's chapter makes clear, support for the PRI continued to weaken. The PAN and the PRD struggled for leadership of the opposition. The PRD beat the PAN in the 1988 and 1997 national elections, while the PAN came out ahead of the PRD in the 1991 and 1994 national elections. This process of pull-and-tug set loose some voters from their partisan moorings. The weakening of partisanship enabled candidate effects to become important.

Mexico's 2000 presidential election, as Magaloni and Poiré demonstrate, showed strong candidate effects. The assessment of a candidate's utility for obtaining better national economic performance proved significant. Magaloni and Poiré also find that valence issues (those favored by everyone, such as peace and prosperity) help to explain the vote. Valence issues are useful when voters are asked to connect them to the expected performance of the candidates. A key valence issue was the desire for change; every candidate, including the PRI's Labastida, favored change. Fox sought to embody the prospects for change personally; his electoral coalition was called the Alliance for Change. Thus, in comparison to the four national elections in the 1988–1997 period, the salience and explanatory efficiency of party identification declined in time for the 2000 election; candidate and valence issue effects contributed more than in the past to explain the electoral outcome. Magaloni and Poiré also show that candidate effects helped to shape the voting choice of strategic voters. There were two effects: expectations of a given candidate's capacity to defeat the PRI, and perceptions of candidate competence.

Another effect of the partisan realignment and dealignment under way during the preceding decade and a half was the enlargement of a pool of independent voters who did not lean toward any political party. Each of the three principal presidential candidates, Magaloni and Poiré show, won a significant fraction of the independent voters, but Fox won the lion's share. Approximately 29 percent of the Fox coalition on election day was composed of independent voters, won over by the appeal of his personal candidacy.

The decline in the explanatory utility of partisanship should not be exaggerated, however. Party identification remained a more important explanation of the voting choice than either candidate assessments or valence issues. The largest component of the Fox vote on election day was core PAN supporters. The largest block of Labastida voters was *priístas*. The decisive segment of Cárdenas's votes came from PRD partisans. Candidate effects had an impact on strategic voters, but such voters represented only about 5 percent of the vote for Fox. Moreover, specific policy issues had very little impact on the vote choice. Voters hold views on corruption, public safety, crime policy, economic issues, and political reforms, but those attitudes on specific issues explained little about their choice on election day. Only attitudes toward the possible privatization of the state-owned electric power industry helped to distinguish Fox voters from Labastida and Cárdenas voters. Specific policy issues also had little explanatory utility in previous Mexican elections.[19]

The strength of partisan attachments constrains the impact of campaigns on Mexican voters. Most Mexican voters did not change their voting preferences at all during the campaign. But the weakening of partisan attachments by the 2000 election made it possible for PAN presidential candidate Fox to use the campaign, his image, and valence issues to good effect in fashioning the first-ever defeat of the PRI. Fox won over significant numbers of independent voters, former PRI partisans, and strategic voters who might have otherwise voted for Cárdenas.

The relative importance of economic voting is analyzed by Magaloni and Poiré. They find that economic voting played a significant role in the 2000 presidential election, just as it had in every election since 1988. Voters were pessimistic about the prospects for the Mexican economy, even though it had performed well since the last (1997) national election, as the introductory chapter reports. The principal reason for this economic skepticism was the overwhelming expectation that there would be an end-of-presidential-term economic crisis, just as there had been one at the end of each of the four preceding terms. Voters were unwilling to give credit to the PRI or Labastida for the economic growth of the Zedillo presidency because they thought that this PRI government would again lead the country to an economic fiasco, and, we suspect, because Labastida did not make Zedillo's economic record a centerpiece of his campaign. Mexicans did not believe in the PRI's promises about the country's economic future. Both retrospective and prospective economic assessments helped to shape the voting choice. They fed upon each other through the means of end-of-term-crisis expectations. Magaloni and Poiré also show, however, that prospective economic assessment was the stronger of these two economic voting explanations. The greater importance of prospective economic voting suggests that candidate campaigns could frame economic perceptions and voting.

Finally, assessments about the political regime had only a limited impact on the 2000 presidential election. Attitudes toward democracy, expectations of electoral fraud, and left-right self-placement (which, in Mexico, worked as a proxy for pro- or anti-PRI regime attitudes),

Klesner shows, influenced evaluations of the major political parties. On the other hand, McCann demonstrates that partisan and factional affiliation had little impact on the assessment whether Mexico had a democratic political system in 2000. Magaloni and Poiré show that attitudes concerning the issue of political reform had no impact on the voting choice, and that left-right self-placement had at most a modest impact. They estimate the change in the perceived extent of democracy in Mexico among PRD defectors, reporting that this change was statistically significant for those who chose to vote for Labastida but not for those who chose to vote for Fox. This variable thus affected just a tiny fraction of the electorate. In short, variables directly related to the prospects for, or the quality of, democratic politics in Mexico were not very salient in shaping the voting choice in 2000.[20] Fox's mandate for change was an anti-incumbent vote more than an ideological embrace of democratic principles. The limited salience of these variables allowed for a greater crafting of the political choice during the campaign.

In short, political campaigning affected voting behavior in Mexico's 2000 elections because social cleavage attachments were weak (as always), partisanship had weakened compared to elections past, prospective economic assessments outweighed retrospective assessments, and evaluation of the political regime was not a salient factor in the voting choice. Valence issues and candidate effects had an impact on the electoral outcome, and their importance grew during the presidential campaign. The effects of political campaigning were still constrained, however, because partisan identification remained the strongest explanatory variable and because retrospective economic voting—the result of the experience of decades—also helped to shape the behavior of voters.

HOW WERE CAMPAIGN EFFECTS FELT?

In U.S. presidential campaigns, "one of the important roles of the campaign," Thomas Holbrook has argued, "is to help move public opinion toward the expected outcome." In U.S. campaigns, "as events unfold ... voters update their evaluations" of the parties.[21] Mexican voters, Magaloni has reasoned elsewhere, have long updated their information about the capacities of their rulers; they did so gradually, as might be expected from a Bayesian learning perspective. And yet the long-term impact of such updating turned voters against the PRI.[22] Further updating during the 2000 presidential campaign moved Mexican voters *toward the unexpected outcome*, that is, to defeat the incumbent party's candidate despite good economic performance, high approval of the sitting president, and strong PRI partisanship facing a split opposition.[23]

Were Labastida's chances hurt because of a divisive PRI presidential primary? McCann's chapter describes the PRI's first-ever adoption of a presidential primary election in November 1999 to choose its nominee, replacing the previous method, which was the incumbent president's de facto appointment of the nominee. McCann shows that the primary campaign was divisive and left a sour taste (evident in our February 2000 poll) among primary voters who had supported someone other than Labastida. The non-Labastida PRI primary voters were significantly more likely to prefer an opposition candidate in the general election than they were to vote for Labastida; indeed, they were more anti-Labastida than voters who had taken no part in the PRI primary election. And yet, as the campaign progressed from February to July 2000, McCann shows that the debilitating effect of the primary on Labastida's chances vanished. Yes, support for Labastida's candidacy dropped precipitously in those months, but the effects of the PRI primary election had little to do with that electoral plunge. The anti-Labastida primary voters remained less likely than pro-Labastida primary voters to support Labastida in July, but all were more likely to support Labastida than those who had not participated in the primary. Between February and July, the likelihood of voting for an opposition candidate increased more among Labastida primary supporters than among his primary opponents. McCann thus suggests that the primary election innovation had no lasting adverse effects on the PRI and, on the positive side, may have contributed to party building. This institutional change does not, therefore, explain Labastida's defeat in July 2000.

Did long-successful PRI practices of mobilization during the campaign determine voting behavior? Did other political parties engage in such practices in the 2000 election? Wayne Cornelius argues that the efficacy of vote buying and coercion declined in the 1990s; it was rather low in the 2000 presidential election. All three major parties engaged in these practices to some extent in 2000, although the PRI, not surprisingly, did so the most. Alas, the PRI also got the smallest payoff from these tactics. Home visits by party representatives worked more effectively for the PAN than for the PRI. Nor did many government social programs targeted at the poor give the PRI presidential candidate much of a boost. In short, old-fashioned mobilization had only modest effects on voting behavior and does not exemplify campaign effects well.

In contrast to such factors that mattered little for the voting choice in 2000, a key instrument for bringing about the "unexpected" outcome was the role of the mass media. As Lawson shows in his first chapter in this volume, exposure to Mexican television network news exercised a statistically significant influence on voting behavior in the 2000 election, controlling for other factors. Those who watched Televisión Azteca news broadcasts were more likely to vote for Fox than were those who watched Televisa news broadcasts. Exposure to Televisa coverage tended to increase support for both Fox and Labastida, reducing the number of undecided voters. TV Azteca depressed the vote for Labastida and increased the vote for Fox dramatically as weekly viewership increased from one to five days. The reason for this effect is noteworthy. Televisa's news was biased against Fox; his support increased, nonetheless, as a result of the exposure but could not grow too much. TV Azteca provided relatively balanced news coverage, enabling many voters to discover that they were *foxistas* at heart.[24]

There were also two televised presidential debates during the campaign. Lawson's chapter on the "great debates" demonstrates their impact. Viewership levels were very high, as is typical of "first" debates in countries that had not had them before. The debates boosted audience impressions of Fox's leadership abilities, solidified his own partisan base, and helped him lure away some voters from Labastida. Fox's political career had put him at odds with some leaders of his own party; the reinforcement of PAN sympathizer commitment to Fox's candidacy was thus an important accomplishment. The debates also reinforced the commitment to Cárdenas of his own previously committed partisans, but they weakened support for Labastida among PRI sympathizers. Some PRI sympathizers switched to Fox.

The comparative scholarship on debates has emphasized their limited impact on electoral outcomes. The two presidential debates in Mexico's 2000 election had an impact on the electoral outcome in part because of their relative novelty (there had been just one presidential debate in 1994, the first ever in Mexico), but they had little impact in other respects. The debates did not increase turnout on election day, change attitudes toward the parties, or contribute to citizen political knowledge. Thus the debates did not foster "issue voting," but they did significantly shape the impressions of the candidates as individuals. This was what mattered on election day.

Fox's effective mobilization of his supporters—through his public personality, use of the mass media, and PAN activism—significantly

increased voter turnout. As Lawson and Klesner show, the 2000 campaign made it more likely that PAN sympathizers and Fox supporters
would vote on election day. The partisan composition of the vote
shifted between February and July 2000, with PAN identifiers confirming their intention to vote in the presidential election.

Political advertising was also significant, as Moreno demonstrates
in his chapter.[25] Negative political advertising through the mass media
worked for Fox by influencing many Labastida partisans to abandon
their candidate. Labastida's own negativity had an unexpected result: it
turned off some of his early supporters. At the heart of the national
campaign, there was a single, clear political cleavage: all the opposition
candidates versus PRI candidate Labastida. Within the opposition,
early in the campaign Fox became the principal alternative to continued PRI rule. Fox built his campaign on a high volume of strongly
negative communication, criticizing Labastida for his politics and also
for his looks and alleged personal character defects.

How did this negativity work for Fox? In U.S. Senate elections,
Kahn and Kenney have argued "that people distinguish between useful negative information presented in an appropriate manner and ir-
relevant and harsh mudslinging."[26] Something like this happened in
the Mexican 2000 presidential election. Moreno concludes that most
strong partisans did not consider their preferred candidate's criticisms
as negative information; they considered them apt and useful evidence.
(One qualifier is that some of the negativity in the Mexican election—
Fox calling Labastida a fag or a drag queen, for example—could hardly
be considered "presented in an appropriate manner.") Most strong
partisans were outraged mainly by the negativity of the candidate who
was criticizing their party's standard-bearer. The odd result in the
Mexican election, as Moreno notes, is that Labastida's negativity hurt
him among some of his own partisans.

Thus political advertising worked in two ways. Labastida's negativity hurt him with some PRI identifiers and did not attract votes or dissuade Fox supporters from such support. Fox's negativity did not hurt
him with his own partisans, but it helped to dissuade some Labastida
supporters from continued adherence to the PRI candidate. Fox gained
few votes from these Labastida defectors, some of whom voted for
Cárdenas and a significant number simply failed to vote. This important campaign effect stands in contrast to more common comparative
findings about the null effects of negative political advertising.[27]

Moreno's findings buttress conclusions reached in other chapters. Magaloni and Poiré show that partisan defectors were a small fraction of all voters—even of Fox's voters—in July 2000 because the core of each major candidate's vote pool was the sum of his own partisans plus a share of the independent vote. Negative ads help to explain Magaloni and Poiré's finding that candidate effects significantly shaped voting behavior in July 2000. The effects of negative advertising contributed to the gap in partisan turnout that favored the PAN, which Lawson and Klesner highlight. All of these campaign effects were strongly mediated by partisanship.

The fact that Labastida defectors were more likely to abstain than to vote for Fox is also consistent with John Zaller's findings with U.S. data. Zaller shows that a highly politically aware person will be attentive to campaign events but also most likely "to resist information that is inconsistent with her basic values or partisanship." Moreover, "conversion" experiences—switching support from one party to another—are relatively infrequent and take considerable time. Citizens "respond to new issues mainly on the basis of the partisanship and ideology of the elite sources of the messages."[28]

These same observations support the proposition that most voters did *not* change their views as a result of the campaign, yet this does not mean that the campaign had no effect on them. Gelman and King have examined election poll volatility during U.S. presidential election campaigns. They conclude that campaigns convey information to voters that enables them to behave according to what might be called "underlying variables," among them partisanship and economic assessments, rendering the election more predictable in the long term. This assumes that candidates and parties have conducted an effective campaign.[29] These findings apply to Mexico as well. In 2000, the effect of the campaign was to confirm *cardenista* partisan voters in their intention to vote for Cárdenas, even if his chances of winning the presidency remained slim. The campaign was even more important in solidifying PAN leaners as Fox voters; Fox's campaign also increased substantially his share of the baseline PAN vote in the electorate. Only an ineffective campaign such as Labastida's lost votes for its presidential candidate. We turn to this puzzle in the next section.

WHY WERE SUCH CAMPAIGN EFFECTS FELT?

Mexican politics changed substantially during the 1990s, and these changes were a key to explain the electoral outcome in 2000. The PRI had been the "party of the state." In the 1990s it had to learn to become a more normal political party, contesting power with fewer advantages than in the past. In his chapter, Roderic Camp notes the gradual changes in Mexican political culture, including the loss of fear to criticize the government or support the opposition. The role and impact of parties changed. The PRD was born from the experience of the 1988 presidential election, and the PAN was reinvigorated by the political contestation of the decade that followed. Cornelius's chapter on the declining efficacy of vote buying and coercion also makes a strong case that Mexico has changed in important ways.

On the eve of the 2000 elections, opposition mayors governed half of Mexico's people and opposition governors headed states that accounted for nearly half of Mexico's gross domestic product. Mexican citizens no longer feared rule by PAN or PRD leaders, who had proven their competence as subnational executives. Electoral institutions and processes had already changed in many states and municipalities, making PAN and PRD opposition victories thinkable. Klesner demonstrates the growth of partisan competition since 1979, when the electoral law for the first time created somewhat better conditions for competition. In 1979, the PRI was hegemonic in 242 out of 300 electoral districts. In 1997, PRI hegemony persisted in only 25 of the 300 districts.

Mexico also built new electoral institutions, especially the Federal Electoral Institute (IFE), as the book's introduction notes. Reforms enacted in 1996 contributed to make the IFE highly autonomous and professional. Lawson and Klesner show that the perception that electoral fraud would decline increased turnout from opposition sympathizers on election day.[30] That same 1996 law, Kathleen Bruhn reminds us, created a vast pool of funds for the public financing of elections. The distribution of public funds to finance the 2000 election was based on the distribution of votes for the 1997 nationwide congressional election, adjusted to ensure a fairly level playing field. In 2000, public financing for the opposition parties was more than twice the public financing for the PRI.[31]

Yet another key change was the emergence and public acceptance of professional public opinion polling and the dissemination of polling information through the mass media. Mexicans could learn that there was opposition, that others critical of the PRI shared their views, and that some opposition politicians were more likely than others to defeat the PRI. Pollsters informed voters about electoral trends and likely winners, solidifying partisan and ideological commitments in some cases but also enabling strategic voters to calculate how to vote effectively. The impact of polling on the conduct of the campaign depended, albeit indirectly, on the long-term development of an increasingly independent mass media willing and able to pay for and print information about professional polling, a public sufficiently well educated to understand that numbers mattered, and professionals who could guarantee the procedural integrity of the process. Significant social, intellectual, and institutional changes are part of the "big picture" of political change in Mexico in the 1990s. Thus the possibility of greater change in 2000 was rooted in slow-moving structural change in the Mexican national experience.[32]

These institutional and electoral reforms, a more vigilant mass media, and well-funded political parties made it more difficult for the longtime PRI machinery to work as before. Electoral fraud was much less probable. Even the assertive use of pork-barrel projects or old-fashioned individual vote buying became more difficult to implement. The PRI's electoral machine under-performed, as Bruhn, Cornelius, and Lawson and Klesner indicate.

Strategic decisions made by politicians and voters before and during the campaign also help to explain the election results. Zaller has argued regarding the United States that "the public changes its opinion in the direction of the information and leadership cues supplied to it by elites.... [C]itizens hold opinions that they would not hold if aware of the best available information and analysis."[33] One illustration of elite shaping of public opinion occurred in Canada's 1988 national election. Johnston and his co-authors call attention to "priming," a key to "the electoral manifestation of the elite struggle for control of the agenda." They show that, for different reasons, Canada's leading party politicians kept the status of Quebec off the electoral agenda even though the recently signed Meech Lake Accord, focused on Canadian federalism and the standing of Quebec within the federation, could just as easily have been the election's centerpiece. Instead, the candidates for prime minister argued about the 1987 U.S.-Canada Free Trade Agreement (FTA), favored by the incumbent Conservatives and opposed by the opposition Liberals and the New Democratic Party. "Opinion shifts on the FTA responded to parties' rhetorical initiatives.... The very emphasis on the FTA was far from inevitable; the subject dominated because party organizations laboured to make it so."[34]

The Mexican 2000 presidential election exhibits these same key characteristics. Fox succeeded in framing the election as being about "change." As Bruhn shows in her chapter, all candidates, including the PRI's Labastida, accepted this framing. The main parties, Bruhn also shows, had blurred differences between them on many specific issues, so the candidates battled over the ownership of the concept of change. For Labastida, this was perhaps a hopeless endeavor, but he embraced this framing enthusiastically. Lawson's "great debate" chapter shows that Labastida's opening statement during the first presidential debate used the word "change" or a variant thereof more often than all the other candidates combined. Yet if change was so necessary, an opposition candidate seemed more likely to bring it about.

The PRI and the Labastida campaign could have embraced President Zedillo's record and personal popularity, which was high and rising steadily in the year before the election, as the introductory chapter shows. Labastida could have run on the government's very good macroeconomic performance of the second half of the 1990s. Gross domestic product grew at a rate from 5 to 6 percent per year, double the economy's growth rate in the first half of the 1990s and nearly triple the growth rate during the 1980s.[35] After so many economic crises under the PRI's stewardship over decades past, jaded voters, Bruhn notes, might have resisted a PRI message of renewed prosperity, but it was even harder to persuade most Mexicans that the PRI stood for change. Labastida and the PRI kept their distance from Zedillo and kept insisting that major economic changes had to be enacted. Labastida endorsed the framing of the election as being about change, and thus kept the PRI's potentially winning issues—Zedillo's and the economy's good performance—off the minds of voters.

A second important strategic decision shaped Mexico's 2000 election: who would be the standard-bearer for the opposition? The Canadian comparison is helpful again. At the start of Canada's 1988 national election, voter assessments of the three principal candidates for prime minister—from the Liberal Party, the Conservatives, and the New Democratic Party (NDP)—were fairly close. On the election's key issue, the FTA, the positions of the Liberals and the NDP were very close. Voters had to decide, however, whether to split their votes between the opposition parties, voting sincerely but ensuring a Conservative victory, or to vote strategically, that is, "to vote for one's second choice the better to defeat one's last choice." As the campaign progressed, apostate Liberals who might have supported the NDP "came home"; support for the NDP waned.[36]

Since the 1988 national election, Mexican opposition voters had faced the same dilemma, giving the edge to Cárdenas and the PRD in 1988 and 1997, and to various PAN candidates in 1991 and 1994. Bruhn's chapter shows that nominating Cárdenas for the presidency for the third consecutive time in 2000 was a poor decision. Cárdenas had not proven an effective presidential candidate in the past, and his steward-ship as mayor of Mexico City since 1997 had not gone well. A key bat-tle within the opposition became how to cast a so-called useful vote, namely, the vote that would ensure the PRI's eviction from the presi-dency. Fox won that fight handily in the televised presidential debates, as Bruhn and Lawson note.

Were the voters strategic in their behavior? Magaloni and Poiré examine this question. They reconfirm the significance of partisanship, prospective economic assessments, valence issues, and candidate ef-fects as key explanations for voting behavior in Mexico's 2000 presi-dential election. Most votes could be predicted without reference to strategic behavior. Magaloni and Poiré then focus on the relatively few but crucial voters who behaved strategically. The strategic and ideo-logical choices facing Mexican voters in a multicandidate presidential context were complex. Strategic opposition voting required a prefer-ence rank ordering whereby any outcome was preferable to PRI vic-tory; strategic voters had to value the PRI's defeat above their own ideological preferences. Voters also had to assess the probability of victory of the different alternatives. The logic of the "useful vote" im-plies that voters defect from the trailing candidate—as they had de-fected from the NDP in Canada's 1988 national election—in favor of the opposition front-runner. Strategic voting implies that there are two elections under way simultaneously, one between opposition candi-dates and another between the opposition and the ruling party. Strate-gic voting became thinkable in Mexico only during the 1988 presiden-tial election, in which the PRI first became vulnerable to defeat.[37]

After 1988, campaigns became vehicles to inform the voters about the likely outcome. Thus strategic voters swung to support the PAN or the PRD in different elections and for various national and subnational offices. Likely strategic voters are also somewhat volatile during a campaign, as they were in 2000, because they need to inform them-selves. Magaloni and Poiré conclude that strategic voting in Mexico's 2000 election was significant for Fox's election, nearly equaling his margin of victory over Labastida. Strong partisans were least likely to be strategic voters, consistent with other findings in this book. Weaker partisans and unaffiliated voters made up the pool for strategic voters.

CONCLUSION

Mexico's 2000 presidential election campaign mattered. It closed the breach between Fox and old-line *panistas*, somewhat distrustful of his candidacy. It stimulated PAN voters to turn out at rates higher than those of PRI supporters on election day. It solidified the Cárdenas base in the PRD. It demoralized the PRI machinery. It detached voters from Labastida, leading them to vote for another candidate or to stay home on election day. It informed opposition strategic voters to support Fox. The proportion of voters influenced by the campaign to change their voting preference was at least two to three times greater than in U.S. presidential campaigns and at least twice Fox's margin of victory. In fact, the proportion of strategic voters alone gave Fox nearly all of his margin of victory.

Significant campaign effects were possible for various reasons. Institutional and legal changes made free and fair elections at long last possible. The PRI's presidential primary even imparted a measure of change to this ancient political party. The voting behavior of Mexicans is, for the most part, not wedded to social cleavages, rendering voters more susceptible to campaign persuasion. Mexicans long ago stopped focusing on a bad economy, which they resented but had come to consider typical. Thus retrospective voting lost some explanatory punch. Mexicans paid greater attention to the future of the economy and were thus open to politicians who framed this issue most convincingly. Prospective economic voting increased the likelihood of campaign effects.

Mexican parties retain a remarkable hold on citizen voting behavior. Partisanship conditions and mediates nearly all campaign effects. Nonetheless, the explanatory impact of partisanship weakened somewhat in advance of the 2000 election, making more room for candidate and valence issue effects on voting behavior. (Specific policy issues mattered little, however.) Mass media news reporting, negative political advertising, and televised debates all affected electoral outcomes, though always mediated by partisan affiliation. The campaign mattered.

Campaigns may matter more in emerging democracies. In many of these countries, partisanship may be even weaker than in Mexico or in the advanced industrial democracies. Fair and abundant television coverage of opposition election campaigns becomes possible only upon democratization. Moreover, in poor countries, widespread access to television is a relatively recent phenomenon. Thus our research may help bridge the interests of scholars in the long-established and the new democracies.

Many of the changes evident in Mexico are, of course, *good*. Mexico has become a freer, more open country. Its citizens express their opinions, contest views, and choose their rulers, giving at last concrete meaning to "the consent of the governed." Voter intimidation and vote buying have ended in most parts of Mexico, though pockets of abuse remain. Yet citizens and analysts should worry that candidate-centered campaigns focused on vague themes, reliant on negative advertising and on unelected media barons, do not make for healthy democratic politics. Weak social attachments, weakened partisanship, and greater attention to prospective economic fantasies rather than actual evidence about the economy are also not attractive elements for the quality of Mexico's democracy. Moreover, Mexico's 2000 election also led Mexican politics to "gridlock," where the president's party lacks a majority in both houses of Congress.

The hero of Mexico's democratic transition has been the voter. Prudently, cautiously, during the 1990s, voters put the PRI on notice that it had better improve or lose power. In the 2000 presidential election, voters gave Fox a decisive victory, but they also chose a Congress in which the president's party was a minority in both the Senate and the Chamber of Deputies. The PRI outperformed Labastida in the congressional elections. As Alesina and Rosenthal have argued for the United States, "divided government is not an accident, but the result of the voters' desire for policy moderation."[38] Mexican citizens were ready to try out a new president from a different party, but they also bought a double insurance policy—against renewed authoritarian lordship and against wild policy implementation. The 2000 election deepened Mexico's slowly evolving democracy, but it may also have persuaded politicians that unsavory campaign practices are effective. It surely enshrined policy gridlock between president and Congress. Mexicans gave birth to their political democracy. Now they must improve its quality.

Notes

1. Book I, chapter 7.

2. For a general discussion, see Amy Gutmann and Dennis F. Thompson, *Democracy and Disagreement* (Cambridge, Mass.: Harvard University Press, 1996).

3. This is not a freestanding chapter. Instead, it highlights themes from preceding chapters. I rely on occasional textual references to other chapters, but the debt to my co-authors is much greater. These are solely my views, however. The book's authors are free to claim that all the errors in this chapter are mine and that all the insights are theirs. All mistakes are mine alone. Versions of this chapter have been presented at Harvard University's Weatherhead Center for International Affairs, the MIT Political Science Department, the University of Notre Dame's Kellogg Institute, and the Political Science Department of the New School University. I am grateful for the comments and suggestions made at these sessions. My general research has been supported by Harvard's Weatherhead Center for International Affairs and the David Rockefeller Center for Latin American Studies.

4. Steven E. Finkel, "Reexamining the 'Minimal Effects' Model in Recent Presidential Campaigns," *Journal of Politics* 55, no. 1 (February 1993): 2–3, 11; quote, p. 2.

5. Gregory B. Markus, "The Impact of Personal and National Economic Conditions on the Presidential Vote: A Pooled Cross-Sectional Analysis," *American Journal of Political Science* 32, no. 1 (1988): 137–54.

6. Michael Lewis-Beck, *Economics and Elections: The Major Western Democracies* (Ann Arbor: University of Michigan Press, 1988): 58–59.

7. It is possible, though hard to prove, that opposition candidates may have won more votes in 1929, 1940, and 1988. The ruling party claimed victory in these three elections.

8. Beatriz Magaloni, "Is the PRI Fading? Economic Performance, Electoral Accountability, and Voting Behavior in the 1994 and 1997 Elections," in Jorge I. Domínguez and Alejandro Poiré, eds., *Toward Mexico's Democratization: Parties, Campaigns, Elections, and Public Opinion* (New York: Routledge, 1999): 233.

9. For a similar view from a different context, see Pippa Norris, John Curtice, David Sanders, Margaret Scammell, and Holli Semetko, *On Message: Communicating the Campaign* (London: Sage Publications, 1999), especially chapter 11.

10. For the classic study, see Seymour Martin Lipset and Stein Rokkan, "Cleavage Structures, Party Systems, and Voter Alignments," in *Party Systems and Voter Alignments: Cross-National Perspectives* (New York: The Free Press, 1967). See also Richard Rose and Derek Unwin, "Persistence and Change in Western Party Systems since 1945," *Political Studies* 18, no. 3 (1970): 287–319.

11. For the United States, the classic is Angus Campbell, Philip Converse, Warren Miller, and Donald Stokes, *The American Voter* (New York: Wiley, 1960). Party identification weakened markedly in the United States in the 1960s. Yet even after the 1960s, "one of the stable anchor points for the American public remains party identification" (Norman Nie, Sidney Verba, and John Petrocik, *The Changing American Voter* [Cambridge, Mass.: Harvard University Press, 1976]: 350). See also Eric Shickler and Donald P. Green, "The Stability of Party Identification in Western Democracies: Results from Eight Panel Surveys," *Comparative Political Studies* 30, no. 4 (August 1997): 450–83.

12. See Alberto Alesina and Howard Rosenthal, *Partisan Politics, Divided Government, and the Economy* (Cambridge: Cambridge University Press, 1995) for discussions of "rational partisan" economic voting. See also Douglas A. Hibbs, Jr., *The*

Political Economy of Industrial Democracies (Cambridge, Mass.: Harvard University Press, 1987), and Lewis-Beck, *Economics and Elections*.

13. David Swanson and Paolo Mancini, "Patterns of Modern Electoral Campaigning and Their Consequences," in David Swanson and Paolo Mancini, eds., *Politics, Media, and Modern Democracy: An International Study of Innovations in Electoral Campaigning and Their Consequences* (Westport, Conn.: Praeger, 1996).

14. Lewis-Beck, *Economics and Elections*, p. 82.

15. These findings refer to the chapters in this book, unless otherwise cited. Our principal empirical basis is a four-wave panel study of Mexico's presidential election in 2000.

16. See, for example, Jorge I. Domínguez and James A. McCann, *Democratizing Mexico: Public Opinion and Electoral Choices* (Baltimore, Md.: Johns Hopkins University Press, 1996); Jorge I. Domínguez and Alejandro Poiré, *Toward Mexico's Democratization*.

17. For previous elections, see ibid.

18. Domínguez and McCann, *Democratizing Mexico*, chapter 4.

19. For the lack of explanatory significance of specific issue variables even in the 1988 election, when presidential candidates posed stark choices, see ibid.

20. Political interest and the preference for "strong leaders" over reliance on laws had no statistically significant effect on the voting choice in the 1988 or 1991 national elections. See Domínguez and McCann, *Democratizing Mexico*, tables 4–15 and 5–9.

21. Thomas M. Holbrook, *Do Campaigns Matter?* (Thousand Oaks, Calif.: Sage, 1996): 156.

22. Magaloni, "Is the PRI Fading?"

23. On the conduct of the campaign, see Joseph L. Klesner, *The 2000 Mexican Presidential and Congressional Elections: Pre-Election Report* (Washington, D.C.: Center for Strategic and International Studies, 2000); George W. Grayson, *A Guide to the 2000 Mexican Presidential Election* (Washington, D.C.: Center for Strategic and International Studies, 2000).

24. On the role of television in the 2000 election, see also Florence Toussaint Alcaraz, "Las campañas electorales del 2000 en televisión: el caso mexicano," *Revista Mexicana de Ciencias Políticas y Sociales* 44, no. 180 (September–December 2000): 39–56.

25. For a general discussion of political advertising in the 2000 election, see Concepción Virriel López, "El problema de la credibilidad de los *spots* políticos," *Revista Mexicana de Ciencias Políticas y Sociales* 44, no. 180 (September–December 2000): 175–90.

26. Kim Fridkin Kahn and Patrick. J. Kenney, "Do Negative Campaigns Mobilize or Suppress Turnout? Clarifying the Relationship between Negativity and Participation," *American Political Science Review* 93, no. 4 (December 1999): 877–89.

27. For a scholarly literature survey, see Richard Lau, Lee Sigelman, Caroline Heldman, and Paul Babbitt, "The Effects of Negative Political Advertisements: A Meta-Analytic Assessment," *American Political Science Review* 93, no. 4 (December 1999): 851–75.

28. See John R. Zaller, *The Nature and Origins of Mass Opinion* (Cambridge: Cambridge University Press, 2002): 267, 282; quotes, pp. 266 and 31, respectively.

29. Andrew Gelman and Gary King, "Why Are American Presidential Election Polls So Variable When Voters Are So Predictable?" *British Journal of Political Science* 23 (1993): 409–51.

30. On the vote-depressing effects of fraud, see James McCann and Jorge Domínguez, "Mexicans React to Electoral Fraud and Political Corruption: An Assessment of Public Opinion and Voting Behavior," *Electoral Studies* 17, no. 4 (1998): 499.

31. This did not prevent the massive illegal diversion of funds from the state-owned oil firm, Pemex, to support the PRI campaign, however.

32. See also Miguel Basáñez, "Polling and the Mexican Transition to Democracy" (Mexico City, 2001, unpublished).

33. Zaller, *The Nature and Origins of Mass Opinion*, pp. 311, 313.

34. Richard Johnston, André Blais, Henry Brady, and Jean Crête, *Letting the People Decide: Dynamics of a Canadian Election* (Stanford, Calif.: Stanford University Press, 1992); quotations from pp. 212 and 243. Francophone Quebecois voters did support the Conservatives in part because their government sponsored the Meech Lake agreement.

35. Naciones Unidas, Comisión Económica para América Latina y el Caribe, *Balance preliminar de las economías de América Latina y el Caribe, 2000* (Santiago, Chile: CEPAL-Naciones Unidas, 2000): 85.

36. Johnson, Blais, Brady, and Crête, *Letting the People Decide*, pp. 195, 201, 224–25; quote, p. 198.

37. Domínguez and McCann, *Democratizing Mexico*, chapter 4.

38. Alesina and Rosenthal, *Parties, Politics, Divided Government, and the Economy*, p. 2.

Appendix. Mexico 2000 Panel Study

Overview

The Mexico 2000 Panel Study represents one of the first major panel studies of political attitudes in an emerging democracy. It was explicitly designed to measure campaign influences on public opinion and voting behavior in Mexico's 2000 presidential race. All data from the study are available to the public.

Organizers of the project included (in alphabetical order): Miguel Basáñez, Roderic Camp, Wayne Cornelius, Jorge Domínguez, Federico Estévez, Joseph Klesner, Chappell Lawson (principal investigator), Beatriz Magaloni, James McCann, Alejandro Moreno, Pablo Parás, and Alejandro Poiré. Interviews for the panel component of the project were conducted by the polling staff of *Reforma* newspaper, under the direction of Alejandro Moreno. Polling for the postelectoral cross-section was conducted by CEOP, under the direction of Miguel Basáñez and Pablo Parás.

Funding for the Mexico 2000 Panel Study was provided by the National Science Foundation (SES-9905703) and *Reforma* newspaper (which covered approximately half of the costs of the project-related surveys it conducted). Princeton University provided additional funding for a project planning conference. The Massachusetts Institute of Technology covered costs of project planning and administration. The Harvard University Weatherhead Center for International Affairs hosted a conference in December 2000, at which participants in the Mexico 2000 Panel Study formally presented findings from the project for the first time. Since that time, project participants have presented their findings at the 2001 conference of the Midwest Political Science Association, the 2001 conference of the American Political Science Association, and the 2001 conference of the Latin American Studies Association, among other forums.

Project Design

The Mexico 2000 Panel Study consists of approximately 7,000 interviews in five separate surveys over the course of the campaign, using a hybrid panel/cross-sectional design. Its first round, conducted in February 19–27 (just after the official beginning of the campaign), polled a national cross-section of 2,400 adults. This sample was then randomly divided into two groups, the first of which was re-interviewed in the second round (April 28–May 7). Because of attrition, this wave included approximately 950 respondents. In the third round (June 3–18), pollsters re-interviewed all of those in the second randomly selected subset of the first round, plus approximately 400 respondents interviewed in the second round. Finally, in the fourth round (July 7–16), pollsters re-interviewed as many of the participants as possible from all previous rounds. This included almost 1,200 respondents who had been interviewed in the second and third rounds, as well as just over 100 respondents who had only been previously interviewed in the first wave. This panel sample was supplemented with a new cross-section of approximately 1,200 fresh respondents.

Figure A.1 summarizes this design. The two white boxes indicate national cross-sectional polls (one in February, one in July). The shaded boxes represent re-interviews of the original respondents in the first round. Sample sizes are given in parentheses.

Figure A1. Outline of Mexico 2000 Panel Study

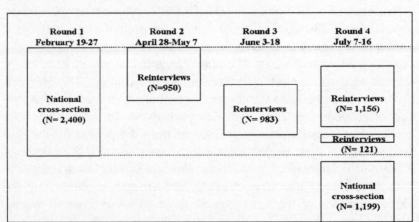

The hybrid nature of the Mexico 2000 Panel Study was intended to capture benefits beyond those of a pure panel study or a series of cross-sectional polls. The panel nature of the data allows analysts to control for individual-level effects—something crucial for most analyses of campaign influence. In the case of media effects, for instance, self-selection of viewers to media that accord with their preexisting views makes conclusions drawn from cross-sectional data highly suspect. It may be, for instance, that regular listeners of independent talk-radio programs are more likely to vote for the opposition. But these listeners may tune in to such radio programs because they already detest the government, rather than the other way around. With panel data, analysts can tell not only whether people who listen to independent radio shows were more likely to vote for the opposition, but also whether, controlling for other factors, they were more likely to switch to the opposition than were their compatriots who relied on more pro-government media.

Pure panel surveys, however, entail certain trade-offs and sacrifices. Because of attrition, panel surveys are not representative of the general population, and conclusions based on them may not be applicable to the background population. For this reason, a separate cross-sectional poll, timed to coincide with the fourth wave of the panel, was included in the project. This separate cross-section was designed to allow researchers to determine whether the sorts of effects identified in the panel also occurred in random cross-sections of the population.

A second trade-off involved in panel studies is the risk of contamination—that is, the danger that repeated interviews might inadvertently influence respondents' opinions. Contamination is an obvious problem for measuring issues like political learning; not only might the survey itself convey knowledge about political issues, asking respondents basic factual questions (such as "Which party uses the Aztec Sun as its campaign symbol?") might stimulate them to find the answers. Contamination, however, may also take more insidious forms. For instance, if repeated interviews stimulate learning about politics and political knowledge is associated with dislike for the PRI, then panel participants might exhibit different patterns of attitude change than non-participants with otherwise similar backgrounds and opinions. Again, the second cross-sectional poll is intended to allow analysts to assess the extent of contamination and, if appropriate, attempt to correct for it statistically.

Survey Items

The Mexico 2000 Panel Study covered a wide range of issues relevant to voting behavior: demographics, media exposure, political knowledge and engagement, opinions about salient public issues, attitudes toward the main parties and candidates, impressions of the electoral process, and (of course) voting intentions. Special attention was paid to campaign influences, such as contact with party activists, exposure to news coverage in the mass media, viewership of political advertisements, and the presidential debates, as well as to attitudes about the main parties and voting intentions. Many of these items—for instance, exposure to television news—were repeated in all four waves of the panel and the postelectoral cross-section.

Both the panel and the postelectoral cross-section contain weights, based on education levels designed to make the original sample populations comparable to the background population. In general, however, the first round of the panel and the postelectoral cross-section proved highly representative. Thus far, project organizers have obtained similar results with weighted and unweighted data.

Polling Procedures

Interviews for the panel component of the project were conducted by the polling staff of *Reforma* newspaper, under the direction of Alejandro Moreno. Fieldwork for the postelectoral cross-section was overseen by Pablo Parás, as well as general administrators Francisco Sarmiento and Carlos López; Juan Balderas managed the sampling and database. (A list of assistants, interviewers, supervisors, and data entry staff is available through CEOP.) All together, two general administrators, five assistants, forty-seven interviewers, and eleven supervisors participated in the postelectoral cross-section.

Polling sites for the first round of the panel were selected at random from the Federal Electoral Institute's (IFE) list of polling stations. Twelve respondents were interviewed at each site, meaning that one hundred sites were selected for the postelectoral cross-section and two hundred for the first round of the panel. At each site, interviewers began at the address listed by the IFE and polled potential respondents according to a pre-arranged formula, using age and gender quotas to secure a representative breakdown of respondents. For the second round of the panel, a randomly chosen subsample of sites from the first round was selected for re-interviewing. For the third round, interviewers polled all sites not included in the second round, plus a randomly chosen subsample of sites from the second round. In the fourth round, interviewers attempted to contact all respondents from the first round.

The postelectoral cross-section was based on a representative sample of Mexicans at least eighteen years old, regardless of whether they were registered or whether they voted. Interviews were conducted in person at the respondent's residence. None was conducted in the street or in an office, unless the office was also the residence of the person selected and the respondent agreed to be interviewed there. Only those who actually lived in the selected residence were interviewed. Interviews were conducted over two weekends (the precise days were July 8, 9, 10, 15, and 16) to maximize the representativeness of the sample.

In the first stage of the selection, 100 sites were chosen from the 63,345 electoral sections defined by the Federal Electoral Institute. These 100 sites included 21 rural areas, 69 urban areas, and 10 mixed areas in 85 counties and boroughs (7 boroughs in the Federal District and 78 counties in the rest of Mexico), covering 30 states. To select the 100 sites, 63,345 sections were ordered from largest to smallest; the first site was then chosen randomly, and every kth site thereafter was also chosen, according to the formula $k = n/(p - 1)$, where n is the total number of potential sites and p is the number of sites to be chosen in the sample. In the second stage of the selection, interviewers began at the actual polling site for the 2000 elections within each section. In urban or suburban areas, each interviewer then polled in a clockwise spiral from the northeast corner of the block where the polling site was located, beginning with that block and proceeding outward to other blocks. Each residence was selected randomly, with the interval between residences depending on the number of houses per block and the characteristics of the neighborhood. Where residences were primarily apartments or condominiums, each building was treated as a block and the same fixed interval between residences was used. Industrial parks and commercial zones were excluded from the polling route. In rural areas, polling routes might be either spiral or variable, depending on characteristics of the zone, but selection of residences according to a fixed interval was still employed.

In the final stage of the selection, respondents were chosen by most recent birthday, subject to preset age/gender quotas. If no one answered at a given residence, or if the person selected declined to be interviewed or did not complete the interview, the interviewer proceeded to the next residence on the interviewer's fixed interval. The final size of the sample was 1,199, yielding a margin of error of +/−3 percent at the 95 percent level of confidence.

Supervision of the postelectoral cross-section was conducted according to standard CEOP procedures. Thirty-eight percent of the sample (457 cases) were supervised; 10 percent (120 cases) by telephone, 20 percent (241 cases) by supervisor visits after the fact, and 8 percent (96 cases) by the supervisor at the time of the interview.

Supervision of the panel occurred at several levels. Before polling, interviewers were screened and trained by Moreno and others at *Reforma* with extensive experience in survey work in Mexico. During the administration of the panel itself, supervisors employed the following method to ensure data reliability. In the first wave, interviewers recorded respondents' birth dates and (for those who agreed to participate in subsequent rounds) exact addresses. Immediately upon returning from the field, interviewers then surrendered all information to the administrator of the project. Before each subsequent round, interviewers were given the address, gender, month of birth, and year of birth (though not the day of the month) for each respondent they were to reinterview. At the start of the interview, pollsters again recorded respondents' complete birth dates, including the day of the month on which respondents were born. By matching days of the month in each round of the panel, supervisors were thus able to verify after the fact that interviewers did not inadvertently contact the wrong person in the household or (less likely) fabricate the interview. Following each wave of the panel, supervisors re-contacted up to 20 percent of respondents in each wave to verify the interviews (including both random checks and checks targeted at those respondents whose birth dates did not match up). Finally, after the entire panel set was assembled, key demographic indicators were matched and suspicious cases flagged for follow-up. Investigation of these cases led to the deletion of a small number of additional interviews, reducing the total number of respondents in the first round of the panel to 2,355. Further detail about the sampling and supervisory procedures for the panel can be obtained through Alejandro Moreno at *Reforma* newspaper.

Index

References in *italics* refer to tables, charts, and figures.